The Wholeness Principle
Stephano Sabetti

The Wholeness Principle

Exploring Life Energy Process*

Stephano Sabetti

Life Energy Media
Sherman Oaks, California

Cover painting conceived by Fritz Horauf, Akademischer Maler und Bildhauer, Ursulastrasse 10, 8000 Munich 40, West Germany.

Cover painting by Dr. Josiane Beauvais C.A., O.M.D., 11 Chanticleer Street, Larkspur, CA 94939, Telephone (415) 924-2082.

Cover design by Stephano Sabetti.

Graphics and text art by Rick Marks, Creative Graphics, 200 Posada Del Sol, Novato, CA 94947, Telephone (415) 382-8044.

Author's photograph by Susan Segal.

Library of Congress Cataloging-in-Publication Data
Sabetti, Stephano.
  The wholeness principle.

  Bibliography: p.
  Includes index.
  1. Vitality. 2. Holistic medicine. 3. Health.
4. Force and energy. I. Title
RA776.5.S23 1986 613 86-15200
ISBN 0-937725-10-2
ISBN 0-937725-11-0 (pbk.)

For Thomaso
whose simplicity
was the
wisdom
of the
heart.

INSTITUTE FOR LIFE ENERGY®

The INSTITUTE FOR LIFE ENERGY bases its work on a universal force called life energy that flows in all phenomena, physical and non-physical. We encourage personal and social evolution in which everyone finds their individual and collective path towards growth. This is facilitated by bringing consciousness to the flow and blockage of this life force through the Life Energy Process (L.E.P.). From this perspective, health is an organic movement which when disturbed results in the diseases and problems of everyday life. Even though physical, psychological, organizational or spiritual difficulties appear to be unrelated they are essentially manifestations of the same energy dysfunction.

The result of the Life Energy Process is a new awareness of the meaning and unique direction of this energetic flow leading us towards innate wholeness.

INSTITUTE FOR LIFE ENERGY
Trautenwolfstrasse 3
8000 Munich 40
West Germany
Tel: (089) 347692
Hours: Mon., Wed., Fri. 9 am—12 noon

DR. STEPHANO SABETTI, founder and Director of the Institute for Life Energy, has a doctorate in Counseling Psychology from Boston University. His extensive training includes work in Bioenergetics with A. Lowen and J. Pierrakos; Gestalt Therapy with I. Fromm and L. Perls; Acupuncture with Dr. James So from the Hong Kong College of Acupuncture; Kundalini Yoga; dance and martial arts.

He conducts training and facilitates workshops in wholeness with individuals, groups and large organizations throughout the world. A Professor at International College in Los Angeles, Dr. Sabetti has published numerous articles and books as well as produced film and videos about his work.

Dr. Sabetti's *Life Energy Process*∗ is a spiritually oriented approach to body work and life style which allows direct contact with your spiritual self through energy vibrations. He has developed several forms of the Life Energy Process: *Life Energy Therapy*® is a body oriented psychotherapy through which an energy channel is opened so that we can contact our unique energy frequency and with process inquiry go beyond the superficial trace problems of everday life to resolve deeper energy disturbances and return to wholeness. *Shinkido*∗ is the massage art of resonation by influencing energy waves in the body to promote physical health, foster emotional expression, enhance sensual pleasure and support spiritual evolution. *Dansergia*∗ is the inner connection and outward expression through movement of the healing channel for psychological and spiritual development. *Il Teatro Energetico*∗ is a newly conceived theater of energy which heightens awareness of psychological patterns and transforms these into new possibilities for growth. *Kinergy*∗ is the physical manipulation in the physiotherapeutic style which through facilitation of energy movement stimulates nerve activity, extends/relaxes muscles and releases physical and psychological holding in the body. *Acquasus*∗ is a program of therapeutic exercises in water in which energy waves in the body are enhanced to help release physical and emotional tensions. *Organetics*∗ is the understanding, diagnosis and intervention in organizations based on energy movement which provides a unique form of organization development and consultation. This constellation of forms has been developed by Dr. Sabetti as part of his *Life Energy Process*∗.

∗Trademark pending.

I would like to express my appreciation
for those who contributed to this whole.

Renata W. Erlemann
Annalea Bennett
Heide Bongers
Susanne Immendörfer
Margo Komenar
Matt Sabetti
Siegfried Weitz
Icilius von Quintus
Thelma Coutts
Deborah Eaglebarger

and H.

OTHER PUBLICATIONS

BY

DR. STEPHANO SABETTI

Lebensenergie (The Wholeness Principle) (Scherz Verlag, Munich)
German edition DM 32

Articles Available for $3 Each

Life Energy Therapy: An Introduction
Life Energy: A Psychotherapeutic Evolution
Energy Concepts of Life Energy Therapy
The Manifestations of Energy
Gestalt Therapy Energized: Theory
Gestalt Therapy Energized: Therapy
Psychoanalysis as Process: Theory
Psychoanalysis as Process: Therapy
Organizational Energy
Shinkido Massage
Emotions on Trial
Perceptual Energy
Common Ground
Life Energy Live
Behavior Modification (Wolpe) as an Energy Process

Life Energy Therapy (Film) 1975
Life Energy Process (Video) 1986

Publications may be ordered directly from the Institute for Life Energy
in Munich, West Germany. *The Wholeness Principle* may be purchased
from Life Energy Media, 14755 Ventura Blvd., Suite 1908, Sherman
Oaks, CA 91403. An order form is available at the end of the book.

CONTENTS

ILLUSTRATIONS

Introduction

Beneath the busy texture of society a quiet (r)evolution is happening. It affects our patterns of life, our understanding of how the universe functions, and our concepts of health and disease. It is a subtle yet radical change and it is finding its way into every segment of modern living. This (r)evolution is the rediscovered sense of wholeness.

Wholeness is a body that loves to be alive, a spirit that expresses itself in every action, and a spontaneous and comprehensive awareness. A whole society responds to all its people, not just to those who talk the loudest or have the most money. In a whole environment all the earth's elements exist in a complementary relationship, free of pollutants and manufactured radiation. These wholes are not ideal states, but they do reflect movement in the direction of greater awareness which is both the means and the natural result.

Unfortunately, this wholeness has been too often forgotten in a world of linear goals and quick production. Slowly, however, we are beginning to rediscover that all human expressions—in the atmosphere, home, and workplace—are circles of energy which will ultimately come back to us. This is the revolution (L. *revolvere*, to roll back)—a return to the nature of wholeness which is the essence of our entire universe. The wisdom of this unity was known by ancient peoples and expressed in their architectures, religions, and healing techniques. The current revolution is also a return to this ancient knowledge.

Similarly, wholeness is also an evolution, for as we experience the circles of wholeness with awareness, the movement of life energy becomes a spiral of evolution taking us beyond our personal worlds to the realm of universal consciousness in which all things are experienced as one. In both the revolution and evolution of wholeness two tendencies are apparent in everyday life: one is a tendency toward new integration, the other is a movement toward dissolution.

Especially in science and related fields of study, the integration of knowledge into larger wholes has taken on new life. For example, in physics the theories of relativity, quantum mechanics, and supergravity demand a wholeness which was antithetical to Newton's classical physics. In medicine and psychology, the development of holistic and psychosomatic medicine is based on the wholeness of mind, body, and emotions. In psychotherapy, milieu therapy, and family therapy, ecosystemic approaches reveal the need to see the individual and his environment as part of a larger whole. In the field of economics, many nations now realize the necessity of developing multi-national and world markets for their goods. Oil shortages and wheat surpluses have forced new trade arrangements which defy the old isolationism. Businesses and organizations of all types are beginning to base their operations on systems concepts. The worker is now seen more clearly as part of a working environment whose relationship to himself, to his fellow workers, and to management affects the quality and innovation of the products produced. Never before have the sciences come together in such an interdisciplinary spirit of cooperation. This union has resulted in a host of new fields such as psychotronics, dermoptics, psychohistory, sociobiology, and photobiology. The ancient sciences of homeopathy, Ayurveda, herbalism, color therapy, and radiasthesis are being rediscovered because of their holistic, nonharmful application to healing.

The media has responded to this interest in wholeness by producing new material on the synthesis of Eastern and Western ideas in physics, religion, and nutrition. Feats of "wonder" from religious cults and healing practices from all over the world are becoming commonplace knowledge in newspapers, on television, and on film. Nowhere is the excitement of wholeness more apparent than in the new consciousness of the healing arts:

In Hong Kong, an acupuncturist eliminates all pain from an inflamed tooth which is to be extracted by simply inserting four needles into the body.

In India, a Yogi is buried underground in a wooden box without water, food, or extra oxygen and emerges forty days later, completely unharmed, to demonstrate the potential of controlled breathing.

In Boston, a middle-aged nurse is relieved of her arthritis by body psychotherapy after her medical colleagues had given up on her as a hopeless case.

In Tokyo, a master of Karate lies on a bed of nails and allows one of his assistants to break a forty-pound cement block on his belly. Not a single nail pierces his skin.

In Rio de Janeiro, a local healer working with medical doctors and spirit mediums helps a paralyzed physician to walk after several thirty-minute healing sessions.

In Munich, a radiasthetist, using his pendulum, locates a missing boy by using the boy's picture and a dowser's map of the area.

Aside from a fascination with the question of *how* such feats are possible, interest is growing in the principles of life energy that make these feats possible. This new interest is part of the evolution. Gradually, as the "wonder" of these phenomena fades, we begin to probe the nature of the life force which they express. In the East, the connection to this life force has been a fact of life for thousands of years. In the West, this relationship has been hindered by the "letter" of technological science to the detriment of scientific "spirit." Because this life force has not always adhered to the accepted laws of science, it has often been dismissed as nonexistent, even though such a common phenomenon as electricity has not ever been adequately explained by these same laws.

This book proposes the idea that electricity, as well as magnetism and all "accepted" forms of energy, are expressions of life energy, a vitalistic force of nature which is the medium of wholeness. This force has been known and used almost universally and has had particular relevance for the Egyptians, the Chinese, the Japanese, the Tibetans, the Indians, the Jews, the Hawaiians, and all native peoples. Early Western physicians and researchers, as well as the early Greek philosophers, knew about life force which I call life energy.

Wholeness is a vibrational field which brings harmony, order, and integration to life through the medium of life energy; it is the basic organizing principle of the universe. It manifests in the body as health, in the spiritual realm as soul, and on the emotional plane as love. In the atmosphere, wholeness is expressed in ecology and in human relations as harmony and compatibility.

To complement this new awareness of integration, a second tendency in the (r)evolution of wholeness has manifested itself as a dissolution of integration into dis-ease, chaos, political struggle, and existential anxiety. This is certainly not a new phenomenon. In fact, it is simply the opposite polarity of life energy movement which operates in our universe. The coherent forces of coming together must be balanced by the distributory forces of coming apart in order to achieve a dynamic wholeness. As the decay of flowers and the dying of leaves produce humus to nourish the next season's growth, so the confusion and collapse of our societies can be the source of a new wholeness when these trends are perceived with a different awareness. It is ironic that the separation from wholeness which causes disease should also be the same energy dysfunction which stores within itself the potential seed of renewed wholeness; nevertheless, this *is* a fundamental law of life energy.

From this perspective, all forms of disharmony or disease are attempts by a particular unit of wholeness—whether the cell, the body, or society—to re-establish a measure of wholeness when a dysfunction of life energy exists. Therefore, all types of disease, including spiritual, physical, environmental, and political, can be understood as disturbances of life energy in the process of seeking balance.

In developing this idea, I was often amazed at how easily most people see the destructive force in the cycle of wholeness while the harmonious and constructive forces are not perceived. Why is it that we recognize what is wrong with our lives rather than the positive steps needed to change? Why do we hold on to parts of ourselves which are clearly unhealthy for us? These questions puzzled me, and I wondered if there was some connection here to the existential problem of meaninglessness so often seen in therapy.

I found that the key to understanding these problems lay in the nature of wholeness. I came to realize that, even though wholeness is the natural state of life, many of us have never experienced wholeness as a conscious process. Consequently, we are frightened of it at a deeper level. Our tendencies to cling to negativity and disease or to run away into flights of fun are learned responses to a fear of wholeness. This could be called *holophobia*, from the Greek words for wholeness and fear. My exploration into the fear of wholeness has led me into many fields of research and experience in both ancient cultures and modern technology, along Eastern paths of knowledge and into Western techniques of therapy. (Eventually, of course, it has led me back to myself, which is the only place any exploration can begin or end—but it doesn't.)

Fortunately, I also found a practical way of returning to wholeness by first understanding the principles of life energy and then experiencing this state of wholeness through a new psychotherapeutic method called Life Energy Therapy.

Life energy is a continuous process which has no organic beginning or end. When we choose to stop this process on one level it is illusory to call this an end. In fact, any attempt to control its flow disturbs our relationship to wholeness, which ultimately leads to some form of disease. Life energy is a (r)evolution in conscious process and form which forces us, especially in these times, to seriously reflect on those theories and ideas which we now believe hold the universe together. Ultimately, the revolution of wholeness is our chance to rediscover our path of evolution.

In Chapter One, we will explore the tradition of life energy in Eastern and Western cultures which has transcended the boundaries of ritual, religion, philosophy, and science. We will see that in almost all cultures an understanding and usage of life energy has existed, along with a consistent set of ideas about the functioning of this force in health, disease, and evolution.

In the East, the traditional use of energy is quite extensive and has been made part of life by incorporating its principles into nutrition, philosophy, politics, and medicine. The West generally lacks this unified perspective, but has kept alive a tradition of natural medicine and scientific research in a small segment of the culture. As though passed from person to person, the spirit of energy concepts has been maintained since the earliest days of Greek civilization, and perhaps even earlier in lost civilizations such as Atlantis. Both East and West have experienced periods of renewal and decline in the development and extension of ideas on life energy (an interesting mirror of the polarized movement of the force itself).

The history of human civilization is filled with "new" discoveries which we later find were already known by previous cultures. In fact, the more we learn about these ancient cultures, the more we find we have given new names or added slight alterations to processes which have been known for a long time.

Chapter Two proposes that current ideas of energy are in dire need of re-evaluation based on recent research findings in subatomic and radiational physics. The present ideas concerning both the spectrum and the qualities of energy are insufficient to explain many well-supported studies of what are considered paranormal, psychotronic, or psi events: people who bend metal without touching it, or have the psychic ability to affect physics instruments (such as the cloud chamber, a subatomic particle detector). Scientific proof is examined as a valid concept in order to establish a possible starting place to transform thinking about our universe and its laws.

The key to a new understanding of these laws lies in radically changing our present models of science and scientific thought. Many scientists have been unwilling to closely examine their colleagues' research because it seemed too unbelievable to be true. This is indeed ironic, because science can only make progress by opening the door to new possibilities, testing new hypotheses, and, when necessary, revising its "laws." Despite this acknowledged necessity, science has generally been reluctant to proceed according to its own scientific rules. Nevertheless, good science demands this openness.

Many present-day problems have been caused by the belief that pieces of the whole could be separately analyzed. Western science operates on the assumption that the key to nature lies in ever smaller pieces of the whole. Current research in many disciplines is proving that just the opposite is true. In fact, it is only in the context of the whole that the part has any relevance. In truth, the pieces themselves are actually smaller wholes; thus, there is no escape from wholeness. From this rediscovered perspective on wholeness, consciousness is examined as a qualitative aspect of life energy.

In Chapter Three, several manifestations of life energy and wholeness are examined. The soul is defined as the spiritual expression of wholeness; its unique process in our universe is represented by the concept of spirit. Thus, the spirit of any person or object is the distinct energy frequency, or frequency band, which identifies it. The relationship of soul and spirit to the body, mind, and emotions is discussed, and a new way of understanding psychosomatic processes is developed. Love is presented as the central expression of the emotional sphere, and sadness, fear, and anger are interrelated with the loss, excitement, and boundaries of love's wholeness. Finally, health and disease are discussed from a life energy point of view.

Life Energy extends from the person to the environment, and Chapter Four looks at the effect of light, color, sound, and form on our lives. Here we also examine the consequences of radiation from the atmosphere, the ground, and our living environments. In this process, the disturbance and enhancement of wholeness is discussed.

In Chapter Five, medical therapy and psychotherapy are examined in their roles as healing media. It is proposed that a new form of therapy is required to meet today's needs. This therapy will have to be based on energy principles and a philosophy of wholeness.

In Chapter Six, Life Energy Therapy (L.E.T.), a system of therapy based on such energy concepts from both East and West is presented. The main thesis of L.E.T. is that disease and healing are forms of life energy processes and that only by understanding and using these principles in the context of wholeness is any deep change and spiritual evolution possible. L.E.T. is a spiritually oriented body psychotherapy and lifestyle based on the premise that physical health, psychological growth, and spiritual evolution are processes directly related to the unique flow of life energy through us. Each of us functions as a transformer of energy as we absorb and radiate this life force on many frequency levels. When all these levels are in harmony we experience health and well being. Otherwise, a state of dis-ease is created which then manifests on various levels as sickness, mental disorders, and meaninglessness. These discoveries prompted me to write this book and I shall elaborate on them in more detail in the last chapter.

I believe that the key to correcting the ills of daily life lies in the understanding of life energy and its functions in the state of wholeness. I also believe that acceptance of greater wholeness in all sectors of society, and in our sciences in particular, has been retarded by a basic fear of wholeness. Seen from a new perspective, our problems are actually messages about wholeness which need to be converted into constructive action. This book is intended to give you, the reader, an overview of the connectedness of the universe, using the processes of life energy. Generally, the concern for so-called physical energies such as nuclear power, electricity, magnetism, and so on, has overshadowed the very real, yet ignored, *human* side of the energy question. The fact is, we can no longer afford the luxury (or better yet, poverty) of separating ourselves from energetic processes, because they all affect us, directly or indirectly. Ultimately, you are the whole from which this book was made.

Los Angeles, 1986

Chapter One

History of Energy

Part One: The East

Introduction

In almost every civilization, modern and ancient, a concept of life energy has existed, understood to be a universal force permeating all things and bringing them into movement. From what we know of prehistoric people, their understanding of life energy was largely based on its relation to aspects of nature such as the sun, moon, winds, and water. Many of these aspects, because of their powerful influence on health, food, and, ultimately, survival, were believed to be gods or demons, depending on their effect.

Early tribal people believed that everything had its own spirit which was a manifestation of this life force. Health resulted when these spirits were in harmony with each other; disease occurred when these spirits were disturbed or displeased. Because the finer workings of life energy processes were not clearly understood, the movement of energy in sickness, weather, war, and so forth was often thought to be of supernatural origin. Nature, therefore, was considered to be the manifestation of super-natural forces which brought life to the various aspects of nature.

As our early ancestors began to see relationships between energy processes, they passed this knowledge on from person to person as part of their oral traditions. Some people became energy specialists because they experienced "callings" (physical symptoms such as fits or delirium were often considered a "calling" from the spirits, charging a person to act as a medium). As physician and healer, it was this person's task to understand the movement of energy in illness and to find out which spirits or tribal transgressions were to blame for the disharmony. Through the ages, this information about energy, spirits, and disease was transmitted to advanced civilizations. This knowledge has been systematically gathered and taught, both to specialists such as doctors and scientists, and to laypersons who practice folk medicine.

In some cases, the "primitive" knowledge of energy and its usage was probably quite superior to that of modern civilizations. In fact, some of the early energy technology was not equalled in modern cultures for thousands of years. Evidence gathered by archaeologists from historically out-of-place artifacts (coined "ooparts") strongly indicates that we generally underestimate the capabilities of our ancestors. According to standard views of history, these ooparts should not exist—but they do. Consider the discovery of electric cells (similar to batteries) in Iraq, dated around 100 B.C.—eighteen centuries before Benjamin Franklin supposedly discovered electricity! Using clay pots lined with an inner cylinder of sheet copper and having an iron rod suspended in the center, the ancient Iraqis were thought to have added an acid, probably grape juice, to make a battery.[1] In Egypt, researchers found a curious piece of sycamore wood which had astounding aerodynamic features. Scientific tests showed that this 5.6-inch long piece of wood, called the saqqara bird, could actually fly; therefore, it has been called an ancient model airplane. Yet, what did our "primitive" ancestors know about flying? (It is interesting to note that the U.S. government had, coincidentally, considered building an oblique winged aircraft which closely resembles this 2000-year-old Egyptian relic.)

Other evidence based on chemical analysis suggests that the mighty structures of the past such as Stonehenge in England, the pyramids in Egypt, the Great Stone Heads of the Olmecs in Central America (each weighing around twenty-four tons), and the Gate of Sun (a ten-ton gate standing by itself on an isolated plateau in Bolivia, 13,000 feet above sea level), may have been created by melting rock. Joseph Davidots, a chemical scientist in France, has presented evidence, based on its molecular structure, that indicates the Gate of Sun was once liquid. He theorized that stone was excavated from quarries, liquified by oxalic acid (which is still present as a residue on the Stone Gate), and transported to the building site, where it was poured into a mould.

Egyptians

One of the oldest recorded sciences of life energy was that developed by the Egyptians, who named this force *ga-llama* or *ka*.* *Ga-llama*

---

*This science may be 142,000 years old (H. Verlag).

was energy taken in and expressed by the breath. It provided the basis for a system of training now known as Caucasian or Egyptian yoga. Not much more is known about this practice except that it may have been the basis for yoga in India.

We do know that the Egyptians believed in an original wholeness, called *nun* which operated through cosmic or vital powers called *neteriv.* As the *nun* began to express itself, Atum, the One, became the creator of all things. In one version of the Creation, Atum creates himself from his own heart and brings forth eight elementary principles.

Throughout Egyptian lore the principle of polarity is used to explain the movement of life energy, such as Osiris (the Nile) impregnating Isis, the Earth, to bring forth life. The concept of spirit was expressed in the root *akh,* which incarnates the body, *kha,* and radiates light (see Figure 1). Akh is also used to designate the third eye, which can be angry or benevolent. The soul, *ba,* had cosmic qualities, was present in humans, and transmigrated after death. Whether a person escaped the cycle of births depended upon the quality of *maat,* consciousness, which also resided in the heart.[2] All of these functions operated through the vital power of *ka,* life energy.

We also know that the Egyptians considered disease to be the result of evil spirits or the soul of a dead person which had managed to enter a living body. The priest-physician was generally called upon to plead with the gods or give a recipe for medication. The symbol R_x, still used in medicine today, stood for the Eye of Horus, a symbol used in healing to represent a magical plea to Thoth, the god of wisdom.

Thoth, it is believed, was a deification of a legendary figure known as Hermes Trismegistus, the supposed founder of an ancient wisdom known as the Kybalion. As far as is known no written or printed knowledge of Hermes or his doctrines exists, but an oral tradition has been passed down for thousands of years in the form of maxims, axioms, and precepts. Hermes is believed by some to have been an Egyptian who lived at the time of Abraham and, according to Jewish tradition, may even have been one of his teachers. Adherents of the Kybalion hold that Hermes developed a "Secret Doctrine" to describe laws of the universe which could only be understood by those who knew the code. Closer examination of these Hermetic axioms reveals that they are essentially laws of life energy describing processes of vibration, frequencies, rhythm, polarity, and so on.

Among these precepts are the following:
—energy exists on different planes
—everything is in vibratory motion
—various forms develop from different vibrations
—a basic polarity is found in all manifestations

—all movement is governed by laws
—chance does not exist
—alchemy is essentially a transmutation of mental, not physical, states
—an absolute state of divine energy, called the All, is the substantial reality of our universe.

EGYPTIAN EQUIVALENTS

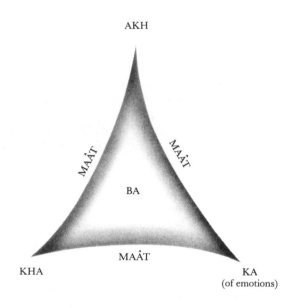

BA = Soul
AKH = Spirit
KHA = Body
KA = Energy, Maintenance of Life
MAÂT = Consciousness

Figure 1.

According to tradition, Hermes taught many scholars from all over the world. Eventually, they returned to their own countries and developed systems such as Chinese medicine, Ayurveda in India, and the Cabala among the Hebrews. In the West, the Hermetic doctrine has been continued by occult schools such as the Theosophists, the Masons, and the Rosicrucians.

Egyptian architecture in the form of pyramids also has a connection to energy and healing. Each granite stone used to build the pyramids was precisely cut for its place. In fact, the stones are so finely cut that the space between them is no more than one-thousandth of an inch. Because of this precision we have to assume that the Egyptians were tremendously advanced technologically about energy usage, or they had help from an advanced culture like Atlantis. In our time, only the laser could so accurately cut these huge stones, which weighed a total of six million tons!

Early pyramid research began when a man named Boris accidentally rediscovered that cats who had entered the pyramids had been "mummified," as well preserved as were the Egyptian dead. Such phenomena have been explained by subsequent studies finding that the energy present in the pyramid is derived from its unique form.

Many effects of the pyramid form have been recorded by using scale models of the Great Pyramid at Gizeh in Egypt. It has been found that meat and plants subjected to pyramid treatments become dehydrated, though decay does not occur; plants grow two to three times as fast; fruit lasts longer; coffee loses its bitterness; animals tend to become vegetarians; and intense heat and tingling in human hands has been reported.[3]

Research has shown that the fifth point, on top of the pyramid, focuses vibratory energy fields by acting as a psychotronic generator for cosmic energy. Airplane pilots are instructed not to fly over the pyramids because their instruments go out of control or stop working completely. In addition, scientists at the University of the Trees, under the directorship of Dr. Hills, have determined that there are:

> ...two basic energy spirals originating at the area of the pyramid's apex where the capstone was located. A positive, clockwise rotating energy spiral comes off the top [moving upwards] while a negative, counter clockwise rotating energy spiral radiates down inside to the base.[4]

Authors Allen et al. point out that the downward flow of energy in the pyramid destroys cell life and therefore retards decay, even leading to mummification. They suggest that the royal chamber in the pyramid was designed to block out most of this negative energy, although it allowed a special ray of concentrated life energy called the Pi-ray to fall on the coffer.[5] Contrary to popular belief, this coffer was not used for burial purposes but to test spiritual initiates to see if they were sufficiently pure to withstand this negative ray (see Figure 2).

Despite the usual apex-upward form of the pyramids, legend has it that in the ancient city of Jemen a pyramid is buried with its apex pointing down. As we shall see in the next section, these different pyramid forms parallel the Chinese symbols of Yin and Yang.

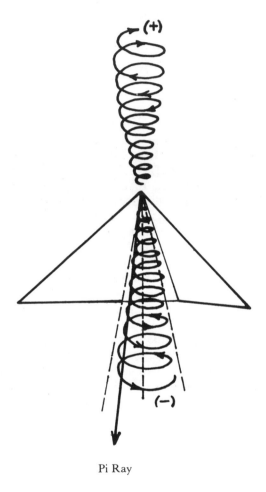

Pi Ray

Figure 2. Energy Stream in an Egyptian Pyramid*

Symbolically, the serpent has always represented some form of life energy because of its activity, its mobility, its adaptability (some

*Reprinted from *Energy, Matter & Form* by Phil Allen et al. by permission of University of the Trees Press. Copyright © 1977.

snakes can swallow a whole deer live), and its power for good* or evil. In Egypt, the serpent has a particularly strong relationship to women, and was often used as a symbol for female deities. The Egyptians used the image of serpent biting its tail as a symbol of wholeness. This symbology of wholeness has remained constant throughout the ages, particularly in relation to other symbols such as the hexagram. With the sun (also a symbol of wholeness) at its center, the serpent with outspread wings represented the voyage to the higher spheres. According to Hindu thought, this path is known as evolution. On an Egyptian headpiece over the forehead the serpent represented protection of an area known in India as the third-eye (or sixth) chakra, a higher energy center.

Chinese

Oriental records of the systematic study and practice of life energy principles originated in China. Like their tribal ancestors, the Chinese had a deep connection to the relationship between this world (expressed as earth) and the world beyond (expressed as heaven). Therefore, it is only natural that their several-thousand-year-old agricultural tradition would provide them with theoretical and practical connections to nature and its elements. This connection came to be expressed as the Tao by Lao Tzu, the spiritual father of Taoism, in the 6th Century B.C., though he neither created the word "Tao" nor was he the originator of its meaning. According to Hackmann:

> Tao means the way and method of maintaining the harmony between this world and beyond; that is, by shaping earthly conduct to correspond completely with the demands of the other world.[6]

In practice, to follow the Tao (originally meaning "the way") was to increase awareness by living in accordance with the movement of life energy as it manifests in the seasons, in elements of creation and destruction, in sickness and health, and in nutrition and philosophy. The Tao was equivalent to wholeness and harmony, and to follow its path meant to resonate with the spirits of life and the energy currents of the universe; this resonance led to health and well-being. Turning away from Tao constituted disobedience to universal laws and was sure to result in sickness and disharmony, as a disturbance of the spirits caused illness for the earlier tribal peoples.

*Snake poison has been used as a healing medication.

The Tao is actually a system of energy principles applied to all phases of life. The early Chinese called this energy Chi; in Japan it was Ki, in Korea, Gi. Chi is thought to be responsible for bodily function, the motion of the planets, and other movements of nature such as the wind.

According to Taoist belief, Chi continues its movement throughout various forms and processes via a polarized flow of life energy. As with heaven and earth, these polarities express the unending relationship between two extremes which flow together to produce harmony. Yin, which originally meant "the shady side of the hill," expresses one tendency of energy as symbolized by the moon, earth, night, water, coldness, negative charge, femininity, and centripetal movement (expressed symbolically as ∇). Yang, its counterpart, evolved from the term "sunny side of the hill" into a representation of sun, heaven, day, fire, dryness, light, positive charge, virility, and centrifugal movement (symbolized by Δ). The modern scientific corollary of Yin and Yang is found in the binary system of "0" and "1" into which all computer languages can be coded. As Yin and Yang tendencies meet in any process they produce a complementary pattern of movement which results in a spiral-like flow, the beginnings of which can be seen in the ancient Chinese symbol, the Wu-Gi.

Figure 3. The Wu-Gi, the Chinese Diagram of the Cosmic Principle. The forces Yin and Yang polarize manifestation of life energy function in a cyclical movement. The light and the dark points show that both forces at the high point of their development already show the seed for the complementary force.

Water and oil, when in the same container, will not mix (to make a modern-day analogy), reflecting the qualities of Yin and Yang, which, though always in harmony, at times exhibit different proportions in terms of both forms and process.

Figure 4. Waves of Oil and Water as Yin and Yang

On a biological level, for example, each man and woman has both male and female sex hormones. Each of us possesses a relative proportion of these hormones, depending on inheritance, eating habits, emotional expression, and spiritual practice. Our wholeness is an integration of all such Yin and Yang components.

Among the many principles of Taoism is the statement that everything is in a state of constant change. This change results from the organic movement of Yin and Yang processes in the whole. In order to maintain this constant flow, the Taoists developed a series of classical dances called T'ai Chi, used both for health maintenance and self-defense. Each movement is also based on Yin/Yang, where the balance necessary for harmony—physical, emotional and spiritual—is found. These exercises, patterned after the movements of tigers, deer, bears, apes, and birds, were practiced daily to improve the movement of Chi, or life energy, through the body.

A related and equally important system is Kung-Fu, generally known as a Chinese martial art. However, the beginning of Kung-Fu, like T'ai Chi, was dance. Kung-Fu originally meant "work-man" or "the man who works with the art of bodily exercise for the prevention or treatment of disease."[7] As an entire system, like the philosophy of the Tao, Kung-Fu taught movement, breathing, postures, and massage to maintain the flow of life energy and to effect cures when stagnation or injury had blocked its movement.

In addition to T'ai Chi and Kung-Fu, a number of other systems of energy flow have developed over the years. Among the more important are Aikido, which was recently developed from elements of spear fighting—jujitsu and eikijutsu, among others; karate (Japanese); Tae Kwon Do (Korean); and judo. In principle, most of the martial arts place great emphasis on the use of internal energy as manifest in the Tan Den (an energy center located two fingers below the navel).

In order to effect cures when necessary, the Chinese developed several widely used systems. Interestingly enough, each particular region of China developed its own style of healing based on the climate and environment of that area. In the Western mountains, minerals and herbs were used to heal. In the East, where more animal food, including shellfish, is eaten, surgery developed. In the colder climate of the north moxibustion (a method of burning moxa (mugwort) for heat) was used; in the south acupuncture developed. In the central area, where the climate is moderate, massage developed as a balancing and restorative approach to life energy.

The theory behind acupuncture describes how Chi flows throughout the body in vessels called meridians. Research conducted in 1980 in Tokyo by Dr. Hiroshi Motoyama, involving liquid crystals which were painted on the skin, has visually confirmed the location and function of the meridians.[8] His findings have been supported by Dr. Kim Bong Han of North Korea, who injected the isotope P32 into meridians and traced their pathways. Kim discovered a fluid called Sanal in these meridians which contains DNA* and RNA** molecules, protein, estrogen, and all the essential amino acids necessary for life. His finding suggests that these meridians together may be a major "energy circulatory system" virtually unknown to Western science. Based on the results of thousands of experiments, he suggests that these energy meridians exist in all multicellular organisms and exhibit themselves in as little as fifteen hours after conception (in chicks).

According to oriental thought, health is maintained by a continual, free flow of energy along these channels which directly effects lymph, nerve, and blood functions. Tiny energy centers, called acupoints (used in both acupuncture and acupressure), gather and distribute the life force along the meridians. These points have been used in treatment for at least five thousand years, although their systematization

---

*DNA is a double helixed molecule which is the key to cellular reproduction and essential to life.

**RNA is a substance in DNA which transmits hereditary characteristics from generation to generation.

came later. Dr. Kim claims to have found a group of small oval cells, surrounded by capillaries in the skin and other cells deeper in the body, which he thinks are these acupoints.

Various researchers, using a Tobiscope, which measures degrees of electrical resistance, have found that acupoints have lower resistance than surrounding skin, thus allowing energy to flow more easily at these sites. One such researcher, Soviet scientist Victor Adamenko has found that these acupoints produce from fifty to one hundred and fifty microvolts of electricity. Autosuggestion can stimulate them to produce up to five hundred microvolts. Because of their energy output these points appear to be highly concentrated vortices or spirals of energy which, on a micro-scale, resemble the Indian chakras.

Acupuncture's curative power lies in stimulating blocked life energy processes locally and along the meridian as a whole. Stones, bone, bamboo, and, more recently, metal have all been used to effect this energy flow by piercing the skin to a depth appropriate for each point and person. This relieves the congestion and toxification which exists. Acupuncture needles inserted into the tissue affect the molecules in the tissue fluid by changing the flow of traditional, as well as nonaccepted, forms of energy.

Contemporary acupuncture also burns moxa at selected points to increase their energy charge, along with recommending diet and herbal medicines to effect a complete treatment. Research on acupoints has demonstrated that they can be stimulated by electricity, laser beams, ultra-sound, and magnets, as well as traditional needling and moxa techniques. Acupuncture seems to be most effective with acute conditions ranging from back pain to arthritis, and may be helpful in chronic conditions if the energy of the body is strong enough. Soviet scientists have even demonstrated effectiveness in reversing tumor growth and the regeneration of new tissue.[9]

Oriental massage, best known as acupressure or Shiatsu, also uses acupoints to relieve acute problems and maintain health. Shiatsu (meaning finger pressure) is actually an integrated system of massage which encompasses acupressure, anma massage (an ancient Japanese practice), Ampaku, therapy of the viscera, and some western techniques. Though many styles of Shiatsu exist, all agree that stagnation of Chi or Ki causes disease and that this stagnation can be felt as nodules which are hardened or granular areas below the skin's surface. Treatment consists of rhythmic pressure, pulling, kneading, and similar movements which remove these waste deposits and bring fresh energy to the site.

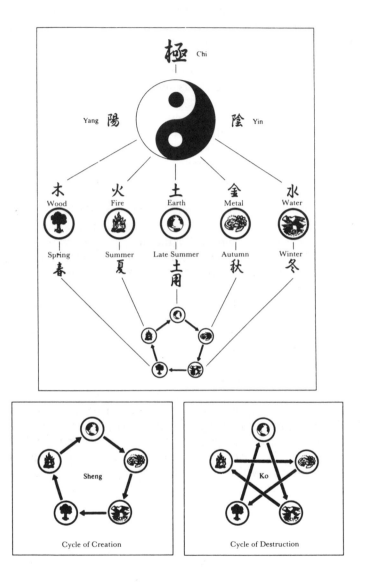

Figure 5. The Differentiation of Life Energy Based on the Chinese Model: from the absolute (Chi, not to be confused with the Ch'i of life energy). The polarized forces Yin and Yang create the function of the Five Elements. According to the "Cycle of Creation" and the "Cycle of Destruction" these elements influence one another.

An interesting thing about these points is that each has several levels of effect. Light stimulation of the points, for example, stimulating a point behind the ear lobes, will produce a sensual feeling; going a little deeper will stimulate heat generated by the organs. If we go deeper still, these points bring about emotional release, while the deepest levels can produce paralysis (as in judo or jujitsu).

As Yin and Yang polarities of life energy flow throughout the meridians, organs, and in the universe itself, they are further manifested in five elements of transformations. Four of these elements—fire, earth, air (in Chinese, metal represents air), and water—are almost universally recognized as four aspects of the life force. The fifth, wood, represents the life energy which gives rise to the other four.

These five elements are expressed in all forms of nature, including human beings. Each organ is related to one of the elements, the seasons, the time of day, type of food, emotions, and so on. In a complete system of medicine, philosophy, or life style, every aspect of life can be understood as a movement of Chi in the polarized activity of Yin and Yang and further distributed into five elements. Every life process is interconnected by an organic movement of life energy in a nontechnical theory of relativity whose basis is wholeness.

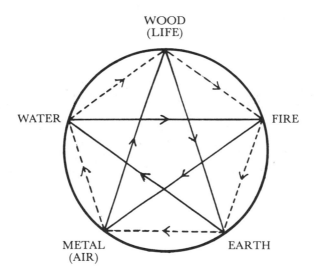

Figure 6. The Five Elements *

*Reprinted from *Energy, Matter & Form* by Phil Allen et al. by permission of University of the Trees Press. Copyright © 1977.

Indians

Like the Chinese, the Indians also developed a comprehensive phi-losophy, a unique approach to medicine, and a spiritual life style that were based on life energy principles. They believed that a life force called *Prana*, more basic than atomic energy, is the universal source of all things material and nonmaterial. All other forms of energy including heat, light, electricity, and so on are considered to be forms of Prana.* As we breathe, Prana (literally, breath) is inhaled and exhaled and may be increased both quantitatively and qualitatively through the practice known as Pranayama.

Currents of Prana, called *nadis*, run through the body distributing this energy completely to all parts. These nadis are numerous; the most important being Sushumna, which flows up the spine, Ida, which opens at the left nostril, and Pingala at the right nostril. Both Ida and Pingala intersect each other as they wind around the spine in serpent-like fashion. In fact, the serpent is the symbol for this rising energy, call *kundalini*, which is often pictured as coiled and at rest. Thus, the Sushumna nadi manifests its central harmonizing force from the negatively-charged Ida, called Shakti in Hindu religion, and the positively-charged Pingala, known as Shiva. This complementarity has been expressed in Yantric** art by the hexagram of the female symbol, Yoni (∇), and the male symbol, Lingam (Δ) being superimposed on one another (✡). Tantric yoga, the yoga of com-plements, uses this polarized male and female energy for good or evo-lution (white Tantra), for evil or power (black Tantra), or for sexual pleasures or personal gratifications (red Tantra). Like Yin and Yang in Chinese philosophy, Shakti and Shiva demonstrate a dual aspect of life energy which flows together by alternately containing and expanding this universal force.

The movement of these three energy canals is depicted in the *meru danda*, an ancient symbol which represents the evolution of mankind from the base (matter) to the divine Atman (spirit).

Instead of two channels representing Ida and Pingala, only the energy influence of each on their respective sides is visible. (As we shall see later, in Greek culture these two channels are separately delineated in the symbol for health, the caduceus.) The center staff

---

*In Greek philosophy Prana corresponds to psychikon pneuma or ani-mal spirits, an intermediate state of energy between spirit and matter (Bailey, A.).

**Yantric art is represented by mandalas (meditation circles) used to wor-ship dieties.

is the Sushumna canal which stabilizes the other two nadis and acts as their energy harmonizer.

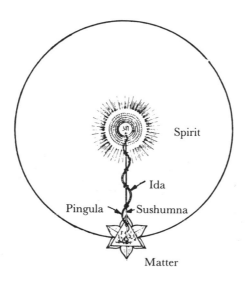

Figure 7. The Meru Danda*

In the body, Prana manifests as kundalini (whose source is said to be magnetic by some scholars of Hindu study).** This kundalini energy descends these three channels, creating whirling energy centers as it envelopes matter from top to bottom. These centers, known as *chakras*, or spinning wheels, are formed as the kundalini slows in both frequency and process. At its lowest point, kundalini rests at a place between the anus and the genitals, until it is stimulated to ascend once again in these three channels.

The chakras are located on the etheric level of energy but are directly related to a network of nerves called nerve plexi in the physical body. Each plexus is related to an endocrine gland which excites or inhibits physiological processes by releasing hormones into the bloodstream. Scientists have found a special neuroendocrine cell,

---

*Reprinted from *Energy, Matter & Form* by Phil Allen et al. by permission of University of the Trees Press. Copyright © 1977.

**This descent into matter is known spiritually as *involution* and will be covered in Chapter Three.

called chromaffin tissue, which is located in all major nerve plexi that both carry nerve impulses and secrete adrenalin. It may be that the gathering and distributing functions of the chakras affect the nerves and therefore the entire body through this chromaffin tissue. These chromaffin cells follow the basic spiral pattern of the double helix found in DNA, as well as the sympathetic nervous chains along the spine which parallel the movement of life energy along the Ida and Pingala channels as they unite all the chakras.[10] Therefore, through a series of transformations, higher frequencied energy from the cosmos may be taken in and distributed by the chakras in a form the body can use.

Figure 8. The Chakras: The position of the life energy centers (chakras) and the movement of the three main streams of life energy in the human body. The vertebrae correspond with the vertical line of the Sushumna-Nadi, the spiral wound double line the Ida-Nadi, and the opposite flowing single line, the Pingala-Nadi.

Dr. Motoyama's work as a Shinto priest and energy researcher has shown that the chakras are also related to acupuncture meridians. Using his AMI* machine, he has found that certain patterns of energy flowing in the meridians correspond to the openness of specific chakras. Each chakra is associated with specific psychic abilities and the functioning of specific acupuncture meridians. By determining the energy pattern he can predict the probability of developing the psychic ability which corresponds to each center.

In the process of spiritual awakening, kundalini begins to manifest as the various frequencies associated with each chakra begin to move.** Although this awakening may occur spontaneously, it usually only happens after years of practice in consciously arousing this life energy process.

This may be done by many methods: in India the most common methods used are various forms of meditation and yoga. Yoga, meaning union in Sanskrit, is commonly known in the West as a system of physical exercise. Nothing could be farther from the actual truth. First, over twenty schools or approaches to yoga may be practiced, either alone or in combination, such as hatha yoga or kriya yoga. Though hatha yoga is *the* yoga of the West and does involve certain physical positions (asanas), it is far more than gymnastics. It is a process of harmony formed on the physical level and is intended to lead to spiritual development by letting go of the body. Breathing, particularly the Pranayama mentioned earlier, is used to control the development of energy. Kriya yoga, on the other hand, is a union produced by movements usually used as purification. Involuntary kriyas or movements often occur in the process of raising kundalini and may be experienced in hatha yoga as well, although this is more rare. The yogas themselves are often seen as meditation or as pre-meditation practices, because their connection to the practice or experience of meditation is so intertwined.

As in Chinese medicine, the concept of health in Indian medicine focuses on balance and harmony. When prana is flowing correctly there can be no disease. However, if this flow is obstructed or weak, the science of medicine called Ayurveda addresses this problem. Ayurveda has been practiced in principle for thousands of years, but it was not systematized until about three thousand years ago. Ayurveda means the science (veda) of health and long life (Ayur).

*AMI: Apparatus for measuring the functions of the meridians and their corresponding internal organs.
**This energy movement upwards from matter to soul is called evolution (see Chapter Three).

Ayurveda sees human beings as composed of soul (mind) and body (matter), and serves to help humanity by alleviation of our mental and physical problems, as well as our attachment to matter. The latter is especially important as it demonstrates Ayurveda's application to the spiritual aspects of energy as well as the physical and mental. Thus, the goal is not only physical/psychological health, but a true salvation from all attachment, which is also the basis of Buddhist thought.

The Ayurvedic doctor is interested in finding out what is being held onto and what treatment, if any, is to be recommended. I knew a Western woman once who went to a Nepalese Ayurvedic doctor for treatment of a bladder infection. She was asked to come into the room where the doctor was drinking tea and reading his newspaper. After waiting for him to say something, she grew impatient and demanded that he listen to her complaint. He politely refused and told her to come back the next day at the same hour. Again she returned, but all was as before; he did not allow her to tell her whole story of pain, but, once again, he told her to return.

Some time passed, and after much resistance she decided to return. This time the doctor looked at her, smiled, and asked: "It's feeling better, isn't it?" To her amazement, she realized that in her frustration she had forgotten about the bladder and the pain was almost gone. He then gave her some medication to finalize the treatment. The complete treatment, however, had consisted of treating her as a whole person, first by dealing with her attitude and behavior, and then giving medication only for what was additionally necessary. Needless to say, she learned more about herself than simply how to cure a bladder infection.

Ayurvedic treatment does not seek to remove symptoms but instead, views symptoms as manifestations of a deeper problem. Medication is only given when appropriate. Ayurveda categorizes symptoms into five elements called bhutas: ether, air, fire, water, and earth, as well as three qualities of energy: *sattva*, a state of balance (analogous to the harmonizing effect of the sushumna channel); *rajas*, the quality of activity (similar to the positively charged pingala channel and Shiva); and *tamas*, the quality of quiescence or inertia (like the negatively charged ida nadi, and shakti).

Ayurveda assesses these qualities as they manifest in patient behavior and attitudes. It then combines this assessment with a diagnosis of symptoms based on the five elements discussed, and considers other information, such as family and life circumstances, to acquire a complete picture of what the deeper problem really is. In many cases, the Ayurvedic doctor also instructs the patient in the regulation of his personal habits, sexual activities, and perhaps even choice of marital partner. The patient, for his or her part, is obliged to direct himself towards purity and to overcome "animal" instincts of mechanistic behavior and life style.

Tibetans

Tibetan Buddhist culture is rich in tradition and practices which promote spiritual development. Some Tibetans practice a form of yoga derived from the Kundalini yoga of India. Like the Indians, the Tibetan lamas (holy men) believe in a force of life energy which actuates all phenomena in its universal flow. The Tibetans use the word *lung* to describe the *kundalini*-type energy and believe it is a force extracted from the universal, naturally-existing *prana*.

Though not unique to the Tibetans, the practice they developed called *tummo* activates and stores this energy in the body to be used when necessary to generate tremendous amounts of psycho-physical heat. The channels for this heat are called *tsas*, and they correspond to the Indian *nadis*. These *tsas* are nonphysical vessels which transport *lung* principally through the central portion of the body and to the extremities as well. The *tsas* serve roughly the same purpose as nerves do in the physical body. The flow through the *tsas* unites all the energy centers, called *khor-lo* (literally, wheel, corresponding to the Indian *chakra*). These whirling transducers of life energy exchange energy both from the cosmic source on the inflow and the personal/spiritual resources of the individual on the outflow.

After years of training, *tummo* initiates are brought to a lake high in the mountains during the winter for a test. Here they sit naked and attempt to dry out wet cloths draped around their bodies. One enjoyable competition involves trying to dry out the most cloths after a whole night of Tummo exercise! Another competition tests the amount of snow that the initiates can melt as they sit on the ground. Western observers have reported that as much as ten feet away from the practitioner snow will melt solely from the heat generated by *tummo*.

Similar but opposite feats are also part of the Indian yoga tradition. One requires the yogin (the practitioner of yoga) to sit surrounded by fires of wood and cow dung which are only a few feet from his body, as the midday sun shines directly down. This feat reveals his immunity to heat. Fire-walking ceremonies in the South Sea islands and elsewhere entail similar processes.

The aim of these feats of immunity to extremes of heat and cold is detachment from physical needs of warmth and coldness. By giving themselves in an act of surrender to a power greater than their own, the initiates of such practices go beyond their individual limits and thereby acquire qualities of the life energy itself—the total regulation of natural forces through internal harmony. They become impervious to the elements because they *become* these elements. Where there is no separation the polarity of heat and cold cannot exist.

The Tibetans also believe an energy called *shugs* manifests whenever a thought is made. They believe thought is energy which can be passed from person to person as well as from nation to person. In both cases, energy is processed in a specific way and extended to another person by touch, idea, trance, and so forth. In the case of a nation, consistent energy vibrations will radiate to all people born in that culture. By implication, this means that each of us is subject to national influences on certain energy levels; through increased consciousness, however, we can transform these influences when they are negative (but first we have to become aware of what these influences are).

Hawaiians

The ancient Hawaiians developed Huna—a system of medicine and healing based on life energy concepts. They identified three main forms: Manab*—body waves; Mana Mana—thinking waves; and Mana Loa—spiritual or psychic energy. Of the three, Mana Loa was considered to have the highest evolutionary status because of its influence over all things. Its symbol was the sun, a major source of life energy—a parallel to the Hindu belief that prana (primordial energy) is emitted from the sun.

For each of these forms of life energy, a corresponding body existed on a different energy plane. These were called Aka bodies** and together composed a Trinity of Man. The Mana Aka dealt with low-voltage energy which could be stored in wood, and could be transmitted from person to person. Mana Aka was the energetic form of what was spiritually called the low self because its nature was subconscious. A large transference of Mana by "will" could paralyze or mesmerize someone into unconsciousness, if desired. Its main function was to vitalize the physical body, transforming it from mere matter into a living transducer of life energy.

Mana Mana was considered to be a higher-frequency force used by the conscious mind and manifests itself in the Mana Mana Aka as the middle self, for thinking and projective activities (like the

*Mana is the medium for waves of energy that are propagated through the body.
**Body here might be understood as an energy field in modern physics.

Tibetan shugs). These procedures also included a type of hypnosis that could place a thought in the mind of another to grow like a germinating seed.

The third manifestation of Huna life energy, Mana Loa—thought to be the most powerful, was manifest in the Mana Loa Aka as the superconscious mind and the higher spiritual self for healing and spiritual development. The Huna healers, called Kahunas, practiced a form of laying-on-of-hands called Lomi Lomi, as well as more traditional massage, bodily manipulation, and baths to effect their cures. The Kahunas practiced breathing-in of Mana, like the Pranayama techniques of the Indians, and visualized Mana rising in them until it overflowed, much like Tibetan Tummo exercises. According to Max Long, who spent years studying Huna medicine, the Kahunas could perform extraordinary healing, control the winds, and foretell the future.

The Jews

The ancient Hebrews knew the concept of life energy as "cheim," the dynamic principle of all life. They believed all living things were infused with this life force which manifested itself as their "spirit." They used the word "ruach" (like the Arabic "ruh") to express this animating spirit, which could be disturbed in illness. One manifestation of "cheim" was koach, which also translated as energy but generally meant power or strength—of either God or people.

The Hebrew connection to life energy intertwined with the traditions and teachings of God, because he was considered to be the totality of this dynamic force. One of the most important sources for understanding this relationship is the Bible. Because of its historical style, however, the Bible is often misunderstood as a simple history of the Jews. Biblical scholars cite four possible levels of interpretation: the historical; the allegorical, which is equivalent to a step-by-step process of spiritual evolution; the cryptic, whereby a secret code of esoteric knowledge is hidden; and the Cabalistic level. This last level refers to a system of religious philosophy which predated even the Bible and has its roots in ancient Egypt.

In addition, the Bible may be interpreted on a fifth level; namely, the energetic, in which the laws and principles of life energy are detailed. Because any extrapolation of this idea goes beyond our present focus, and because the cabalistic tradition contains components of this energy perspective, we will examine the Cabala more closely.

Cabala comes from the Hebrew *qabal*, which means to receive and reveal. Sometimes known as the Secret Wisdom, the Cabala is believed to have been passed from generation to generation since the time of

Moses by a tradition of initiates who were taught energy secrets. From this ancient tradition and the more recent interpretations of its meanings, some important understandings of Hebrew thought and lifestyle concerning life energy have emerged.

God was central to Jewish thought; however, in the Bible God as Jehovah is described as being inexpressible. The four Hebrew letters which represent this inexpressibility are:

Yod

Heh

Wav

Heh

Figure 9. The "Yahweh" Tetragrammaton

According to author Jeff Love, God is not really a name but a "formula describing a universal process."[11] Each of the letters expresses a quality which is a manifestation of God in what is knows as a tetragrammaton. *Yod* provides the basis for all the other letters. It is symbolized by a flame and represents the quality of *force*, which is considered to be male and active; it also denotes the quality time as expressed through a sequence of forces. *Hay*, the second letter, denotes the quality pattern which relies on *structure* for its existence. Because of its positioning patterns it also implies the condition *space*, a located-ness. In its fourth position, *hay* denotes a formal structure called *form*, which indicates a certain solidity or substance known in physics as mass. The third letter, *vav*, concerns us most, because it represents *activity*. In physics this quality of activity is connected with energy.

The inexpressible concept of God may be indirectly alluded to through his physical manifestations of *force, time, pattern, structure, space, form, mass, activity,* and *energy.* As I shall later point out, energy is the center of all other physical manifestations. Therefore, God as symbol and focus-point is equivalent to the totality of all energy manifestations which express different quantities, constellations, or levels of life energy. In the Bible, eleven names of God represent different states of consciousness or levels of energy. Several of these names begin with "El," which is composed of the first Hebrew symbol, aleph (א), meaning divine, energy or outpouring of breath, and lamed (ל) which refers to "that which stimulates." Thus, "El" means the divine energy or breath that stimulates.

Using the cabalistic code he discovered, Samuel Bousky, an American research physicist, encoded El Shaddai, one compound name of God, to mean the life force, equivalent to the Hindu prana and the oriental chi or ki. El Elohim refers to mind and spirit, and El Elyon means soul. Elohim, the name used in conjunction with the creation of the world, may be seen as the organizing principle for the other three manifestations of life, spirit, and soul. Because Elohim is masculine and feminine as well as plural, it expresses the energetic harmony of both polarities (Yin/Yang, Shakti/Shiva) as well as the wholeness of the "one from the many."

According to allegorical tradition all Biblical names may be seen as stages of consciousness, and Biblical places are conditions under which these states arise.

One major key to understanding the ancient Hebrew connection to life energy and its dynamics is the symbol of the Tree of Life. The Hebrew word for Tree of Life can be translated as the "plan or concept of existence," a meaning, by the way, also shared by the early alchemists, who used the symbol of the tree to express the relationship of tranformational elements.

Each of the circles on the Tree of Life is called a *sephira,* which means light or emanation. Sephira may also be understood as a unit of the universal whole or an energy quantum in a cosmic field of energy interchange. As such, the Tree of Life may be viewed as an energy blueprint which can be applied to many areas of study including astrology, ontology (the study of the nature of existence), optics, metaphysics, religion, mathematics, and so on. The path from one sephira to another, and the three vertical lines that run through the sephirot (pl. for sephira) create an energy flow diagram similar to acupuncture's system of points and meridians, and the Indian (or Tibetan) system of *nadis* and *chakras.*

Like the symbology of the Indian Meru Dandu, the Bible mentions a serpent in the Tree of Knowledge of good and evil in the Garden of Paradise. Generally, the serpent is believed to have enticed Adam and Eve into sin. From another point of view, the snake—an ancient symbol for life energy—is only tempting to those who remain attached to the polarity of good and evil. Otherwise this neutral energy is merely a medium for the knowledge of wholeness.

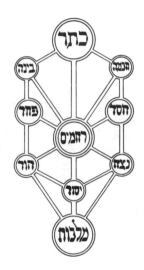

Figure 10. The Tree of Life: The cabalist diagram of the changing function between the different manifestations of life energy.

Like the Indian Yantric symbol and the Chinese symbols for Yin and Yang, the Hebrews also used two triangles as a symbol for balance which are known as the Star of David. By superimposing these two triangles atop one another, the six-pointed star is created ✡ . Incidentally, this form is also represented by the first six sephiroth of the Tree of Life, (the bottom four sephiroth form a Latin cross ✝ when the fifth sephira is shared by both the star and the cross). The Star of David, also known as Solomon's seal, Magen (Mogen) David, and the Shield of David, is an ancient hexagram dating at least as far back as the Egyptians. It has always symbolized the balance between two complementary polarities such as the dark and light forces, the conscious and unconscious, and the earthly and heavenly realms. Eliphas Levi has defined one occult meaning of this symbol as the union of the magical triangle of fate, will, and power with the godly triangle of lawfulness, freedom, and reasonableness. Its earliest attested Jewish use is found on a seventh-century B.C. seal belonging to Joshua ben Asayahu of Sidon. It was later found on a second-century A.D. Galilean synagogue, alongside a pentagram, a radial star, and a swastica! Solomon, it is believed, used this symbol as a manifestation of power; he is also thought to have received an image of this seal as a symbol for Hebrew victory.[12] Attributed to a strong Zionist movement, the Star of David became the symbol for the Hebrews and was later adopted as the national emblem of the Jewish State of Israel.

Of course, not all Jews believed in the Cabala. In the seventeenth century Spinoza, an outcast Jewish-Dutch philosopher, explained that God was the prime energy behind the wholeness of the universe. Though Spinoza did not believe in the Cabala, he did believe that the life principle in all things was God and that this indivisible God was pure energy, the principle of movement in an ever-changing world. Albert Einstein, himself a Jew, when asked if he believed in God, said, "I believe in Spinoza's God."[13]

The philosophies of the East had a great influence on the history of life energy principles as seen in the Orient's complete systems of learning and medical practice. In addition, several individuals from the East also stand out as having made significant contributions to important aspects of energy concepts.

Galen

Six hundred years after Hippocrates' time, Galen, a native of Perganum in northwest Asia Minor, made a major contribution to medicine by organizing all medical knowledge from Hippocrates onwards into a comprehensive whole. He believed in a force he called *physis* which pervades all of life and manifests in physical form. Through properties of attraction, retention, and expulsion, *physis* functioned to promote health and growth. Galen also postulated a *pneuma* or vital air through which the *physis* became operative. This concept corresponds closely to the Indian *prana* that charges all other energy processes and the later physics concept of ether. Galen thought that his *pneuma* was carried through vessels of nerves throughout the body (a parallel to the Chinese system of acupuncture meridians). He also recognized that life energy dispersed itself throughout the body according to natural principles, based on the needs of the organism. In addition, like Hippocrates, he believed in the system of *humours* which were necessary to maintain balance and health.

Food also played an important role in Galen's concept of wholeness. He believed that foods modified the body, based on the *humours* of which all foods were made, the soil in which they were grown, and the diet of the animals who provided meat.

Avicenna

Another nine hundred years were to pass before life energy principles in medicine would again be revitalized, this time by Avicenna. Despite the fact that Avicenna could be considered one of the fathers of nature-cure systems and pharmacology, he is practically unknown in the West. Born Abu Ali al-Husein ibn Sina of Bokhara in Persia, Avicenna authored the Canon of Medicine (Qanun-fi-l-Tibb), an eighteen-volume compendium of existing medical knowledge. In the Near and Middle East, as well as in India, it still remains the bible of medical teaching and practice for thousands of people.

According to Avicenna, health is based on the flow of life energy called *ruh* in Muslim. *Ruh* is a quasi-material substance acting more like a ray of light than Galen's *pneuma*. It was thought to be formed by the lighter, vaporous portions of the *humours* in the heart. In Avicenna's belief system, *ruh* is carried by the blood vessels, conditioned by respiration, and forms the basis of all functional activity in the body. Organs of the body are thought to develop based on the proportion of the *humours*.

According to Shah,[14] the concept of *ruh* may be identified on the physical level as glucose or blood sugar. Avicenna's concept of a vital force might equate with the basic metabolic energy that underlies the life and activity of all organs and tissues. Reminiscent of the Tibetan *tummo*, *ruh* manifests as an innate heat regulated by the breathing.

The quantity of *ruh* is regulated by the vasomotor center, through the contraction and expansion of the pulse. This, in turn, is heavily influenced by emotional changes which, when outwardly expressed, may produce the physical and emotional coldness so often seen in clinical practice. When anxiety and anger are mixed, both an inward and outward movement of life energy is experienced.

Clearly, Avicenna believed in the polarity of energy when he spoke about the hot, dry air and fire qualities as being male, and cold, moist matter and water as being female. In his system, a mutual interaction of these polarities leads to a balance which can never be perfect. Rather, balance (or, as he called it, a "pattern of the body") must only be seen from a whole perspective as being appropriate for the human being at any one time. He was advocating a *dynamic balance* of energy flow quite similar in concept to Aikido.

Balance, therefore, is always relative, depending upon a number of factors:

—the species as a whole,
—geographical location,
—general pattern for an individual,
—temporary balance of the individual in relation to his organs,
—the equilibrium of the organ itself,
—racial patterns—different races have varied proportions of energy,
—patterns of age—children possess moderate excesses of moisture and warmth for growth; adults for maintenance functions; and older people tend to be colder and more dry, and
—patterns of sex—women tend to be colder and more moist than men.

Throughout Eastern thought there has been a continual usage of life energy concepts both in its world view (Weltanschauen) and its healing practices. There is a remarkably consistent understanding of how life energy functions and about its role as a medium for integrating all aspects of life such as food, seasons, organs, spirit, body and mind. Though the forms they developed were often quite dissimilar, Western researchers also saw life energy in ways quite similar to more traditional cultures in the East.

Part Two: The West

Introduction

It is not widely known that Western philosophies, like those of the East, have clearly pointed to an understanding and development of life energy principles. In fact, the history of Greek philosophy reads like a textbook on what is being called here a philosophy of "energism."* Energism holds that all phenomena can be described as processes of energy, and that energy has both qualitative and quantitative properties, including spiritual evolution, consciousness, information, field, and form. It further says that all experience (thinking, feeling, acting, and so on) ultimately leads to a universal whole.

If we examine the early philosophy of the Greeks from this energy-oriented point of view, we find many seeds for thought about life energy principles which closely parallel systems of life energy in the East. Among the major tenets of life energy we will examine in this book, several are quite apparent in Greek philosophy. These include

---

*An earlier concept of energism exists in ethical theory which states that right action consists of exercising one's normal capacities efficiently.

the nature of wholeness and the function of the soul, the nature of
the universal medium by which all phenomena come to exist, the
nature of movement, and the extension of wholeness as medium and
its movement into form.

The Greeks

Thales (624-546 B.C.), one of the first recognized Greek philosophers, headed the group of seven philosophers known as the Ionian
physicists or Miletians. They believed in the theory of hylozoism,
which stated that matter and life are inseparable, that life is a property of matter, and that matter has spiritual properties. Every substance which existed in the three forms of liquid, solid, and gas was
thought to have a life or soul, and was filled with God. Water was
believed to be the cosmic "stuff" of the universe. This meant that even
inanimate objects had life—a belief also supported by life energy
principles.

Anaximander, one of Thales's colleagues, called life energy *apeiron* (literally...unlimited), an indestructible substance from which all
matter (earth, air, fire) is derived. Matter, Anaximander said, was
infinite in essence but perceptible in existence. He shared the Hindu
belief in the transmigration of the soul, whereby matter creates and
disintegrates, only to be recreated again and again in a perpetual cycle
of transformation.

Anaximenes, the third member of the Miletian school, believed the
basic substance of existence to be air, which he called the *originator.*
Air was omnipresent and essential to the growth of all natural objects.
Xenophanes of Elea, the precursor of the Eleatic School of philosophy, thought that God and the universe were one. God (the *arche*, originator) was seen as the cosmic principle which was unchanging and
present in all things.

Heraclitus, on the other hand, stated that all things were in flux,
always undergoing change, a view similar to the Taoist belief that all
change is a manifestation of the dynamic interplay of opposites. Heraclitus used the symbol of fire to represent the force responsible for
the genesis of the world, which he called simply *motion.* In addition,
he used the word *logos* to express the universal order, wholeness, or
principle of law by which nature functions. All of the "laws" of modern science are based on this principle of wholeness, as seen in the
names of our scientific areas of study: bio-logy, psycho-logy, and so
on. For Heraclitus also, the soul was the spirit of the universe which
transmigrates at death.

Parmenides, the founder of the Eleatic School, saw the universe as a single permanent substance. All things which we perceive are actually only "Being," the ultimate essence. Being is unique, indivisible, unchangeable, and homogeneous. Leucippus of Abdera, founder of the school of atomism and the true father of ancient atomic theory, carried Parmenides's "ultimate reality" one step further. He believed that the actual embodiment of Being was a proliferation of qualitatively identical elements known as atoms. Both he and his successor, Democritus, were among the first philosophers to emphasize a mechanistic approach to life. They believed that all phenomena could be reduced to mechanistic terms based on an atomic structure. This trend in mechanistic thinking prevails even today in the physical sciences and behavioristic psychology, where the human being is reduced to a biomechanical machine manifesting chemical, physical, and behavioral activity.

Zeno of Elea was a disciple of Parmenides and was considered by Aristotle to be the originator of dialectic. He scoffed at the atomists, saying that if atoms had even the smallest dimensions they could be divided. (The notion that matter is made up of basic particles still plagues modern-day subatomic physicists as they search endlessly for *the* basic particle.) Zeno instead reaffirmed that reality is one—permanent and indivisible.

Empedocles, the first of the metaphysical pluralists, said that everything was composed of four basic elements: fire, air, water, and earth. These elements are moved into various arrangements by two polarized forces—love and hate—closely resembling the Yin and Yang of Chinese thought. Love, he stated, was the universal law which was responsible for unity, order, and wholeness, whereas hate caused separation, disarray, and decay.

Anaxagoras, another of the metaphysical pluralists, believed that the forces of nature must be controlled by mental or psychic energy, which he called *nous*. *Nous* resembles the logos of Heraclitus which was thought to be responsible for order, beauty, and intelligent functioning.

Pythagoras, known for his "Pythagorean theorem" in mathematics, was also one of the first Greeks in the 6th century B.C. to talk about a vital force that could heal. He referred to this life energy as the *central fire*, which he believed had its origins in a divine source, although it was also present in us as human beings. He believed health depended on the foods we eat, the thoughts we create, and the degree of balance and moderation in life. Proper health depended on the correct attunement of the body and soul, which created a harmonious pattern or rhythm of energy. Both music and color therapy were used for healing.

For Plato, a well-known student of Socrates, the soul gave beauty, order, direction, and purpose to life by uniting with matter through the physical body. The soul, he believed, had three parts—an immortal, rational part coming from God; an intermediate part, will or spirit; and a mortal, animal, or sensitive part which was the seat of appetites and belonged to the body. He felt that even though matter is imperfect because of its nature, all objects, including human beings, are impelled by *nous* to move toward the good in order to achieve divine purpose. He also distinguished between the relative truths of the senses and the absolute truth of the mind.

Aristotle, often referred to as *the* philosopher due to his influence on scientists and philosophers alike, systematized and organized the scientific knowledge of his time. Among these studies was psychology, considered to be the rational study of the soul and mental functions. Aristotle's students organized his writings on matters beyond or after physics, leading to the term metaphysics. Aristotle himself developed the term *energeia* to describe that which transforms potentiality into activity. He saw energia as the means by which essence was brought to full expression in its present existence. The *form* of an object was considered to be a manifestation of this essence, which was brought into reality through energeia, and would come to a useful end by virtue of the principle of *entelechy*. He believed that existence in the present leads automatically to the reality of the future (teleology). He thought each form possessed a pattern or design whose essence manifested itself in the existence of form. Aristotle even predated the development in physics of holograms (to be discussed later) by suggesting that objects which he called *homolomeries* could be divisible into parts which were qualitatively identical with the whole. He believed the soul was the sum of vital principles, the true Being in the body.

Despite the differences among the early philosophers, their conclusions about life can be seen as an inclusive development of the nature and function of life energy principles. One of the chief problems for philosophers and most thinkers of the West is the tendency to see differing positions or viewpoints as antithetical. However, seen from a holistic point of view, each thesis, when brought together with others, lends itself to a new understanding which need not be contrary. The polarities of love and hate (according to Empedocles), or the relative and absolute truths of Plato, even the phenomenological and metaphysical realities of Democritus, are really only complementary aspects of life energy.

The nature of the universe in relation to order and wholeness was of great interest to the Greeks. The oneness of matter and life for the Miletians, the unity of God and the universe for Xenophanes, and the oneness of the universe for Parmenides and Zeno all attest to this fact. Several referred to the soul as this wholeness (Plato and Aristotle), yet saw different aspects of the physical, spiritual, and cosmic in the manifestation of the soul (Plato). Like the Hindus, several Greeks saw the basic spirituality of life (Anaximander, Heraclitus, Empedocles, and Aristotle) in the transmigration of the soul and its life-giving properties. In fact, the body was seen as a form of the soul to be used in each lifetime.

Aristotle even developed principles of energy in his entelechy, teleology, and form concepts by which the structure and final evolution of objects was thought to be due to a design or a pattern (of energy) whose sole purpose was to fulfill itself in its movement from the present into the future. Others, such as Heraclitus with his concept of logos and Anaxagoras with his idea of nous, demonstrated the importance of life's holistic principles which are based on an organization and subsequent order, an intelligence, a sense of law based on the nature of change, and a harmony which leads ultimately to beauty.

The concept of a medial substance or life energy by which the universe of objects was created ranged from the atom of Leucippus and Democritus through the being of Parmenides, the nous of Anaxagoras, the logos of Heraclitus, the central fire of Pythagorus, to the apeiron of Anaximander and the element theories of Thales (water) and Anaximenes (air). Of course, for thousands of years previous to the development of Western thought about elements, the Chinese had already realized that the universe has five manifestations of life energy (Chi) which are actually phases of transformation.

With the exception of the atom theory, all the Greek ideas of the genesis of the universe are basically dynamic and vitalistic. But even the atomic theory of Leucippus and Democritus shows that an atom is also a unit of wholeness. Even the word atom (from the Greek *atomos*) means indivisible. If we take the atom to be indivisible on its level of energy, it too represents a whole which functions like other wholes such as a cell, a molecule, a body, and so on, in a particular frequency band of life energy. Pythagoras saw that life energy had healing qualities, and Aristotle perceived not only the fundamental relationship of energy as a medium of activity but that living in awareness of this activity became a lifestyle of fulfillment and evolution. These ideas were carried over into medicine and healing by another great pioneer, Hippocrates.

Hippocrates

Around the 5th century B.C., Hippocrates, often called the father of modern medicine, took the philosophical principles and practices of Pythagoras and developed a practical approach to health based on a vitalistic idea of life energy. His belief that life was a basic unity and a special power of nature, called *enormon* (indwelling power), paralleled the then developing idea in Greek philosophy of life-specific energy (*spira* or spiral one).[1] Hippocrates based his philosophy of health on the concept of physics, which meant for him both the organism in its unity—its whole nature—and the spiritual-restoring essence. Life, he felt, was larger than the organism, though the organism and the environment worked in reciprocal harmony. This parallels the Gestalt idea of the organism/environment relationship which becomes disturbed in neurosis.

In the medical philosophy of Hippocrates, the relative proportions of the four humours (or body fluids)—blood, phlegm, black bile, and yellow bile—determined the health of a person. He further believed that an innate heat kept these fluids in movement and that a particular form of this heat, called *sacred fire*, protected humans from disease. In many systems of healing and therapy, this healing quality has been given the name "vis medicatrix naturae," or, simply, life energy.

Paracelsus

In the mid-1500s Paracelsus, following Hippocrates's thought, was convinced of the wholeness of nature. He is credited with the discovery that celestial bodies such as stars, the moon, and the planets affect human beings by means of a subtle force called *munia*. This form of life energy was thought to be a power inherent in the flesh which could cause disease or heal, depending on its usage. However, it was also thought to radiate within and around living organisms like a luminous sphere, to have magnetic properties, to be applicable from a distance as well as directly onto the body.

For Paracelsus, energy and matter were bound together in the concept of *iliaster* which expresses both vital force and vital matter. Health resulted when both were in harmony. He used the concept of *archeus* to describe the connection between the macrocosm of the universe as a whole and the microcosm of the individual with all his parts. He believed archeus operated through metabolizing subtle emanations of munia. The physical body was thought to mirror a semicorporeal *star body* which inhabits and maintains the physical form; thus paralleling the Greek concept of soul and closely resembling the idea of an etheric or aura body.

Paracelsus believed *quintessence* was the energy essence of a substance which, when purified, could be used to treat illness. Homeopathy later incorporated this concept into its principle of minimal dosage. The true healer, for Paracelsus, was the *fire* which was triggered by medication and was thought to operate by burning out disease. A good example of this is the common fever, which has been shown medically to speed up metabolism and inhibit the growth of virus or bacteria.[2]

Anton Mesmer

Anton Mesmer (1734-1815) used life energy principles in a rather dramatic way to develop Mesmerism and to assist his partial "discovery" of hypnosis, along with Dr. Braid, a British doctor. Mesmer believed that a vital force which he called *animal magnetism* manifested itself throughout nature. This force differed from *mineral magnetism* in that it worked without chemical action. The properties of animal magnetism included its ability to penetrate all matter, to operate at a distance, to cure nervous disease, and that it can be accumulated and transported. These findings were an extension of Paracelsus's ideas on *munia*.

Mesmer used a tub, called a *baquet*, in which people would sit holding hands. Below them, powdered glass and iron filings covered with glass bottles gathered life energy and transmitted it upwards to the rows of patients via ropes and metal chains which were attached to their bodies. Among the common phenomena resulting from such gatherings were emotional catharsis, convulsions, and states of languor, all resembling the spiritist meetings in Brazil where embodied spirits are exorcised.

Mesmer believed that health resulted from being in harmony with nature's laws; when disturbed, however, this wholeness became disease. He described the pulsation of life energy as processes of intensification and remission of energy units, called streams, which developed from the breakdown of universal fluid (animal magnetism) into smaller movements. Furthermore, Mesmer apparently developed and used the concept of body armoring in his work with patients. He called such armoring *occlusions* which resulted from chronic expansion or contraction of muscles. These ideas parallel the later work of Wilhelm Reich, whose patients felt *streamings* of pulsating life energy when they were freed from their characteristic muscular tension or treated in his orgone box. As a result of Mesmer's work, his mode of treatment has gradually come to be known as "laying-on-of-hands."

Karl von Reichenbach

Karl von Reichenbach was a nineteenth-century philosopher who, unlike Hahnemann, came to the existence of life energy by way of his technical research in magnetism, electricity, heat, light, and crystals. He was inspired to conduct this research by Goethe, who was one of his teachers, when Goethe spoke about the nature of vibration and the luminosity around plants as biological energies. Also of German descent, Reichenbach began his professional life as an industrialist, but later turned his full attention to the study and research of life energy, which he called *odyl* or *od*. According to Reichenbach, od pervaded all living bodies and penetrated through all matter. It was thought to possess polarity—positive and negative od—which could be felt in the body when crystalline substances were passed over it. Upward movements tended to produce warm, unpleasant feelings that could lead to spasm, while downward movements were cool and agreeable.

Od could be seen by gifted clairvoyants as a luminous glow that radiated from the body, which itself was believed to be a natural accumulator and transferrer of these rays. In addition, od emanations were thought to fluctuate in intensity depending on emotional state and time of day.

Samuel Hahnemann

In the late eighteenth century a physician named Christian Friedrich Samuel Hahnemann (1755-1843) developed a system of life energy. In agreement with Ayurvedic doctors, Hippocrates, and Paracelsus, he believed in the principle that "like cures like." Unlike allopathic* medications, which achieve their potency through the large size of the dosage used, homeopathy is based on administering infinitesimal doses which are unique to each remedy. Their healing power is released from the material form by a process called succussion.** Succussion consists of the calculated shaking of a remedy, so that the energy particular to each plant, mineral, or animal substance is released into the solution; this is also known as potentizing. Energy researcher Mark Gallert believes that succussion causes the

---

*A term coined by Hahnemann to denote the treatment by opposites, typical of Western chemistry processes; also known in Germany as school medicine.

*It is interesting that allopathic medicine recognizes that minute doses of an irritant can cause allergies, but does not accept a cure by the same process.

molecules of the substance to spread out, thus altering its nature and freeing the unique signature of each substance as an energy process, similar to the negative radiation effect of nuclear energy. Because the drugs share similar patterns with the disease, they meet little resistance in the body and even stimulate the body's defenses.

Health, Hahnemann believed, was due to the free movement of a life force he called *dynamis* or *vital force*. He believed this vital force to be endowed with formative intelligence; it was "constructive" in that it continuously controlled the body; it had adaptive qualities for keeping the body healthy under most conditions; it was subject to change, both in order and disorder; and it dominated the body it occupied.[3]

Homeopathic remedies reflect the dynamic interplay of health and disease. Due to this similarity of energy patterns, homeopathic remedies must be exact in their unique correspondence with the disease. Otherwise the symptoms may take an unnatural turn or there will be no effect. In either case, homeopathic medicine results in few of the harmful side effects so common in orthodox medicine. As in Ayurvedic medicine, correct homeopathic remedy treats the whole person in his or her living situation, according to prevailing geographical conditions and the patient's mental attitude. The lower potencies (which, ironically, contain more of the material used in the remedy) are effective for energy disturbances on the physical level, while higher potencies (containing less material) work more on the emotional and psychological levels.

The principle behind homeopathic remedies is that the medication and the disease will resonate at similar frequencies until the disease pattern is destroyed, as glass will shatter at a distinct energy oscillation. Other nondiseased elements of the person will not be affected because these vibrate at different rates, thus minimizing unwanted side effects.

Disease, Hahnemann believed, was not caused by virus, bacteria, or even poisons; rather, the patient became susceptible through the energetic disruption of this vital force. The so-called "germs" of disease were the results, not the cause. However, illness was not considered an entity by itself; it was only an aberration of health. Hahnemann clearly emphasized wholeness, not disease. In fact, disease was seen as the body's attempt to maintain wholeness in the face of morbid agents. This position on the nature of disease has been championed by the so-called "vitalistic" school of medicine which held that life could not be explained solely by mechanical/chemical processes but must include a principle of vitalization such as the soul.

In acute forms of disease the body is assumed to falter and then regain its wholeness, perhaps with the help of a homeopathic remedy which supports the body's healing abilities. Chronic conditions result when the healing process has been severely disturbed and the regenerative forces must first be activated. As healing takes place, the disease shifts from more vital organs to less vital ones, often manifesting in the reverse order of its original path. In many cases the disease must go through a healing crisis in which the symptoms become worse. This is a sign that the vital force is working. When symptoms reach their worst point, the disease breaks and symptoms gradually disappear.

Rudolph Steiner

In Germany during the late 1890s, Rudolph Steiner developed a system of perceptual knowledge called anthroposophy which had its early roots in theosophy* and natural science. At the heart of anthroposophy lies the belief that man's knowledge is limitless and that reality must be an integration of perception and conception (mental), though both are, in fact, distinct. Steiner attempted to bring the primary experience of the spiritual world together with the secondary perspectives of the physical world through a holistic, vitalistic approach towards both. Consciousness, he believed, results from a continuous death process of nerve cells releasing organic life from the cellular matter.

Illness was understood as a potential chance for further wholeness; therefore, health will never be achieved by simply eliminating symptoms. In general, illnesses were classified into two polarities: overactivity of the metabolic pole (inflammation, warm and active) or overfunctioning of the nerve sense pole (degenerative conditions and tumors, still and cool). The blood was thought to move between the yang of the metabolic system and the yin of the nerve and sense system.

Steiner also believed that all known "physical energy forms" such as heat, light, warmth, and so on were manifestations of more basic forces which he termed *etheric-formative forces* or ethers. They include warmth ether, light ether, chemical or sound ether, and life ether. All four may be distinguished by their rate of energetic vibration or wave length, as well as by the unique qualities of each. Life ether, the most evolved along the phylogenetic scale, contains in itself the other three formative forces. The four ethers, similar to body systems, are polarized;

*Theosophy is an esoteric philosophical system known as the wisdom religion, which claims to be the divine wisdom and true knowledge of the deity.

thus, heat and light ethers are expansive or centrifugal (yang), and chemical and life ethers are centripetal or inward-drawing (yin).

These ether manifestations may be understood as four types of life energy motion which act as specific media for other energy forms. As such they represent particular processes that create currently accepted energy forms. Light ether creates light as we know it, while life ether develops into magnetism and gravity.

Albert Abrams

Around the beginning of this century (1910), a medical doctor from San Francisco named Albert Abrams made an important discovery that later developed into the science of radionics. While percussing a patient (tapping on the body), Abrams heard a certain dull sound in the abdomen which he could only detect when the person was facing west. Thinking that this finding may have been evidence of a magnetic effect, he continued his research and discovered that the mere proximity of diseased tissue near a healthy person would cause the same dull sound. Eventually he found that every disease had a specific sound which could be quantified scientifically using an apparatus known as "Abram's black box."* Each disease he found could be determined by its vibrational frequency, called a "rate." Once he had developed a diagnostic ability using radionics, Abrams created another apparatus, called an "oscilloclast," which could radiate a healthy frequency, eliminating the need for ingestion of chemical medications.

Naturally, this was a tremendous medical breakthrough because it meant that, for the first time, disease could be treated in a scientific way without medication. In 1924, an English scientific committee reluctantly admitted that Abrams's claims were valid. Like homeopathy, radionics works through energy vibrations, but unlike homeopathy the need for all medication was eliminated, although some natural herbs or homeopathic remedies may be given to support the healing process.

Later research has even shown that electricity is not necessary to operate the radionics apparatus because the major element of radionics treatment is the ability of the operator to receive and transmit energy emanations; the apparatus is simply a focus for those who need it. Similar to the early radiasthetists, who worked with pendulums and divining rods, radionics operators are only as effective as their own energy sensitivity and clarity.

*This was done technically by introducing a variably resisting electrical current which passed through his instrument.

A sample of the person (blood, hair, saliva, picture, and so forth) can be used to diagnose and treat most diseases because each part of us radiates a unique energy field. By tuning in to this frequency, treatment may be carried out even at a distance.

The advantages of diagnosis and treatment by radionics are numerous: it is possible to diagnose disease even before "germ" elements are present;* different levels of disease may be identified; healing is without side effects; it supports the body's own healing power instead of "fighting" disease; it is holistic, integrating mind, body, and spirit in its treatments; and it may lead to spiritual development if the energy transmission is connected with a source higher than us.

Georges Lakhovsky

In the 1920s, a French engineer named Georges Lakhovsky developed a theory that cells were oscillators vibrating at a unique frequency and that all organisms could be considered high-frequency oscillating circuits. Lakhovsky felt that life energy from cosmic waves, called telluric energy, was received on earth and charged all living entities. This was presumed to be possible through the energy conduction of filaments and chromosomes in the cell nucleus which are covered by an insulating material and contain a liquid-like serum similar to sea water.

Lakhovsky held that disease resulted when cells were in oscillatory disharmony, and he developed an apparatus called the multiple-wave oscillator which produced weak electrostatic waves to correct these disturbances. Lakhovsky's oscillator was so designed that all electromagnetic waves, from the smallest to the largest (three meters to infra-red), would be generated. In this way, all cells could vibrate in harmony with these frequencies, each in its own range.

Like homeopathy, these radiated frequencies affected only the appropriate cells, although they allowed a greater breadth of treatment because of their multiple frequencies. Lakhovsky's treatments did not attack the microbes of disease but reinforced the vitality of the cell, which, in turn, could better defend itself against the microbes.

As a preventative and treatment measure, Lakhovsky also developed belts made from insulated copper spirals which were worn around the body (e.g., waist, arm) or placed around sick plants to concentrate energy from the cosmos. This belt design is quite similar to Buddhist and Indian belts used for the purpose.

*Research has found that germs are often a byproduct of disease and exist only after an energy disturbance is already present.

Harold Burr

In the 1930s, Dr. Harold Burr, working in conjunction with other associates at the Yale School of Medicine, discovered fields of life energy which have been called electrodynamic life fields or L-fields for short. These L-fields, according to Burr, may be seen as electrostatic, electromagnetic, or electrodynamic, depending on how they are measured. In essence however, these fields are organized bodies of force which exist in all species, and maintain a balance between the growth and decay of cells, despite constant changes in physical material. Burr claimed that L-fields provide us with a "design" that remains relatively constant throughout our lifetime, although it is affected by the "electric tides" in the atmosphere created by planets, sun, moon, and so on.

Unlike the radiations of energy used in radionics, L-fields are of the same nature, though more subtle, than other fields known and accepted by modern physics. In many thousands of experiments Burr found these L-fields could be measured by microvoltmeters which show a steady-state energy level for each organism, rather than electrical flow. In health these states are relatively consistent, but in disease a negative change occurs. Burr even found that it was possible, as in radionics, to detect a disease state *before* any physical change was apparent. Research done on nearly a thousand women in New York using L-fields showed that it was possible to diagnose cancer in ninety percent of these women who were later diagnosed by conventional means as having malignancies.

In conjunction with Burr, Dr. Leonard J. Ravitz, Yale psychiatrist, showed that emotional conditions also manifested in the fluctuation of energy patterns. Based on his study of emotional intensity under hypnosis, Ravitz equated emotions with energy. As far as L-fields are concerned, emotional and physical stimuli are indistinguishable, a finding similar to one Wilhelm Reich made in his explanation of character armoring in the 1940s.

Like radionics, L-fields respond to the whole person, because any aberration of a part will be reflected in the whole energy field. They also point to the amazing sensitivity of our nervous system to be able to respond to such a variety of energy influences and still function. In addition, L-fields form a bridge between the known energy processes of orthodox physics and the more subtle energy radiations which have not been fully accepted by hardcore science.

Wilhelm Reich

In the early 1900s Sigmund Freud described a psychic energy of the mental apparatus as "libido." Wilhelm Reich, one of his illustrious students and colleagues, went a step further by declaring that life energy manifested not only a psychological level but biological, physical, and emotional levels as well. Reich called this life force *orgone*, a combination of the words orgasm and organism.

According to Reich, life energy normally flows harmoniously through the body unless it is held back by unexpressed emotions. This holding, he observed, is performed by muscles, individually and in groups, which may become chronically "stuck." This leads to what Reich called *character armoring* because of the rigid quality of such muscles. Eventually such armoring leads to sexual frustration and psychosomatic problems, in addition to unhealthy secondary drives such as sadism. Reich showed that both mind and body functioned as a whole and that difficulties in energy flow in the body were also expressed in the mind, either as tense muscles or destructive mental attitudes. After developing these ideas, Reich moved away from classical psychoanalysis and developed *vegetotherapy* and later *orgone therapy* which dealt expressly with the energetic aspects of psychological problems. In doing so, he became the father of western body psychotherapy.

Through experiments, Reich proved that inorganic materials such as coal, dust, and rust, when heated and placed in a sterile nutritive solution, would swell into vesicles he called *bions* and display movements similar to organic particles. Reich said that bions are microscopically visible vesicles of functioning energy and transitional forms from non-living to living matter.[4] Bions are units of energy consisting of a membrane filled with liquid and imbued with orgone (life) energy. They are constantly being produced and they develop into protozoa or degenerate into cocci and bacilli.

When Reich treated sand in the same manner as other inorganic materials, it produced a bluish color, caused eye inflammation if gazed at too long, and would burn the skin if held. He had discovered a radiation of life energy unknown to science at that time. In relation to other ideas, orgone appears to be quite closely related to the chemical ether of Steiner and to the electrostatic energy of physics.

Further research revealed that orgone could be seen in the atmosphere in the form of arc-like movements of white dots; these were also noted thousands of years earlier by the Indian yogis, who called them prana, the primordial life energy. Reich found that he could concentrate orgone in blankets and boxes (called orgone accumulators) which could be used to restore vitality or treat physical/ emotional problems by exposures of short duration. Extrapolating his research results, Reich found that weather could be influenced and a motor made to function without "physical" energy. Perhaps Reich's most significant contribution to life energy principles was the development of a psychotherapeutic approach using the medium of the body for healing. His theories and research were brilliant, extending from the biology of cells through the emotional disturbances of the body and even later into UFO research. Unfortunately, like Ruth Drown, a radionics practitioner and pioneer of life energy research, Reich was imprisoned for his ideas, where he died in 1957, one day before his scheduled release.

J.E.R. McDonagh

From 1929 to 1954 Dr. McDonagh, a medical radiasthetist, developed a theory of life energy based on the evolution of matter. According to this theory, matter is formed from the primordial movement of life energy, which he called *activity*, as it proceeds in an evolutionary series of developmental spirals from pure process to matter. Beginning at the level of subatomic particles, life energy evolves in the second phase into atomic elements. McDonagh proposed that life energy in matter has three fundamental functions: storage, radiation, and attraction which manifest themselves in matter by alternately expanding and contracting. Metals predominantly exhibit the functions of radiation, nonmetals manifest attraction properties, and the inert gases are involved in storage functions.

In the third phase of the cycle, crystalline products such as carbon and its compounds are formed. Carbon is especially important because it forms the basis of all organic life. The fourth phase of life energy in evolution produces colloids, to which group protein belongs. It is on this level that all three energy functions can be exhibited simultaneously, unlike the crystalline molecular, or subatomic levels, where energy can only exhibit one property at a time. In the fifth phase, protein becomes differentiated into the structures of the vegetable world where interdependence (harmony) becomes evident. The last phase of evolution is marked by the development of animal products in which protein becomes the matrix of tissues and organs—man being the final product, exhibiting complete interdependence.

In McDonagh's view, activity (life energy) pulsates with movement as it manifests itself in the form of varying high energy rays (called *climates*). When all functions operate harmoniously, health exists; but when disharmony is present, disease develops (we will discuss the details of this dynamic in a subsequent chapter). In McDonagh's theory, we see close parallels to Reich's idea of orgone, which also pulsates, contracts, expands, and is the basis for health when it flows freely. Dr. George Lawrence, a surgeon and general practitioner, took up McDonagh's thesis, tested it, and applied it in his therapy as a medical radiasthetist. He found he could test any imbalance in the body's proteins and could prescribe medications (mostly homeopathic) to rebalance any disturbance. The application of McDonagh's concepts to disease has come to be known as the *Unitary Theory of Disease.*

Eastern Europe

It is known that many cultures were aware of bluish or bluish-white flames or emanations coming from the body. In the Bible, many references occur such as the description of a burning bush (Moses on Mount Sinai) or flames appearing over the apostles on Pentecost. During the late 1880s, research in Eastern Europe supported the idea that these emanations were actually a form of life energy. In the late nineteenth century, Professor Navratil, a Czech physicist, and Yakov Narkevich-Todko, a Russian electrical engineer, independently obtained photos of what have been called electrical discharges. Later, in the 1930s, a Soviet electrician Semyon Davidovich Kirlian, and his wife, Valentina, began producing photographs of an energy field that surrounded everything but which was especially active with living things. The Kirlians showed that everything radiates a life energy which can be recorded on film by a process of high-frequency voltage called Kirlian- or electrophotography. Further studies have indicated that the manifestation of this energy may vary considerably during emotional states such as anger, love, and fear, as well as different states of disease, including psychological disturbance, and weather movements, such as storms. Breathing has a strong effect on the increase or decrease of this energy radiation as well.

As this energy radiates, a field is created which surrounds and permeates all that is being photographed. Some have claimed this to be the "aura," a nonphysical energy body which is seen by clairvoyants. Both in ancient traditions and occult sciences, the aura is thought to be an organized field of subtle energy which attracts and distributes energy from the atmosphere. Actually, many energy fields exist outside our physical body, so we need to speak of many auras to be accurate.

Through Kirlian photography, it was also tentatively shown that even when two to ten percent of a healthy leaf is cut away from the rest, an energy field still remains where the physical form no longer exists. Applied on a human level, it is quite possible that the "phantom limb" effect, experienced by amputees who claim to feel pain where the body part has been severed, might be the result of such an energy field. Even though the physical limb is no longer present, the energy field may still be sending information. According to Dr. Worsley at the Chinese College of Acupuncture in England, "The more pronounced the 'phantom' pains are in the amputee, the more visible is the amputated portion of the body."[5] Though more research is needed, if it proves to be true that a field of life energy remains intact without the physical counterpart of a body part, it might prove that the energy field creates the body rather than the reverse. But what is this energy?

Scientists generally refer to four states of matter: solids, liquids, gases, and plasma (a special type of gas stripped of its nuclear electrons). Plasma exists in outer space and can be demonstrated in the lab at very high temperatures as well. In 1944, Soviet scientist V.S. Grischenko proposed the word *bioplasma* for a fifth state of matter which radiates in living organisms. Since then, much research has been done to substantiate Grischenko's idea. According to V.M. Inyushin, bioplasma is a field (the biofield) of energy consisting of ions, free electrons, and free protons, all of which are free-floating subatomic particles existing unattached to a nucleus. His experiments show that bioplasma is relatively stable, though affected by environmental forces, and that it radiates a bioluminescence, as seen clearly in some insects such as fireflies. It appears to be concentrated in the brain and spinal column, and is radiated from the eyes and exchanged with the atmosphere during breathing. Inyushin also asserts that channels of bioplasmic particles called *microstreamers* may be released during the Kirlian photography process, partially accounting for its photos.

All this research points to the existence of a new form of energy not yet accepted by Western scientists. Other data indicates that life energy is specific to each organism's tissue and possibly each biomolecule. Despite this specificity, bioplasma has a very complex organization which relies on the whole field of energy forces to function. In other words, bioplasma is holistic. Though different molecules, tissues, and people, for that matter, have special bioplasma fields, they all still act as a whole when there is harmony and health.

Dr. Ivan Dumitrescu of Rumania, using an adaption to the Kirlian apparatus which he calls an *electronograph*, has claimed to be able to see the quality of energetic glow in a single cell. He has found that healthy cells appear darker than unhealthy cells and has been able to detect the presence of cancer in forty-seven chemical workers, forty-one of whom were later confirmed to have cancer. His hypothesis suggests that the other six will also eventually develop the disease. This supports the idea that the energy field governs the energy flow to the body and that a disharmonious field will produce a bodily disease unless steps are taken to alter the field.

In the 1930s, Russian biologist Alexander Gurvich found that all cells radiate an invisible emanation which he called *mitogenic radiation*. According to Gurvich, muscle tissue, the cornea of the eye, blood, and nerves are all senders. Further research in Paris has shown that these rays are emitted most strongly by parts of the body which are rapidly replaced by new cells, such as the palms of the hands, soles of the feet, and the fingertips. Later experiments by Dr. Alexander P. Dubrov, a Russian biophysicist, concur that an energetic radiation is given off during cell mitosis (the splitting of a cell during development) which also produces a bioluminescence and ultrasonic waves of a high frequency. Mitogenic radiations can be explained by the fact that cell walls operate as semiconductors of life energy in conjunction with liquid crystals which make up the cells. Liquid crystals have the ability to gather and radiate life energy which produces both a biological glow and energy transference into field organization.

Czech engineer Robert Pavlita has shown how his psychotronic generators are able to charge energy from his thought waves and transfer this energy to small moving devices. Pavlita is able to magnetize wood, then reverse the polarity by simply bringing one of these small generators to his temple, thereby changing the energy pattern. He is even able to kill flies at a distance of twenty feet, simply by programming a generator and directing it to them. The interesting feature of these generators is that they have no electrical or mechanical components, the way a normal generator does; they simply function by processing life energy in a way as yet unexplained by modern science.

According to Western researchers who have visited Eastern Europe, one of the main differences between energy studies in the East and West is that the Eastern European scientists are convinced of the existence of another type of energy which presently defies our scientific categories. They are looking for new ways to research and understand this phenomenon, whereas in many cases Western researchers are still trying to prove its existence to skeptical colleagues.

In addition to the scientists and medical doctors mentioned, other researchers have discovered new forms of life energy in the West. Although they have called this life force by various names, its properties have remained fairly consistent throughout the years. A list of various cultures and notable figures, along with their names, including X Energy, "for life energy," follows:

The X Energy: A Universal Phenomenon

Discoverer	Name of X Energy	Approx. Date	Reference
Australian Aborigines	Arunquiitha, Churinga	''	''
Australian Tribes of the Torres Strait	Zogo	''	''
Malaya	Badi	''	''
Gelaria (New Guinea)	Labuni	''	''
Ponape (Pacific)	Ani, Han	''	''
Palau (Pacific)	Kasinge, Kalit	''	''
Bataks (Pacific)	Tondi	''	''
Maoris (New Zealand)	Atua	''	''
Malagasy (Philippines)	Andriamanitra	''	''
Kusaie (Pacific)	Anut	''	''
Tobi (Pacific)	Yaris	''	''

LATER SOURCES (After 1500)

Discoverer	Name of X Energy	Approx. Date	Reference
Paracelsus	Mumia or Munia	ca. 1530	W.E. Mann, *Orgone, Reich, and Eros*
Johannes Kepler	Facultas Formatrix	ca. 1620	A. Hardy, R. Harvie, and A. Koestler, *The Challenge of Chance*
Jan Baptista van Helmont	Magnale Magnum	ca. 1620	S. Ostrander and L. Schroeder, *Psychic Discoveries Behind the Iron Curtain*

Discoverer	Name of X Energy	Approx. Date	Reference
J.B. Rhine, Robert Thouless, B. Weisner	Psi Faculty	1947	J.B. Rhine, *The Reach of the Mind*
L.E. Eeman	X Force	1947	L.E. Eeman, *Cooperative Healing*
Gustav Stromberg	The Soul of the Universe	1948	G. Stromberg, *The Soul of the Universe*
Oscar Brunler	Dielectric Biocosmic Energy	1950	O. Brunler, *Rays and Radiation Phenomena*
Carl Gustav Jung	Synchronicity	1951	C.G. Jung, *Synchronicity*
Robert Pavlita	Psychotronic Energy	1955	D. Hammond, *The Search for Psychic Power*
John W. Campbell	Psionics	1956	J.W. Campbell, *Amazing Science Fiction* (Feb. 1956)
Henry Margenau	Quasielectro-static Field	1959	W.E. Mann, *Orgone, Reich, and Eros*
Abraham Maslow (after Benedict)	Synergy	1960	A. Maslow, *The Farther Reaches of Human Nature*
Andrija Puharich	(1) Psi Plasma	1962	A. Puharich, *Beyond Telepathy*
	(2) Inergy	1973	A. Puharich, *Uri*
Cleve Backster	Primary Perception	1966	J. White, *Frontiers of Conciousness*
George De la Warr	(1) Biomagnetism	1967	G. De la Warr, *Biomagnetism*
	(2) Prephysical Energy		
Nikolai Kozyrev	Time	1967	N. Kozyrev, *Possibility of Experimental Study of the Properties of Time*
Arthur Koestler	Integrative Tendency	1967	A. Koestler, *The Ghost in the Machine*

Discoverer	Name of X Energy	Approx. Date	Reference
Ludwig von Bertalanffy (after Woltereck)	Anamorphosis	1967	A. Koestler, *The Heel of Achilles*
L.L. Whyte	Unitary Principle in Nature	1969	L.L. Whyte, *The Unitary Principle in Nature*
Dubrov	Biogravitational Field		*Future Science*
Buckminster Fuller	Synergy	1970	B. Fuller, *Operating Manual for Spaceship Earth*
Ambrose Worrall	Paraelectricity	1970	O. Worrall, *Explore Your Psychic World*
Colin Wilson	X Factor	1971	C. Wilson, *The Occult*
Charles Musès	Noetic Energy	1972	C. Musès and A. Young, *Consciousness and Reality*
William A. Tiller	Magneto-electricity	1973	W. Tiller*

*Reprinted from *Future Science* edited by John White and Stanley Krippner by permission of John White. Copyright © 1977.

Chapter Two

Toward a Physics of Life Energy

"The most apparent thing about energy is that there is nothing else. Its rhythms are not only outside and within us, but they are us...."—Blair

The physics of energy is really a description of the dynamics of life's very foundations. Because energy is a universal phenomenon, found everywhere and involved in everything we do, it often escapes our immediate attention except perhaps when we think about household appliances or take a course in physics. In both cases, energy is described generally by its "capacity to do work" (Gk. *ergon*). But in this case "work" (W) is only the transfer of energy, equal to force (f), over a particular distance (d), such that: (W = fd). Energy in the physical sense is often used to explain electricity, magnetism, and nuclear fission, but these forces are existent aspects of how energy manifests itself. Rarely, however, is it described in terms of essence; in other words, what it is. This is because energy is a *process* which cannot fully be explained as *content*, no matter how hard we try. In fact, the ultimate "stuff" of life is better described as an energy process,[1] not a substance, as in the classical perspective.

One of the original meanings of energy (Gk. *energeia*) is Aristotle's definition: "that which brings all things into activity"—quite a different emphasis than its classical usage in connection with work. In order to distinguish the two usages, I have called the "vitalist"* concept of this force "life energy." This life energy is essentially a medium which activates everything, including us, and brings an aliveness to all things and processes in our cosmos. If we look to the roots of physics we find

---

*Vitalism is the philosophical doctrine which states that there is an inherent life force in all phenomena which is self-determining.

that according to Fritjof Capra, "physis" (Gk.), from which physics is derived, originally meant "the endeavor of seeing the essential nature of things."[2] The physics of life energy could therefore be seen as an exploration into the essential nature of the animating force in the cosmos. Naturally, this is an undertaking which couldn't be completely satisfied in this limited work. However, we can describe some aspects of this life force.

As we can see from the brief history of life energy outlined earlier, the vital aspects of this medium were present in cosmological thought from its inception. It was not until a mechanistic, reductionistic perspective of the world emerged that energy concepts took on a quantitative emphasis to the exclusion of qualitative analysis.

For the early Greeks, the search for essence was primarily philosophical in nature. It wasn't until the time of the Renaissance that the concept of "physis" became more experimental, with greater emphasis being placed on observation and mathematical calculation. In time, experimental theory and research gave rise to what is generally known now as classical physics, which bases its existence on three major pillars of thought: Euclidean geometry, Newtonian physics, and Cartesian dualism. Euclid, for his part, developed a geometry based on theorems and axioms which produced a consistent and logical system of interactions. Newton, in his development of mechanics, used this geometrical basis to create the laws of moving bodies, thermodynamics, and so forth. In philosophy, Descartes postulated two separate aspects of nature, one called mind (res cogitans) the other called matter (res extensa). Though neither was thought to interact with the other, together they made up the entirety of life.

In the Newtonian world view, space was considered three-dimensional, empty, absolute, always at rest, and basically unchangeable. The entire universe was seen as a closed energy system in which little exchange took place with the outside, like a great machine created by God. Newton saw matter and the forces acting on it as being carefully thought out beforehand and simply put into motion by the divine power. Life and its processes were considered continuous, dualistic in nature, and predictable according to well-defined laws. From this perspective, matter consisted of solid, indivisible particles which could be freely interchanged. This atomistic model had its roots in the early Greek philosophies of Democritus and Leucippus, and it was later supported by Newtonian mechanics.

This mechanistic model dominated physics for several hundred years until a dynamic new wave of thought, spear-headed by Albert Einstein in the early nineteen hundreds, began to shake its foundations. The new wave, however, also had prior roots. Beginning in the late nineteenth century, Faraday and Maxwell showed that electricity and magnetism were not two separate forces but were, in reality, one force which is now called electromagnetism. In addition, they developed the concept of a force *field*—a major departure from the idea that forces are related only to material bodies. For the first time a more subtle energy process, independent of matter, was being considered.

Then came Einstein. Believing in nature's wholeness, he showed that electromagnetism and Newtonian mechanics could be brought into unity through his special theory of relativity—but only if the accepted concepts of time and space were changed. According to Einstein, space is neither three-dimensional nor separate from time. Therefore he proposed a space/time continuum, which meant that the absoluteness of space or time alone was replaced by a relative perspective of each to the other.

ASPECTS OF ENERGY

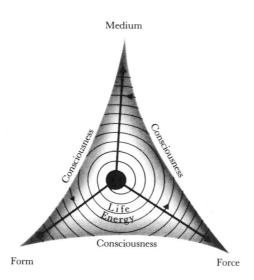

Figure 11.

With the discovery of fields and the gradual erosion of the isolation model of classical physics, it became impossible to separate different aspects of the whole. Although it *is* possible, theoretically, to isolate elements from the whole, such as mind from matter (Descartes), or one physical event from another (Newton), life energy, the basis of all movement, does not function in this schizophrenic way. Rather, it acts according to laws of wholeness; therefore, it always seeks completion and unity. Because of this wholeness, energy can only be understood as an entire phenomenon.

In developing an overview of the physics of life energy, four aspects of its wholeness emerge as relevant to our present discussion. These include aspects of form, force, medium, and consciousness. Working together, these manifestations help explain how life energy functions as a whole.

Form

The concept of *form* initially proposed by Plato was further developed by Aristotle, who saw form as an intelligible structure whose essence made the formation of matter possible. For Aristotle, matter achieved its mass, weight, content, and motion through the process of form (whose animating activity is directly related to the function of life energy, in my view). Form was thought of as the spirit through which substance emerged.

Saint Thomas Aquinas, another renowned philosopher and theologian, saw matter as contracting the free-moving form. He saw matter as the principle of individuation, because its contraction of form's process created separate entities from the whole. Aristotle, on the other hand, believed that only the union of form with matter created such individuation. His concept of *entelechy* (discussed in Chapter One) was proposed to explain how matter and form came together. According to this idea, all matter is subject to an inner purpose or sense of completion which is derived from the design of form. Without this design, matter would have no form at all. To extrapolate this to life energy terms, we could say that all process or form has a sense of wholeness which produces matter in its movement towards completion. Matter is therefore only an extension of form, both of which exist and function in harmony as manifestations of life energy.

In the realm of physics, Einstein came to a similar conclusion. In his famous equation $E = mc^2$ (Energy (E) equals mass (m) times the speed of light (c) squared), matter was shown to be a form of energy. As with electricity and magnetism, matter and energy are not separate but are part of a larger whole. In fact, all dualities exist only on lower levels of perception as complementary manifestations of each other; on more complete levels, only wholes exist. According to Einstein, matter is merely a crystallized form of energy and therefore a manifestation of light as well. Even the smallest mass (matter) has a tremendous amount of energy, because the speed of light in the equation above is 186,000 miles per second.

Thus, relativity theory took the existing theories of the day, electromagnetism and Newtonian mechanics, and created a larger, more complete whole from them both. In so doing, it unified time and space into the time/space continuum and showed that energy and matter are interchangeable, each being transmutable into the other. It also pointed out that matter is alive with activity, thus destroying the idea of a separation between "living" and dead matter.

In addition to relativity theory, classical physics lost more ground to a new world view with the advent of quantum theory. This new direction in physics originated with Max Planck's discovery that heat radiation is produced in noncontinuous energy packets, which disrupted the Newtonian belief in continuous energy emission. Einstein postulated that these "quanta" or units of energy were basic to every form of electromagnetic radiation, including light. In fact, light quanta, called *photons*, gave quantum theory its name. Because photons have been accepted as particles, though they also have wave-like properties, it was not clear at first whether they should be classified as matter or waves. Quantum theory resolved this duality by demonstrating that matter is not really physical substance with a definite place in space or time, but can only be described by its "tendency to exist." Physicists describe this "tendency" in terms of mathematical waves which are abstractions unlike the physical waves of sound or water, for example.

These waves cannot be isolated from other energy interconnections; thus, the basic wholeness of matter is once again affirmed. As Capra pointed out:

Quantum theory has thus demolished the classical concepts of solid objects and of strictly deterministic *laws of nature*. At the subatomic level, the solid material objects of classical physics dissolve into wavelike patterns of probabilities, and these patterns, ultimately, do not represent probabilities of things, but rather *probabilities of interconnections*. A careful analysis of the process of observation in atomic physics has shown that the *subatomic particles have no meaning as isolated entities*, but can only be understood as interconnections between the preparation of an experiment and the subsequent measurement. Quantum theory thus reveals a basic oneness of the universe. It shows that we cannot decompose the world into independently existing smallest units. As we penetrate into matter, nature *does not show us any isolated "basic building blocks,"* but rather appears as a complicated web of relations between the various parts of the whole.[3]

If the essence of matter is really only patterns of energy probabilities, why does a wall look and feel solid? It turns out that two "building blocks" of matter are actually the energy interactions of atoms which compose it. One of these interactions is the force exerted on electrons to bind them to the center or nucleus of the atom. Electrons, however, react to this confinement by spinning very quickly at about 600 miles per second. In fact, the more they are held, the faster they spin. Because of these two complementary and simultaneous interactions of confinement and acceleration, it is difficult to compress the atom any further and matter takes on its familiar solid appearance. Ironically, it is the aliveness of these atomic movements which makes matter appear static and dead.

With the introduction of relativity theory and its subsequent proof through quantum physics, the old classical theory of matter being built of "basic blocks" such as atoms is rapidly fading as a tenable thesis. In four lines of research modern physics supports the contention of relativity theory that matter has no ultimate building blocks of life. In the first, early experiments in subatomic particles, in which the atom was split, researchers began to discover so-called "elementary" particles, which would have supported a basic "stuff" theory, but that theory later was destroyed when more and more "elementary" particles were found until they totalled over two hundred—hardly basic!

Next was the discovery of antimatter. Scientists found that almost all elementary particles of matter may have a corresponding particle of equal mass but opposite charge (which probably moves backward in time) called an antiparticle. It is theorized that somewhere in the universe are particles complementary to our world's particles, which, if brought together, would cancel each other out. It is believed that only energy would be left from this union; no particles would remain.

Third, it appears that bombardment of particles at high speeds produces a splitting of the particle, but the two or more resulting particles are duplicates of the original, having been formed out of the energy used for separation. Thus particles are destroyed and created at the same time, and no smaller particles could be obtained.

Finally, matter may also be created spontaneously in a vacuum in space out of nothing we presently know about.[4] This could mean that either particles in space are undiscovered as yet, or matter is being created by an unknown energy process. In either case, because particles are also energy, energy is creating matter, directly or indirectly. Even though physicists are still looking for more basic building blocks called quarks, all the evidence seems to suggest that although particles and subparticles ad infinitum may be discovered, no particle as the essence of matter will be found. Capra sums up this state of affairs quite well:

> In classical physics the mass of an object had always been associated with an indestructible material substance with some 'stuff' of which all things were thought to be made. Relativity theory showed that mass has nothing to do with any substance, but is a form of energy. Energy, however, is a dynamic quantity associated with activity, or with processes. The fact that the mass of a particle is equivalent to a certain amount of energy means that the particle can no longer be seen as a static object, but has to be conceived as a dynamic pattern, a process involving the energy which manifests itself as the particle's mass.[5]

Thus, matter can be seen as an aspect of energy whose form is dependent on the nature of the energy processes inherent in its movement. Therefore, what we see in our physical world as different shapes of matter are really the living (i.e., constantly in motion) processes of distinct energy patterns or designs of form. Later on we shall see that form is related in the metaphysical world to the evolution of soul and its manifestation through the spirit.

An indirect but interesting substantiation for the relation between form, matter, and energy comes from the work of the eighteenth-century German physicist Ernst Chladni, and, more recently, Hans Jenny in Switzerland. Both have shown that sound will produce specific patterns of energy. Working with sand scattered on steel discs, Chladni demonstrated that playing notes on a violin caused the sand to arrange itself in patterns unique to each note. Of special interest is the fact that the sand would settle on parts of the disc where the *least* vibration occurred. When applied to matter, this could mean that the most active or energized parts of material are not what is seen as mass but what cannot be seen as process. In effect, the substance quality of matter is the least alive aspect. This has important implications for body psychotherapists, as I shall point out in Chapter Five.

Jenny later found that circles, the universal symbols of wholeness (as in Mandalas), mediate patterns of energy unequalled by other forms. He also found that inorganic matter, when vibrated, produced organic patterns and that raising the pitch of sound (i.e., increasing the energy frequency and intensity) caused static patterns to suddenly begin moving. This could be a clue to the connection between inorganic (nonliving) and organic (living) matter, which will be discussed at the end of this chapter.

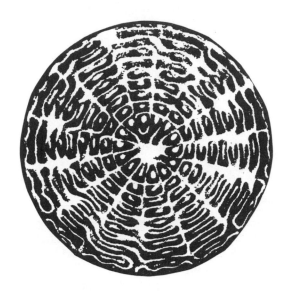

*Figure 12. Chladni Figure**

It is interesting that the Chinese, according to Zukav, use the character "Wu" to describe both matter and energy as an inseparable entity. The Chinese word for physics consists of the two characters "Wu" and "Li," which, among other things, mean "pattern of organic energy," and in another context, "enlightenment." At least from the Chinese perspective, physics—the seeking of the essential nature of things—is also related to spirituality through the concept of enlightenment. Enlightenment is described by the great teachers as a state of perfect truth in which relative realities are seen as complementary aspects of absolute oneness. Absolute truth lies within the experience of complete wholeness. Enlightenment might be understood as a state of evolution in which one lives continually in the light of truth.

*Reprinted from *Energy, Matter & Form* by Phil Allen et al. by permission of University of the Trees Press. Copyright © 1977.

When Einstein spoke of light and its relationship to mass and energy he was referring to physical light as we know it. On a spiritual level, light is also used as a symbol of clarity and perfect vision. I believe that scientific interest in matter, energy, light, and related ideas is really a longing for a connection to the spiritual realm. Matter and energy are interchangeable; both are related to light. The world of physics is approaching the ancient wisdom which held that in essence, everything is one, though at the level of relative existence different forms may manifest. Isn't it the metaphysical goal of physics to discover the basic truths of life? Therefore, we might say that the physics of energy is really an exploration of the essential nature of the life force which leads to enlightenment. The study of matter as a form of energy is also a path toward enlightenment, as are its complementary aspects of force, medium, and consciousness. All paths lead to the same essence—wholeness.

Force

It is well known in physics that matter is composed mostly of space with a minute amount of mass. Mass, as we have seen, is not substance in the classical sense, but energy which is bound in a particular pattern; this pattern is unique for every form of matter. In order for a pattern to exist, mass must be separated in space; otherwise, all things would automatically converge into one point. In physics this would mean that all mass would be drawn together by attractive forces into a huge lump. The fact that this doesn't happen implies the existence of another force which separates matter, thereby maintaining the patterns of organic energy. So it is this balance of forces, like the ancient Chinese polarities of Yin/Yang or the Indian Shakti/Shiva, which directs energy and matter into patterns.

At present, orthodox science has recognized four types of unique forces. These include, in order of strength: 1) strong nuclear forces, 2) electromagnetism, 3) weak forces, and 4) gravity. Strong forces hold the nucleus of the atom together and are over one hundred times stronger than electromagnetism. Electromagnetism is generally the most familiar of the forces and includes radio waves, microwaves, infrared, visible light, ultraviolet, X-rays, and gamma rays, and so on. It also binds atoms together in molecules, and, within the atom itself, it maintains electrons in their orbit around the nucleus. However, the more electrons are bound to the nucleus, the quicker they spin around, thereby creating a dynamic balance between the Yin of attraction and the Yang of repulsion. The weak force is the least researched of the forces. Its existence is inferred from subatomic interactions and derives its name from the fact that it is weaker than electromagnetism. The last of the recognized forces is gravity. It is thought to be responsible for the long-range interactions of large cosmic bodies such as solar systems, galaxies, and universes.

Other forms of energy including light, sound, mechanical energy, chemical energy, and nuclear energy are considered to be manifestations of the above forces. Nevertheless, according to a holistic concept of energy, all these forces would have to be unified into some larger whole. We have several good reasons to assume that this unification will eventually happen. For one, it is unreasonable to presume that different forms of energy are not derivatives of the same source simply because they have different properties. In nature's realms, this difference does not isolate one form from another. Apples and oranges, for example, have many different qualities, yet both are considered fruit. A recent discovery in physics of a "supersymmetry" in matter has already allowed scientists to organize once-isolated subatomic particles* into one larger whole (called a subatomic "family").

A second support for unification derives from the solid, old tradition found in both the East and the West (and discussed in Chapter One), of a unified concept of life energy. However, many qualities of this basic force do not coincide with our present scientific ideas; therefore, today's accepted properties of energy would have to be reconciled with other qualities of life energy which have been used theoretically and practically for thousands of years by native peoples, philosophers, and scientists alike.

In addition, even physics research suggests that the isolation of four separate forces probably does not depict the true state of affairs. Beginning with Newton, who unified celestial and terrestrial gravity into a single model of gravity, the history of physics tells us that apparently differing phenomena related to energy are often later revealed to be different manifestations of the same entity. This was the case with electricity and magnetism, which eventually came to be viewed as electromagnetism, and with the concepts space and time, which became space/time. In fact, Einstein spent the last twenty-five years of his life working to integrate the four known forces in to what has been called the *unified field theory*. At the time of his death he had still not succeeded.

However, in 1968 another piece of the energy picture became clear when Steven Weinberg and Abdus Salam proposed that the weak

*These particles are bosons and fermions.

nuclear force and electromagnetism were fundamentally the same. This was later proved to be accurate. Some physicists call this newly combined force the "electroweak" force. Thus, only three forces must be united for a holistic energy picture to be complete. New hope has arisen in physics that this unification may occur. A new theory called "supergravity" employs the concept of supersymmetry mentioned earlier as a unifying concept which needs to be tested in the laboratory. According to the theory, when the universe was first formed all of nature's forces were one, but because of a decline in cosmic energy this single force was broken down into different forms of lesser intensity. The originators of this theory also propose that more powerful accelerations of subatomic particles will verify that at higher levels of energy all energy forces become one.[6]

It is quite likely that in time physicists will be talking about "polarized movement," rather than "different forces." Since the development of quantum field theory, some scientists already prefer the word "interaction" to "force," because the action of forces influences matter and facilitates the exchange of particles. Particles, however, are matter and matter is patterned energy; forces, therefore, are simply manifestations of energy which interact with each other. Two movements have been noted in these interactions: a movement towards (attraction) and a movement away (repulsion). If we apply these movements to the four forces, their basic unity is automatically understood.

Electromagnetism displays both attraction and repulsion. Gravity, on the other hand, is always attractive; however, evidence suggests that a complementary force among large bodies, known by some physicists as *radiation pressure*, occurs when gravity has compressed a star into an excited, dense mass of whirling gas. Physicist Christopher Hills has called this force *levity*.[7] Evidence also points to the existence of gravitational effects in living organisms (as researched by Russian scientist Alexander Dubrov), and to a biogravitational field, both of which produce attractive and repulsive movements.

The weak nuclear forces in the atom always attract. However, we now know that the weak force is a manifestation of electromagnetism which also manifests repelling movements. The strong force, much more powerful than electromagnetism (which causes protons approaching the nucleus (also made up of protons) to be repelled), will, if a proton is pushed beyond this repelling field, actually suck the proton into itself. Thus, strong forces are considered to be attractive in nature. However, in some cases the strong forces also repel, as, for example, with strongly interacting particles called "Hadrons." It is quite probable that strong forces and electromagnetism will, in time, be seen as manifesting the same force, though strong forces bind like charges (positive) in close proximity, while magnetic forces act on opposite charges over greater distances. As salt in the body restrains the free flow of water to create a balance, strong and electromagnetic forces may provide a Yin/Yang energy homeostasis whereby binding and expansion of particle activities are maintained in equilibrium.

It is quite likely that the separation among the four known forces is arbitrary and will, in time, be perceived as academic. Life energy will be found to have several forms, some corresponding to our known forces, other as yet undiscovered.* All known forces—such as strong nuclear, gravity, and weak forces—will be recognized as special forms of an enlarged spectrum of electromagnetism, differing slightly only in form, strength, and orientation. The stronger the force, the greater are the restrictions on its quantity of interactions, again demonstrating a dynamic balance whereby greater power is limited by restrained activity.

The result of integrating our present knowledge of forces in terms of energy movement (attraction and repulsion), and replacing the concept of "forces" with "interactions" will stimulate a broadened view of electromagnetism which would include weak and strong nuclear forces as well as gravity as a special case of magnetism on large bodies. In this process we will have to include qualities and quantities of energy which have not as yet been accepted by orthodox science but which nevertheless have been proven to exist in other areas of research by competent scientists throughout the world.

In fact, in the early 1960s a new field of study called Psychotronics (from the Greek *psyche* meaning life principle or soul, and *tron* meaning an instrument) was developed by several international scientists to research energy phenomena not explained by the current laws of science.** Their research includes areas such as subatomic physics and astrophysics, parapsychology, biology, and radiasthesic physics.*** Their findings to date support the existence of a form of life energy which vibrates beyond the speed of light (thought impossible by conventional physics) and is more powerful than electromagnetic, nuclear, or gravitational forces because it can counteract them. Often called "X-energy"

*Researchers at the De La Warr Laboratory in England have found an east-west force apparent in electromagnetism which is neither magnetic nor electrical but which operates according to the known laws of physics (p. 12 & 18).

**These early adherents included Dr. Zdenek Rèjdak, Czechoslovakia; Dr. Victor Adamenko, Russia; Dr. Stanley Krippner, U.S.A.; and Dr. Smilov, Bulgaria, among others.

***Radiasthesic physics is the science that studies and describes dousing and pendulum radiations.

because it is unknown, this form of life energy may provide the connection between the healing energy of the East and the early Western scientific findings of radiational forces by Lakhovsky, von Reichenbach, Reich, Galvani, De La Warr, and others.

In the 1960s, the American Institute of Electronic Engineers set up a special committee to study forms of energy (no matter how bizarre in appearance) which appeared in nature but did not coincide with known forces. Based on the investigations of this committee, Chairman Rexford Daniels made the following comment about a force that exists, unknown to science, which:

> ...penetrated everything; could not usually be measured by conventional electronic instruments; did not attenuate according to recognized formulas; and could cause instantaneous reactions at incredible distances....

He later concluded:

> Because of the diversities of use of this force it appeared that it might even have a spectrum of its own.[8]

In Tokyo, Dr. Motoyama has shown that a psychic's concentration on a person sitting in a room shielded from all *known forces* was able to produce changes in pulse, blood flow, and respiratory rate during test trials. Obviously, some force was being transmitted. At Stanford University in California, psychic Ingo Swann has demonstrated his ability to alter the temperature of a heat-sensitive instrument (thermistor) located a foot from his body, as well as deflect a magnetic indicator for thirty seconds, doubling the actual measurement in the room when all known physical radiations had been screened out.[9] Such ability to affect matter with mental or psychic force is known technically as psychokinesis (PK).

Psychic healer Dr. Olga Worrall, in another PK experiment was able to cause pulsating waves in a cloud chamber (an instrument used to detect subatomic particles) simply by placing her hands near it. Later, from a distance of five hundred miles, she achieved the same effect for periods of three and eight minutes.[10] These results cannot be explained by contemporary laws or forces in physics. Taylor has studied children who, simply by rubbing a plastic tube with sealed ends which contained a foot-long aluminum bar, were able to bend the form into an S-shape. In fact, the more rigid the bar, the easier it was for the children to bend it! This is the opposite effect from what we would expect of accepted laws of physics.[11]

Research done on *both* psychic healers and magnetism has shown that the effects of treatment on *both* produce similar results, suggesting that psychic healing may entail some form of magnetism.[12] However, the same research was unable to detect any magnetic field surrounding the healer. Most probably healing is a type of life energy expression which displays properties of magnetism, because megnetism is also a property of life energy but does not appear in the physical spectrum of electromagnetism as we now understand it. This would support the ideas that some manifestations of life energy exist in a dimension other than what are currently accepted as forces, and that a direct and immediate connection exists between accepted forces such as magnetism and other, as yet unaccepted, energy forms.

Some studies have shown that the distance such information can travel may be limitless. In one, a mother rabbit exhibited an electric brainwave signal as each of her babies was touched in an underwater submarine, some three hundred miles away. This effect has been called "rapport" and has been demonstrated in interspecies research as well. For example, a plant used as a monitor reacted almost instantaneously when live shrimp were dropped into boiling water or when grass was cut.[13] Psychogavanometrist Cleve Backster who did the research has called the near-instantaneous energy he found in his plant studies *primary perception.* This concept seems to suggest that information is traveling very quickly from one living entity to another in a way untypical of accepted forces in physics.* There must be something else, but what is this unrecognized energy?

Physicist Jack Sarfatti offers a clue. He postulates that information can only be received at such speed over such distances if it travels faster than the speed of light. But according to relativity theory no signal can travel at superluminal (faster than light) speeds. Some theoretical physicists who work outside traditional realms, however, are proposing the existence of particles called *tachyons* which would travel faster than light. Scientists suggest that if these particles exist, they should be detectable through the emission of Cerenkov radiation—a bluish light emitted by highly-charged particles. This bluish light is reminiscent of the symbolic Hindu portrayal of Vishnu (universal consciousness exprienced inwardly), who is sky blue in complexion, as well as the Buddhist deity Samantabhadra (Skt.); astronomers' observations of bluish formations during increased sunspot activity; and the bluish radiation of Reich's orgone. It is possible that in the East and West, Yogi and scientist have unknowingly shared a common experience of life energy.

*Other plant signals pass chemically through the air (Boling).

Sarfatti suggests that "energy communication" is indeed happening, as specific research experiments* prove it to be, but no signal is generated; thus, no transport of energy is detectable. Although this theory is considered impossible by orthodox science, it does explain the research findings, which traditional physics cannot do. If Sarfatti is correct, this would prove that everything in the universe is connected—not by signals, but by a wholeness in which all parts "know" what the other parts are doing and respond accordingly! This leads us to the question of energy as consciousness, which I shall take up shortly.

Based on the previous discussion, it is clear that a new spectrum of energy must be developed which would account for research findings to date. I propose this spectrum be termed a "Life Energy Continuum." This new model would include all known forces which are presently accepted, as well as other forms and manifestations which have been experienced by many people throughout time and have been shown to exist theoretically/experimentally by modern physics but are not yet officially accepted by science.

A schema has been developed by Dr. William Tiller, professor of material sciences at Stanford University, which could be used as a suprastructure for this new model. He suggests a three-dimensional paradigm which includes positive space/time, negative space/time, and deltron energy. Positive space/time would include commonly accepted forms of energy such as electromagnetism, nuclear energy, and gravity. In the new Life Energy Continuum model, we would have to expand our concept of electromagnetism to include vibrations that are both lower and higher than those which are presently accepted.** This would include all lower vibrations such as "inanimate objects" (stones, crystals, and so on) and higher vibrations such as thought, although these have not yet been physically measured. Positive space/time could include all vibrations from zero to the speed of light.

Negative space/time would include all vibrations which travel faster than light (superluminal) and would account for such phenomenon as telepathy, levitation, psychokinesis, and precognition. Dr. Tiller has even coined the term "magnetoelectric" to identify energy in this realm.

*Clauser-Freedman experiment; for a further description, see Zukav, p. 309.

**Dr. Hills has proposed just such a spectrum based on the fact that all matter radiates magnetic waves, although some may not, as yet, be measured.

Table I

Space-Time Substance Manifestations

X	X†
Electric monopole	Magnetic monopole
Forms atoms, molecules, etc.	Forms atoms, molecules, etc.
Coherence state I	Coherence state II
Positive mass	Negative mass
Slower than light	Faster than light
Electromagnetic radiation at speed of light	Magnetoelectric radiation at $\sim 10^{10}$ speed of EM light
Positive energy states	Negative energy states
E increases as v increases	E increases as v increases
Positive time flow	Negative time flow
Gravitation	Levitation
Frequency	Frequency
Screened by Faraday cage	Not screened by Faraday cage
	Magnetic cage screening
I_e generates H	I_m generates E
Space I	Space II

("Mirror Relationship" labelled between the two columns)

X = physical   X† = etheric   E = energy

Space/Time Substance Manifestation*

*Reprinted from "Toward a Future Medicine Based on Controlled Energy Fields," in *Phoenix: New Directions in the Study of Man* (Summer, 1977) by William A. Tiller by permission of William A. Tiller. Copyright © 1977.

In negative space/time, particles have a negative mass and are known as antimatter. These particles are not visible to the unaided eye and are magnetic in character. When activated to superluminal speeds, these particles would appear to dematerialize, although they actually only change character at these higher frequencies. In addition, energy at a negative space/time level would produce a force with a levitation quality which would balance the gravitational effect of positive space/time. Finally, negative space/time would also account for the psychic's ability to transmit energy through all known force shields.

According to Dr. Tiller, energy traveling beyond the speed of light in negative space/time cannot directly interact with slower-than-light energy. He has therefore proposed the existence of a "deltron" energy zone which would act as a connecting medium between these two forms of energy. It is beyond the scope of this book to further speculate on this life energy spectrum, though such a model seems necessary in order to bring our knowledge, past and present, together in an organized whole.

Medium

Besides the processes of life energy evident in form (matter) and force, life energy also exists in a third manifestation—medium. For many years, in scientific circles the medium was known as ether; the Chinese word Chi, meaning energy, also means ether or gas.* From the early Greek concept of ether, Newton proposed the idea of a medium through which heat, light, radio waves, and so on traveled. He claimed it to be more subtle than air, to have its own vibrations, and to penetrate all matter. In early physics textbooks, ether was described as transmitting radiant energy to matter and absorbing it as well. We were thought to exist in a sea of ether which permeated the entire universe as an ever present medium which did not move. This Newtonian concept of inert ether fit perfectly with the classical model of a mechanical universe. Ether was thought to exist because it *had* to exist. Something must be creating wavelike motion, for example, in order for light to travel in waves; that "something" was supposed to be ether.

In 1887, the Michelson-Morley experiment tested this ether theory and "proved" that it was not valid. Einstein's theory of relativity in 1905 further destroyed the theory of an energy medium by claiming

*In Hindu thought ether is called Akasha.

that "the ether does not exist." This seemed to be the end of the ether theory but even Michelson could not believe his own research— perhaps with good reason. According to Dr. H.C. Dudley, professor of Radiational Physics, the Michelson-Morley apparatus foreordained a proof against ether which was not experimentally valid. Specula- tion by Paul Dirac and later Victor de Broglie, both Nobel Prize win- ners, as well as astrophysical studies of the space between the planets and stars, points anew to the feasibility of ether existing. Research has shown that space is not empty, as Einstein thought, but filled with interlocking magnetic and electric fields as well as neutrinos.* This is important, because both relativity theory and quantum physics *require* that no ether exist, just as Newtonian physics requires its exis- tence. Therefore, to admit the presence of ether is to destroy relativ- ity theory and quantum mechanics as currently stated.[14]

Research by Von Sezeele in the late 19th century, confirmed independently by Drs. Hanshka and Spindler in the 1940s, has shown that mineral substances such as iodine are manufactured by plants, although no known physical source was provided due to specially "closed" environments devoid of earth and external watering.[15] This research may be comparable to the experiences of people, like Theresa von Konnersreuth in Germany, who were able to survive many years all with little or no food; both cases may be evidence of an ether-like energy which supports life in a nonphysical way, similar to the etheric- formative forces of Steiner. Even quantum physics, according to physicist-author Gary Zukav, resurrects a new concept of ether as a vacuum state which is as "featureless" as the older ether theory. The most plausible contender for an energy ether might be a sea of the aforementioned neutrinos. Could this neutrino sea found by the astrophysicists be one manifestation of the Indian prana, Chinese Chi or Reich's orgone?

It is most probable that, like matter, the medium of energy will not prove to be composed of any single substance but will be, instead, a sea of movement which may display aspects of both positive and nega- tive space/time. This pervasive sea may prove to be a particular manifestation of life energy which, at higher or lower frequencies, could create other forms such as matter, thought, or healing. Because life energy is process rather than content anyway, it would of neces- sity have the transmission properties seen in healing sessions, as well as the dynamic property of "being" without signal transmission. It

---

*Neutrinos are a subquantic medium of uncharged particles in flux which can pass through all matter.

would be a mistake to see ether as a substance. It is far more plausible to view it as an emanation of life energy at a particular state of being which is related by movement to matter and force as part of a larger whole.*

Michelson and Morley's "proof" that ether did not exist and the later discoveries of their probable research error, as well as other evidence from astrophysics that suggests space is not empty but contains a sea of neutrinos (an ether sea?), raises the issue of scientific proof. With the advent of relativity theory and quantum mechanics the entire foundation of science was overturned. In the old-world view, the scientist could be objective, impartial, and precise about his findings—at least so he thought. Quantum theory disturbed this preordained order by declaring that at the subatomic level no-thing is so dependable, predictable, or precisely measurable as to warrant such scientific expectations. It is often thought that a scientific "proof" with machines and measurements is a guarantee of truth. But as Zukav points out:

> A scientific proof is a mathematical demonstration that the assertion in question is logically consistent. In the realm of pure mathematics, an assertion may have no relevance to experience at all. Nonetheless if it is accompanied by a self-consistent 'proof' it is accepted.[16]

A physics theory which is "true" may better be described as useful but not necessarily an indication of reality. Quantum research has shown that there can be no objective truth because even the researcher sets up the experiment in certain ways, sees the problem from his or her perspective, and even designs the equipment—all subjective experiences. So where is the objectivity? In the numbers perhaps? The answer is unfortunately "no." Kurt Godel's Incompleteness Theorem (as yet unrefuted) has shown that so-called logical systems of deduction also have a nonlogical component, and that this nonlogical aspect is necessary to deduce some of arithmetic's true statements. This means that a set of axioms (upon which logic is based) is incomplete in and of itself to explain the theorems that are developed. Moreover, false statements could also be deduced from these same axioms.[17]

*One such integration of matter, force, and ether has been suggested by physicist Pat Flannagan in his ether-vortex theory developed from research with pyramids.

What about the axioms themselves? Again, Godel has stated the impossibility of ascertaining whether even the axioms with the system are consistent. Based on this, Pelletier concludes:

> ...the scientist who remains a pure logician has no real base from which he can reason with absolute assuredness. Adherence to a particular personal, scientific or cultural paradigm is a function of belief or faith rather than a matter of necessity dictated by objective information.[18]

And according to Einstein:

> Pure logical thinking cannot yield us any knowledge of the empirical world: all knowledge of reality starts from experience and ends in it. Propositions arrived at by purely logical means are completely empty as regards reality.[19]

Those among us (scientists included) who would hold onto the objective science of the classical era will be surprised to learn that even Euclid's geometry, which served as the basis of Newtonian mechanics in the old-world view, was based on assumptions which cannot be "proved." In fact, it has been shown that several other "logical" systems, equally as consistent yet contrary to Euclidean geometry, can be and were developed.[20] Einstein has shown that space is curved, rather than flat as Euclid predicted, and phenomena such as black holes and gravitational collapse in outer space defy the laws which seem to be true in classical physics. The point is that science is just as subjective as any other discipline, though it may aim for greater clarity,* and that mathematical proof, the basis of our natural sciences, is fallible.

This state of affairs has prompted scientists such as John A. Wheeler to insist on replacing the idea of an *observer* in science by a *participator*. Interestingly enough, this shift from objective to subjective, from observer to participator, is derived from the age-old Tantric belief that the observer and the observed are one.** ***

---

*Even the arithmetic numbers we use are arbitrary, unlike the units of the Druids or the Egyptians which were based on proportions from nature. (Blair)

**Krishnamurti, a modern spiritual teacher, also postulates this belief in his philosophical discussions.

***Bohm has proposed the term rheomode for a new holistic, flowing mode of thinking.

The true scientist is someone who seeks the essence of life; a physicist as well as a spiritual seeker. He or she has the courage to open wide the door of possibilities and go beyond the limits of the personally known, sometimes leaping into a new perspective or experience without guarantee or security that it will be right or accepted. At the same time he or she is clear enough to know that seeing one light is not equivalent to living in the light of truth (enlightenment). Over and over again the doors of perception must be allowed to open to admit new growth and eventual evolution. For science (derived from the Latin *scire*, to know), like all human endeavor, is in the end an adventure in consciousness which cannot be predicted but can only be accepted as it is. Like the physicist, the spiritual seeker must conduct "research," which is a continual seeking (or better, a remaining in contact with that which is already, somewhere, known) of life's essence.

In focusing on the essential in science, "energy" provides a convenient, researchable, and experiential process which can be used to integrate our present knowledge in various sciences and disciplines and to forge new paths in knowledge which eventually lead back to us and our spiritual evolution. It is a myth to suppose that science will discover any really new "finds;" all we can do is rediscover what is known and expand our general consciousness so that more people open to and accept these truths. For this purpose, formal science is extremely useful.

An interesting development in physics called Scatter or S-matrix theory demonstrates that form, force, and medium can be seen as three aspects of a larger energy whole. S-matrix theory takes its name from the mathematical table of probabilities used for strongly-interacting particles called "hadrons." According to Fritjof Capra, the "scattering" or colliding of hadrons in subatomic research represents a flow of energy through nonphysical pathways called "reaction channels." These channels resemble cavities in which energy forces react with each other in the formation of particles. One type of short-lived particle, called "resonances," is created when a specific vibratory frequency of the reaction channel is reached. In this way particles are more in the sense of an event rather than the longer lasting objects of classical physics.

From this subatomic world view, particles of matter (form) are intermediate stages of the interaction of energy processes (forces) which are created through the resonation of distinct vibrations in reaction channels (medium). From a larger perspective this suggests that everything in our world is in a transitory state and depends on the continual interaction of energy for its existence. Furthermore, it implies that everything exists through the resonation of energy frequencies.

It is my contention that consciousness, acting as a medium for "sou-lar" processes, functions as the energy source for vibrations which create the physical world. Our spirit field operates as a reaction channel which allows energy to be processed in specific frequency areas, thus creating our bodies, personalities, and social milieu. Later I shall show that one manifestation of this spirit field, called the *healing channel*, is associated with our physical and emotional health as well as our spiritual evolution. How aware we are of the processes of the spirit as it extends itself in our everyday lives is dependent on our level of consciousness.

Consciousness

Perhaps the most-overlooked phenomenon in modern science, an omission as serious as personal bias and professional skepticism to new approaches, is consciousness. Many scientists in their ill-fated search for complete objectivity, have forgotten that their interests, ideas, and energy may also play a part in their research results. Quantum physics has shown us that the observer and what he is observing are one. We cannot separate the two, anymore than we can see single particles isolated from the context of their existence in matter. Werner Heisenberg (1927) stated in his famous Uncertainty Principle (which was later demonstrated experimentally) that any attempt on our part to observe something automatically influences (and alters) it. The moment we attend to something or focus energy on it, it is affected by our attention. This is as true in research as it is in everyday life. If we continually focus on life's difficulties, for example, we invest more and more energy in their continuation. This then reinforces a belief that life is difficult. Our focus and investment of energy depend on our state of consciousness (which can never really be described but only directly experienced).

In the concept of life energy presented here, consciousness is the qualitative and directional aspect of energy. Without consciousness we couldn't even think about energy; in every energetic process consciousness is present.

In the words of physicist Jack Sarfatti: "We have come to know that consciousness and energy are one."[21] Charles Muses has called consciousness noetic energy. From its roots, consciousness (L. *conscius*) means to share knowledge. Therefore, when we speak about consciousness we are referring to an awareness of information: to be conscious is to be cognizant of knowledge. Such knowledge, however, does not refer to content or how much we know but rather to the *quality* of that knowledge. If we return to the essential nature (physis) of energy, consciousness is the knowledge about the essence of life or movement. Through the movement of life energy, consciousness binds structure of form, the quantity of force, and the medium of process, into the whole of life.

Thus form, force, and medium are three aspects of energy held in dynamic pattern by consciousness. Any one aspect may dominate at a time, though all remain in relative proportion with the others. It is the consciousness aspect of energy that dictates how, where, and in what form energy is to be allocated. In an elaborate sharing of knowledge, without need for energy transfer, all aspects of energy "know" from their sense of unity in which proportion they need to be. I call this the Law of Wholeness. The Law of Wholeness, as I define it, states that the gathering, dissipation, and maintenance of energy wholeness is dictated by a universal consciousness of the form, force, or medium needed in any given time or place. But how is this "knowledge" possible?

Several ideas have been suggested. Teilhard de Chardin believed that in the evolution of organisms from the most primitive cell to humans there developed an increasing complexity whereby human beings, the most complex of earth species, also developed the greatest ability to be conscious. As far as we know, we are the only organisms who are aware of our awareness. Other forms of matter (therefore energy), have awareness but are not able to reflect upon this fact.

Teilhard de Chardin's hypothesis is complemented by the research of Dr. Sheldrake, mentioned earlier. According to Sheldrake, we evolved by "morphogenic radiation," whereby developmental leaps in our evolution were "known" by other members of the species. In support of these evolutionary theories of knowledge sharing (consciousness) are William McDougall's research, done in 1920, and more recently the work of F.A.E. Crew in Melbourne and W.E. Agar in Melbourne, who duplicated and extended McDougall's original findings. Their collected research indicated that successive generations of rats trained to escape from a water maze improved in this ability in each following generation. This would be expected if learning is passed on genetically.

Interestingly enough, though, even the rats in control groups, who were not raised from trained parents, performed the task with improvement. What this means is that, although learning is passed on genetically to other generations, consciousness is passed on to the whole species, though no biological connection or training is present. Somehow these "control" rats received information without direction, communication or biological connection.

If further research confirms these conclusions it would lend support to the concept that the medium for consciousness is a tuning-in to the highest state of awareness in the species by all the other members. This would mean that when any one of us increases our consciousness, all the rest of us tune in to this, if we are open, and increase our consciousness at the same time. Therefore, the more open we are to being whole, the more information we share with others and the more we learn about the essence of life through this increased consciousness.

In the process of evolution, many civilizations rose and fell according to their ability to maintain a certain level of consciousness. Those cultures which evolved a measure of consciousness but lost the essential connection to this state began to decline, while those on the "up" side were in various stages of consciousness development.* The fact that no major civilization remained at its peak of evolution means that as a species we have not yet learned to live permanently at our potential height of development.

Physics provides another perspective on the "knowledgeability" of the consciousness phenomenon. In 1803, Thomas Young set up an experiment which showed that light functions as a wave.** He demonstrated that shining light through two slits in a screen produces not two slits of light but bands of light and dark, depending on whether the waves respectively overlap or cancel each other out. If we perform the same experiment with a single unit of light (photon) and close one of the slits, a fascinating thing happens. The photon goes through the open slit and is registered in an area that was dark when both slits were open. In other words, it behaves differently when one slit or two slits are open; otherwise it would not go to the dark area in the one-slit situation. Somehow the photon "knows" there are two different situations and responds accordingly.

But how does the photon know this? Quantum theory claims it is only by chance that a photon goes one place or another. This theory cannot predict with certainty the path of one energy event. Einstein couldn't accept this theory, and commented that "God doesn't play dice." He tried to account for the individual path of a photon by postulating a mathematical, though nonexistent, wave called a "ghost" wave. In the world of physics such an explanation is generally considered to be too contrived to be real.[22]

---

*Atlantis may be a culture that, though highly-evolved, misused its knowledge of energy.

**Known as the Young double-slit experiment.

On the other hand, according to the Law of Wholeness light may respond to a given situation with an action that is most appropriate— most whole. Einstein's "ghost" wave could be the spirit or essence of the photon which guides its way. This implies that photons possess primitive consciousness in order to know whether one slit or two are open and respond with "whole action."

Whole action, in terms of life energy principles, means an awareness of appropriate action based on the situation. The photon, like the amoeba, knows which action it has to take and does it. Therefore, even at this primitive level there seems to be conscious action based on the awareness of wholes and its built-in sense of completion.

In a monumental work entitled *The Reflexive Universe*, Arthur Young has substantiated his research findings that matter manifests a particular type of consciousness manifests itself at every level of organization, from fundamental particles in physics to biological organisms. From the uncertainty of the photon to rational man, consciousness operates at discrete levels of awareness, differing only in complexity and degree of freedom. It may be that more elemental matter serves as a graded potential for higher states of awareness in biologically more highly evolved species. This primitive consciousness may create a "building block" effect, not of content but process, for more complex energy systems and forms. Higher stages of evolution could be experienced by using the knowledge of lower realms to go beyond our present state of consciousness, thereby allowing us more free energy at the higher frequencies. This knowledge would allow a member of a biological species to "tune in" to the most advanced developmental frequencies of its species and provide the impetus for further evolution.

Gordon Globus, at the University of California, Irvine, drawing on evidence from philosophy, physics, and medicine, contends that conscious activity is present down as low on the scale of animal evolution as the metazoa. He found a "selective attention" even at these elemental stages which is part of consciousness at higher developmental levels. The difference, he claims, between inorganic matter and sentient beings lies only in the quantity of consciousness. All forms of energy have the same basic awareness. It is possible that we humans are reluctant to accept that everything has consciousness because we hold ourselves to be "special." Globus reflects:

Although it may seem absurd to propose that all organizations are conscious, this apparent absurdity may reflect human chauvinism about consciousness.[23]

In physics, the problem of a photon's "choice" raised the issue of consciousness as a matter for inquiry. According to physicist E.H. Walker, photons may be conscious. He postulates:

> ...the universe is "inhabited" by an almost unlimited number of rather discrete conscious, usually nonthinking entities that are responsible for the detailed working of the universe.[24]

Dr. Tiller has called these units of consciousness "perceptrons." Could these units be floating in a sea of energy (neutrinos), awaiting appropriate activity for a continuation of the state of wholeness? If this were so it would mean that photons, like all quanta or units of energy, "know" at all times what must be done because they have an inherent sense of wholeness. As part of this organized whole, they simply supply activity (energy) in appropriate ways (such as the correct quantity or direction), depending on the needs of the moment to maintain a state of wholeness. Their information about any situation is not transferred but arises in awareness from the universal consciousness within each process of energy. There is no need to even admit the concept of choice. They simply do what has to be done. Even chemicals know with which other chemicals they can unite and which they must avoid. In chemistry, this primitive consciousness has been "scientifically" ascribed to laws of reactions. However, the essence of all laws of nature is a self-consistency in its organization. Speaking about the Chinese "Li" symbol, the principle of organization, philosopher Needham says:

> There is a "law"...to which parts of wholes have to conform by virtue of their very existence as parts of wholes...The most important thing about parts is that they have to fit precisely into place with the other parts in the whole organism which they compose.[25]

In order for anything in the universe to fit in with other processes it has to have some sense of what the whole is. Without this our entire cosmos would be a chaos of chance events. Laws of nature are simply special applications of the Law of Wholeness. They are processes of consciousness which form a consistent pattern amongst themselves.

I believe that every process, from the lowest-graded potential of matter to the ultimate movement in the cosmos, has consciousness. All these processes are governed by the Law of Wholeness. They are floating in a sea of energy (perhaps neutrinos) and are aware of and participate in activity which maintains wholeness on their level of functioning.

According to some physicists, consciousness is the hidden variable that goes beyond space and time, a "fifth force" which generates the material universe from its clusters of being. This is supported by the quantum idea that matter is only an energetic probability. According to Heisenberg we cannot determine with certainty the location of matter—only the likelihood that it exists.

So what determines what actually becomes matter in our universe? Given so many possibilities for energy structure, can it really be mere chance, as the quantum physicists suggest, that certain forms develop and evolve whereas others do not? No. I suggest it is due to a universal awareness of what is needed. No form develops when there is no need for it. Everything has its place in the whole and therefore is created for a reason, even though that reason may not always be clear to us. The universe is actualized exactly the way it is because consciousness of the whole dictates that from myriad possibilities only those structures, forces, and media develop that are essential for further evolution. The forms of religions, cultures, and even physical buildings only last as long as there is an energetic need for them. When their need has been satisfied they, too, pass away, transformed into the next expression of consciousness.

It is precisely the uncertainty of energy formations which enables us to evolve. If everything was fixed with certainty, no new forms could develop and no quality of aliveness would remain. This is true for researchers, spiritual seekers, and the average person on the street. In the indeterminacy of energy lies the power of creativity, innovation, and potential for more complete wholeness.

Like the laws of thermodynamics which govern heat and other energy forms, an increase of consciousness means that energy is lost in some other part of the universe.[26] According to Dr. Tiller, higher consciousness is possible because the order of the universe is decreasing (positive entropy), a view which parallels Steiner's earlier thought.

We need to experience the chaos of modern life as a manifestation of the universe's loss of order so that we can evolve. If our stability were not destroyed, we would not have any free energy to invest in the evolution of new forms or processes. The challenge of modern life, simply explained, is whether or not we as a species can learn from this chaos by transforming destruction into construction, dissipation into wholeness, and thus eventually evolve into higher levels of consciousness.

In order to talk about everything as having a consciousness, we also have to recognize the vast qualitative difference between different forms of energy. Although everything has (or is) consciousness, a stone is not a plant is not a human. Different levels of consciousness correspond to varied qualities and frequencies of energy expressions or forms. The higher the consciousness, the higher the energetic frequency and the more complete the quality of wholeness.

Scientists talk about the ground state as being the lowest energy state of any atom. In order for an electron to jump into a shell outside its normal ground state it needs an amount of energy to overcome the tendency to remain at ground level. Once an atom has been heated and then cooled off, the electrons that jumped to other levels now return to ground state. When any of us attempts to increase our consciousness we require a certain amount of energy to overcome a similar ground state. We could call the basic level of consciousness for any form of energy "ground-level consciousness" (GLC). In human terms we can read the tendency to remain at GLC level as laziness or comfortableness.

Like atoms, we can also experience a jump in awareness due to increased energy, but unlike atoms, we can stay there. This is basically the physics underlying personal evolution. A lot of effort is generally required to stay at this peak of consciousness, because our tendency is always to fall back to GLC where we *think* we feel more secure. Quantum physics believes that energy comes in quanta or units but does so noncontinuously—only a piece at a time. This is contrary to the classic idea that energy is continuous. If we apply these ideas to consciousness, they would imply that consciousness either increases by a certain amount at one time or it increases gradually. Actually, both views are correct. Consciousness is elevated when any new input in the quality of awareness and wholeness is received, although it may not stabilize until a particular as yet unmeasurable quanta of new consciousness is allowed. Thus, while any energy increment increases the potential for greater evolution, a certain amount of focusing at this new level of awareness is necessary before we can remain at that consciousness level.

This is why an altered-state-of-consciousness experience, in which a person goes beyond the GLC using drugs, psychosis, meditation, or other practices, generally leads to an increase in consciousness only if the state is frequently induced and experienced and eventually integrated. Otherwise, an intensive experience remains only a "happening" with no increase in stabilized consciousness. On the other hand, once a higher level of awareness has been experienced it becomes easier to experience this state again. Like a door which has been opened suddenly, energy flows in a new channel of perception, making a further step in evolution possible.

Evolving to a higher energy/consciousness level reflects a shift in awareness from a lower-frequencied vibration to a higher one. Generally this requires much preparation in order to be able to fully integrate the new level of consciousness into everyday life. Like an electron which returns to the ground state and gives off light in the process, we too, upon re-entry into ordinary life, reflect this new awareness in all that we do.

Anthropologist Roger Westcott has offered the suggestion that consciousness is an internal bioluminescence. In this regard, enlightenment may be thought of as an ultimate state of consciousness in which energy in the form of light simply radiates from inside out, going beyond the personal into universal wholeness. For the few who become enlightened, the light which is experienced above is brought to the ground in such a way that they are here with us *and* still there in the other reality. In their absolute wholeness these beings experience no separation between here and there because they exist beyond space and time.

In a conceptual sense, consciousness is the awareness of degrees of wholeness such that lower levels of consciousness are characterized by less complete degrees of awareness than higher levels. In its own way, the scientific community is also becoming interested in greater degrees of wholeness. Because of new theoretical insights and experimental findings, physicists are being literally forced to think more holistically. Probably the most important aspect of this new scientific perspective is that any complete picture of the ways of nature must be predicated on wholeness as much as possible. This is true in relativity theory and quantum mechanics, as well as in all research design. According to physicist David Bohm, professor of Physics at the University of London and frequent conversationalist in the Krishnamurti Discussion Series:

> ...science itself is demanding a new, nonfragmentary world view....It is shown that both in relativity theory and quantum theory, notions implying the undivided wholeness of the universe would provide a much more orderly way of considering the general nature of reality.[27]

It is important to realize that our scientific truths are relative to our present understanding, which could easily change with new insights. The isolation work of the Newtonian era carried us away from our wholeness by focusing only on the individual experience. Ultimately, this focus narrowed our scientific perspectives about reality due to its noninteractive orientation. However, all research—be it formally scientific or personal/experiential—is influenced by our consciousness which is a definite, though nonphysical, source of energy.

Numerous examples from everyday scientific theory and research support the importance of wholeness as an essential energetic concept. In an overview of the new path of physics, David Bohm has said:

We must turn physics around. Instead of starting with parts and showing how they work together (the Cartesian order), we start with the whole.[28]

And in another context he states:

Parts are seen to be in immediate connection in which their dynamic relationships depend in an irreducible way on the state of the whole system....Thus one is led to a new notion of *unbroken wholeness* which denies the classical idea of analyzability of the world into separately and independently existent parts...[29]

These are certainly radical comments from a quantum physics viewpoint, even though quantum theory is holistic in concept. Quantum mechanics assumes that individual events occur by pure chance, whereas Bohm asserts that even these individual events (which are cherished by classical Newtonian thinking) are part of the whole as well. Thus, with a more complete sense of wholeness, it is possible to replace the dichotomy of individual or separate (Newtonian) vs. whole or unseparate (quantum physics) by a complementary relationship in which the individual parts are a function of the whole. We then could develop a theoretical whole which is more complete than the whole of the quantum principle by showing the relationship of the part to the whole as well.

Any analysis of particles or elemental building blocks can make sense only when done in a larger context (not in and of itself, because this is reductionistic and ultimately belies a greater truth)—the part in service of the entire. If, for example, we look at the process of fission, wherein atoms are split to yield nuclear power, we see that dividing the whole will give us energy, but at what cost? Because dividing the nuclear whole is unnatural, we are left with millions of tons of nuclear waste that cannot be readily absorbed back into the whole of nature. Some nuclear waste has a radiating lifetime of 100,000 to 300,000 years! Fusion, on the other hand, is a holistic process: it unites two hydrogen nuclei, yields little nuclear waste, and produces an energy output of five million times that of fission. Fusion occurs naturally in the sun and is used in building hydrogen bombs, though with more research peaceful energy uses could be developed. Thus even at the atomic level wholeness manifests itself as an essential aspect of physics today. Nevertheless, many scientists are still reluctant to acknowledge this unifying principle.

According to Zukav, quantum scientists noticed a certain "connectedness" among research phenomena but ascribed this to accident.

However, mathematician J.S. Bell developed a theorem, which was later scientifically substantiated in the laboratory,* that all separate parts are connected in a holistic way; this disproves the "accident" theory. Therefore, those scientists who do not believe in the nature of wholeness either have to accept the fact that they have been wrong or accept that a fundamental building block of their science, mathematics, is inconsistent and fallible.

If the concept of wholeness was absent from physics, it would be difficult to explain how light acts both as a wave and a particle, unless they were manifestations of some fundamental process. Technically (according to classical science), light can only be one *or* the other but not both. In the 1930s, Niels Bohr developed a theory of *complementarity* which held that the manifestation of light, either as a wave or a particle, is a reflection of how it is measured. This implies that the scientist will determine, with his instrumentation, whether light in one circumstance will be a wave or a particle. It must be clear, however, that light is holistic—it is simply what it is. But when we measure it, we see it dualistically.

Bohr's concept of complementarity contends that light has no properties by itself; what we describe as light is our interaction (force) which it. In other words, we create the image of light with our consciousness. The "wavicle" (wave and particle) properties of light are consistent in themselves; otherwise, light could not exist. But because our perception of light is split we see it as either particle or wave, though both are necessary to understand the phenomenon of light completely. According to Zukav: "...complementarity leads to the conclusion that the world consists not of things, but of interactions."[30]

It is precisely these "interactions" among energy processes that produce matter (particles) or media (waves), though both are movement. Our state of consciousness creates the impetus for these energy forms to develop. It is not that we control this energy but we do have an influence upon the forms in which we have invested our energy. Though we cannot effect the essence of energy, we can, through our consciousness, create the forms that emanate from that essence. In short, we create our own existence. By creating the research in physics, we also create the problems. In the universe there are no problems; only processes that function according to explicit laws of wholeness. Instead of experiencing this wholeness, scientists try to explain the cosmos, often without connecting it to wholeness at all. By denying the unity in the universe and then trying to analyze this

*By Clauzer and Freedman at the Lawrence Berkeley Lab (1972).

self-created disharmony, many problems are created in physics that do not exist in nature.

The wave/particle of light simply points out the dualistic (split) nature of our perceptions on holistic processes. Because of this dualism our consciousness is also unfocused and split. Although polarity of every dimension—day/night, black/white, male/female—exists in our physical world, it is our perception of these as basically contradictory (instead of complementary as in the Chinese Yin/Yang concept) that impedes our progress in scientific or personal development. Wholeness, on the other hand, is the acceptance of life's polarities as confluent (L. flowing together) energy processes. Our consciousness creates the framework for either separation or wholeness depending on our state of development.

We also see the application of wholeness in other areas of physics. For example, the laser graphically demonstrates the application of wholeness in instrumentation. An essential tool in industry, communication, as well as more recently in surgery and acupuncture, the laser projects a form of integrated illumination called coherent light. In contrast to the normal light formed in our homes and offices, which diffuses much of its energy (not to mention its waste), coherent light is concentrated in one frequency and emits rays that are in phase (time coordinated) with each other. It is precisely this unity of frequency and pinpoint directioning of coherent light which make it so powerful; yet in surgery, doctors are able to penetrate the outer layer of eye tissue to cauterize a rupture in the iris without damage to the superficial layer of tissue. American telephone companies are using the coherency of the laser to modulate messages across microscopic filaments over greater distances—in a fraction of the space and with greater clarity than conventional cables. Thus, a high degree of energy wholeness transmits information with little interference or resistance. This will be an important consideration in our discussion of therapy in Chapter Five.

In yet another application of lasers—modern research into holograms—the fundamental quality, as well as the explanatory power, of wholeness is again substantiated. The idea of a hologram (Gk. holos, whole, and gamma, draw) developed as a result of holography (Gk. holos, whole, and graphos, instrument or something written), a photographic process in which three-dimensional pictures are produced by the interaction of two or more light-wave fields. Optically, a holographic picture appears solid in space and can be "frozen" to be reproduced later. An interesting feature of the hologram is that due to the fact that the informational pattern is distributed throughout the image evenly, any part of it may be used to reproduce the whole. Each part of the image is intimately tied to the whole, in the same way that each of us is connected to and creates the society in which we live. Each individual (L. individius, indivisible) cannot be divided or isolated from the rest of that society because no division of society as a whole is possible without leading to disease. In a similar way that even and odd numbers are not identified yet still are part of the set of integers in mathematics so too each so-called subdivision of society is a part of that society as well. Though both the whole and parts of the whole are distinct in their own way, it is we who create the artificial separation that does not exist without us.

Similarly, physicists can describe components of a whole as a wave. By either bringing these waves together or separating them, they can mathematically describe a unit of anything, even consciousness, by a process called Fourrier superpositions. We could, if we wanted to, describe a whole society based on such waves in which members of that society would be expressed as the superposition of all their individual waves. Society then might be thought of as a standing wave whose wholeness is defined and composed of the individual vibrations (and hence waves) of each person. Likewise, life energy can be explained as the superposition of wave components of form, force, and medium, whereby consciousness acts as the integrative factor. The result of such a superposition is the creation of wholeness.

Perhaps the most important manifestation of wholeness in physics is the concept of the field, which might be described as an energetic influence in space. Ever since its Western discovery by Faraday and Maxwell, force is no longer seen as connected to material bodies alone but is understood as being a manifestation of force fields independent of matter. This discovery caused a shift away from classical physics' dependency on matter as the essence of life to a nonmaterialistic approach involving subtler energies. Once again, Einstein was in the forefront of this radical change in perspective. For Einstein, matter could best be understood as a function of its field; like Aristotle, he believed that matter had no existence by itself. In his own words:

> What impresses our senses as matter is really a great concentration of energy into a comparatively small space. We could regard matter as the regions in space where the field is extremely strong.... There would be no place, in our new physics, for both field and matter, field being the only reality.[31]

The field, then, is the spatial influence of energy which, when concentrated, creates matter. Because matter is composed of nonsubstance particles which are really energy patterns, the field is an organizing influence in space which holds energy patterns together. In fact, even when particles are seen by physicists in specially designed enclosures called bubble chambers they see only the traces of some interaction, not particles as substance. According to quantum theory, currently the most successful theory in physics in terms of explaining phenomena, particles are actually fields which are interacting at a single point in space. A further extension of quantum physics, called quantum field theory, even asserts that each particle has a separate field. Though there are some mathematical difficulties with this theory because so many particles exist, quantum field theory is quite successful. An interesting premise of this theory holds that the physical world as we know it is made up of fields—and fields alone. Matter is simply the temporary expression of fields that interact. In order for matter not to disappear before our eyes, the fields which organize energy into particles must continue to interact.

It would seem that fields hold our universe together. Matter is created by energy fields, and forces can be seen as interactions in those fields. So both matter and force can be explained by field theory. Fields are the process components of wholeness. They are teleological environments which aid in nature's overall design of wholeness. In biology we speak of homeostasis—the means by which the body retains physiological stability in temperature and energy transference despite the variety of stimuli that impinge upon it. The German biologist Hans Driesch theorized that cells are guided by what he called "entelechy" (after Aristotle), the way their position in the whole governs their biological development. Each cell influences the whole and in turn is influenced by it. Research scientists Dr. Harold S. Burr and Dr. F.S.C. Northrop with their exploration of L-fields discovered that every living form has a distinctive field, paralleling the quantum field theory's view that every particle has a unique field. This suggests the possibility that cells are governed by "biofields" which determine how they grow. Russian scientist Viktor Inyushin has found such a biofield, formed by bioplasma and thought to be made up of other subfields—electrostatic, electromagnetic, acoustic, hydrodynamic, and possibly others not yet discovered. One of these new fields might be Dr. Dubrov's biogravitational field. According to Dubrov, this biogravitational field could be the basis for a unified field theory which is necessary to integrate all the forces of physics under one rubric. He comments:

> By the term biogravitation we designate a field-energy system. The biogravitational field is universally convertible, i.e., it is capable of

transition into any form of field and energy—and therefore a unified field theory must be worked out especially for it.[32]

Dubrov also suggests that the biogravitational field might explain the psychic phenomena of mental telepathy, psychokinesis, and clairvoyance, as these feats demand an energetic explanation that goes beyond our present ideas of space and time into the realm of negative space/time. A unified field theory would provide us with a wholeness from which all energy processes could be understood. Einstein called this organizing structure the universal field. The Hindus called it Asat—the unitary field of pure potentiality—and the Chinese simply said it was the Tao, the undefinable reality, the essence of the universe from which everything flows. The neo-Confucians believed Chi was the form of nonperceptible substance by which universality could become physical matter if condensed enough. Chi creates matter and acts like an ether medium. According to Capra, it also is a field:

> As in quantum field theory, the field or the Chi is not only the underlying essence of all material objects, but also carries their mutual interactions in the form of waves.[33]

Life energy (Chi) activates everything to "become" and contains within its processes the patterns of cosmic interaction. It is the medium by which all things come alive; it is the organizing fields which matter grows into; it is the forces by which matter evolves; it is even the form of matter itself. Thus life energy is the process that uses form, force, and medium through fields and matter to create the whole. Consciousness is the universal field that directs its activity. "Surely consciousness...is a localization in a primal field, presumably that one in which all else originates," says Kunz.[34]

Research on the connection between the brain and consciousness has shown that a holographic field model of the brain's functions is the most likely candidate to explain the role of consciousness. Karl Pribram, noted brain researcher and major contributor to the brain-hologram model, states that because the brain is able to store huge amounts of material in such a small place, the hologram concept is most probably the explanatory mechanism. According to this theory, information is not stored as small packages but as wave functions in which each piece can recall the whole, because the whole is stored in each piece.

Research done by biologist Paul Pietsch supports this position. For example, Pietsch found that if he removed pieces of a salamander's brain, destroyed their physical wholeness (by cutting, shuffling, juxtaposing, or mincing), and then replaced them, there was no change in the animal's eating patterns. In other words, despite all types of *physical* manipulation, the pattern of eating returned to normal after a few weeks of recovery.

Other research on nerve activity in the brain points to the fact that in addition to nerve impulse discharges of either firing or not firing, as has been the accepted theory, there is also a graded, slow potential wave that is influenced by infinitesimal amounts of energy. This means that brain nerves (neurons) are affected both by a gross component and a more subtle component which could account for any change in consciousness. Wholeness as a field phenomenon is not dependent upon the gross mechanisms of the physical brain but shows a consciousness which is beyond materiality. This nonmaterial aspect may have a direct connection to physical activity through the medium of a subtle energetic process.

As further indications of the field relationship of consciousness, we might recall that psychic phenomena such as influencing particle chambers, bending metal, and sending information across shielded walls are all mental expressions of life energy. As such, they reflect a developed consciousness which is able to affect matter. Even on a lesser scale, the ability of one's emotional/psychological state to affect the body is supported by a multitude of research in psychosomatic medicine. Both psychic and psychosomatic processes certainly reflect the power of consciousness to affect matter. As Kenneth Pelletier points out:

> A model of mind-body interaction emerges whereby the subtle properties of consciousness can be shown to have profound effects upon physical processes.[35]

In addition to the negative effect our consciousness can have on the body, the potential for healing, though less researched, is just as great when consciousness is turned in this direction.*

Radionics and dowsing are also areas of energy research which lend credence to the idea that consciousness is a field. In the later years of development in radionics, Arthur Young found that the use of a circuit diagram and symbols of the apparatus's components to "broadcast" vibrations worked as well as when the physical box itself was used! This demonstrated that it was not the radionics apparatus, but rather the coherent consciousness of the operator which was healing. The box had only served as a focus for this consciousness. Edward Russell has accounted for this phenomenon by saying that the operation of a radionics apparatus projects thought- or T-fields which may

---

*The mind-body interaction will be discussed further in the next chapter.

draw "nature's attention" to normalize its forces. This suggests that coherent consciousness as a field projects itself in space and is received by the patient's energy field, effecting his wholeness accordingly. French radiasthetist Louis Turenne, who had successfully dowsed for many years, found, like Young, that a symbol of his apparatus (a dowsing rod) would work as well as the instrument itself. Again, this suggests that the consciousness of the operator is the important factor in radiasthesic field functioning. Instruments may therefore serve as a wave guide for their operators.[36]

Even though fields explain much in contemporary physics, a few scientists have even gone beyond the acceptance of fields as the organizing processes of the universe. One of these was Albert Einstein. He was of the theoretical persuasion that fields were a product of our mental creations, even though earlier he had said they were *the* reality of the universe. In his ultimate vision (mathematically unproven as yet), Einstein said that all the concepts in physics can be reduced to space/time and motion, and these are equivalent. He considered matter and energy to be curvatures of space/time and fields to be motion. According to Einstein, we have created the phenomena of physics to explain in complicated detail the simple fact that everything moves in space/time the way it does simply because it is the easiest path. I would suggest that the easiest path is the path of wholeness.

Charles Muses has suggested that even more basic than fields are the "singularities" which generate them. He defines "singularities" as sources of waves with marked individuality. Physicists theorize that these singularity points* exist, for example, at the base of those burnt-out stars known as "black holes." At these singularity points "all the laws of physics collapse and anything becomes possible, for singularities are entry and exit points which link different universes together."[37] Closer to home, Muses claims that the "self" is a singularity which generates consciousness fields. Working with a mathematical model of hypernumbers, Muses has shown that "selves" exist which transcend physical form and "live" after the death of the physical body, and that these "selves" generate fields through consciousness. Whether these selves are protons or human beings, each produces a field which goes beyond its own physical existence into a negative space/time continuum.

The evidence suggests that consciousness is a universal field that generates other fields which in turn affect and create matter, but

---

*Singularity points may be connected to other points in the etheric body called nodal points, which unite all energy fields together, or acupuncture points, which integrate the Chi in meridians.

which are independent of it. On less complete levels, consciousness may simply be the awareness of energy movement in space over time, whereas on more complete levels it may transcend space/time at points of singularity and exist only as a process of the Spiritual Self or Universal Being.

An inquiry into the physics of energy leads us through the form, force, and medium of life to fields which govern these processes and eventually to consciousness as the universal field. In time, life energy may be shown to be the cosmic motion which transcends positive and negative space/time to attain the simplicity and eternal consciousness of wholeness in the "now." We therefore might describe life energy in the following equations:

$$
\begin{aligned}
\text{life energy} \ &= \ \text{matter} \\
&= \ \text{form} \\
&= \ \text{force} \\
&= \ \text{interaction} \\
&= \ \text{medium} \\
&= \ \text{information} \\
&= \ \text{field} \\
&= \ \text{consciousness} \\
&= \ \text{space/time curvature} \\
&= \ \text{wholeness}
\end{aligned}
$$

To aid in conceptualizing how the various processes of energy physics fit into wholeness, a brief developmental sketch of the energy components necessary for the next chapters seems appropriate.

The essential underlying concept of life energy is that everything by nature is whole. Every form and process of its many manifestations fits into an organized unity which cannot be justifiably separated, without losing completeness. Energy is a convenient concept to describe how wholeness functions in the world of physics as well as in our daily lives. It is a universal concept which can be applied to all problems and therefore to all solutions.

Energy is everywhere; it exists in space; it surrounds us in a sea of activity and permeates us. Therefore we cannot be separate from it—any separation in ourselves or between us and our environment constitutes an automatic splitting from wholeness. In examining the functions of energy more closely, we find two important aspects: energy's cyclical nature—its periodic movement such as seasons, climate changes, or energy transfers—and its evolutionary aspects as it moves from lower, less complete energy processes to higher, more complete ones. The evolutionary aspect occurs in physical and psychological development and, even more importantly, in spiritual unfolding.

In both of these aspects, energy has no real starting point, because all is in movement and space is infinite. However, we can speak about its initial phases in a new cycle, for example. Out of a primordial nothingness, which we can call the *great void*, energy manifests itself as pure potential. Scientists might refer to the void as the ultimate field or simply space (the gravitational field is curved space), whereas mystics refer to it as Brahman, Tao, or the Great Emptiness. The Chinese refer to it as the Wu-Chi—the Great Whole from which all creative potential arises. Ironically, this great void is precisely the Great Whole, both in physics and mysticism. Because no-thing is present and no form exists, all is process and therefore all is possible.

Energy in the void moves in patterns which appear random and unfocused (random is our term for not seeing the greater wholeness); however, even here order prevails. In describing the chaos beneath the order of particle physics, Sarfatti states:

> ...it is a Marx Brothers hyperkinetic pandemonium, Charlie Chaplin slapstick, Helter Skelter now you see it, now you don't....It's psychedelic confusion—until one sees the subtle order.[38]

Gradually, out of the chaos, minute energy movements begin to organize themselves into larger wholes. Because basic energy processes are primarily unstructured (though organized according to potential), they have no form *per se*. As they evolve they seek larger wholes which necessitates greater consistency. Because wholeness is a universal phenomenon, all things are subject to its influence (laws). This is also true of elementary processes which until now have been gradients of activity rather than actual higher-level forces, for example, the graded potentials before neuron activity occurs in the brain. However, under the influence of universal order these elementary movements gradually develop into consistent activity. It is this greater consistency which forms what we know in physics as subatomic "particles." As we know from quantum physics, these so-called particles are not really material in the Newtonian sense of inert, solid entities, but rather alive, predominantly space processes which have properties of matter.

Some of these particles give rise to electrons, protons, and neutrons which form atoms. Let us not forget, however, that in the transition from elementary energy processes to atoms no movement is lost. This could be called the conservation of movement.

Less-structured movement in the void becomes increasingly more form-oriented, and loses a degree of freedom for the sake of greater wholeness. Early atomic forms created by this movement gradually develop into molecules, cells, and higher forms of material such as metals, stones, plants, animals, human beings, and stellar masses (such as planets and stars). In these formations, which appear to us as matter, life energy still functions as movement, albeit changed in process. When energy moves from less structure to more structure, or when basic processes become matter, energy is slowed down because of its loss of freedom. This is due to the fact that matter binds energy in consistent forms. Form, as we discussed, is the structure created from the interaction of fields; therefore, as long as these fields continues to act on one another, form persists. Otherwise, it dissolves into other processes, as seen when ice returns to water.

All energy movement will create *radiation* or *emanations* that stream from a concentration of activity. Regardless of how small or large the movement is, some radiation exists. Most such radiation, of course, cannot be detected by our present technical equipment because of its subtle nature. Nevertheless this radiation does exist. Western science is beginning to accept the possibility of such radiation on the atomic level. According to Dr. Rabi, faculty member of Columbia University and American Association for Advancement of Science prize winner:

> Atoms can act like little radio transmitters broadcasting on ultra short waves...man himself, as well as all kinds of supposedly inert matter constantly emit rays.[39]

One important point here is that even inert or so-called nonliving things radiate energy. In my sense of "life," everything which has movement is a living process. It may not be biological life with reproduction possibilities, but movement does seem to be a fundamental characteristic of everything we know. In that sense everything is alive due to its life energy process. As medical inventor Itzhak Bentov points out:

> We seem to project our own behavior onto other systems, by saying that starting from the atom and going to larger aggregates there is no 'life,' and then suddenly, when the aggregate of atoms have reached a certain stage of organization 'life' appears because we can recognize our own behavior in it.[40]

Medical physicist Andrija Puharich, like scientists Andrew Cross, Martin Morley, and Wilhelm Reich before him, has shown that inert materials can produce biologically alive forms. When inert atoms are put into laboratory bowls and energized with electrical impulses they develop into amino acids (the basic building blocks of biological life). This leads us to question the academic distinction between living and inert, and supports the idea that inert materials are another form of life, perhaps latent in a biological sense but nevertheless alive in their own way.

We might think of radiation as movement from an energy source with a particular quality. This means that different radiation—such as electromagnetic, nuclear, or sound—have different qualities which define them. The medium for these radiations is *waves*. A wave, simply defined, is a shape, form, or pattern that moves. Among the variety of waves, the most important is the so-called "physical" waves such as sound and light, which actually disturb the environment by moving energy and information along a particular path. Thus, all radiation is also information which is coded in the qualities of the waves and enables us to differentiate, for example, between nuclear and electromagnetic radiation. When wave movement is periodic or cyclical we call it a *vibration*. A wave, then, is a patterned vibration which radiates in space and time.

In the process of evolution, random movements of life energy become more rhythmical. Diffuse movements focalize into more definite patterns which simultaneously cause periodic vibrations. These vibrations radiate waves which transmit energy from the source along with coded information about these particular emanations of life energy. We interpret this information as living or inert, depending on the qualities and effects of this energy.*

In order to encode some of this information, science has determined several qualities of vibration (therefore, waves) which enable us to learn about nature's functions and messages to us. Because most of our present science concentrates on physical and gross functions we have only learned about information on the lowest levels of consciousness. However, several qualities of vibrations are useful in describing both the lower and higher levels of energy. One of these is the speed or rate of vibration, known as the *frequency of energy*.

The frequency of energy determines how often energy periodically oscillates between a set of time values. For example, each radio station on the FM band registers a separate channel because the frequency—the rate of emission of electromagnetic waves per second—varies. Channels with lower frequencies radiate fewer cycles of electromagnetic energy per second than those of higher-frequency

---

*In European languages, words for life are derived from the Latin *vibrare*, to vibrate or shake.

stations. In another example, physical matter has a lower frequency of radiation than thoughts.

It is the frequency of the waves that determines one aspect of energy radiations. The greater the vibratory rate of energy transmission, the higher the frequency. In addition to the frequency of the vibration, the amplitude (or height) of the waves and the wave length also play a part in transmitting information about every form of life energy. Although all waves in the electromagnetic spectrum—such as radio waves, visible light, and X-rays—travel at the speed of light, other radiations with different frequencies outside the electromagnetic range travel at superluminal speeds. Because all physical matter contains atoms and all atoms vibrate, all matter should radiate waves. What differentiates individual forms of matter, such as a rock from a plant, lies in the frequency of the energy vibrations. Although classical science has not accepted that inert materials have radiations, this follows from the law that all matter vibrates.

Relativity theory has shown us that matter is not indestructible substance; it is really energy in a particular form determined by its rate of vibration. At the subatomic level it is even clearer that matter in the form of particles is not inert "stuff" to which its form sometimes alludes. As Capra observes:

> The particle can no longer be seen as a static object but has to be conceived as a dynamic pattern, a process involving the energy which manifests itself as the particle's mass.[41]

Because all matter is in motion—vibrating, sending out waves—these patterns retain their form consistently, according to quantum theory, through *energy fields*. It is these fields which are the basis of the universe and not physical matter as was earlier thought. Matter appears when fields of energy interact with each other. For many years in physics, Bohr's theory that electrons rotated around the nucleus in energy shells like planets around the sun was held to be true. Quantum research, however, has shown us that even the position of these electrons is a question of probability, not certainty. An electron, like other subatomic particles, is no longer considered substance but is viewed as a pattern of activity at any given time in space. Therefore, the movements of electrons in their orbits are more appropriately described as energy fields. In fact, it is the interplay of these subatomic energy fields which makes up the atom and, consequently, all matter.

As human beings, we radiate energy like everything else. In these radiations we set vibrations into motion which produces waves. As in all other forms, it is a field which keeps our body in basically the same shape despite the constant change of cells; this field which defines our form is composed of many subfields.

An important corollary to the fact that everything—including us— radiates, vibrates, produces waves, and creates fields is the fact that we also absorb energy. Experience has shown that not all types of energy manifestations or all frequencies are equally absorbed by us.

The key to what we radiate and absorb rests with energy qualities like rate of vibration (frequency), amplitude, and wave length. Let us say you would like to play some music with your friend. Both of you tune your instruments so that you are playing the same notes. What you have done is tune your instruments to the same rate of vibration so that the recurring waves of sound (the energy patterns) correspond exactly with each other. This is *resonance,* a state in which both the maximum and minimum wave values occur at the same time, producing harmony between two energy systems. Obviously, when two instruments are in resonance a harmonious sound is produced, while two people in resonance create compatibility, peace, and love—all of which reflect the whole.

It is interesting to note that the wave values created by the resonance of two identical but separate wave patterns exceed that which either wave pattern alone could produce. This is why the gestalt of love between two or more people exceeds the harmony which is produced if each person loved only him- or herself.

When two energy systems resonate with each other they create what is known in physics as *standing waves.* Standing waves are the "stationary" vibratory patterns of two or more traveling waves which are superpositioned with one another in a confined region of space. A good example of standing waves happens when you pluck a guitar string. Standing waves occur when one object absorbs the same frequency it emits; this causes its oscillations to reinforce each other.

The results of this reinforcing phenomenon can be physically destructive. Foot soldiers crossing a wooden bridge always break their repetitive march; otherwise, the steady rhythm of their feet in unison can cause the bridge to collapse. In fact, the Tacoma Bridge in Washington collapsed because of forty-five-mile-an-hour winds which resonated with the movement of the bridge's suspension supports. The vibrations continued to reinforce each other until the bridge was shaken to destruction. Later I shall discuss how resonation can lead to positive results such as further evolution, if certain criteria are met.

In addition to wave patterns resonating together, another set of vibratory rhythms works both internally and externally to create a larger energy whole. Each simple frequency like the note of a musical instrument may be subdivided into other frequencies which are integral multiples of the original. These subdivisions are called *harmonics* and are important for understanding how different frequencies (parts) are still members of another larger entity (the whole). In physics, harmonics represent wave patterns that are quicker and have a shorter wavelength than the fundamental pattern. Harmonics exist on every scale of vibration from the atomic to the cosmic level and hold the key to any explanation of different energy levels. Because every form of energy radiates emanations in its unique range of frequencies, all energy processes must be understood as participating in the whole while at the same time belonging to different energy levels depending on frequency groupings. This explains how every form of energy can have its own field and still participate in the universal field. Remember that unique fields, like all other entities, cannot be isolated from the whole. So even though there are differences in energy levels, the essence of these processes remains the same; only the quality and quantity of the expression differ.

Concerning consciousness, we could say that the frequency of energy vibrations determines the level of consciousness. Matter has (is) a lower level of consciousness because it cannot respond to subtle radiations as, for example, our minds do. Consciousness is also concerned with the degree of refinement of energetic responses to stimuli: the more refined the ability to react, the greater is the level of consciousness. Because different manifestations of energy radiate specific frequencies, they also have particular degrees of refinement and levels of consciousness. Just as light must be explained by particle (quanta) and wave properties to get a complete picture, consciousness must be viewed as being both continuous and noncontinuous.

In evolution, certain critical points are experienced in which the quantitative aspects of consciousness, which have been building up in intensity, suddenly become a qualitatively different state. This would explain why the path of spiritual development may be followed both stepwise (noncontinuously), as in kundalini yoga; and continuously, as in bhakti yoga. It also explains how the brain functions both at the level of gross neuron firings and at the subtler level of slow-wave functioning. Continuous and noncontinuous aspects of consciousness are part of the dualistic paradox of wholeness which defies our Western ideas of "this" or "that," but not "both." In a more complete wholeness, not only do continuous and noncontinuous comprise a complementary relationship, they also cease to be different—continuity becomes discontinuity and vice versa. This seeming paradox leads us beyond our understanding of the physical world to other energy levels in the metaphysical realms.

Chapter Three

Wholeness and Energy

Just as the energy of wholeness expresses itself functionally as form, force, and medium, it may also be observed and experienced as a spiritual manifestation. In effect, what we behold from a functional or spiritual perspective is equivalent aspects of the same wholeness, only with a different orientation. While the functional orients us to how energy processes work, the spiritual connects us with the deeper meaning of these processes. Therefore, the physicists and the mystic are basically talking about the same processes, but in different languages and naturally from different experiences. The concept of energy allows us to unite both perspectives in a larger whole. Relativity theory did not supplant Newtonian physics but incorporated the classical perspective into modern framework; similarly, the spiritual outlook does not negate the functional, but it supplies a deeper meaning from which to see it instead. Therefore, each reality is appropriate in its own way.

In this regard we need to clarify that reality has both relative and absolute aspects. This helps explain why the reality of physics and science in general keeps changing, though that of the spiritual realm always remains the same. Each new scientific perspective expresses a reality which is relative to what went before and will come afterwards, but in no way can it claim to be *the* reality. Reality is a manifestation in wholeness of what is real. The "real" is essence, pure nature. It cannot change; otherwise, it would not be essence. Reality, therefore, is that which is permanent and unchanging; to our senses, the present reality is an absolute reality. The paradox, however, is that because energy is constantly in motion, it is always changing. If, therefore, Absolute reality is also manifest in energy but the Absolute is unchanging, how can we reconcile these two differences? Even though the Absolute is unchanging, its expression may constantly change without its essence being disturbed. The paradox is easily resolved when we understand that the nature of reality is not dependent upon its expression. Regardless of form or pattern, essence is always essence, the Absolute is always Absolute. The world of the Relative supplies the needed processes to account for the Absolute in varied expression. So, although the existence in our universe of the Absolute may vary from time to time and place to place, the nature of the Absolute is permanent. However, manifestations of this reality may seem true within a certain period but may also change at another time. Such reality is therefore relative, because it is dependent upon our perspective.

Because the world of science is relative and the mystical universe (the spiritual) is absolute, it is more appropriate to view the relative from the perspective of the Absolute rather than the other way around. In so doing we come closer to the true state of the universe. However, we need to be aware that speaking from an absolute perspective is actually possible only when we experience this absoluteness. Only those who are "realized" or "enlightened" are qualified to do so. The Absolute manifests completeness so by orienting ourselves to wholeness we can come as close as possible to the absolute without actually being there. This is the spiritual perspective. Every step we make which is connected to this wholeness automatically brings us closer to the Absolute, because the Absolute is merely wholeness. This is also true of our understanding of energy levels.

Each level or manifestation of energy/consciousness expresses itself in distinguishable qualities. These include: vibration, color, sound, density, laws, and relative reality. It is beyond the scope of this work to explore these in detail; however, a few general comments can be made.

Energy levels are distinguishable by their frequencies. All manifestations of energy which vibrate can be described by frequencies, and because everything in our universe must vibrate in order to express its "life," everything functions according to its relative frequency. Two of the most obvious expressions of energy are light and sound. Light is a universal phenomenon present in every manifestation of energy, even though our physical vision can only see it to a very limited degree. Other forms of light, both above and below the visible spectrum (as detected by clairvoyants), exist in every energy manifestation. Einstein demonstrated that anything which has energy—and that is *everything*—can be expressed in terms of its light. Light may be broken down through a prism into different colors which correspond to specific energy levels. The Hindu chakras (see Chapter 1) also express this relationship between energy levels and colors which can only be seen by those whose vision extends beyond physical sight.

Likewise, sound can be used to describe qualities of different energy levels. Technically, sound results from the disturbance of air by waves of vibration. As everything vibrates, we could say that each energy manifestation has a sound which corresponds to it. Again, many of these sounds are inaudible to us because of our limited hearing range.* Because of their universality and their qualities of vibration, from the earliest times both light and sound were often used in color and music therapy.

Each level of energy can also be differentiated by its density. Matter is an expression of energy that has been brought into form by the intense influence of a field. Without this field matter would not exist. Even the word "substance" reflects this truth. Sub (L. *sub*, under) and stance (L. *stare*, to stand) expresses that which "stands under" or underlies. We now know that matter does not underlie the structure of the universe, so it can no longer be called substance. Substance in our present understanding is actually energy, because energy is the dynamic web through which the entire cosmos is built. What we call substance is actually contracted energy. As the level of consciousness increases, energy becomes less and less contracted; therefore, the density (compactness) decreases due to the expansion of the energy fields. At the higher levels of consciousness practically no density exists because all is space. At each of these levels the laws which govern the order of energy movement differ. This is necessary because each plane processes energy in a different way; the resulting forms must correspond to each level perfectly. For example, if our bodies functioned in as confused and scattered a manner as our minds, we couldn't survive. Therefore, in order to survive we split our awareness and disturb our mind/body connection.

The higher levels of consciousness and the laws that govern these states of being take precedence over the lower laws, as the law of the absolute controls the laws of the relative. This is why our mental condition has a much greater impact on the physical body than the body on the mind, although both interact with each other. In the words of the Kybalion:

Nothing escapes the principle of cause and effect, but there are many Planes of Causation, and one may use the laws of the higher to overcome the laws of the lower.[1]

*Sound below the threshold of hearing is called infrasound; that above the threshold is suprasound.

the Soul, the Spirit, the Body, and the Emotions.* Each of these manifestations is an expression of the Whole, though each has unique properties, laws, reality, information, and consciousness. It is not by chance, for example, that we have bodies or emotions; rather, these manifestations are necessary at this point in our evolution so that we might develop further. Therefore, the information we receive through each of these channels enables us to learn about different aspects of the Whole. It is interesting that the Greek "physis," in addition to being a "seeking for the essential nature of things," is also the principle of growth and change. Therefore, the physics of energy discussed in the last chapter naturally becomes the energy of evolution.

Soul

The concept of "soul" is an ancient idea which has been used in almost all cultures. The Egyptians used the term "BA" to express the soul as the carrier of the self through a divine ray which acted on men via a fluid-like compound similar to the akasha of the Hindus or the ether of early western science. The Hermetics of Egyptian tradition believed the soul to be best expressed as the ALL—source of everything. The Jews knew the soul as the "vital principle," while Aristotle called it the "sum of vital principles." Other Greeks such as Heraclitus saw the unity of complements like the Chinese Yin/Yang as a manifestation of soul or Logos, the principle of wholeness. Anaximenes believed that the soul held matter together. The Greek word "psyche," meaning soul, also meant spirit, mind, and life, all of which are manifestations of soul. For the early Christians, the soul was the expression of light as contrasted with the darkness of the body.

On the spiritual plane, the soul is the principle of organization. As with energy on the functional level, the soul reflects the dynamic quality of harmony or integration which leads to wholeness. The soul stands at the very core of our being, serving as the middle point, the source and organizer of all life's energy. As such it radiates energy in all directions like a sun whose pulsations bring light to everything.

The soul is often seen as an entity separate from the body, but this is a mistake. Although the soul is not dependent on the body for its existence, it functions through the corporeal form. To be correct, we would have to say that the soul is really the sum total of energy processes which organize all of life's functions, including the formation of the body itself. Like other energy principles, the soul expresses

*I have explored other manifestations such as the etheric, astral, and mental levels of consciousness in *Manifestations of Energy.*

its qualities as movement with a unique purpose and place in the entire scope of energy manifestations. Strangely enough, many people tried to assert that the soul was located in the physical body. Hippocrates, Galen, Plato, and Roger Bacon all believed the soul was to be found in the brain, while others thought the soul resided in the heart.

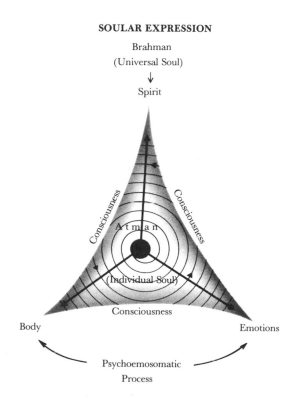

SOULAR EXPRESSION

Brahman

(Universal Soul)

↓

Spirit

Figure 13.

The soul, however, is not a material phenomenon but a holistic principle; it cannot therefore be in one part and not in another. It is in all parts because they are pieces of the whole. The soul is the life principle by which individual and collective life processes become activated.*

*This belief is expressed by the 17th century philosophical concept of Stahl's called *animism* which says that the soul is the principle of life and health and is responsible for all organic development.

We are souls who have bodies, not the other way around, and like a spiritual holograph, each part of us reflects this whole. The state of our wholeness is therefore also reflected in the quality of aliveness we express. In English, the eyes are the windows of the soul, while in German, the eyes are the soul's mirror (Spiegel). Although we cannot accurately talk about more or less soul in our expression, because the soul is infinite, we can say that one person reflects this "soular" energy or light more or less than another. The degree of our evolution is clearly expressed in the ease and clarity with which we do everything.

It is the "soular" process that accounts for the universal consciousness by which all things know what is occurring in their own species and other species, as well. This has sometimes been referred to as cosmic intelligence or universal mind. In this regard, the soul as the fundamental integrator of energy movement expresses as a concept the totality of knowledge and accounts for the distribution of this wisdom throughout the universe. It is through the influence of the soul that all energy processes seek wholeness and know exactly what is needed in every situation.

The soul, however, is more than functional energy. It gives meaning to all movements of energy. Without the process of the soul, energy would have no specific direction; it would remain meaningless activity. "Soular" process adds a new dimension to the neutral activity of functional energy: unfocused activity gradually aligns itself into organized wholes as needed in the process of evolution. It is from this unfolding of greater wholes that forms of all types are created. Forms by themselves have no reason to exist, except in the service of wholeness. We do not *merely* have bodies; neither do we have these shapes only by chance. Our bodies are forms which are necessary vehicles for our development. The presence of the soul's influence provides the overview, the knowledge, and the means by which these particular physical forms develop. It is not the survival of the fittest that guides evolution, as Darwin suggested, but the resonation of standing waves of consciousness which reinforce each other in such a way that a form is created when needed. In fact, consciousness of the whole is one of the main characteristics of the soul. It is only through this awareness that any development is possible.

In this capacity, the soul serves as a field of influence which supports our growth. It beckons us to fulfill its potentiality of wholeness. Fortunately for us, this growth into greater wholeness is an automatic process, although it depends on two premises. The first is that we don't hinder the flow of energy as it moves along its course; and secondly, that we remain conscious of this organic energy flow. Because most of us are frightened by the power of this developmental process, we block the flow of energy with narrow thinking and constricted musculature. This, in turn, limits our consciousness and slows the growth of wholeness.

Two basic movements of energy in the developmental process have been alluded to earlier but now require greater specificity when we refer to the processes of soul. The first of these is a Yin, downward movement of energy* (from the viewpoint of the earth), and the other is a Yang movement upwards. On the spiritual plane, this downward movement is called involution, while its upward counterpart is known as evolution.

Involution

As I briefly mentioned in Chapter One, involution (L. *involvere*, envelop or roll into) consists in the descendancy of energy from the Absolute as it involves itself in the relative. As energy descends from the cosmic realms to the earth, it passes through the chakras until it becomes focused in the lowest chakra. Here the Absolute rests as latent potentiality awaiting its stimulation by active consciousness, or more rarely, involuntary stimulation through sudden physical injury or special practice like kundalini yoga or meditation.

In terms of energy, "soular" involution is the descent of an endless source of vitality from an infinitely high-frequencied force or interaction into a physical, and therefore slower, energy form. Like an electrical transformer which reduces the current of a high-alternating voltage into a lower voltage, the body serves as a medium of transformation for the soul. The Absolute of the soul becomes expressed in the Relative of the physical plane. This descendance of energy from the highest energy frequencies to the lowest creates matter and simultaneously decreases the level of consciousness. When the descendancy of energy takes place as a part of the involution/evolution cycle, consciousness becomes more alive and tangible to the senses.

Matter as a denser form of energy is a contracted field of life which can be used to gain a glimpse of the principles of which life energy operates. At the higher frequencies these principles are quite difficult to perceive because our state of consciousness does not resonate in harmony with the information being presented. Therefore, we cannot understand their messages. The creation of matter, on the other hand, provides the possibility of learning about these life energy principles

---

*The emotional counterpart of bodily energy moving in the direction of the earth is known as "grounding" in body psychotherapy.

because of the reduced frequencies on the physical level. As energy is slowed down it is more readily perceived by the five senses, which is exactly what gives matter qualities such as hardness, smell, and form. This greater "concreteness" enables us to see the patterns of energy in a slowed-down version, as when we look at the frozen form of a nautilus sea shell, or even a piece of fruit. Each has developed a form as a result of a particular pattern of energy.

If we were fully aware, we could see the perfection (wholeness) in all of our everyday forms. By perfection I don't mean a lack of flaws in these forms but rather how exactly and appropriately the form expresses its energy information to us. The human body, for example, is perfect in its expression of the whole, even though its shape may not reflect perfect external harmony. This seems to be a paradox. How can a shape which is imperfect reflect the perfection of the whole? The body, like all form, is one aspect of the manifestation of wholeness at a particular point in the development of the cosmos. As such, it reflects the soul or essence of energy processes, even though its present existence may not be as whole as the essence from which it springs.

As "soular" activity extends its essence through form, the neutral energetic activity of matter becomes aware. The most developed biological form of this conscious matter is human life. As the soul manifests itself in human life, matter becomes infused with the wholeness of the Absolute. This is most evident in the conception of a child. Contrary to a mechanistic view, conception is not only the biological coming together of sperm and egg, but a manifestation of "soular" unity. Therefore, the quality of physical loving also dictates the quality of the child. When a child is conceived in love, this state of emotional wholeness manifests in the form and vibrancy of the child. The spontaneous infusion of soul at a moment of love floods the entire being of the child with this very same quality. The wholeness (love) of the parents simply fosters more wholeness. Thus, later in life, this quality of mutual consciousness on the part of both parents will enable the child to more quickly open his or her latent spiritual expression; the child's lifetime will be an experiencing of this wholeness as it becomes more and more conscious.

In discussing the process of involution we need to make a distinction between universal soul, known in Hinduism as Brahman, and the individual soul or self, called Atman. In the movement of energy processes which are awaiting focus and, later, form, the universal mind (sense of cosmic wholeness) called Brahman becomes aware of the necessity for another human form in which the Divine light might be expressed. Through the physical act of two parents a child is conceived.

Through their love Brahman becomes expressed in another unit of living wholeness which reflects the essence of the Absolute but the existence of the Relative.

This relative form becomes Atman, the soul of the individual. In this process, the Divine or Absolute has involved itself in a smaller, more relative whole, which is nevertheless absolute as potential, residing within the consciousness of the new baby. The seed of total consciousness has been planted. Therefore, each of us is the relative manifestation in form of the absolute potentiality of the soul. Parents only give a biological component to a process of soul which they mediate through their interaction. They do not create a child, but a child is produced through them as "soular" influences seek physical form. This state of affairs is somewhat paralleled in subatomic physics, where matter is always being created in a way which reflects the prevalent state of consciousness. We create many of the forms (including our bodies) which we later come to despise due to our incomplete and confused state of consciousness! Even though the biological form of a child is more stable than the almost random creation of matter at subatomic levels, the conception of that child is equally subject to the laws of consciousness.

In involution, matter is infused with the higher consciousness, enabling it to be charged energetically with the Absolute. The Absolute remains undisturbed in us until it finds its path back to the higher frequencies of greater wholeness. This, then, becomes the journey of evolution.

Evolution

Evolution (L. *evolvere*, to unfold, roll out, unroll) is an unfolding of our true nature or essence through the opening of energy centers (chakras) until all are free to take in and give out energy at their respective frequencies. In a step method of evolution, the chakras on the bottom with the lowest frequencies are opened first, and higher-frequencied centers are opened one by one in succession. Other methods, like Sri Aurobindo's Integral Purna Yoga, begin at the top and descend the chakras until all are opened. Still other methods involve focusing on one chakra (as in Bhakti yoga, where the focus is on the heart) and expanding this energy and consciousness until all the others are included. In every case, spiritual evolution involves opening up all the frequencied energies until a state of absolute unity is experienced. This wholeness or state of complete light is known as enlightenment. The Hindus call this liberation from matter "Moksha;" the Buddhists refer to it as "nirvana," and the Zen Buddhists of Japan know this state of bliss as "satori."

Evolution may best be described as the progressive opening to light, truth, and wholeness. As we begin to open up our latent potential for wholeness, the power of its truths become manifest in us. We begin to see clearly what before was confused and cloudy. What is necessary, however, is an honesty in our perception. We need to accept exactly what we see in ourselves without denigrating or beautifying any aspect, for this would only lead us back to unreality. The real is what is. Evolution can only occur if we accept our state of being on the physical, emotional, and spiritual planes and move gradually beyond lower states of energy consciousness, guided by the light of truth. Evolution is seeing the reality on all planes of consciousness and allowing ourselves to bring this awareness into realities of higher frequency. For example, what is real on the physical level is not true on a higher level. A table seems solid, yet appears so only because of its set pattern of vibration. It is "really" hard to the senses but to the consciousness of wholeness which apprehends energy as movement, the table is non-sense and therefore only stabilized activity. By moving beyond the relative reality of the physical world we open ourselves to the potentialities for seeing other realities, such as those on the emotional level, and further along, even glimpses of absolute reality.

Both involution and evolution may be schematized as circular movements which are drawn either downwards (involution) or upwards (evolution). A spiral is created through their movement as changes in energy and consciousness are reflected in space. Nature also mirrors these spiral movements in its myriad shapes, such as shells. The feeling of widening space in meditation or the narrowing space experienced as we focus in psychotherapy both reflect this spiral motion in experience as well. Despite the continual movement of energy in its involutional and evolutional processes, all activity of consciousness is bound in a life energy weaving, like an ever-changing mosaic of charge and discharge.

As we grow and change, the soul maintains stability by providing the blueprint for orderly development. Even though these stages of change may seem strange—even bizarre at times—they are directed by an absolute sense of wholeness which can be trusted implicitly. This is why it is usually important to have a spiritual teacher who can assist us in both the understanding and support of these developmental phases. In the evolutionary process, change and stability become one when there is a connection to wholeness; otherwise, we experience a deep splitting of our energies. The part which is open to change will be resisted by the part that demands stability. But in wholeness, change is stable because nothing will open in consciousness unless it is also appropriate. However, if we are split by mental difficulties or by forcing the door of perception with drugs or unsupervised kundalini yoga* practice, then the chances are much greater of a psychic split taking place.

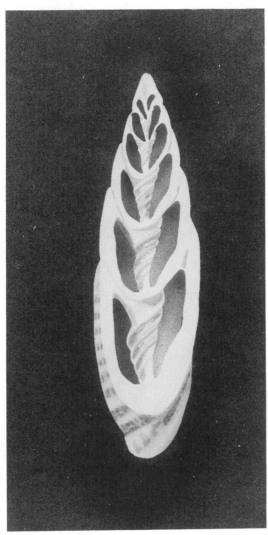

Figure 14. Spirals in Shell

*Kundalini yoga is a practice which forces the energy up the evolutionary tract from lower to higher chakras by rapid breathing techniques and the contraction of muscular "bandas" or centers.

Although energy movement in evolution is sometimes quickened by spontaneous kundalini-type experiences, it usually is a gradual unfolding of clarity and true vision. As we evolve, latent consciousness becomes manifest consciousness. In its course back to absolute wholeness, the manifestations of soul are brought through the physical into the emotional and beyond. We often experience old diseases or unexpressed emotions which seek a way out of their dormancy. Staying with this gradual cleansing, we evolve to purer soul whereby the wholeness on each level of consciousness is experienced and lived increasingly. All that is not whole in us is driven out to be reabsorbed in the energy void. There the unwhole energy processes await further activity which will reintegrate them later into another whole.

Some of the difficulties encountered in life are incomplete energy processes which did not originate in this lifetime. Whole, like unwhole, processes are passed through time as "soular" functions continue from one lifetime to another. Processes which are not finished seek completion in another way at another time through a process known as reincarnation. Reincarnation continually brings into form those energy processes which need to be completed, especially those related to the evolution of the soul. If we consider the soul as a unification of wholeness processes, then reincarnation of the soul means the repetitive expression of the soul in new forms so that wholeness can be completed. Each one of us, as a transformer of energy, serves as a medium for these unfinished "soular" gestalts; therefore, we are influenced in this lifetime by energy processes of another time and space. Karma, the Hindu concept for action, prescribes that every energy process has a consequence which must be brought to a conclusion before a new cycle of movement can be activated. According to the law of Karma, all processes are related to each other; there are no accidents or expressions of fate—only consequences of action.

Some of the physical, emotional and spiritual problems which we experience are actually the unfinished consequences of other "soular" processes which may or may not have come through another person at an earlier point in time. Karmic problems in our present lifetime are indications of the existence of previous soul processes which now continue through us. Karmic processes from the past are referred to as *sanchita*, while the present working-out of these influences is known as *pranabdha*. Even in our present lives we create new karma (*agami*) which goes beyond our lives into the future. Therefore, there is a tremendous responsibility entailed in how we conduct our lives. Most of us are caught in the wheel of birth, death, and birth again which is known to the Buddhists as "samsara." In this constellation we are like a spinning top—merely movement without clear direction until we become aware of how we live. In evolution, however, we have the chance to break away from this unaware activity. By seeking wholeness, the influences of incomplete gestalts from the past or the present gradually become resolved. Those who are able to break completely free of these endless cycles of samsara are the liberated ones—those who have become spiritually realized.

The soul is the organizational principle of harmony by which energy on the functional level achieves purpose, meaning, and direction in its activity. It is the principle of wholeness through which consciousness is manifest in a universal knowledge of all energetic activity. This wholeness principle dictates at any given moment what appropriate action should be taken and directs the creation of all forms as needed in all situations. It even influences which "soular" processes will be infused into human life based on universal need and our level of consciousness.

The soul is a nonmaterial influence and a vital aspect of all matter which allows us to participate in the movement of the Absolute through the processes of involution and evolution. This movement is effected by an infusion of potentiality which needs to be awakened and made manifest by more complete consciousness. Even in our difficulties from this or previous lives, this evolution from matter to the Absolute enables us to grow into a higher consciousness and out of the endless circle of birth and death. In its central role as integrator, the soul serves as a pivotal point for spirit, the body, and the emotions, all of which express wholeness in their individual aspects.

Spirit

The spirit is the main evolutionary expression of the soul as it moves from its latent state to dynamic activity. In a general sense, the spirit of anything is the vital quality which brings potentiality to actuality; it is the medium of the soul, similar to ether or Prana which served this purpose for neutral energy on the functional level. After the universal aspect of soul (Brahman) becomes infused in the material plane (involution), it shows itself as the individual soul (Atman). This individual soul or self is the spirit. Therefore, when we talk about our "self," what we really mean is the expressed essence of the spirit as it moves through us.

The word spirit itself is derived from the Latin *spiritus* which means air or breath. In German the word for breath (*Atem*) is related to the Indian *Atman*, the spirit or individual soul. Even further back in the Bible we read in reference to creation, "In the beginning was the *word.*" The Hebrew term for "word" means exhalation. So we should

healing qualities of each were concentrated for use as health remedies. Homeopathic drugs and Bach flower remedies* both use this
principle to infuse energy patterns into solutions which are used for
treatment. In addition, homeopathic remedies extract essences from
minerals and animals and use a system of succussion to achieve different degrees of drug potency.

The process of the spirit also influences our reactions. In German,
the expression "geistreich" (literally, rich in spirit) signifies a quick
reaction to something. When we are filled with the spirit our response
to everything is also swift and clear. Nothing stands in our way
because the path to wholeness is very precise, yet simple. It is we who
put the obstacles between ourselves and the movement of the spirit
through us. Left to itself, evolution is a rapid matter. The energy knows
where to go in order to complete itself. Confusion (in German, *ent-
geistert*) only occurs when we are not one with our spirit. Otherwise
clarity is a natural process of wholeness.

Naturally, spirit is related to religious experience of all types. Religion (L. *Re*, again, *lig*, tie or kind, and *io*) had the function of uniting
us to wholeness. Except in the East, where this tradition has been
maintained, most religion has lost its connection to wholeness.** However, the renewed interest both in Eastern and Western religions suggests the need to return to some organized form of reunification.

In the Christian church an essential aspect of its doctrine is the Holy
Trinity, comprised of the Father, the Son, and the Holy Spirit. The
Father represents the universal wholeness (Brahman, Absolute soul,
or cosmic intelligence) or the divine aspect of spirit. On the other hand,
the son, Jesus Christ, manifests individual wholeness (Atman, personal soul, or Self) and the corporeal aspects of spirit. The Holy Spirit,
symbolized both by the dove and the element fire, is the transcendent
aspect of spirit. The element fire expresses the transformation potential of the spirit as it destroys matter (form) to draw our energy

*Edward Bach, an English physician, found that by putting flowers in the
sun he was able to transfer the healing properties of these flowers to water
which he then used for treatment.

**In America there is a growing interest in new forms of so-called reli-
gious membership; much of this is an expression of a new wave of moralism as exemplified by the title "the moral majority." Others whose
membership in Jesus cults expresses a desire for an alternative lifestyle
do show strong elements of holistic living, if not necessarily the highest
spiritual pursuits.

upwards on the path of evolution.* The death of Jesus showed us that the spirit needs to be free of its corporeal form.

Easter, several days after Christ's death, celebrates the resurrection of this transcended spirit. Once free, the dove of peace (wholeness) is able to continue its journey in evolution. Thus the Holy Spirit is the transcendent, transformational aspect of wholeness as energy evolves from one plane of consciousness to another, from one lifetime to the next.**

In the language of energy, the message of the spirit is clear and precise. We know from physics that everything in the universe vibrates; it is the different vibratory frequencies (among other qualities) that distinguish one thing from another and provide the universe with its unique form and function. Moving from the very quick vibration of subatomic particles to the slower movements of physical matter, then again to the quicker vibrations beyond material form, energy frequencies dictate the existence of energy. When energy is slowed down, matter is created; when speeded up, matter dissolves, as water turns to ice when frozen, or to steam when heated. Matter is created and dissolved by a fluctuation of energy processes.

Research into the finer aspects of these energy frequencies also shows that within the general category of forms, such as human beings or planets, unique frequency bands are radiated by each member of this category; each of us has a unique energy frequency which distinguishes us from all other people. This is our spirit. Therefore, the spirit of anything is the particular energy frequency band which defines it as a unique process.

It is exactly this spirit which, when manifest through the physical level, expresses itself as unique faces, fingerprints, ear shape,*** genes, voice patterns, handwriting, smell, blood samples,**** and EEG brainwave patterns. One of the most recent discoveries by research scientist Dr. von H. Rohracker of Vienna is that even the sound of skin for each of us is unique.[6] Working with microvibrations, Rohracker found

---

*The medieval alchemists also believed the spirit was one of four elements necessary for transformation.

**In the 13th Century the Catholic Church officially condemned belief in reincarnation.

***Crimonologists, looking for another way to identify people, found that even though criminals removed their fingerprints with acid, they could still be identified by ear shape.

****This is true on a fine energy level, as recorded by pendulum or radionic instruments.

that skin emits complex sound waves which differ with each individual. Likewise, metals can be found in the earth by their unique radiations when tested by dowsers. In fact, all matter emits distinct frequencies which are called "rates" in Radionics. Because every state of disease, like health, has a unique vibrational quality,[7] the newly developing science of vibration can be used to diagnose and treat disease. For over fifty years Radionics has confirmed both the feasibility and efficacy of such a science.

As the universal wholeness expresses itself in energy realms close to the physical plane, it radiates a unique frequency through the spirit field which is often called the aura or energy body. This field radiates our unique vibration to the outside world as a coherent source of energy and absorbs or transforms external sources of energy into this same frequency. This transformation takes place through the energy centers, or chakras, and is also connected to the physical nerve plexi. Though Kirlian photography probably does not reveal the aura (or spirit field) directly, according to research done by Dr. Tiller it does picture a unique shape for each individual, suggesting that it may be an indirect reflection of this spirit field.

Because all matter and energy are related to light, and all things are defined by their spirit, we could say that everything manifests its unique spiritual light in the universal whole. As Allen et al. point out:

Everything in nature is a living energy system which is a unique transformation of pure light into a particular wave field which radiates its own special vibratory "signature." No two signatures are the same, yet all arise from the same source.[8]

The universal soul as the source of all things distributes its whole light, as a prism separates sunlight into colors, by manifesting itself through the spirit in the myriad processes and forms which we see in our universe. The spirit as an energy blueprint enables us to see our singularity in the whole, though our source, like all other manifestations, is the same. Therefore, we are unique in existence but one in essence with all else in the universe. Our purpose in life is to realize this truth by returning to the whole through spiritual evolution.

The unique qualities of the spirit have been a traditional belief of many native peoples. Among the Machu Picchu of Peru, the Uxmal of Mexico, or the Aborigines of Australia, each person is known to have a special note and pitch which expresses his or her spirit. Among the ancient warrior class of Japan, the Samurais, a forceful expression of this note (called Kiai) was able to heal or paralyze (or even kill). Healing resulted from first contacting the spirit frequency, and then raising this vibration until a purification of the energy field and body took place. Destruction, on the other hand, occurred by remaining in "note resonation" until the physical form (the body) broke from wholeness. Like a glass will shatter when a specific pitch is sung or played, the body's integrity is destroyed when the vibration of its form is contacted and reinforced. This is caused by standing waves which increase in strength until they overload the boundaries of the form, leading to collapse the same way the Tacoma bridge was destroyed. As another example, a researcher interested in the frequencies of French police whistles once made a six-foot model of one using forced air to create the sound. Unfortunately, the technician who first "blew" this whistle was killed by its shrill tone. An autopsy revealed that all his internal organs had been "scrambled" by the vibrations.[9]

For the people of Bali and the Theosophists of the West, knowledge of the secret name given to them is equivalent to directly contacting their spirit. Knowledge of this name by others is believed to result in their being controlled. Therefore, these names are guarded with great vigilance. Many natives believe that if their picture is taken, their spirit is also captured—therefore they are reluctant to be photographed.

The unconventional science of radiational physics has revealed that any contact with this unique frequency of ours is enough to cause effects on physical and emotional levels. By using samples of hair, blood, saliva, or a picture, it is possible to diagnose and treat disease through Radionics. Practitioners skilled in pendulum or dowsing radiations are able to find missing persons, locate water, diagnose disease—all according to the unique frequencies of each type of matter.

Connected to the universal wholeness, such practitioners simply allow themselves to become mediums of an energy channel which tells them by way of their questions what the exact nature of the disturbance is (in the case of disease), or the location of the sought-after object. All of their work is based on the principles of vibration. When attuned to the unique frequency of someone and the connection to the universal whole, the pendulum, dowsing rod, or radionics instrument, through the mediumship of the operator, transmits information according to its movements or radiational resonance. In the case of Radionics, the resonating "rod" exhibits a "stick" or point of vibrational harmony when a medication or diagnosis fits the frequency of the sick person. Thus, there is no "guesswork," as in allopathic medicine, as to which medication best suits the patient. Through radiational energy the practitioner is told exactly which drug is suitable.

The spirit also defines us as an energy process. We are not, therefore, mind, body, or emotions; we have these, but they do not define us. They are simply extensions of the spirit which is the manifest essence of soul.

Everything we think defines us is simply the limit of maya or illusion. It looks like us, feels like us, but it is not us, in essence. If you lose an organ through surgery, are you less *you*? If you become depressed, are you not still essentially *you* at a deeper level? This essence, which expresses itself on several levels of existence as body, mind, and emotions, is our spirit. Generally, we define ourselves by our limits, our possessions, our bodies, our titles, or our emotions. Our true identity, however, is an energy vibration expressed as a specific movement of life which develops in us a *process identity* if we stay in contact with it.

To identify (L. *identitas*) means to repeat. By repeating the connection with our spirit we renew the nexus to the core from which we, as matter, first arise. Gradually we come to identify ourselves with this deeper vibrational self. Like an energy mantra,* repetition of the spirit strengthens our sense of who we are and what our presence in the universe means. By repeating this we also connect ourselves with the absolute essence of all things, the universal soul or Divine Spirit. There is no difference in essence between our Self and this universal whole; therefore, connection to one is connection to both. The true spiritual path is an increasing identification with spirit which renews our connection to the Absolute Whole.

Children often repeat songs, games, or words both psychologically, as a function of mastery, but more importantly as a process of meditation. In the Hindu religion, mantras are often repeated so that a particular image will penetrate deep into the core of the believer, thereby increasing the likelihood of his achieving a desired state in his spiritual development. The word "mantra" itself means an instrument or protection of the mind. One Sanskrit mantra, "om mani padme hum," meaning Pure Consciousness is the Jewel in the Heart of the Form, reminds us that consciousness is the essence of all matter. By repeating the mantra of our spirit we protect ourselves from falling into the illusion of seeing this physical world as essential.

At conception, the pattern of spirit will manifest itself on several levels of energy simultaneously. On the physical level, the body receives the genetic coding which will govern the growth of the child. At the mind level, the state of consciousness of both parents at the time of conception crystallizes a state of potential evolution which may restrict or help the child in its path towards wholeness. At the emotional level, the child receives its first primitive experience with feelings through its parents. These may include the nature of contact, the feeling of being wanted, emotional intensity, and the nature of love, among others.

*A mantra is a word or series of words which are repeated for their spiritual effects. The Western prayer has a similar purpose.

The crystallization of these different energy planes takes place at a negative space/time in which the energy influences of each realm combine themselves to form an energy field. This field, once established, influences the child throughout his years, serving as a harmonizing influence in all that happens.* Like a nodal point, an acupuncture point, or a chakra, this spiritual field is an energy locus regulating energy transmission and absorption. Although they exist on different energy planes and, therefore, in unique realms of consciousness, all three centers operate as whirling vortices of energy directly related to our unique frequency of spirit. Because all form has a manifest essence or spirit, we are related to it and it is related to us in an energy interdependency.

Body

As the processes of the Spirit move along the path of evolution they seek shapes or forms which will provide adequate media for further development. The Spirit "breathes" life into those forms which have been organized by "soular" needs and have come into being based on the needs of wholeness. At every stage in the development of the universe, forms are created to aid in the expansion of universal evolution. I call this spirit of form a *form-geist* because it continually senses what forms are needed and directs the formative forces of life energy to fulfill these needs.

Everything in our physical world has been created with just such an expression of Spirit. It is not mere coincidence that the more plastic materials we create, the more we appreciate natural goods. Even the development of the atom bomb, with its potential for destruction, brings us closer to our inner need for peace. No form is useless; each serves to bring us to greater wholeness—that is, if we are conscious. Whether we call these forms rock, plant, or human body, their essence is the same. Their shapes and energy processes differ to suit their respective functions, but this is only a perceptual difference of the senses, not of the Soul.

None of these forms which we call matter are solid or permanent. According to quantum physics, matter is actually ever-changing patterns of energy which cannot be seen in isolation but must be understood as an integrated part of the whole. Though the body looks and feels solid,

*An analogous idea has been proposed by Frances Dixon in her system of Vivaxis, whereby at birth a person is thought to create a signal generator in space which continually interacts through bipolar waves with that person.

it, like all other forms of matter, is really an interconnecting web of energy movement defined by the unique vibration of Spirit. It is simply a conglomeration of molecules which have been limited to a prescribed movement within a very small radius. The limits of this movement are dictated by the energy field which I have called Spirit.

In fact, it has been suggested that if we were to condense the so-called matter of the body into a tight, almost space-free, mass it would probably be about the size of a mustard seed![10] What appears to our eyes ("I's") as reality is deceptive. Russian scientist Albert Szent-Gyorgi offers a possible explanation of why the body seems to be firm when it is actually anything but solid. He suggests that the flow of electrons from molecule to molecule maintains the patterns of matter that we call tissue, muscle, or organs. The body only seems solid because of the incredible speed at which these electrons rotate about the nucleus.

We perceive the body as being solid because our physical senses of sight and touch operate at a slower level of vibration than the movement of the energy in the body. In actuality, the body is not matter all, but crystallized energy or light confined to a particular field of Spirit. The principle of wholeness manifest in the Soul provides the body's boundary and evolutionary potentiality, which is further influenced by our spirit as a channel for energy transformation. It is interesting that the proportions of the body are expressed in an endless ratio phi,* as though it reflected this boundlessness in space.

Even bone, the most "solid" part of the body, is continually changing through the polarized activity of bone-absorbing (osteoclast) and bone-forming (osteoblast) cells, so that a complete turnover of bone material takes place every twenty years. During this activity, bone may change its shape and increase or decrease in size. Wolf's law of bone structure even dictates that bone will grow in different locations, depending on the stress put upon it.[11] Stress shifts the center of activity to the place where the greatest energy interchange takes place. This is probably due to a change in the life energy field on the physical level as it acts in conjunction with other higher-level fields such as the Spirit. All fields of energy are interactive; a shift in one field affects all other fields. Because the sense of wholeness is innate in field activity, the place of greatest stress in the bone increases the need for more support (technically through *trabeculae* or supporting tissue) which is initially supplied by a shift in the physical strain field. Following a shift of ions and molecules to the stressed site, specific tissues and struc-

---

*The ratio phi (φ), called the golden mean or sacred cut by the Greeks, is also a fundamental measurement in the Great Cheops pyramid.

tures of bone then grow into matter based on this new energy field. Each level of consciousness acts like a wave guide to direct the formation of fields from initial stress to healing by passing on information that results in new bone growth. Every level in this process has a different rate of change, the physical being the slowest.

Despite our usual attachment to it, the body itself is not as important as its role of transformer. Because all energy levels from the highest to the lowest come through the body, it is the optimal medium for change. The body itself, however, is only a product of the energy fields which create it. Bentov's research with energy fields has shown that a chicken embryo will grow into an energy field which is present in the egg and which precedes the next stage of development of physical matter. Thus, the physical form grows into the energy field. This correlates with an ancient Chinese belief that life energy (Chi) precedes physical form. As an example of this belief, a fetus grows in relation to the Yin forces of the earth and the Yang from heaven. These cosmic forces align themselves in an individual field of the baby, extending themselves into Yin and Yang meridians. Eventually organs grow along these meridians. This theory has been confirmed by the research of Dr. Kim Bong Han in North Korea, thus providing yet another affirmation that energy pathways precede physical matter.

It is often our mistaken belief that our body is almost impervious to outside influence. We assume that if we are not aware of some outside influence, we are not affected. This is a perceptual error. Because the body is a form of matter (albeit, not solid), and matter is merely vibrationally slowed-down energy, our bodies are basically energy processors operating through field and wave functions. As such, they are quite sensitive to external energy influences.

Despite its solid appearance, the human body is composed of from forty to eighty percent water, depending upon the amount of fat, age and gender.[12] Muscle is about eighty percent water, while fat is fifty percent, and bone only twenty percent. Healthier people have a greater percentage of water, children have proportionally more water than adults, and men, with their greater muscle weight, are made up of more water than women. Water, like earth, is a Yin element which is related to women. Because men have a greater percentage of water than women, this shows that men have a strong Yin or female side as well. But because the male body is more compact (Yang), its water content is more confined than a woman's. As we go from the outside of the body to more internal levels, the body becomes more watery; thus, our core is more fluid than our surface. When a man enters a woman in physical love he is, in one sense, going into a sea! Although sea water is several times saltier than human fluid, some researchers believe there may have been greater similarity ages ago.[13]

Water, which is composed of hydrogen and oxygen (H_2O), is quite sensitive to energetic influence and adapts to the most varying circumstances.* This is due in large part to the susceptibility of hydrogen's nucleus to be influenced by fields. Research in magnetism has shown that hydrogen's nucleus will align itself with any local or applied magnetic field which is greater than the earth's own field.[14] The earth's magnetic field is relatively weak, so almost all magnetic fields have some effect on water. Naturally, as the body is mostly water, it, too, will be affected by these fields. This fact has led to the medical use of a diagnostic technique called nuclear magnetic resonance (NMR) imaging, in which the hydrogen atoms in the body's water are subjected to radio frequency energy and magnetic fields to yield a picture of physical structure and tissues that is far superior to X-rays and seems to pose less danger to the body.[15]

Other life energy fields also affect the body. It is widespread knowledge that the moon's gravitational pull can raise sea levels by as much as fifty feet in some places. The effect of gravity on water, and especially water in the body, has been well documented by Dubrov through his research on biogravitational fields. But even land will be affected: the city of Moscow rises and falls an average of twenty inches twice a day due to this gravitational pull. So the body, which is less dense than land but more dense than sea water, is certainly affected by these influences as well.[16] Healthy women, for example, experience regular menstrual build-up and release according to the phases of the moon. According to Chinese medicine, menstrual flow at full moon is a regulated Yang flow, suiting a woman's innate cycle, while a period at new moon (Yin) means the life energy is being blocked from its organic movement. It has also been observed that even women with irregular periods, when living together, will gradually begin to have their menses at the same time.

In addition to field influences, water is known as a good conductor of energy because its atoms have the tendency to both lose and gain electrons. This makes water an active medium for electron transfer and life energy processes. In fact, biological life itself depends upon water; without it, life couldn't continue. It is precisely this quality of water that enables even primitive cells, that are thousands of years old but dormant, to come to life in only a few drops of water.[17] Water

---

*Elements such as hydrogen and oxygen are two of more than two hundred simple substances which cannot be broken down without losing their wholeness.

is truly a physical manifestation of the Spirit, as it is *the* medium of biological life. Any change in energetic influences on the body will be transferred through its water. So body water has a twofold energy function: it reflects influences of energy fields from outside, and it will transfer these to all other areas of the body through its high conductivity.

The above research and knowledge about the effects of fields and energetic processes of body water have a direct bearing on the health of the body. Water is the main constituent of body fluids, which are the principal agents of homeostasis. Therefore, any field effect on these fluids should affect specific parts of the body as well as the body's balance as a whole. Affected body fluids include blood, lymph, cerebrospinal fluid, endolymph and perilymph fluid of the ear, and aqueous humour of the eye. Blood alone comprises one-thirteenth of the body's total weight.

Biomagnetic researchers know that the blood's leukocytes (white blood cells), essential for the body's health defenses, may increase or decrease depending on the nature of magnetic field influence.[18] Dr. Davis's research suggests that over-acidic blood may be treated by magnetic energy of north polarity because the North Pole influence increases the alkaline quality of the blood. One of the main factors which accounts for this effect on blood is the relatively large amount of iron it contains. As an electrolyte* iron conducts electricity, and because electricity and magnetism are different manifestations of the same force, it will also be affected by a magnetic field. Soviet researcher Dr. Madeline Barnothy has shown that the magnetic influence on blood will modify the likelihood of chemical bond formation under certain conditions which will affect the entire biochemical process.[19]

Like blood, lymphatic system fluid, called lymph, also contains leukocytes necessary for the body's defense mechanisms. In addition, lymph is composed mostly of fluid plasma (ninety percent water), carbon dioxide, and oxygen. In addition to lymph, the lymphatic system is made up of lymph nodes, which more or less disinfect lymph while adding to it lymphocytes and antibodies; and lymphatic vessels, which transport lymph throughout the body. Lymph results from the filtration of tissue fluid taken from the spaces between cells and returned to the blood. Later we shall see the importance of the lymph system as it relates to emotions.

*An electrolyte is a substance in solution which is capable of conducting an electric current.

Another body fluid, called cerebrospinal fluid, is produced in the fourth ventricle of the brain. On the physical level, this fluid bathes the entire brain and spinal cord with rich proteins, while on a more subtle energy level these proteins serve as tiny receivers for energy vibrations with which they resonate. According to energy researcher Dr. Christopher Hills, the chemical PH* of this cerebrospinal fluid determines its resonance ability with other energy fields, much like the special oil some whales use in communicating. Whales use this fluid to resonate over long distances like a radio set that transmits and receives signals. By enhancing the charge of cerebrospinal fluid it is possible to receive higher-frequencied energy characteristic or more developed levels of consciousness.** Both chiropractors and osteopaths, who work with the spine directly, facilitate the flow of cerebrospinal fluid by manipulative adjustments of the vertebrae or more subtle cranial techniques. During many diseases the quality of cerebrospinal fluid changes (pressure, volume, and composition), and these effects are sometimes used in traditional medicine as part of a health diagnosis. Over the years, finer and finer techniques of spinal adjustment have developed in the United States, and today, with the addition of cranial adjustments,*** a subtle but powerful treatment possibility is available for numerous conditions often not curable by allopathic medicine.

From the fourth ventricle of the brain, cerebrospinal fluid passes through the third ventricle, which ancient Sanskrit texts called the Cave of Brahma and which is known as the place of resonance with the cosmic whole. It is therefore possible that our degree of wholeness affects the PH-quality of cerebrospinal fluid and thus dictates our level of consciousness.**** Conversely, techniques and movements which increase the quality of cerebrospinal fluid might contribute to greater consciousness and resonation with cosmic or absolute wholeness (Brahma). Like lymph, cerebrospinal fluid is mostly water and may also be expected to be influenced by magnetic fields. Because we know that every magnetic field radiates waves, and that waves are generated by vibrations, any fluid which is affected by a magnetic field

---

*PH is a chemical scale ranging from zero to fourteen used to indicate the degree of acidity or alkalinity of a solution.
**Technically, this may be accomplished by yoga breathing techniques (pranayama), meditation, Tai Chi, Aikido and special micro-movements developed in Life Energy Therapy (see Chapter Six).
***The bones of the head also move slightly.
****This has been proposed by Dr. Christopher Hills.

will also be affected by vibrations. Further research will be needed to determine exactly what types of vibration affect us and how.

Cell

In order for body fluids to regulate the homeostasis of the body, they need to work in direct relationship with a basic building "block" of life—the cell. Like other forms of matter, the cell is neither solid nor permanent. Rather, it is best understood as a complex organization of dynamic interaction in which all parts serve the whole. The cell in its own right is also a relative whole of life energy. Despite the fact that every second we lose about ten million cells, and that most cells in the body are replaced every seven years, new cells are produced exactly when needed according to a blueprint of wholeness. In design, the cell is a microscopic replica of the universe with a central "sun," the nucleus; and a surrounding "atmosphere," called cytoplasm. On an even smaller scale, the cell also resembles an atom with its nucleus surrounded by spinning electrons. Unlike the universe and the atom, the cell generally has a membrane wall to indicate its limits. Research into the origins of life, however, has recently indicated that the original cell from which all others derived on this planet may not have had a cell wall.*[20] This suggests the possibility that as the forms of biological life developed, it became necessary to enclose the cell's wholeness in a structure with boundaries.

In understanding the principles of life energy, we need only apply what we learn in one area of knowledge to another—all aspects and areas are connected. This is true of the cell. If we apply what we know about the cell to energy centers, this point becomes clear. Not all cells, for example, have a singular nucleus—some cells have several. The nucleus of a cell is not only located in the middle of its form, but it always serves as the center of activity, as the chakras do on the etheric plane. Like multiple-nuclei cells, the chakras may be understood as a center of activity from which our etheric "cells" generate different-frequencied energy, depending on the nature of our spiritual evolution. In the East, much emphasis is placed upon one of these energy chakras, called the tan den, located just below the navel. It is here that all directed activity of the martial arts begins and is focused.

The flexible boundaries of the cell correspond to the martial arts sphere of attack and defense, which relies heavily on the hara (belly) as a center of power. Different martial arts respond uniquely to the

*This cell, found in Indiana and Japan, is known as *thermoplasma acidophilum.*

intrusion of an attacker (such as a foreign body) just as cells differ in their response. But in all cases the attacker is neutralized.

In its relative wholeness, each cell radiates the unique frequency of our spirit in its form and processes, and it responds in unison with other body cells to create a larger, more complete whole. Thus, each cell is a hologram that radiates the vibratory pattern of the entire body. This helps explain how cells may be exactly replicated in a process known as cloning. Each cell seems to record in its genes information about the entire body. Such knowledge has led to a major breakthrough in cancer research. It has been known that when a foreign body (called an *antigen*) is detected in our system, antibodies are quickly sent to counteract its effects as the first line of defense. Many forms of cancer, however, do not stimulate enough antibodies, if any at all. So there has been an attempt to find antibodies which could be developed outside the body in large quantities and introduced later into the body to defend against cancer. Because of the knowledge of cloning, it has recently become possible to identify and multiply specific antibodies in mice which are then injected into humans. The results so far have been quite encouraging, with apparent complete remission of the cancer in a high percentage of the small number of test cases.[21] But how do cells know what is healthy and what is disease? How is information being passed from cell to cell?

One key lies in the energy function of the cell. Because most body cells have a double outer membrane, they are able to function like a wet-cell battery, producing electric currents both within and between their walls. Due to the laws of electromagnetism, every source of electric current will also generate a magnetic field. Thus, cells that have the ability to generate wholeness at different energy levels of the ONE. Because we know from physics that one field cannot exist within another field without being influenced by it, a singular cell or atom is as equally influenced by the wholeness of the cosmic field as is any other part of us. Therefore, on whatever level an energy influence is felt, that effect will be transmitted to the other levels. By the nature of energy laws, those influences from the higher levels will affect those on the lower, rather than the reverse, though every level is cognizant of the other levels.

Under a microscope we see that the cell walls are folded and convoluted like a semiconductor. Internally, the cell contains liquid crystals (*cytochromes*) which also act as semiconductors by absorbing and emitting energy. In addition, these liquid crystals transmit important information about subtle temperature changes necessary for the body's homeostasis. The *mitochondria*, important components of the cell, number in the hundreds for each cell. These act as small transistors by first gathering energy, then concentrating it, and finally amplifying it. This energy is then released for use in electrochemical cellular processes which include the production of DNA, the genetic code of life. Similar to nodal points in the geomagnetic field, chakras in the etheric field, acupoints along the meridians, and lymph nodes along lymphatic vessels, mitochondria serve as centers for energy channeling in the cell. All of these centers for life energy operate as whirling vortices the way a cyclone (sometimes called a "twister") funnels its power into an electric charge also form biomagnetic fields. As American physicist Dr. Beasley clearly points out:

> Each cell can be viewed as possessing its own magnetic environment or magnetic field which combines with the fields of like and adjacent cells, thereby giving rise to the magnetic field of a particular system within the human body.[22]

Because it is also known that cells perform specific and different functions depending on their location, though all arise from the same original source and are structurally basically identical, some communication of work functions between cells is implied in order for them to function uniquely. One likely possibility is that fields establish a governing influence on cells by dictating in a particular organ the specific activity(ies) to be done. Thus, each organ and body system, like each cell, has a specific field which, when integrated in a larger whole, results in a *body field* comprised of all the lower fields. Although each body organ and system is unique, they come together through the principle of energy harmonics and express in their entirety a new field of the body which is also an extension of the spirit. The soul field, as it becomes distributed among the different manifestations of spirit, is further divided into bodies, and these bodies, in turn, are divided into systems, organs, cells, and ultimately, atoms—all expressing the wholeness at different energy levels of the ONE. Because we know from physics that one field cannot exist within another field without being influenced by it, a singular cell or atom is as equally influenced by the wholeness of the cosmic field as is any other part of us. Therefore, on whatever level an energy influence is felt, that effect will be transmitted to the other levels. By the nature of energy laws, those influences from the higher levels will affect those on the lower, rather than the reverse, though every level is cognizant of the other levels.

Under a microscope we see that the cell walls are folded and convoluted like a semiconductor. Internally, the cell contains liquid crystals (*cytochromes*) which also act as semiconductors by absorbing and emitting energy. In addition, these liquid crystals transmit important information about subtle temperature changes necessary for the body's homeostasis. The *mitochondria*, important components of the cell, number in the hundreds for each cell. These act as small transistors by first gathering energy, then concentrating it, and finally amplifying it. This energy is then released for use in electrochemical cellular processes which include the production of DNA, the genetic code of life. Similar to nodal points in the geomagnetic field, chakras in the etheric field, acupoints along the meridians, and lymph nodes along lymphatic vessels, mitochondria serve as centers for energy channeling in the cell. All of these centers for life energy operate as whirling vortices the way a cyclone (sometimes called a "twister") funnels its power into a spiral movement. Any deleterious influence on mitochondria upsets the function of the whole (as is true of the other energy centers). In fact, all the body's centers need to vibrate in unison for complete health to exist:

> The degree to which the mitochondria vibrate in rhythm or harmonic resonance with the surrounding field determines the ability of each cell to crystallize or trap the etheric life energy to which our body owes its physical existence.[23]

As I shall point out later in greater detail, disease is actually a state of disharmony between vibrations within the body and/or between the body and the external environment. Because mitochondria are the respiratory centers of the cell, they are directly affected by the quality of physical air, as well as the subtler qualities of prana as it connects with oxygen. Though it is possible to separate Prana from oxygen—as Yogis have demonstrated by living underground for several weeks without new oxygen—generally speaking, prana is the cosmic aspect of life energy which unites with oxygen, to comprise the in-spir-ation we call breath.

When we breathe, oxygen ions are brought into the bloodstream via the lungs. During this process (oxidation) oxygen combines with other chemicals to form a complex molecule called ATP* which stores and transports energy throughout the cells when needed. Therefore, the nature of our intake of breath and spirit reflects on several levels the degree of wholeness which we experience in life, ranging from the "soular" Absolute to the energy transfer in the mitochondria as it charges the whole body.

It is interesting that in the nucleus DNA, like the mitochondria which supply it with energy, also shows a spiraling movement of activity,

*ATP stands for adenosine triphosphate.

though its shape is a double helix of oppositely charged protein chains. Despite its almost ten billion mile length in the human body, DNA manages to maintain an active stability. Philosopher of science Dr. Reiser contends that this stability is due partly to the opposite charges of its chains. DNA is directly related to the spirit because it serves as the genetic blueprint for our physical development. Therefore, implanted in its coding is an energy pattern which governs our wholeness on the material plane. Genes, which are a segment of DNA, are thought to carry hereditary information from both parents to us.

There is a revived debate about whether genes can be influenced by outside agents thereby making them susceptible to factors of health and disease. If you ask the traditional western community of medicine if genes can be influenced, their answer is an emphatic NO. Based on zoologist August Weismann's work with rats which had their tails amputated and British scientist Francis Crick's work with the establishment and structure of DNA the medical physicalists say we are born who we are and nothing we do can influence our genetic code.

The vitalists on the other hand refute this. Late in the eighteenth century, French naturalist Jean Baptiste Lamarck developed a theory now known as Lamarckism which postulated that habits or adaptions to change in the environment can be inherited. Often ridiculed by "hard-line" scientists, Lamarck's theory is presently all but forgotten. New research, however, suggests that under certain circumstances our genetic code may be influenced by information from external agents (e.g., viruses).[24]

Based on his research with tumors or cancerous viruses, scientist Gustav J.V. Nossal has stated that:

> DNA viruses can infiltrate themselves directly into the genetic material of the host cell. The RNA tumor viruses contain an enzyme, reverse transcriptase, which can cause a DNA copy to be made of RNA blueprint, thus reversing the normal genetic dogma.[25]

In relation to enzymes, biologist C.H. Waddington has produced a model for how genes change based on the adaption of enzymes.[26] This gene/enzyme connection serves as a vital link in our understanding of life energy and wholeness as we shall see in the next sections.

Outside the purely chemical sphere there is a growing number of scientific speculations about the affect of other energy influence on genes. German physicist Dr. Pascual Jordan believes that resonation of energy waves plays an important part in the formation of antibodies, the growth of bacterio macrophages (virus that causes bacteria to disintegrate) and the reproduction of genes.[27]

Reiser also speculates that a resonance exists between DNA in the chromosomes and RNA residing in the cytoplasmic envelope surrounding the nucleus. This would certainly make sense, because RNA acts as a messenger for DNA; instead of a chemical transfer of information alone, Reiser is proposing that a vibratory communication exists between the two protein molecules. If this proves to be true, it would again demonstrate the importance of harmonic resonance in all parts of the body. Biophysicist Fritz Popp has suggested that there is also a resonance between DNA and the mitochondria from whose energy DNA is produced. There is some support for this idea, based on the ability of cells to respond to and communicate through radiations.

These research facts and theoretical models suggest that genes may in fact learn. If resonation is a key in the reproduction of genes, could it be that disturbing or healing radiations of energy not only affect the physical body as a form but also the genetic code which determines future generations as well? It is quite possible that genes act as a hologram in whose facets millions of bits of information are stored,[28] and that by a process of developed consciousness or harmful interference it would be possible to change that biological information!

One key may lie in another important component of cells: *microtubules*. These spindle fibers (called MTs), found inside as well as between cells, are formed when mitosis occurs to help guide chromosomes. They are especially important as builders of cell membranes (cytoskeleton); they serve as an energy matrix on a microscale for the formation of our whole body. Dr. Hameroff of the Tucson Medical Center believes that MTs may function as fiber-optic waveguides in which electromagnetic waves resonate and dwell in place, thereby serving as a guide for energy which is developing into the physical form of a cell.[29] It has been suggested that acupuncture meridians are a form of, or at least have a similar structure to, MTs. Like MTs, the meridians govern organ formation, as discovered by Dr. Kim's research cited earlier. If you recall our previous discussion about the chicken embryo and the energy field that preceded it, you will see a parallel here in MTs. Energy fields, acupuncture meridians, and MTs all serve as energy guides through which form occurs on different levels. Because of their size, shape, and configuration, MTs may function as tuned resonators which respond to certain frequencies of energy, thereby acting as communication antennas such as those found on moths and other insects. Other animals, such as homing pigeons and dogs, use this radiasthetic ability to find their way home or find a mate. It is quite possible that mitochondria and microtubules act in resonation with each other, responding to slightly different but connected information.

Dr. C. Kervran of France has shown that cells experience the natural transmutation of elements outside the radioactive series, which was previously thought only possible inside nuclear reactors. Soviet scientist Dr. A. Gurvich discovered some fifty years ago that cells radiate an ultraviolet emanation which he called *mitogenic radiation*. Dubrov's later work showed that cells did indeed radiate a dim glow, called "bioluminescence," as well as ultrasonic oscillations (106 to 10 Hertz) and other forms of energy fields.[30] Albert Nodon's research, for example, has shown that plant radiation is as great as that of radium or uranium, while that of insects is from three to fifteen times as great. Cells in the human body radiate even more energy.[31] This research shows that cells are even more important as energy processors than we presently realize.

Dubrov has further demonstrated that two biological cultures separated in closed individual containers with a quartz window between them, which is supposed to screen out most known radiations, were able to "communicate" a lethal infection from one culture to the other with no physical contact. The cells in the first container were infected with lethal agents (radiation, viruses, chemicals) which caused them to die. However, the cells in the second container in the same room also died, although no direct infection took place. Further investigation (based on some 5000 experiments) showed that the effect could not be duplicated with glass. When the quartz shield was used, a noticeable change in the photon flow between the cultures was recorded. Because crystalline quartz allows ultraviolet and infra-red ranges of light to penetrate, it might be that cells communicate with each other in a way as yet unaccepted by traditional science. Interestingly enough, the fluids in our cells also act like crystalline quartz structures. This suggests a possible relationship between the transmission of disease and unknown energy processes. Could it be that we radiate both health and disease through energy vibrations as yet unrecognized by classical science?

In 1981 yet another study of life energy by research scientists Dr. M. Rattemeyer and Dr. Fritz Popp in Germany found evidence that DNA was the most important source of "ultraweak" photon emission (electromagnetic radiation), which appears to differ from bioluminescence. It is their belief that DNA controls gene activity, cell metabolism, and cell communication through photon storage and emission. This would mean that DNA governs cell activity through light radiation (a photon is a unit of light).

Based on considerable research, Popp theorizes that cells communicate with each other through signals which also regulate growth. Through such communication the cells are able to monitor which cells in every second have died and which are to replace them. But this decision must be made almost simultaneously to be effective; otherwise, we would soon shrivel up and die. Popp suggests that cell nuclei send out both standing infrared waves and sound waves which complement and stabilize each other. These waves in turn create a field of consciousness which monitors cell activity by the feedback it receives; the mitochondria are thought to be the energy source for these fields.

Dr. Dubrov believes that we need to include an entirely new concept in physics to explain such findings. He explains that the mitogenic radiation of cells does not conform to the laws of classical physics and therefore constitutes a possible new form of energy. He believes that a special biogravitational field exists in living things which has properties of both gravity and living matter and could account for current research findings. If substantiated, it would mean that living systems receive and are affected by gravitational waves, as well as generate them, which is not a possibility accepted by the current laws of physics.

We might even have to go a step further with our new scientific perspective. Dr. Rupert Sheldrake, a former research fellow at the Royal Society of England, has independently developed a theory of evolution based on radiations. Sheldrake contends that changes in the forms of cells, tissues, organs, or crystals do not take place according to some objective law of science outside life, but are developed by a "morphogenic resonance" or a biological tuning which in turn affects energy fields specific to each species. This would mean that health, diseases, and evolution could be affected by radiations of other biological entities which resonate with parts or all of us. Radiational waves are therefore information which is dependent on the quality of energy.

Gradually we are led to the conclusion that our current scientific perspective on the functioning of cells is not sufficient to account for new research findings. The evidence suggests that cells are powerhouses of life energy which radiate and communicate information in ways that are not yet accepted by traditional science. The time has come to reexamine some of these beliefs and inquire in a truely scientific way about the truth of these latest research findings.

Enzymes

As on the physical level, the chemical functioning of cell enzymes also provides evidence that energy influences affect the body. Enzymes are biological catalysts which enter chemical reactions but do not become part of the reaction themselves. They are considered to be the "brain" of the cell because they dictate and control all cell reactions. Each cell has its own enzyme, showing again the uniqueness of each body aspect.

Enzymes stimulate the breakdown of ATP so that energy held in this molecule can be released. Because enzymes control ATP, the molecule responsible for transporting energy to the cells, any disturbance of enzyme activity will negatively affect ATP production, hence, energy transport. But enzymes also control the nervous system, which is responsible for our behavior. So in a sense, enzymes have the lowest level of biological control over our behavior.[32] Enzymes have been shown to be influenced by magnetic fields, as well as the fields produced by healers.* It has also been shown that the earth's magnetic field activates enzyme activity in fruits and vegetables, causing them to ripen. This research demonstrates that field influences can affect enzymes which control energy transportation (ATP) and ultimately our behavior as well. As a good therapist acts quite similarly to an enzyme in the therapeutic milieu, it is quite possible that the "ripening" of personal issues and the outcome of therapy are more influenced by the field of the therapist or the vibrational interaction between client and therapist than the techniques themselves.

Taken as a whole, then, the mitochondria, microtubules, and enzymes of the cell provide a very powerful basis for energy accumulation, transfer, and transformation within the body. These energetic processes are also influenced by other internal and external sources and can be positively affected to provide greater wholeness or negatively influenced to create greater disease.

As we saw in the shift from Newtonian mechanics to quantum physics, nothing can be isolated from the whole if we are to gain a complete picture of how it functions. Research with the basic energetic functioning of the cell has reflected the same wholeness. Each cell has its own unity, like each part of the cell itself, but only in the connection among these isolated parts do we really see the intricacy of wholeness, the "pattern of health."

Brain

Just as the nerve plexi function as the physical correlate from the energy chakras, so does the brain function as the physical correlate for the mind. The mechanistic trend in science equates brain and

*The enzymes tested were trypsin, a pancreatice enzyme; and catalase, a blood enzyme.

mind, but this is inaccurate. Mind represents a state of consciousness which is present to a greater or lesser degree in all energy processes, including those without a brain. In the human body, the brain functions as an intermediary between spirit and physical activity. In this capacity the brain is the organizer of all neurological activity expressing the wholeness of soul on the physical plane. The most recent brain research bears witness to this fact.

The latest findings indicate that as many as 100,000 neurons per second are active in transmitting nerve impulses to and from the brain. This network of activity has the estimated capacity of storing ten billion bits of information per cubic centimeter; the only known information processing system which can operate in such a small space is the holograph. The functioning of the brain is so holistic that even the removal of large amounts of tissue hardly interferes with perceptual and memory functions. According to researchers Allen et al.:

> This indicates that perception and memory are functions of the entire brain as if an overall wave field or mentally imaged hologram is present.[33]

This brings us back to the idea that matter, including ourselves, is a manifestation of standing waves of light. Consciousness, which is a state of relative wholeness, reflects that degree of light as well. In order for the brain to function in some holographic way, light needs to be used. How would this be possible?

As we have discussed, all matter radiates light as a function of its atomic activity. Several previously mentioned researchers have shown that cells radiate light in the form of ultraviolet, ultraweak, bioluminescence, and perhaps infrared—all of which are contained in the electromagnetic spectrum. In addition, both the nerves of the brain and the nervous system (called neurons) as a whole are filled with microtubules which probably act as light waveguides. Therefore, the brain seems to function as a holograph. Other evidence also supports this conclusion. Although both brain hemispheres seem to have different functions, this should not be seen as two types of consciousness but as specialized foci. The left and right brain operate as a Yin/Yang complementarity; their co-functioning creates a whole.

If the body is an extension of the spirit, as I contend, then this should also be apparent in the brain. It turns out that everyone's brain pattern (EEG) is unique, like their smell, fingerprints, voice, and so on. This would support the idea that the radiation of spirit as a unique energy field extends its particular frequency band to us through the body. Both the hypothalamus and the reticular formation, two units* of the brain, are the major emission centers of these brain waves. Just as the brain serves as an organizer for the entire body's communication on the physical level, the cerebrum, the largest part of the brain, integrates brain waves by creating a single wave from several waves. Thus, just as the body field integrates the individual fields of every cell, organ, and system, so the cerebrum creates a single brain field which is measured as a wave. Biomagnetic researcher Dr. Becker even believes that the magnitude, and perhaps the polarity, of the cerebral energy flow is directly related to the level of consciousness.[34] Russian research in brain-generated frequencies has reported on an ultra-Theta wave which is supposed to vibrate at the rate of one-hundred-million cycles per second.[35] More research is needed to substantiate this claim, but if it is correct it would physically corroborate the existence of mental energy, which might account for all psi phenomena.**

Higher levels of consciousness probably tune in to these higher frequencies as well as generate them. This might explain the extraordinary powers exhibited by those who are spiritually evolved.

The brain, which is ninety-eight percent water, is extremely amenable to influence by magnetic fields. Iron oxide (known as magnetite or lodestone) has been found in the brains of homing pigeons, as well as dolphins and certain migrating birds. These deposits are believed to be responsible for the magnetic sense of these animals. Most insects and birds use these fields to find their way, build homes, and remain together with others of their species. In humans we find a similar sensitivity to these fields. Zoologist Dr. Baker of Manchester University in England believes that these magnetites could exist in the human brain in the region where the skull joins the nose.[36] He conducted research on students wearing helmets with magnets in them which showed that those whose magnets were activated were unable to find their way home after being left in a strange place outside from the city, whereas those without activated magnets were left in a similar place blindfolded and could find their way.[37] This suggests that we have an internal magnetic sense of direction which can be influenced by external magnetic fields. Recently an ultrasensitive magnetic field detector (called SQUID) has been developed at the University of Colorado and is being used to measure magnetic fields in the brain as well as the heart.

*The reticular formation is not a physical unit but a functional unit of nerves working in an organized way from the medulla, pons, and mid-brain of the brain.

**Psi (Gk. *psei*, mind) is the psychotronic expression for direct thought transfer in paraphysics, ESP, and parapsychology.

Evidence indicates that the brain will respond directly to magnetic fields, affecting the cerebral cortex, the central nervous system, and the spine. The brain, after all, generates what are called "bioelectric waves;" these waves are used to measure encephalographs (EEGs). Because it is recognized that electrical flow corresponds with magnetic fields, the brain is actually producing magnetic fields of its own. All fields interact, so the brain fields will be affected by outside fields. Among the negative effects of such outside influences are: weariness, distress in sleep, and a decrease in mental processes.[38] Biomagnetic researcher Dr. A.K. Bhattacharya has reported that only male offspring have been produced by men working in a magnet plant in India.[39] Thus, magnetism may have a "red light" affect as seen in certain plants and animals that produce male offspring. This is discussed further in the section on colors. Animal researcher Dr. Kholodov of Moscow has shown that magnetic fields increased the number and size of glial cells (associated with brain neurons) through metabolism interference. Other experiments by biomagnetic researcher Dr. Hanoka in Texas demonstrate that powerful magnetic fields raise or lower the brain's response to stimuli. Changing the magnetic field impairs the ability to control body motion.[40] This is particularly important because the central nervous system organizes our different functions into organized wholes. This would indicate that disturbance of these organized wholes disrupts not only the parts of the whole but the entire integration of energetic processes, at least on the biological level.

As for the positive effects, magnetic fields have been used to stimulate the brain's activity, reduce consciousness to the point of anesthesia, and activate nerve plexi.[41] Evidence presented by several physicians and researchers indicates that epilepsy,[42] brain palsy,[43] cancer,[44] and even the extension of animal life[45] may be affected by selective use of magnet therapy. According to Kholodov, an unidentified center in the brain acts as a receptor for magnetic energy which can be developed for a magnetic sense. These results indicate that magnetic fields can have a wide range of effects, both positive and negative. In fact, Dr. Kholodov has stated that the "brain is the first organ of the body to respond directly, without intermediate stages, to the appearance of a magnetic field."[46] This, of course, raises the possibility that other fields may also effect the brain; more research is needed to ascertain what these effects might be.

Nervous System

The entire nervous system is quite responsive to energy vibrations. The main physical stem of the nervous system is the vertebral column or spine. The word spine (L. *spina*, thorn) means outgrowth or extension and is related to the Greek "spira," for life energy,[47] and the Latin "spira," for anything coiled, as in "spiral." From an energy viewpoint, the spine is the physical structure which has arisen in our development as the physical extension of the spirit. The vertebrae are the joints of that energy movement which facilitate its physical extension. At the base of the spine lies the sacrum, which is derived from the words "holy bone" (L. *os sacrum*) because of its connection in sacrificial usage. The essence of sacrifice was the destroying of one substance for a higher good. The true sacrifice was performed as a way of transforming lower forms into higher, more complete energy forms. The sacrum, at the spinal area of the pelvis, represents the place of sacrifice, whereby the involuted energy which has coiled in the base of the spine spirals upward and becomes transformed again into its more complete aspect of the soul through evolution.

It has generally been thought that the nervous system is strictly a physical network. However, research in radiasthesia has shown that the nervous system may have far more important functions. According to structural engineer and energy researcher Dr. William Tiller, the human body is an ideal antenna for both transmission and reception of various energy information. The autonomic nervous system serves as the power source for transmission, and the myelin sheaths (the fine spiral coverings of the nerve axons*) act as wave guides for energy transmission to the skin surface. Tiller says that the body's antenna system could function over a wide range of wavelengths (vibrations) and obtain good broadcasting and receiving capability with its six-hundred thousand miles of "wire." Thus information from inside could be relayed to the surface of the skin as well as guided to the brain from outside.

On the receiving end, what we "sense" is not only a mechanical response but a rate of energy vibration which we tune in to and a connection to the place in the brain where it is received. This is why, under hypnosis or other altered states of consciousness, what we would normally think of as "objective" pain is not experienced when tested. We do not experience pain unless we are attuned to it. In reality, the nervous system is an antenna for a wide range of energy vibrations; through our level of consciousness we are able to select the types of energy and information to which we will respond. The aura or etheric body is a local energy field which serves as the patterning mechanism for higher frequencies, enabling the nerves to function as antenna.

---

*An axon is a nerve fiber which transmits impulses away from the cell.

All of this, of course, has significant implications for our behavior and psychological well being. In the words of Dr. Becker:

> We have discovered that the electromagnetic field in our environment has a profound effect on behavior and biological cycles. We believe the mechanism for its action is within the central nervous system.[48]

Based on his research, Becker further believes that the bioelectric field (the human body field) is the connection between cosmic forces and human somatic and psychological functions.

Any effect on the brain and spine should also influence the functioning of the senses and sense organs, as they are directly related. Simple examination of a few sense organs reveals that they operate according to vibrations of different types.

Consider the ear, for example. Any elementary textbook on anatomy and physiology will show that vibrations in the form of sound are gathered by the outer ear, guided through the eardrum to the middle ear, and finally to the inner ear where the body fluid, perilymph, is set into motion. In the cochlea, these fluid waves are translated into nerve impulses which go to the brain. The inner ear is also responsible for balance, which is controlled by endolymph movement. Throughout the hearing and balance processes, vibrations regulate information using guiding waves, mechanical vibrations, fluid movements, hair sensitivity, and finally, nerve activity. When the amplitude of the vibrations is too great, the stapedius muscle defends against this intrusion by minimizing the intensity.

Almost all hearing loss is a function of disturbed vibrations. For example, ringing in the ears (tinnitus), accompanied by an inability to hear sound in noise, is generally a sign of a hearing problem called high-frequency hearing loss. This means that the higher-pitched vibrations, such as consonants, are not distinguishable. This is often due to a degeneration of the cochlea's hairs, which normally respond to the vibrations of sound. Thus, even though the bones of the middle ear and the eardrum are normal, the movement of sound energy is disturbed in its transformation from vibratory waves to nerve impulses.* As we shall see later, much hearing loss is caused by our environment; noise pollution has recently been recognized as being a major health risk.

Similarly, the eye functions according to vibrations. In order to see, we need light; light, as we know, is energy vibrating at a particular

---

*This type of problem is known as sensorineural or nerve deafness.

frequency and wavelength. Light passes from the cornea on the outside of the eye, through the lens, then through the aqueous humour (an eye fluid), and finally these vibrations are focused on the retina. (Like all watery fluids, the aqueous humour should be affected by magnetic fields and perhaps other fields as well.) Our ability to see at normal distances depends on how light is bent or refracted through the lens. Contrary to popular belief, near-sightedness and far-sightedness are rarely the fault of the eye apparatus. Instead, they are adjustments to the fear of focus. Near-sighted people focus on the foreground and miss the visual target further away; in far-sighted people the opposite is true. In both cases, the focal point represents something we do not want to face. To avoid this, we focus away to minimize the energetic charge of impact on us. This method of not confronting life becomes a lifestyle. Technically, this is accomplished by an abnormal tension or relaxation in the eyes.* Muscles normally exhibit a certain healthy tension called "tonus," which consists of some muscle fiber being in contraction at all times. Muscle contraction, however, produces fine vibrations which are always present if tonus exists. It is these vibrations in the eyes, which must correspond to what we see, that creates holistic vision on several levels. What we see is not an objective but a subjective phenomenon, depending on our openness to perceive reality. True vision goes beyond seeing with the eyes alone; rather, it is our ability to perceive wholeness on many levels. Physical problems in seeing often reflect emotional and/or spiritual problems as well.

Another holistic aspect of eyes is their ability to produce a single image from two eyes; technically, this is called "convergence." This ability is another simple example of how two complementary aspects (such as Yin and Yang) form a whole when they work together. The eyes reflect the degree of connection to the whole and express themselves as a sense of aliveness, which sparkles. Recent research on radiation from the eyes has coined the term "eye beam" for these energy emanations (which can be recorded on film).[49] This knowledge has been put to good use by the IBM corporation, which has developed an infra-red receptor for a computer which enables the focus of anyone's eyes on the computer screen to make selections. Originally developed for disabled persons, the computer registers eye focus as light beams and responds accordingly.

The nose is also an energy organ. In addition to its function as a physical tube for breathing, the nose serves other important energy

---

*The iris, which controls the constriction and dilation of the pupil, has been shown to respond to emotional stimulation.

processes. Biomagnetic researcher Dr. Davis has found that each nostril is oppositely polarized—the left cavity being negatively charged and the right positively charged. According to Eastern belief, this would correspond to the energy channels called Ida and Pingala that run up the front of the body and end at the nasal cavities. Davis also found that the tiny hairs (cilia) in the nose are electrified and are used to electrocute bacteria or viral germs entering the body. The cilia also ionize hydrogen atoms in the air we breathe by releasing its electrons. According to acupuncture researcher Greg Brodsky, these free electrons travel to the sphenoid bone, which acts as a storage area for life energy, directly affecting the pituitary gland, controller of all the body's hormones.

The production of sound in the voice, like hearing, is almost totally a product of vibration. Speech is produced when the normally tense vocal cords are forced apart by the expulsion of air. The result is discrete puffs or pulses of sound which we identify as syllables of speech. It is interesting that the vocal cords, which resemble parts of the vagina in appearance, are often related to sexual dysfunction in both males and females. Energetically, the body often holds a charge both in the throat and in the pelvis as a way of controlling sexual, as well as other emotional, expression. One voice researcher, Dr. Paul Moses, has written an entire book on the subject of voice and psychological difficulties, entitled *The Voice of Neurosis.*

The skin—not generally considered an organ—is actually a tremendous network through which we receive and transmit energy. A new science called "dermoptics" has shown that all skin can be trained to react to different colors. According to energy researchers Allen et al.:

> Those light frequencies that we think we "see" as colors and brightness are actually virtual images created in our minds in response to patterns of electro-chemical reactions triggered by frequencies which resonate with our biological tissues.[50]

Dr. Tiller notes that the skin has resistance and capacitance qualities which lend themselves quite well to energy absorption, discrimination, and transference. The higher the level of consciousness, the finer the discrimination of these energies. Training in the form of energy sensitivity can enhance these abilities.

Of course, other bodily functions and processes which operate by rhythmical pulsation do exist, but they are too numerous to explain in detail here. These pulsations are the biological counterpart of vibrations. These include the movement of the trachea (slow and fast), swallowing in the esophagus which sends waves to the anus, the peristalsis of the intestines, the pulsation of the heart, the movement of the cilia in the lungs, the rhythmic pulsation of orgasms, and the vibration of muscles as they shake to cause heat. All of these are governed by the autonomic nervous system and are directly affected by a wide variety of emotional reactions.

Considering all the research presented above and the ensuing discussions, it should be clear that the human body is more than a machine—even a great machine. Rather, it is a dynamic organization of energy vibrations held together by energy fields and brought to life through the manifestation of the spirit. With all its complexity, it still remains a simple product of energy processes which can be understood through life energy principles.

One of the main principles discussed here is that wholeness is the natural state of all processes and any disruption of this leads to somatic distress and eventually disease. The study and usage of fields may be used to comprehend how wholeness functions in its expression of life energy. It is also quite apparent that as far as the body is concerned, we need a more comprehensive approach to the nature and influence of body energy. Clearly, one way is through the use of energy vibrations—magnetic or otherwise. This is essential if we are to get a more complete understanding of how the physical realm of matter and biological life fit with other energy manifestations.

A considerable amount of research supports the idea that the body is quite amenable to magnetic influence. Magnetism, as we know, operates according to waves and creates energy fields in its operation. Because waves are produced by vibrations, the effect of magnetism on the body shows that our physical processes can be influenced by vibrations, at least within the magnetic spectrum. But magnetism and electricity are two manifestations of the same force—electromagnetism. Therefore, what is affected by magnetism should also be influenced by electricity. The latest research in atomic physics suggests that electromagnetism and weak nuclear energy are probably the same force. This extends the range of energy vibrations which might affect us considerably, especially if we look at the micro-doses of energy as potential influences on a subtle but powerful level. And because all matter is crystallized vibration (our bodies included), there must be a tremendous amount of interaction between various vibrations which are currently being scientifically "discovered," but which have been known for centuries in the East.

It is my contention that life energy will one day be accepted as having a broader spectrum than currently accepted energies, but it will include them within its range. Therefore, the effects of electromagnetic phenomena on the body can be said to be effects of life energy within the electromagnetic range. It is also interesting to note that the organism *as a whole* is more sensitive to magnetic radiation than separate organs or tissues.[51] This suggests that in all interaction the nature of wholeness plays a crucial role, a role that shouldn't be overlooked merely because it doesn't fit accepted perspectives.

Emotions

As our spirit moves through the medium of the body, it creates the realm of emotions which regulates and vitalizes our physical form. As long as they are uninterrupted, the processes of this realm gather and discharge energy to the outside world. Current understanding of emotions generally focuses on their physiology and/or adaptation because these are easier to study in a laboratory.

Research in physiological psychology indicates that emotions are the product of complex interactions between the brain, nerve activity, and social adaption. The most recent findings suggest that the brain's hypothalamus acts as a mediating center between several other parts* of the brain in a type of biofeedback looping. It has also been found that emotional activity will occur when areas in the midbrain are stimulated, even if the hypothalamus has been surgically severed. This would indicate that though emotional activity is organized in the hypothalamus, emotional expression is far more than the simple mechanistic function it was once thought to be. According to Richard McFarland, professor of physiological psychology at California State College, Fullerton, current physiological data suggests that

> ...in higher organisms neural output from subhypothalamic nuclei may produce individual parts of an emotional response but that neuronal networks converting a hypothalamus-to-cortex [brain] system of nuclei are responsible for organizing the fragments into unified, effective emotional behaviors.[52]

This implies that physiocranial interrelations are rather involved functions of a holistic network of energy processes which as yet have not been isolatable. Only in the whole do we get a more complete picture of how emotions are connected to their physiological components.

In addition to the physiological aspects of emotions, which are generally known as "arousal" factors, research begun by Fritz Heiderland and continued by Stanley Schachter has shown that once we are aroused by an emotional stimulus we also look for something to which

*The amygdala, cingulate gyrus, hippocampus, and thalamus (McFarland).

we can attribute this arousal. This has come to be known as *attribution theory*. According to research findings and extrapolations made from them, emotions begin as general arousal states and become emotions only when we are able to place this arousal in some concrete situation.* Under anxious circumstances this general arousal might lead to fear, while in an aggressive context it could lead to anger. Evidence indicates that different emotions such as fear and anger will release different physiological responses,** suggesting that an element of emotional specificity is also involved.

Despite the general trend in seeing emotions as essentially physiological in nature, this perspective tends to minimize the true significance of emotional expression. Emotions are basically energy processes, manifestations of our spirit or unique energy frequency. Part of their function derives from physiological components, but this aspect only expresses their relationship in existence to the physical realm—it says nothing about the essence of emotions. Scientists have confused the physical workings of emotions with their essential nature because the physiology of emotions is easier to examine.

In the first phase of psychoanalysis, Freud equated emotions with psychic energy; psychoneurotic symptoms were seen as attempts to discharge abnormally large quantities of a pent-up psychic energy. Even after he later revised his theories, Freud maintained that emotions were a product of energy. In fact, this entire energetic perspective came to be known as the economic viewpoint, from which all phenomena were seen as energy processes. Wilhelm Reich furthered this energy perspective by demonstrating through research that emotional energy and mental energy had a biological basis in his concepts of orgone. More recently, Dr. Ravitz, a psychiatrist and co-researcher with L-field theorist Dr. Burr, also found that emotions can be equated with energy.*** Based on their findings, the emotional stability of a person is reflected in the consistency of his or her energy field (L-field). Unstable people, for example, display an erratic pattern of voltage rhythms, whereas emotionally stable people display little change in their energy rhythm over time. Emotions, like other stimuli, involve

---

*Subjects who are injected with adrenaline, a hormone released during emotional excitement, fail to become emotional when they are told the shot will make them aroused but nothing more.

**A.F. Ax found that greater amounts of the hormone epinephrine were released in a state of fear, while in anger, both epinephrine and norepinephrine were involved (McFarland).

***Strong emotions expressed under hypnosis caused a fifteen- to fifty-millivolt rise in energy. (Ravitz)

a mobilization of electrical energy when measured by finely-tuned microvoltmeters such as those used to plot the L-field.

Emotions are also related to electricity and magnetic fields. Radiasthetists know that emotional radiations are expressed in horizontal waves (magnetic), while mind vibrations function in the vertical direction (electrical).* This fact has led some energy researchers to wonder whether the Star of David or Solomon's Seal was used as a protection against unwanted emotions, because its form radiates only vertical waves. Actually, in Hebrew the Star of David is also referred to as the *Shield* of David.

We also know that emotional conditions can be caused by magnetic fields as well as treated by them. A reversal of the brain's normal magnetic polarity can cause a state of depression, while a magnetic field lined up in accordance with normal brain polarity will induce feelings of calm and contentment.** In fact, in 1921 inventor A.E. Baines developed an apparatus called the "Vitic" device which was used for treatment of emotional and psychological disturbances—particularly nervous breakdowns. The patient placed the left hand around a steel rod mounted between two horseshoe magnets and the right hand on a graphite rod, and magnetic currents were then passed through the body. About ten minutes a day of this treatment was sufficient to vitalize the emotions as well as the body's internal organs. Biomagnetic researcher Dr. Ralph Sierra has been able to calm irritation and lift depression by having people lie in the field of several large horseshoe magnets.[53] This magnetic treatment of emotions is reminiscent of Wilhelm Reich's use of the orgone box—in which people would sit in the cabin for ten to thirty minutes a day to revitalize (or charge) themselves. Like the experience with magnets, an overextended stay under the influence of these energy fields would produce an overcharge, leading to insomnia or hyperexcitability. Emotions are really energy fields which can be treated by other fields and which produce electrical, chemical, and magnetic manifestations as they operate in the body.

In another area of research, color and music were used in treating psychotic patients at the end of World War II. This treatment was useful in eliciting calmness, weeping, sobbing, and anger simply by showing films of abstract colors with accompanying music.[54] This suggests that the vibrations of color and sound can affect emotional expression.

---

*Electromagnetism is thus a composite field of vertical and horizontal waves (Allen et al., p. 225).

**The front of the head has a negative charge, while the back is positive (Dr. Davis, as cited in Beasley, p.78).

More research is needed to specify at which vibrational frequency particular emotions are evoked.

From a life energy perspective, emotions are really waves of energy focused on a particular frequency band of the life energy spectrum.* They are movements caused by the vibratory effects of life energy as it is channeled through the body. Later in our discussion of Life Energy Therapy, we shall see how pent-up emotions are brought naturally to the outside for expression as the healing channel of life energy is opened.

People often speak about emotions as though they were things— the heavy heart of sorrow or the burden of one's problems. Emotions are processes, however, not content. In fact, it is only when emotions are held by being blocked that they take on a thing or content orientation. Their nature, however, is movement. Emotions, by definition (L. *ex*, out, and *movere*, to move), are energy movements outward, each with its own frequency; when confusion among these exists (such as "I don't know exactly what I'm feeling"), either several frequencies are being quickly shifted or one frequency is not being clearly attuned.

The body serves as the resonating background for emotional vibrations, much as the board or cabinet used in hi-fi speakers for stability. When the body is not healthy, the signals from inside cannot clearly be received or expressed. Breathing acts as the bridge between the body and emotions and connects the body to the spirit through the inspiration and expiration of prana. Prana charges the individual soul with energy from its universal source, just as oxygen charges the body. Breathing is also directly related to feeling. In order to feel, a minimal amount of breathing is necessary; this is why people who are depressed don't feel much of anything. They have de-pressed (pushed down) their emotions by decreasing their breathing.

With the intake of air into the lungs our entire field expands; it becomes excited with life. Russian research with life energy (called bioplasma) has shown that breathing increases the brightness of the energy field (aura) which can be photographed by Kirlian or electrophotography. Breathing actually ionizes the body, including the body fluids which are essential to health. Therefore, disturbed or depressed breathing will automatically affect our wholeness. Clinical research has shown that not everyone breathes alike. In fact, the quality and quantity of breathing are good indicators of our emotional and physical health. Every emotional problem is registered as a breathing problem—no mater how slight or unobservable to the untrained eye. Nobel Laureate Szent-Györgi maintains that cancer is the result

---

*As yet technically unproven.

of oxygen deprivation in the cells; this is an idea long held by Wilhelm Reich in his own cancer research with emotional expression that oxygen charges the life energy (orgone) level in the body. Healthy breathing is a balanced, charged, inspiration and a discharged expiration; it is a breath that unites the body to the emotions and the spirit to them both.

EMOTIONAL FLOW CHART

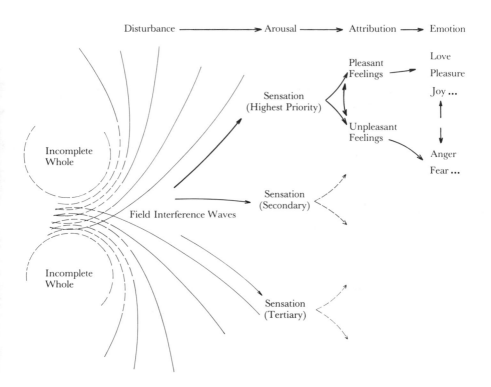

Figure 15.

As emotions develop, four interrelated phases emerge (see Figures 15 and 16). First, an interaction (disturbance) of fields takes place, either within the person or between the person and the environment. This is followed by a physical sensation which corresponds to the arousal state described by physiological psychologists. Next, a phase

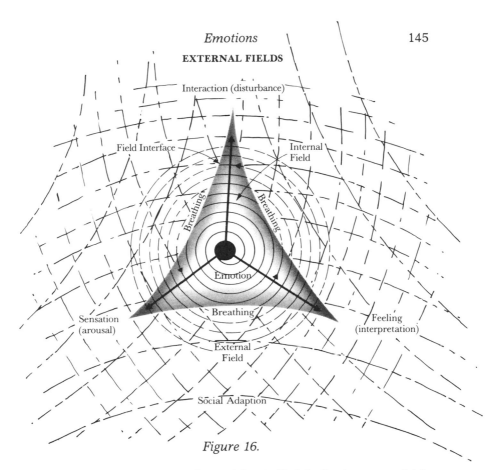

Figure 16.

of interpreting these arousal activities (called feeling) occurs which corresponds to the attribution component proposed by social psychologists. In the feeling state, the relative neutrality of sensation begins to evolve into a meaningful energy gestalt. Based on biological survival, past experience, and degree of openness, we judge these stimuli to be pleasant or unpleasant so we know how to respond to them. Healthy breathing increases the clarity and strength of these gestalts, whereas faulty breathing prevents us from precisely feeling and interpreting these sensations.

Once a feeling has become clear, we are ready for the expression of the emotion itself. Each emotion is simultaneously an extension of feeling and a response to it. By allowing the gestalt to build through successive energy charges, a peak is reached in which, as a sexual climax leads to an orgasm, emotions are expressed and an energy discharge results.

Emotions are expressive waves of energy which have a distinct meaning to us in terms of understanding ourselves and our paths of evolution. Because the meaning of processes brings all aspects of energy together into a greater whole, the *raison d'etre* of emotions is an important consideration for the exploration of life energy principles. The key to the significance of emotions lies in their evolution. Sociobiologist O.E. Wilson has gathered impressive evidence to show that emotions, like behaviors, exist in many animal species and may have been there for millions of years. We also know that plants exhibit strong reactions to being cut or negatively thought about, indicating that they, too, are capable of primitive emotional response, if not emotions per se.* One major difference between emotional response in lower organisms and humans is the range and variety of possible responses—humans obviously exhibit greater individuality in expression.

The longevity of apparently emotional behavior in the evolution of species leads us to believe such behavior has a useful function. As we rise on the psychogenetic scale, emotions are more differentiated. Children mirror a somewhat parallel phenomenon by expressing early in their lives more primitive, undifferentiated responses of quiescence or activity, and slowly beginning to show greater differentiation until several distinct emotions are displayed. As early as 1932, clinical observations revealed that "distress" is not generally seen until one month, while at three months differentiated signs of pleasure (such as smiling or vocalizations) were noticed. The emotions of anger, disgust, and fear were observed distinctly at about six months, while elation and affection occurred at about one year, and joy at age two.[56] Naturally, from a "scientific" point of view we would have to specify more precisely the behaviors labeled as joy, fear, and anger, but the point seems to be that emotions also evolve. Even from their earliest days, babies display emotional expressions such as crying, frustration, and loving—all fleeting forms of more developed emotions. I suggest that emotions develop on a continuum of energy processing that is always present but becomes more focused and changed as a baby grows. Some researchers, including Watson and Morgan (1917), and, more recently, Carroll Izard, have argued that emotions are inborn and their function is rooted in our evolutionary history.

Emotions and emotion-like behavior are an almost universal phenomenon in all biologically alive organisms; there appears to be an innate quality of emotions which are physically produced by a

*Called primary perception.

combination of physiological sensations and feelings. These internal impressions are affected by energy fields within and outside us and may lead to emotional expressions which are strongly affected by social situations. To a large degree, skeletal muscles, soft tissue, and body organs influence the quality of movement and storage of this emotional energy which may become blocked at any stage of its process.

A number of reasons can explain why emotions evolved and have remained a part of the development of living organisms for quite some time. In the first place, they help discharge excess energy which has accumulated over time. This means they serve a homeostatic function by maintaining a healthy level of energy charge. By manifesting both excitatory and inhibitory processes, emotions provide a milieu in which change and stability are both possible. Behaviorally, this is seen in our simultaneous spontaneity and caution about new ventures. Emotions also provide a direct feedback mechanism about who we are, based on our response to certain stimuli. They are existential indicators of what frightens or makes us angry. For example, they tell us which people we may feel open to and which not. All this information enables us to develop some concept of who we are, by providing an identity (I-dentity). In fact, even if we don't respond at all, we learn about our own deadness. This realization in itself would automatically lead to change if we could fully accept its potent impact on us. Because of their feedback qualities (only when they are expressed), emotions provide necessary help in the development of our egos, personalities, and self-image. They help us see the organization in our psychological make-up based on a history of interaction with others in our milieu. Other people's reactions to our emotions in turn help shape our sense of how others see us and therefore provide us with a partial picture of who we are. Of course, limitations in this process exist: the holding on to our ego, identity, personality, or self-image prevents a furthering of spiritual evolution. However, on the less-complete energy levels, these facets are generally important psychological issues and are therefore valuable aspects of our development, even if at a future point they need to be transformed.

Emotions are also important as powerful indices along the path of energy flow. They serve as acupoints on the energy meridians— vortices of gathering and dispersion. They are the spirals of activity which erupt from the flow of moment-to-moment awareness so necessary for our evolution towards greater wholeness; they shake us out of our boredom and lethargy. However, if we were able to stay more fully aware, we would have less need of the grosser forms of emotions.

Energetically, emotions provide a vital power that is essential to life. Emotional people exhibit an aliveness in the eyes that shows their eagerness to be here in this world. They are excited by their life's work and the opportunity to grow. Such people are active; they perceive meaning in their lives and are glad to share that with others. The Indian sage Sri Aurobindo has called emotions "vital consciousness" to describe this awareness of physical aliveness.

The most important function of emotions is that of unification. Emotions gather the forces of life energy together and create appropriate forms of expression as new and important feeling gestalts emerge. They help integrate all that is body and mind into a total experience of the moment so that we are completely involved in our expression. Emotions tie us in a spontaneous, though sporadic, way with the wholeness of life, which has many levels of operation. It is, for example, a common clinical finding that people who are unable to express their emotions manifest a splitting from wholeness. They tend to be confused, unconcentrated, and have no clear lines of development. In its extreme forms, these people exhibit such schizoid characteristics as isolation, lack of human relationship, and a typical sense of being out-of-touch with themselves and their environment. Even more extreme is the schizophrenic process by which the unification in life becomes so disturbed that a splitting-off from physical reality occurs.

At the more complete levels of energy our emotions show us how far along we are in our spiritual growth. If little things still irritate us or we find we are often vulnerable to the words of others, we can conclude that we are still attached to the superficial and external in life. So the nature of our relationship to our emotions feeds back to us the unfinished energy gestalts as well as showing us where our next evolutionary steps lie. By recognizing where we have difficulty we can focus more energy on emotional resolution; every resolution of a difficulty leads us to greater wholeness.

Most of us come to identify ourselves in terms of our likes and dislikes, our needs, and so on. We become tied to these preferences as defining characteristics of who we are; yet, if we remain at this level we cannot evolve further. Spiritual evolution demands we let go of all desires; even our personal needs. However, people who fail to develop strong egos or identities often become dependent on a group consciousness; they *are* the people with whom they socialize. How can we resolve the need for identity while letting go of the ego? In coming to a wholeness of emotional expression by letting go of the need to repress or act out emotions, we are free to learn about ourselves from these expressions without defining ourselves by them. Each emotion expresses wholeness in its unique way through its functions, direction, and connection to the body's energy circuits.

Love

Though all emotions, when expressed directly and completely, bring wholeness to our actions, love is the most harmonizing because it is the most complete. All other emotions are whole in their polarity of energy, but love has no polarity—it knows only oneness. Love is also the most encompassing of the emotions because it transcends all levels of energy, including our personal boundaries, by extending itself into states of transpersonal consciousness. Love lies at the heart of all other emotions as a focus of energetic activity (see Figure 17). In the presence of a spiritual master it may be experienced as pure being in which the boundaries between you and the master dissolve. You become the love the master radiates because your essence is the same. The only difference is that a true master lives that love continuously, whereas we experience it only temporarily, if at all. At the highest levels, love has no direction and therefore cannot be called an e-motion in the same sense as a personal expression of love. Because love can manifest on many levels of energy, it is unlimited as a medium for evolution. It cannot be directly taught, but it can be experienced and learned because it lies within us. A good teacher will help bring this learning into movement.

Certain evidence suggests that love may even be present at the level of genes. According to sociobiologist* E.O. Wilson, love in the form of altruism is transmitted in the genes and may be expressed as the sacrificing of one's own possessions, safety, and comfort for the welfare of another. According to Wilson's controversial thesis, animals at many phylogenetic levels (including humans) pass on genes for love because this trait can benefit the lineage of related organisms (such as brothers, sisters, or daughters) and support their future survival. The question remains whether these loving (altruistic) behaviors are transmitted or learned or a combination of both. In any case, there seems to be some justification for the idea that love is as necessary for survival as anger or fear.

Hans Selye, the now-famous pioneer in stress research, has commented that in our physical evolution this "altruistic egotism," as he calls it, has developed out of necessity because even single cells needed to cooperate with each other in order to become multicellular

---

*Sociobiology is the scientific study of the biological basis of all forms of social behavior in all forms of organisms, including man.

LOVE AND OTHER EMOTIONS

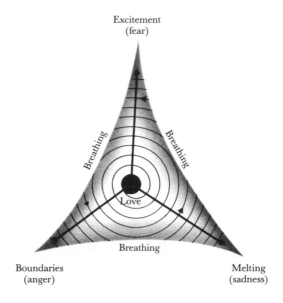

Figure 17.

beings. He further states that evolutionary advancement based on altruistic egotism takes place without the cells being aware of it.[57] I prefer to believe that cells, even from the beginning, have been very much aware of evolutionary principles, especially wholeness, and that in the evolutionary process, they have learned to develop larger, more complete wholes by going beyond their individual limits (cell egotism). In a sense, love on the cellular level is simply an openness to more complete wholeness, which can be passed on from one generation to another because it has both survival and creative potential. There can be no division between the individual and "others"—whether they be cells, people, or nations—so every holistic behavior affects each part of the whole and the whole as an entirety.

Love also has an important effect on the body. Most Western societies believe that the heart is the seat of love. We often speak of a "broken heart" or of having a "heart-throb" for a loved one. When something touches us deeply we say we have "taken it to heart." When we memorize something, we learn it "by heart." One of the heart's main functions is to pump enough blood under sufficient pressure to meet the needs of the body's cells and maintain the movement of body fluids. The heart pumps blood using muscle contractions which eliminate the need for an extrinsic stimulator. However, scientists still don't know how the first heart impulse arises. I believe it originates from a nonphysical source: the spirit.

As the spirit extends itself into matter, acupuncture meridians are formed which channel energy into the formation of physical tissues and organs. At a critical point when the body form is sufficiently developed, it is transformed by the spirit onto a higher level of wholeness. I contend that the first heartbeat marks this physical and spiritual event. Heartbeats are actually sounds made by the closing of internal valves; when the heart muscles relax, a contraction of biological waves is discharged. An electrocardiogram measures the changes in potential of the contraction and relaxation phases. Heart vibrations are probably also affected by other energy waves in both positive and negative ways because all wave fields influence each other. Because the heart pumps blood throughout the body, and blood is a body fluid subject to wave dispersion in fluids, the heart should transmit the quality of these waves to all parts of the body. Therefore, any vibratory effect on our heart or blood should affect us directly. In fact, so important is a coordinated heart vibration that when heart muscle fibers vibrate or twitch alone a fatal condition known as fibrillation may occur; when it does occur, the heart stops beating. We know that electrical vibrations from a defibrillator may shock the heart into whole contractions again, but technically we know little about the subtle vibrations in and around us which may adversely affect the heart.

We do know that the autonomic nervous system regulates the heart, although it does not originate the heartbeat itself. The autonomous nervous system includes both the brain and spinal fluid, both of which are amenable to change by magnetic influence. This then suggests that the regulation of the heart is also influenced, directly or indirectly, by vibrations to the autonomic nervous system. According to researcher Dr. P. Schneider:

> ...the living body is not merely one pulse 'heart beat' but the composite of several pulsing systems, perhaps a different frequency for each of the seven major body tissue systems.[58]

Research implemented through SQUID, a sensitive apparatus used to detect magnetic fields, has demonstrated that the heart has many subtle fields of magnetic force which are only now being fully delineated. Schneider believes that brain-heart and mind-heart connections are operated by specific centrally directed biomagnetic fields, and that the brain-heart design is established at the moment of fertilization. He says this design is unique for each member of every species. Like the brain, the heart emits a composite field of the whole made up of individual vibrations or waves. The energy fields formed from such waves influence one another and these smaller fields unite to form larger and more inclusive fields, the largest personal field being the spirit. It is quite probable that the quality of love we receive and give has definite biological effects on our system. Kirlian photographs reveal conclusive evidence that when thinking about or feeling love, the human aura expands, while in isolation, anger, or fear it contracts.

It is conceivable to speak about the love of our bodies as actually being the maintenance of healthy bodily functions. Proper rest, balanced nutrition, and healthy stimulation are all aspects of wholeness which are included in this love. This should not be confused, however, with an obsession with how the body looks or how perfectly it functions. Love of the body means simply maintaining a wholeness in its operation as a medium of the spirit.* It is important not to become attached to either body beautification or body debasement. Love of the body is a path in the center.**

Like all emotions, personal love begins its bodily manifestation through waves of energy from the hara (or belly) which move through the viscera into the heart. From there an expansion of openness spreads to all parts of the body, filling its form with light and clarity. In sexual love, the warmth of its radiations generates an all-encompassing fire which melts the boundaries of two individuals by transforming them into a single, expanded whole. Love is a union of vulnerability and complete trust. The embrace of lovers is the true alchemy of form and process. Nietzsche once said that after lovemaking partners feel sad. This is only true if sex is dissociated from love; in holistic love, the physical waves generated through sexuality carry over into higher energy levels, lifting lovers beyond their physical limits.

Love is the essence of life. In German, the words *Liebe*, for love, and *Leben* meaning life, come from the same root. Even the word *Leib*, for body, has its roots in the word for life. Thus, we see the connection between the body, love, and life—all of which originate from the expression of soul or wholeness. A body without love has no life—a

---

*This idea has also been voiced by Christians who view the body as being a temple of the Holy Ghost.

**The heart of anything is its center in common parlance. The French word "coeur," meaning heart, also means center (core).

fact that clinical observation supports daily. Heidegger even coined a new verb: *leiben*, for the process of living in one's body.

Love is an attractive force, drawing all to itself while at the same time radiating only light. It is like a black-white (w)hole with simultaneous attraction and emanation. All that is whole or on the path to wholeness is drawn to it as a resonation of likeness, while all that is not whole seeks its completeness. Therefore, the more whole we become the more attractive we become, both of "good" and "evil." Love is also transformational. It brings together all that is in disharmony and changes it into an integrated whole. Every experience of wholeness increases the likelihood of greater wholeness, because of its complete feeling. Rama Krishna, a spiritual teacher, talked about "going to the heart" as a coming home; our task in life is simply to discover what we already know within, that the way to the heart is love itself. Our spiritual home is really a process of loving—and that knows no physical boundaries.

Tantric yoga (the yoga of polarized union) speaks about the heart as the seat of *jivatma* (embodied spirit), while the Upanishads profess it to be the very home of Brahma, the universal soul.* They further proclaim that the heart is the home of the vital breaths, the five pranas or manifestations of life energy. In Ayurvedic medicine the vapory portion of the humours so essential to the vital force resides in the heart, and it is here that the three elemental forces (*tridosha*) are gathered.** The Vaidik system (another Indian system of knowledge) believed that the heart was the chief center of consciousness, as do the teachers of bhakti yoga (the yoga of devotion). For Eastern mystics the heart, much more than the brain, is a center of spiritual transformation. In this regard, the nature of our loving is not determined by sexual activity or personal relationship but on our openness to transcend personal boundaries of physical and emotional love into spiritual wholeness.

Love might be called the holy emotion because it unites the body with the spirit in an unbounded process of wholeness. It is manifest on every level of energy and through every chakra, though its area of focus is the heart. The heart chakra, known as anahata, is the balancing center between the three lower chakras, which are concerned with the harmony of the physical body; and the three upper chakras, which deal with spiritual development. Its symbol is the hex-

---

*The heart is known as hridiayam, for "it is he" who dwells "in the heart," (Bailey, p. 101)
*Tridosha is the Indian theory of elements, whereby pitta (fire and earth), kaph (earth and water), and vayu (air and ether) are balanced in health.

agram of the ancient Egyptians, the Indians, the Hebrews (Star of David), and the superimposed Yin/Yang of the Chinese. The heart chakra also transforms the Sephira Hesed (No. 4), symbolizing love, and Din (No. 5), representing power on the Cabalic Tree of Life. Generally speaking, the heart chakra is usually depicted as being located in the center of the body on the chest bone. However, according to ancient vedas (holy Indian scripture), there are also two minor chakras, one on either side of this center. In his experience of enlightenment, Indian sage Sri Ramana Maharshi rediscovered that the spiritual heart was to be found on the right side of center.[59]

If we use the anahata chakra as a middle point and extend lines to both sides, a Latin cross is formed, which symbolizes for Christians Jesus Christ with his message of love. The cross, by the way, united the ancient symbol —, for earth, with the |, for heaven, creating a mixture of heaven and earth which was the realm of the Son of God. In Christian symbology, a circle is often placed around the meeting point of the two lines ✛ (of Celtic origin), so that the wholeness of this nexus stands out. Even the hexagram itself is often surrounded by a circle, sometimes of a serpent representing the infinite wholeness of life energy. The heart chakra, generally associated with the element air (the *pneuma* of the early Greeks), is a major center of transformation. Through its energetic functions passion is balanced with compassion, courage transformed from anger, and openness developed from closedness. Here the constructive and destructive, the love and hate of Empedocles, unite with each other in a new harmony. Even on the physical level the heart transforms energy by serving as a minor chamber for various hormones. The thymus gland functions through the heart chakra as an important center in the immunization system in the bodily defense against foreign bacteria.

Thymus stems from the Greek root *thymos*, literally meaning thymelike outgrowth and came to be defined as the raising of mind, soul or spirit,[60] quite similar to the Greek "psyche." Originally, thymos was related to smoke, fire, breath (Indo-European dheu), vibration, movement (Skt. dheua), and later extended to emotions such as anger and wrath, as well as courage and stormy upheaval (Gk. thuo). Greek anatomists believed the thymus gland to be the seat of the soul, while Plato believed the seat of consciousness resided here between the desire of the lower body parts and the reason of the upper. In early psychiatry "thymopsycho" referred to the realm of all affective or mood processes. Philosopher Paul Tillich has developed what is known as the *thymos doctrine* to show the relation of health and religion to the existential question of courage and self-affirmative vitality.

There is evidence that the protection provided by the thymus heart/chakra connection is also related to DNA, the blueprint of life. Originally DNA was called Thymo)nucleic acid whose main chemical substance is thymine. Thymine was first discovered in a calf thymus gland and has been since found in all animals where it has been researched.* Dr. Paul Lee, herbologist and founder of the Platonic Academy in California, suggests that there is a strong relationship between thymine, the thymus gland, and the herb thyme. Despite the traditional medical doubt about such word coincidences, there appears to be some evidence that such a relationship may in fact exist.

Consider cancer researcher Dr. Leonell Strong who has spent most of his professional life working to find a cancer cure. In 1935 he demonstrated that oil of thyme could reduce the incidence of spontaneous cancer by forty to sixty percent in mice by causing a stimulation of the production of while blood cells called thymus or T-lymphocyte cells so important in the defense and immunization of the body. We know from ancient Mesopotamian, Egyptian, and Greek texts that thyme was particularly used as an antiseptic, liniment, and anti-inflammatory medicine. On the other hand it was also used as a religious incense (Gk. thuos) because of its particular smoke or vapor. In Chinese medicine a burnt or scorched smell refers to the element fire and is related to the blood and blood vessels, the heart and small intestines as well as the affective states of manic-depression. How then might thyme with its anti-inflammatory quality and its fiery component both be a key to the function of the thymus and its role in cancer and DNA (via thymine)?

According to researcher Julian Jaynes the ancient concept of thymos refers to the emergency response of the sympathetic nervous system and its liberation of adrenalin particularly as a precedence for violent activity, as for example a warrior produces in battle.

Although still speculation it is quite possible that thymus activity may affect DNA material through thymine. Research cited earlier has already shown that DNA can be affected by outside influences such as viruses. Can it also be affected in a positive way by health practices, herbal treatments, and so on? The key seems to be ability of an outside agent to duplicate a DNA message through RNA. Clearly the similarity between the outside agent and the host DNA is an important factor. Although on a different level such a similarity also seems to exist between thyme and the thymus gland.

We know from homeopathy that the essence of a plant, animal, or mineral can heal a sick person through the ancient law of similars.

*The De in Deoxyribonucleic acid (DNA) is thymine.

In practice this meant that a remedy which would produce specific symptoms in a healthy person would cure a sick person who already had these same symptoms. This same law was practiced by Hippocrates and Paracelsus from the ancient medical systems before them. In the 1930s Swiss medical doctor Paul Niehans developed fresh cell therapy which used the cells from unborn mountain sheep to cure tumors. Niehans found that by injecting healthy fresh organ cells into sick people their organs would go through a regeneration. His research showed that diseased thymus glands for example could be rejuvenated by healthy thymus cells of sheep. Again we see another example a "similar curing similar." But how does it work?

The research of Albert Abrams (Radionics), Harold Burr (L-fields), and Georges Lakhovsky (multiple-wave oscillator) have all shown that any disease can be seen as a disturbance of energy radiation. Every organ too has its own vibration frequency which when disturbed leads to disease.

Homeopathic practioners like their technical colleagues using various instruments of energy radiation are able to tune into the correct healing frequencies in their potions or energy broadcastings. Like the Tacoma Bridge, or even a simple glass will testify when a form is confronted with its own resonation pitch it will collapse. The same is true of any disease state when its frequency has been replicated. It reaches a peak of form identity and begins to subside.

Part of the effect of thyme on the thymus gland may come from its similar radiation when used in minor dosages. Another effect may be produced when used in large quantities as an allopathic remedy. Still another part of its effect may lie in the resonance similarity of their shapes. One ancient theory suggests that the thymus gland received its name because of its resemblance to a cluster of thyme flowers. This would be a nice story alone except for the fact that many effective early medications were discovered because of such connections. In fact, according to Dr. Norman Farnsworth, an expert in pharmocognosy* at the University of Illinois, Chicago, modern medicine still uses about 50-75 percent of drugs known to early civilizations. According to a once-popular *Doctrine of Signatures* certain plants give an indication of their medical usage through their external markings, color, or shape. Ayurveda still uses such a concept which has proven useful over literally thousands of years.

A modern version of the effects of similar form on another has been researched by Dr. Serge King, director of Huna International in

*The science of crude drugs (from plants and animals)—their physical, botanical, and chemical properties.

California. King suggests that geometric form, e.g., pyramids, cones, spirals, tetrahedrons and others, induce the same energetic effects without any apparent outside sources. These forms are known in the world of psychotronics as psionic generators. King calls this life energy *neoenergy* and says it is due to a "resonant shape" effect which concentrates or intensifies this energy. He cites laser specialist Dr. Florent Bailey whose work with lasers demonstrates that related forms strengthen each other. Another example of this form resonation might be the Chinese use of Ginseng whose shape is said to resemble the human form and is used as a total body rejuvenator.

Gradually a picture of the entire thymos influence emerges based mostly on facts and partly on speculation of possible relationships. Let us say for example that the thymus gland is a physical organ of the thymos spirit working through the heart or anahata chakra of the etheric-body. It acts on the etheric level as an energy transformer between the lower chakras (elements: Yin, Shakti, mother, God the Son, earth, water) and the upper chakras (elements: ether, Yang, Shiva, God the father, air). This functioned according to its intermediary position between heaven (|) and earth (—) to form an energy cauldron (+) through its elements (fire, Holy ghost, love, etc.).

On the physical plane the thymus gland served to immunize the body through its production of certain white blood cells (lymphocytes) in the blood and its vessels. These lymphocytes we know are especially important in the formation of body defense through the production of antibodies. What if thyme which resembles thymus in appearance acted in both a resonance and chemical capacity, through its suppression of fire as an antiseptic (water and earth both control fire) and as a stimulator of fire when it creates smoke, promotes sweating and prepares us for strong physical activity? This would mean that thyme also acts as a balancer of yin and yang energies.

What if both the thymus gland and thyme helped balance the yin depressive side and the yang manic side of us on the emotional plane? What if these quiet and strong sides of us could be learned and passed on genetically through reversal of DNA's usual one)way communication to the cells? This would mean Lamarck was right. But what if Darwin was also right that evolution also developed from a survival of the fittest, not as he thought by natural selection alone, but by a learning through gene education? Would biological evolutionists have anything to fight about? Of course, it is partly speculation, but what if such a wholeness really existed? What if we learned to use our healthy yang aggression to be courageous and vital about our personal and collective paths and our yin quiet side to enjoy peace, pleasure, and love? What if?

It may be that our openness to love, acting through the heart chakra on the etheric level and the thymus gland on the physical level, stimulates our defense system against antigens. From current medical knowledge we know that the thymus gland plays an important role in the formation of antibodies which are essential in the war against (really neutralization of) foreign elements or antigens that disturb the body. Cancer viruses of course are major antigens. Dr. Lee suggests that the thymus gland in its immunological activity against various antigens including cancer virus can be stimulated into greater production of T-cells by rubbing oil of thyme onto the skin outside the thymus gland.

An external medication like thyme or one of its derivatives may support this protective process through its chemical and resonant influence. If this is true, it might demonstrate on several energy levels what spiritual teachers and Aikido or Tai Chi masters have taught: the best defense is openness. When all in us is open, there can be no point of attack; therefore, at a further level of evolution we don't even need a defense. We simply let everything through. It is also possible that this love could be passed on through DNA coding in a way not yet known but hinted at in the work of Wilson, Strong, and Lee.

In the emotional/spiritual sphere an expressed ability to love literally opens up many possibilities for wholeness of body, mind, consciousness, and emotions. The stronger love is, and the more often it is repeated, the stronger the binding energy to this wholeness.

The relationship between the heart, the anahata chakra, immunology, love, DNA, the thymus gland, the soul, and courage is pointed out to show that wholeness is present everywhere. It is only necessary to go far enough into the roots of any subject or experience to show their interrelatedness. In our societies, so full of complexity and vibrational incompatibility, only a connection to a universal wholeness like love can establish order based on harmony, organicity, and mutual respect.

Excitement (Fear)

Every movement of energy through the emotions brings an excitement with it. As love becomes charged and begins to move upward, the excitement which is felt is often called joy. The Chinese believe that joy resides in the heart and in cases of excess or depletion it may be treated by acupuncture. In psychotherapy, an excess of joy corresponds to manic states; a depletion leads to depressive moods. People who become manic with their joy often need the depressive state to counterbalance their energy. Once a "high" is reached, fear often sets in as a warning that the boundaries of acceptable energy experience have been reached or exceeded.

Excitement quickly becomes fear, if outward expression is denied. In fact, fear is retroflected excitement (driven back on itself), as Fritz Perls, founder of Gestalt Therapy, accurately pointed out. But fear is not only blocked excitement; it is also a separation from wholeness. We cannot be afraid if we are whole. Fear is both the recognition and concomitant physiological processes of separation from well-being and integration. A rat phobia, for example, is often a separation between the person and the movement of behavior (generally) of the animal. Sometimes there has been a life-and-death experience where rats have run over the young baby. Unable to defend itself, the child separates from the intense experience by denying the emotions or actions which might have righted the situation. In these early years a child generally lacks the experience or strength to deal with such a life-and-death situation.

Fear is perhaps the earliest emotion to develop due to its survival mechanism. It is derived from the Latin *periculum*, which meant peril or trial. Something dangerous is experienced as a peril only because we feel it would separate us from wholeness. A would-be attacker is dangerous because he could separate us from our living by killing or harming us. Aikido master Uyeshiba once allowed a man with a loaded gun to stand in front of him and pull the trigger when he wanted. Uyeshiba Sensei (teacher) knew that at the moment of pulling the trigger the man would express his separation from this act and so Uyeshiba simply (!) stepped out of the way seconds before this moment. A mind at peace has no fear because there is no separation. Even death is not frightening if it is accepted as part of life.

Fear is often experienced as we cross a particular "I-dentity" boundary. Our usual identity defines (L. *finis*, limit) us by its boundaries, unlike love, which defines us by our potential. If we define ourselves by set actions, responses, or codes of conduct, then we experience fear whenever we step outside these walls. Our identity can become a prison in which we are afraid to experience freedom. So we escape this fear by staying in the prison of false security. For example, a child of seven or eight months will suddenly begin to express fear of strangers, but only if it has been forming a "focused relationship" for several months with specific other adults such as the parents.[61] It is as though identity with its parents may somehow be destroyed by the stranger. When there was no wholeness of a deep relationship to lose there was no fear, but after this bond was established, it could be lost or detached.

Physiologically we tend to show more sympathetic nervous responses in fear because we are stimulated to respond in a stress situation as the hormone adrenalin is secreted into the bloodstream. Anxiety, which is an anticipatory fear, is caused by projecting our awareness into the future. It, too, is a separation—in this case, a disconnection from the wholeness of the present. We cannot actually live in the future, so any attempt to predict such events is really a fear of living totally in the present and accepting things as they are. Some of the symptoms of anxiety include: increase in muscle tension, muscle tremors, dizziness, need to urinate often, decrease in appetite, and rapid shallow breathing. Muscle spasms and rapid muscle trembling will be experienced in some cases. Energetically, this shaking is the body's attempt to generate heat. It is as though the introversion of life energy excitement in fear is forced outwards in muscle trembling in an attempt to create an "as if" state of wholeness.

When fear is experienced, life energy moves from the hara upwards, and is held, as a frozen diaphragm, strangulated throat, dry mouth, and dilated eyes. As our spirit moves with this energy rush, it moves to leave the body. In fright we use the word aghast (Old English, a *gaestan*, from *gast*, ghost) to describe the phenomenon of the spirit leaving us. This is what causes the hair to stand on end as it stimulates erectile tissue in the scalp. If this fear is not expressed, it is held in the body as frozen energy. Typically, the shoulders are held up, the feet do not make full contact with the ground, the eyes are enlarged or their energy withdrawn, and breathing remains shallow.

Fear and anxiety are basically parts of a warning system, sensitive to all stimuli which are considered to be dangerous. The greater the split in our lives, the greater is the danger of falling apart; therefore, the greater is our fear. But the greatest fear of all is that of letting go of our fragmentation. We are afraid to be whole. I call this state holophobia (Gk. *holos*, healing, wholeness; Gk. *phobia*, fear). In wholeness we have no more excuses, games, or struggles. Letting go of these life patterns is equal to losing an old identity with our problems. It is the death of familiar strategies. Wholeness, on the other hand, is a new identity based on honesty, and this is why we are frightened. True love demands that we let go of our emotional isolation. It follows us into every blind alley until we are one with its wholeness.

Melting (Sadness)

As the excitement of love opens our hearts, we think there is a danger of becoming vulnerable to the outside world. In our illusion of what love is we often open ourselves to the wrong people, at the wrong times. Maybe we are blind to the physical realities of other people and conflict develops; perhaps we let ourselves be deceived and later learn to distrust others. Our idea of love is often filled with illusions which lead us to emotional pain. At the lower levels of evolution, love's openness (Yin) must be balanced with a protective (Yang) side; otherwise, we become easily unbalanced. This is true both physically and emotionally. In the martial arts one learns that physical injury can only occur if we are unaware, untrained, uncentered (too fast or too slow), or moving beyond our protective limits. The same is true on the emotional level. We can only be emotionally hurt when there is an openness to being hurt.

When we love a partner, we don't usually do so openly. Rather, we expect something in return. When our partner doesn't reciprocate we often feel rejected (L. *rejicere*, throw back), although this is not due to our partner's rejection, as we think, but is caused by our own misplaced desires. Actually, we are brought back to ourselves to see what we have done—this is our chance to learn. We are hurt when our expectations have not been fulfilled. But an expectation is an energy movement in the future which cannot be supported by universal wholeness because we are not living totally aware in the "now." Perhaps we have ideas about the way a relationship should be and are disappointed when it does not function so. Again, we feel emotionally hurt because we have not been with the experience of the moment but rather in our ideas. This shows us again that we have been away from the true center of appropriate action, our "visceral brain" in the belly. The "high" of our ideational images of love, much like manic flights from the truth, is brought to the ground sooner of later. These head "trips" of ours are energetic movements that lack any real connection to our spirit. Our being in "high spirits" is quickly reduced to feeling low or being in "low spirits" when our feeling good has not been connected to an organic energy movement. The true path of the spirit has little to do with highs or lows because its way is the road of balance, harmony and wholeness—not polarized disconnectedness. True love knows no up or down—only a center. It knows no hurt because there is no point of attack from the other; it lets every negativity through.

Much of our emotional pain is created because we are not aware. On the physical level this lack of awareness leads to bodily pain as we bang into an open cupboard door or stub our toes. Generally, we yell a few words that help us let go of the pain. Health practitioners often hear about a pain in the back or heart region which really covers for an emotional hurt; because it is easier to say that our body hurts, instead of "I hurt," the pain remains physical.

We know that physical pain often gives rise to reflex and autonomic activity and increases tone in the skeletal muscles. Like physical pain, emotional hurt forces us to become aware, to "a-tone" for the suffering we inflict on ourselves. Only in understanding what our suffering is indirectly telling us can we experience atonement (at-one-ment) or reconciliation with the universal wholeness.

Suffering is a refusal to accept our hurt. If we could accept the feelings we have and let them go as easily as we scream when we physically injure ourselves, we would not suffer. Life is full of difficult situations, but these are chances to grow, if seen from a holistic perspective. Pain is not to be done away with but transformed into learning. "Suffering," said the Buddha, "is the attachment to our delusions."

Sometimes we feel that someone else has hurt us. However, no one can hurt us unless we are open for that hurt. This openness is based on unfinished energy gestalts which seek completion. Every unfinished energy gestalt remains open to awareness. Actually, we should thank our friends who are direct for their painful comments, because they have shown us an unaccepted part of ourselves. Those who are "sensitive" to emotional pain are actually people who have not expressed their emotional hurt from the past. They are sensitive because they are sitting on a mountain of pain.

In the process of energetic flow, feelings of emotional hurt lead naturally to sadness, an emotional expression. Though animals feel some sense of sadness, and they have a fluid cleansing mechanism for their eyes, humans are the only known creatures who cry because of sadness. This suggests that our evolution has combined several processes to create a whole greater than that of lower creatures. Researchers have found that during sadness the cardiovascular system undergoes continual fluctuation. In order for the feeling to be released in sadness, crying is necessary. Crying occurs when the veins of the eye build to a climax of tension (like an orgasm) and become distended. The eyelid then, as in a sexual release, contracts in spasmodic vibration against the eye socket which produces tears. If tears are not released, the expansion in the eyeballs remains as a tension in the capillaries and edema or swelling of the tissues is experienced. Such chronic blockage of tears can result in vision difficulties because the eye cannot operate in a relaxed way. Again we see that even in crying, vibrations play an important role. Without these energetic pulsations, no release would take place and the energy gestalt could not be finished. In fact, many eye problems are due to just such emotional holding. Eyeglasses deal with the symptoms but almost never treat the deeper energetic problem.

In sadness, life energy arises from the hara; moves up the body into the throat, mouth, and eyes; and returns downward to the belly. The voice is generally a bit broken as sobbing takes place. Sometimes only one eye will tear or one eye later than the other. This shows a splitting mechanism where the emotional release is not spontaneously whole. The general movement of sadness is downward, and is expressed in such feelings as "being low" or feeling "down in the dumps."

Sadness may also exist when we experience the loss of an important person through death, or even the loss of a part of ourselves through accident or surgery. In both cases, our loss usually leads to a particular condition called grief. Grief, like the more general sadness, also has a heavy quality to it. In fact, grief (L. *gravis*, heavy) itself means heavy. Our sadness and grief often revolve around a loss of wholeness.

The energy fields which remain after we lose a limb or a loved one remind us, even in our physical body, of the pain of separation from the whole. The greater our attachment to anything, the greater will our pain be when separating from it. Love is the emotional wholeness necessary for our well-being. When we lose this wholeness we become sad. Unlike Nietzsche's concept of love, complete love cannot be lost unless we somehow push this away. It is natural to feel some loss when we are no longer with our lover, but this is only because our love is still attached. We cannot lose shared love, because this wholeness continues within ourselves through the universal whole. We actually lose (reject) our connection to love in a larger sense because *we* cannot have the love *we* want. Our sadness is really the product of our realization that love does not function according to will but rests on the principle of universal wholeness. We become spiteful when we do not get what we want. This is our true pain; through our spite we lose the wholeness of peace and close the way to the same love which we wanted and still need.

Unwilling to express the hurt we feel, our emotional wounds stay open. Over time, emotional scar tissue brings our wound into an "as if" wholeness. Just as physical scar tissue is more durable than normal skin, so do we become hardened by our pain; our muscle tone increases to the point of rigidity; and we die on the inside. We become cold to ourselves and others. This is often seen as the cardiovascular problem of cold hands and feet.

Letting go of sadness by crying restores the energetic balance once again. Pent-up energy is released and a tremendous relief is felt, like a dam which has suddenly been opened. New energy is freed for creative pursuits as the blockage has been transformed from holding to flowing. A deep warmth is felt as the fire of life energy is released and the hardness melts. This is true love—to be in harmony with ourselves and the universal soul.

Sadness also clears our awareness by cleansing the "dirt" of confused consciousness. In letting out the tears, we simultaneously let down our image and the barriers that stand between us and love— we allow others to see our soft side. Culturally, women are more prone to cry than men because they are allowed to be soft. (However, this can work to their disadvantage, especially if they habitually respond in this way, because sadness is often used as a cover for deeper anger.) But as we know from the martial arts of Tai Chi and Aikido, soft does not mean weak. On the contrary, letting go of our chronic defense of coldness allows us to develop a dynamic defense when needed because we are free to see, feel, and respond.

Boundaries (Anger)

Sadness is directly related to anger, which comes to us from the Old Norse *ange*, meaning grief. Anger is the antagonism we feel against someone or something which we assume has injured or wronged us; often, we want to get even. Energetically speaking, this need for "vendetta" is really an attempt to close an energy wound. Feeling that the boundary we define as us has been violated through injury, as though an invader had attacked us, we fight back in defense of our walls. This wall is our identity, the image we have of ourselves. If we think someone has hurt us by assaulting this image, we tend to fight back by assaulting them. In fact, the earlier physical attacks on medieval city walls correspond energetically to what we still do now on an interpersonal level. The principles are the same.

Anger can be understood as a protective process which allows us to gather our strength into a focus for defense. Constructive anger occurs at all boundaries of contact between us and others as a way of letting them *and* us know exactly what we will tolerate. It helps us develop boundaries around the psychological self if we define by exclusion. "I" becomes defined as everything within our psychological and physical limits; everything else is "not-I." Even on a biological level, the ability to express anger shows itself in a vital and rapidly responding immune system. Bacterial and viral invaders are quickly identified as "not I" and killed. People who can express their anger are almost never sick from such infections; those who are often sick are spoken of as having "little resistance" to disease.* In reality, anger provides an emotional defense which is also manifest on the physiological level as resistance to illness.

It is important to distinguish between the ability to be angry and the need to always be angry. The ability to be angry means that our defense energy is available to us in need but is only expressed when a true threat is indicated. The person who is chronically angry has never really expressed his anger directly to those who have offended him. Instead, the whole world becomes his unfocused target. This leads to social acting out and provides only a symptomatic discharge of pent-up energy at best.

The expression of anger is often maligned because it is so poorly understood. Being aggressive, for example, does not necessarily imply that we are angry. Aggression (L. *aggressus*, from the roots *ad* and *gradi*, to step) really means to go towards. This step forward might be a request for help as much as a punch in the face. Both are aggressive acts. Anger is really only destructive when:

1) there is no clear or appropriate focus
2) the intensity is inappropriate for the act or situation
3) a large build-up of previous grievances exists
4) there is a tendency to act out with physical violence
5) the individual often loses clear consciousness in the
   situation (usually through alcohol consumption or
   in a blind rage of passion).

According to research findings, primitive forms of anger may be expressed as early as six days of age when a desired object is not acquired. This is an anger that results from frustration; social scientists call this the frustration-aggression response—a frustrating situation wherein we don't get what we want and respond aggressively. Even if the object of our anger is not present, we may displace this anger onto someone else. This is what happens to people who are always angry. They displace their anger onto almost any other person or object rather than deal directly with the real object of their anger. Though frustration leads to aggression early in life, it is not until later that this aggression becomes the hostility of wanting to hurt someone.

*People who are frequently ill present a clinical picture of having difficulty expressing anger outwards, feeling strong self-hate (retroflected anger), and possessing ego-centrism, as well as getting reinforcement for illnesses in the form of attention from others.

In addition to frustration, many internal and external states may produce anger. Among these are helplessness, loss of control, unexpressed fear, jealousy, refusal to accept life situations, thwarted plans, intolerance, and confusion. Instead of asking for help, we become angry because no one is there for us. Losing control generally implies giving up our power in some way; many people respond to this loss with the potency of anger. Sometimes we are too frightened to admit our fear so we re-act defensively before the fear can get to us; here, anger serves as a good cover. Jealousy occurs when we want to possess someone; the loss of this possession is rooted in early childhood insecurity and often causes us to angrily express our displeasure. This is true of other situations in life, whether we plan them or they simply happen—if we cannot accept the flow of energy we also become angry. In this same vein, we often expect people to be the same as us because this fits our ideas of a controlled reality. When people are different, we have difficulty tolerating them and become angry because they force us to think and feel in novel ways which do not fit our stereotyped living patterns. When we are confused, we seek something to give us a direction because very little is clear; anger gives us a temporary direction though it covers our basic energy scattering. So many means are at hand to avoid love; anger, unfortunately, is used in many of them.

Physiologically, anger produces a rise in blood pressure following emotional expression, although heart rate is decreased. Autonomic responses to anger tend to involve more parasympathetic components which act in the body to control excitement. Although fear is a withdrawal of emotional energy during which the body responds with heightened alertness and excitement, anger expresses emotional energy outwards and is controlled by its physiology, although both emotions are acted upon in varying degrees by both sympathetic and parasympathetic processes. This shows in another way how the body seeks homeostasis or biological wholeness through a dynamic balance of polarized energy processes. In fact, physiological researchers R.L. Solomon and J. Corbit have proposed an opponent process model of emotions to account for chemical findings. In this model, the initial bodily response to an emotion will automatically be followed by its opposite process as a balancing mechanism.

In anger energy moves upward and downward from the belly— up to the voice, eyes, and especially the back, where the power of the arms is experienced; and downwards into the legs and feet for kicking action, if necessary. The heat and redness felt in anger are caused by the rush of blood to the extremities from the energy of the hara. In Chinese medicine, the small intestine governs circulation, so a strong hara is essential for a forceful and focused expression of anger.

On the lower realms of energy, healthy anger expression leads to constructive creation of psychological and emotional boundaries. It will also allow us to feel our physical strength, the power of our wholeness in defense, and the sense of emotional solidity.

As a hand must open and close to remain functional, so do the boundaries created by anger need the balance of love's infinite space. Unfortunately, many of us get stuck in one extreme or the other, either being hard and protective or too open and perpetually hurt. In a relationship, the healthy expression of anger reveals our trust and confidence in our partner's acceptance of such powerful emotions. Unfortunately, much of our anger expression is destructive and hostile; as such, anger can only lead to greater disharmony and separation.

At the higher, more complete levels of energy, anger is less needed because our sense of identity is not based on boundaries but on the process of openness or love. We cannot be hurt because hurt is something we do to ourselves on the basis of our expectations, lack of clarity, and dishonesty—though we blame others to keep the focus away from us. If we could flow with the excitement of life energy processes we would need no limits. However, because evolution for most of us is a slow, steady process we often need the limits provided by physical reality. Otherwise, in our confused states, we would lose our spiritual way completely.

As we have seen, one emotion may be supplanted by another—sadness for anger, anger for sadness, anger for fear, and so on. Depression is a good excuse for not expressing sadness and anger. In general, we could say that in most cases our fear of love's harmony keeps us bouncing from one emotion to another. We are sad because we have lost love, frightened because we are separated from love, and angry because we are frustrated by not getting the love we need. While women tend to be more sad (yin) and frightened (yin) than angry (yang), men show the opposite pattern in most cultures. Because of their cultural upbringing and slower energy vibrations, most men tend toward anger and defense, rather than openness. Even in sex we find a similar pattern. Men often accept love to "get sex," women allow sex to get love. It is really only by seeing the complementarity of the sexes and their energy tendencies that couples can ever come to the love that unites them both in universal wholeness.

Psychoemosomatics

Emotions are energy movements of a particular quality, and even though they are blocked from direct expression, they look for other avenues of expression. Among many possible avenues of discharge, four are used most often: psychopathology (craziness), acting-out behavior (crime), sublimation (becoming a "workaholic"), or psychosomatic illness (some manifestation of physical disease). Of these four avenues, we are concerned with the last one, whereby bodily symptoms can be seen as indirect expressions of a deeper emotional message which is trying to express itself.

Colloquially, we talk about someone "being a pain in the neck," or not being able to "stomach" a relative. In anger, we often say that a situation "made our blood boil" or we "blew our stack." In sadness, we talk about having a "heavy heart." The Germans refer to something being important by saying that it lies on the heart (Es liegt mir am Herzen.). In anxiety, they speak about the fear in the neck (Angst im Nacken), and that anger sits in the belly (Ich habe einen Wut im Bauch.); anger makes people see red because of its intensity (Ich sehe rot vor mir.) and even stimulates the gall bladder to release bile (Die Galle kommt hoch.). In fact, every emotion has specific connections to body organs, activated by emotions which are in turn, supplied by the organs with energy in a type of reciprocal activity. Anger is connected with the liver and gall bladder, while fear is associated with the kidneys and bladder, for example. It would be oversimplistic to say that these organs are the only ones associated with these emotions, but they have been proven over the centuries in Chinese medicine to have a specific relationship, both in diagnosis and treatment.

Generally, the study of the body and its relationship to mental conditions has been called psychosomatics, and its treatment is known as psychosomatic medicine. However, several aspects of this term are inappropriate. In the first place, psyche is more than mind alone. Originally it meant soul, spirit, and breath as well as mind. In German, we speak of the "Seele und Leib" (soul and body) as the two components of psychosomatic medicine. This interpretation comes much closer to the original Greek meanings for psyche and soma. Secondly, emotions are somehow unclearly defined as being part of the body (in English) or part of the soul (in German), as though they were identical. Because it is possible to focus on the soul or use the body without necessarily involving the emotions, the body/emotion and soul/emotion identities are inappropriate.

Emotions, from a life energy perspective, play the major role in the physical symptoms of the body, but aren't even clearly part of psychosomatic expression. In view of these facts, I propose a new term, psycho-emo-somatics (PES). Part of the problem to date with our terms for understanding of the complex mind/emotion/body interaction is that it is too holistic for us to analyze into isolated components. The mind, for example, has many levels of operation, only the least of which is the physiological brain connection. Mind refers to a state of consciousness and as such reflects different aspects of awareness on unique levels of energy, as I have discussed more fully in *Manifestations of Energy*. In addition, a complete concept of PES would also have to include the soul, spirit, and breath, as well as the effects of food and nutritional supplements (such as vitamins) on the body, and its relationship to emotions, physical health, mental activity, and states of consciousness. This is beyond the scope or interest of most physiological researchers; thus, psychosomatics has been limited to physiological measurements of body/emotion interactions. We must go beyond these limits.

A new concept of psycho-emo-somatics emerges which incorporates the energetic relationship of the soul, spirit, and mind (consciousness), as influenced by the breath and emotions and external influences such as food in health and disease. This last aspect of health is important because almost all psychosomatic medicine to date has focused on the negative effects of the mind on the body, rather than the mind's positive influences. In recent years this trend has been somewhat reversed by increasing research into and success of biofeedback technology* and holistic medicine, both of which are integrative approaches focused on the positive effects of mental functioning.

Let's briefly go back to the beginning to see where our current ideas of psychosomatics went astray. You will recall that the earliest civilizations believed in concepts such as spirit and soul which were seen as the external causes of disease. Scientists like to say these people were misled by belief in magic. In view of the fact that much of our medicine today is slowly reverting back to holistic thinking in the areas of nutrition, belief systems, healing, and self-cures, we have to question whether the magical thinking of our ancestors wasn't, in fact, part of the answer to an expanded idea of health on several energy levels.

Three of the ancient systems of medicine—the Chinese, Unani (from the Middle East), and Indian Ayurveda—all believe in the basic wholeness of the psyche/emotion/body relationship. They see no sepa-

---

*Biofeedback is the use of electrophysical instruments attached to parts of the body which send physiological data about internal body and mind conditions back to the individual so these conditions can be regulated and trained, if desired.

ration here; merely the varying specification of energy levels which are parts of the whole and different manifestations of the same vital force, life energy (called Chi, Ruh, and Prana respectively). They always considered the mental state of the patient to be part of both the diagnosis and treatment in regard to the flow or disturbance of life energy.

This tradition of energy wholeness was practiced by the Egyptians, though, like Ayurvedic and Chinese medicine, they had specialties in many aspects of medicine, such as surgery and obstetrics, among others. Even the early Greeks, whose traditions included a synthesis of religion, science, and philosophy, were interested in the physis or essential nature of things, rather than their divisions. Heraclitus saw the polarities of life as a dynamic interplay of energies which formed a unity called the *logos*.

Although the concept of wholeness regarding the body and mind has a long history, there has been another tendency among smaller factions to see the body and mind as two separate entities. One of the first people to explicitly express this idea was Anaxagoras, a Greek philosopher of the fifth century B.C. It is interesting that he is generally considered the father of scientific inquiry for contributing this dualistic view, as though scientific inquiry demanded such a split in wholeness. Anaxagoras's belief in a life force called *nous* has often been falsely interpreted as mind in the limited Western sense of mental activity. Although he considered nous to be distinct from the body, he did believe that it was a self-regulating entity which had complete mastery over life functions. Nous had the quality of spirit and animate materiality or soul and operated as a universal intelligence or reason. This, however, is more in keeping with the intelligence concept of Krishnamurti, which is more a basic wholeness and harmony than mental activity in the physiological sense. Thus, reason and mind could be seen as functions of soul or psyche for Anaxagoras. Plato also believed that the laws which govern the psyche cannot apply to those of body, which he held to be multiform, dissoluble, and changeable. In this belief, he was quite in accordance with Buddhism, Taoism, and Hinduism, all of which agree that the body is simply an illusion of the true reality.

By far the most influential figure on the maintenance of a mind/body duality, however, was Rene Descartes who lived during the seventeenth century. For keeping alive this split he has sometimes been called the "father of physiological psychology," though he made not one single scientific discovery. Descartes was one of the first to specifically distinguish the mind from the Greek psyche as being an instrument of thinking (res cogitans) as separate from matter (res extensa). This Cartesian duality became the basis for Newton's physics, which isolated all matter into separate pieces and saw the body as a wonderful machine. This has had broad implications for psychology and spirituality because man came to identify with his mind rather than his whole being. Based on Descartes's famous proclamation, "cogito ergo sum" (I think, therefore I am), consciousness of existence has depended on our mind being a rational apparatus without which, presumably, we could not exist. Thus a dependency has developed on thinking as the central channel of living, instead of feeling or simply being. However, as David Bohm has pointed out in *Wholeness and the Implicate Order*:

> ...in a certain sense Descartes was perhaps anticipating that consciousness has to be understood in terms of an order that is closer to the implicate than it is to the explicate.[62]

Bohm goes on to explain that matter as extended substance can be called "explicate" because of its explicit arrangement in space, such as rows of objects or a series of events. This leads to an explicate order. Implicate order, on the other hand, is based on a total or whole organization which cannot be separated into parts. What Bohm is suggesting is that Descartes's "thinking" is better described as consciousness of an implicate or indivisible order and that this implicate order is fundamentally different from the explicate or divisible order of matter.

But this difference between divisible and indivisible is an ancient philosophic discussion. Descartes's use of this thematic polarity has no basis in theory or fact. Theoretically, the essence of life may be a whole whose existence in form can be subdivided *ad infinitum* yet still retain that wholeness in each part. This is because wholeness is a process, not a content (substance). Therefore, it is possible to see the body (matter) as explicate or divisible as structure, though its essence—spirit—is implicate or indivisible. As Aristotle pointed out, form is only the design or pattern of essence. The body and mind (consciousness) are not separate, even though they express different observable manifestations. In essence, they are the same.

From a spiritual point of view, the more we hold on to, the less we are connected with our essence. Therefore, the more we hold the mind in awe, and the more content we hold in the mind as "matter" or frozen energy, the less chance we have of really experiencing the spirit which enables that rational mind to exist. Ironically, holding on to the mind as life has actually deadened us to the deeper processes of life energy. Many people have actually become controlled by their need to think and are therefore "frightened to death" of letting go of this thinking process.

A major advance in our return to wholeness took place in 1884 when Dr. Daniel Hack Tuke gathered a compendium of mind/body interactions together and asserted quite convincingly that the mind can influence the body in both positive and negative ways. In the psychological realm, Jean Charcot's work with hysteria under hypnosis, and Freud's later work with Joseph Breuer on hysterical conversions, began to expand the realm of psycho-emo-somatics.* In Freud's time it was believed that the mind and body operated in a mirror fashion, wherein each part reflected the activities of the other. This was known as psychosomatic parallelism.

Wilhelm Reich found that Freud's so-called "psychological energy" (libido) could be better explained as a biological energy (orgone) which could be physically measured. He showed that in fear life energy diminished, while in pleasure life energy expanded and increased. He posited that the mind and body function as one unit with different points of reference. He called this wholeness *psychosomatic functionalism* because of their working harmony.** Thus, little by little, the path toward wholeness in the mind/body dimension has been rediscovered in psychotherapy but still awaits its comeback in physiological psychology. Descartes's influence is unfortunately still very strong.

Much of psychology as a science has come from physics, so the discoveries in the new physics may eventually bring about a new revival of wholeness. Until the advent of Einstein's theory of relativity and quantum physics, Newton's classical physics and divisionism were the prominent modes of perceiving the world. With the acceptance of quantum physics, science is now returning to a wholeness which was always present but could not be seen. The key in this return is the relationship of the psyche to the body.

From a life energy perspective, the psyche represents the soul aspect of energy as well as the mind aspect. Soul is the unchanging process of energy which manifests itself in many forms, including the body. The difference between the soul and body is only a matter of relative levels of energy. The body as em-bodi-ment (em-bodhi*** ment?) of the soul represents its involutionary phase as it descends into matter. Therefore, in an absolute sense, the body is also

---

*It is interesting that Breuer's patient, Anna O., actually discovered the cathartic method—a clear manifestation of self-healing.

**Reich thus became the father of body psychotherapy, from which systems such as Bioenergetics and Gestalt Therapy later emerged.

***The bodhi tree is the place where Buddha sat until he became spiritually whole or enlightened.

the soul or psyche, while in a relative sense, the laws which govern the body are laws of a lower energy level. The aspects of both body and soul which remain the same are their adherence to the principle of wholeness. The mind as part of the psyche, which Western physiologists relate most closely with brain functioning, is actually consciousness operating on several levels. On its lowest level, mind is equivalent to brain functioning, but even here the mind still reflects a consciousness of electrical enervation both to and from it, and according to research, functions according to the wholeness principle. The same wholeness can be found in the body's homeostatic regulation.

Homeostasis, a term coined by Walter Cannon, one of the pioneers of physiology, was used to describe the built-in regulation of the body's internal states, from the Greek words *homoeo* (similar) and *stasis* (position).* On the biological level, homeostasis is the *sine qua non* of wholeness. Literally thousands of control systems make up this self-regulation,[63] which raises the question: how does the body know how to keep all these processes functioning at the same time?

There must be a built-in sense of wholeness which need not concern itself with conscious divisions. I have called this level of awareness *maintenance consciousness* and would define it as an energy field, connected with the fields of emotions, spirit, and soul, which preserves a level of wholeness in the body unless one of the fields is disturbed by emotional reaction (over- or under-reaction), extreme bodily deprivation, chemical insult, or spiritual learning,** among others.

Despite the importance of wholeness in general and homeostasis in particular, greater emphasis in research has been placed on the factors and physiological functioning of how we lose our energy balance than how we maintain it. The key to both appears to be stress. Stress is defined by the pioneer in this work, Hans Selye, as "...the nonspecific response of the body to any demand made upon it...." A stress factor, called a *stressor*, may be pleasant or unpleasant. According to Selye, it is not the content of the stress which most affects us, but its intensity. His research has shown that stimuli elicit both specific and nonspecific responses in the body. The nonspecific response is the body's way of adapting to change; this is stress. The specific response to

*Wilhelm Reich also spoke about an emotional (especially sexual) self-regulation.

**Sometimes we need a certain sickness or physical disturbance to shock us into an altered state of consciousness in order to evolve. Many enlightened people were sick to the point of near death when they became enlightened because of their surrender at that point.

certain stimuli such as heat, cold, or shock is not stress, though it will produce physiological changes specific to the stimuli. The interesting point about Selye's research over the last forty years is that all stressors produce the same nonspecific response which he called the general adaptation syndrome (GAS).

Apparently, the body responds holistically to stressors in three stages. The first stage is *alarm*, in which we sense the threat is immediate; the second stage, *resistance*, occurs when the body's defenses are even more mobilized. However, long-term exposure to the stressor brings on stage three, *exhaustion*, in which the body's ability to resist is limited, and death ensues.* Dr. Selye claims the body's ability to adapt to stress is a measure of its adaptation energy. Once the exhaustion level is reached, the adaptation energy becomes very low, even though physical intake of energy-producing substances (such as food) is sufficient. This is a well-known phenomenon in children's hospitals, where all physical conditions for living are provided and yet some children still die. In both cases there is a loss of the so-called will to live,** which is really a loss of spirit, whereby our connection to the higher energies is severed. Without the spirit of life the body cannot function by itself.

The important point about stress is that it is useful, even necessary, in small doses to keep homeostasis functioning. In the words of French physiologist Charles Richet:

> ...[the body] is stable because it is modifiable—the slight instability is the necessary condition for the true stability of the organism.[64]

It is stress which keeps the tonus in the muscles,*** the heart pumping, and the brain active, even in sleep. In fact, the absence of stress is death. Only when stress is prolonged does it become distress and consequently dangerous to us. Therefore, stress is an energy process which maintains the wholeness of the body (homeostasis) by constantly forcing us to adapt. Change is an essential aspect of stability and both are represented in the process of life energy. According to Pelletier, the effects of stress depend on four main factors: the amount of stress, its duration, the pre-existence of long-term reactivity to

---

*Psychological stress rarely leads to this third stage.
**For a little child, the will to live is very much connected to demonstrated love. When physical holding and touching are not present, young children often die.
***Hypotonic muscles display too little stress; hypertonic too much. Pelletier (1978)

stress, and the degree to which the stressor activates the pituitary and adrenal medulla. Research has indicated that the absolute amount of stress is not as important as whether the person feels pushed against his basic nature in the stress situation. Although negative life events generally cause more stress than positive ones, the real factor in illness was also whether the adaptation was too great in too short a time. Another study by psychologist Richard Lazarus has shown that the day-to-day nuisances, frustrations, and unpleasant surprises, rather than major life crises, have the greatest effect on our health. These studies indicate that change takes time and that each of us has a particular rhythm of change to which we need to adjust if we are to stay healthy. Particularly important is the day-to-day handling of potential stress situations. Even professionals in helping fields such as medicine, psychology, social work, and physical therapies experience a type of stress which has come to be known as "burn-out." One of their greatest stressors is the assumption that they themselves don't need help. But how does stress affect the PES process?

Research has shown that stress activates two important systems of the body: the autonomic nervous system (sometimes called involuntary*) and the endocrine system. The autonomic system— controlling the internal organs, blood system, and sexual activity— operates mainly through visceral reflexes and internal sensory receptors. Generally, autonomic functioning is the result of balanced activity between the sympathetic nervous system, which normally restricts involuntary muscles,** and the parasympathetic system, which dilates smooth muscle, leading to a state of relaxation. In distress, however, there is an excess of sympathetic activity typical of a fight or flight reaction as exhibited by accelerated heart beat, rigid pelvis, numb genitals, tight neck and throat, and tensed leg muscles,[65] among other responses. Ironically, at the same time, breathing becomes more shallow. Thus the body burns more energy but closes down at the same time, so that the entire energetic charge stays within, prepared for a fight or flight response. But what if we prepared for fight or flight and didn't do either? This is our perpetual condition when fear (flight) or anger (fight) is not expressed. We are constantly prepared to wage war or run away, except we don't do either and live with this constant distress.

*Research on Yoga and biofeedback proves that the autonomic system can also be put under voluntary control and is therefore not really involuntary at all.

**The sympathetic also dilates in some cases, although it is too complex to go into that here.

If we were able to release this constricted energy, the body would regulate itself again. If, however, there is no release, the body takes on a frozen appearance in which all these processes become "fixed," as it were.* Clinically, many people exhibit symptoms of physical and mental rigidity, particularly in cultures where order is a fixation and there tends to be a strong emphasis on what is right and wrong. Typically, such people lack spontaneity, exhibit passive aggression such as one-upmanship** while driving, and fear pleasure or anything else which is outside their sense of order.

In addition to the autonomic nervous system, the neuroendocrine system is greatly affected by stress. The endocrine system includes the pituitary, pineal, thyroid, parathyroid, (thymus),*** adrenals, gonads, and pancreas. During prolonged stress, the hypothalamus stimulates the pituitary (the master gland) and hormones are released into the bloodstream and other specific endocrine glands to prepare for stress action. Although the neurological activity of the sympathetic and parasympathetic nervous system initiates a quicker response to stress, the endocrines are brought into play when the release of adrenalin from the adrenal glands is stimulated by sympathetic nervous activity. Because the adrenals are important in maintaining resistance to disease, any disturbance in their normal activity will have PES effects such as arthritis and bursitis when the release of emotional energy is blocked.

Another important gland, which also acts as lymph tissue, is the thymus. The thymus plays a central role in the immune system which is governed by the hypothalamus. It produces white blood cells, which make up eighty percent of the body's entire blood supply.**** By producing thymus cells (or T-cells), the thymus enables the body to defend itself against disease by directly destroying or secreting toxins against antigens. According to physiologist G.F. Solomon, T-cells act in a surveillance capacity by screening out antigens from the body's own substances. Stress, however, weakens the T-cells' ability to recognize antigens; thus some antigens may slip through the defense screen[66] and limit its potential for removing dead or damaged tumor cells.[67] Medical researcher Sigmund Grollman has suggested that

---

*Reich has discussed this at length as muscular armoring.

**One-upmanship is a term used to describe the act of always trying to be better than the next person.

***The thymus gland is not always included, although recent research is discovering more about its function, as part of the lymph system.

****The other twenty percent is produced by B-cells in bone marrow.

stress creates a conditioned reflex whereby over time, less and less thymus hormone is released.

Dr. David Baltimore, a Nobel Prize winner in physiology and medicine, says that each of us has a unique set of antibodies which fights antigens, and that these antibodies have gathered as the result of a learning interaction with the outside world.[68] In other words, we learned to defend ourselves even on the biological level.

Selye says that the body responds defensively to stress in two complementary ways: either a syntonic reaction, which creates a state of peaceful coexistence with aggressors, or a catatoxic response, in which aggressors are attacked and destroyed. Whereas on the lower levels of defense we need to attack and defend ourselves (catatoxic), a higher form of consciousness, like love, acts more like a syntoxic response by neutralizing any toxicity in our milieu. Self-love eliminates the bulk of life's stressors from our denied self by completely accepting who we are.

On the emotional level, love's universal field of openness is actually a perfect defense because it does not need to protect itself against anything in its advanced expression—there are no limits or boundaries which can be grasped or pushed against. Like a spiritual Tai Chi or Aikido, our defense becomes our openness; movement is speeded up or slowed down to suit the situation. Love is the peace we experience when we totally accept ourselves and are able to live in this completeness. Excessive stress disrupts that peace and therefore disturbs our openness as a natural defense.

Not surprisingly, the greatest stressor for the body is unexpressed emotions. As it is constantly struggling to maintain a resistance against ourselves, the body often produces a symptom(s) which both declares the nature of the problem indirectly and at the same time tries to relieve stress by an indirect expression of bottled-up emotions. But as Pelletier points out:

> An individual's physiology is ill suited to cope with an extended duration of stress and anxiety common in contemporary society— from which no *physical* escape takes place.[69]

Under undue stress each of us is in a no-win situation. The body responds as though every minute were a matter of life and death, but it cannot live or die completely. One of the main centers of the brain affected by this distress is the diencephalon, of which the hypothalamus is the main agent. Here emotions of fear, hate, passion, rage, and euphoria would constantly vacillate unless controlled by higher centers of the brain's cortex.

Another important agent is the limbic system of the brain. This system governs various aspects of behavior and emotion such as approach and inhibition mechanisms and the fight or flight response.[70] It plays a major role in certain emotional activities such as sexual behavior. Both the hypothalamus and limbic systems work in close unison, because the hypothalamus responds to the emotional/psychological stimuli of the limbic system in addition to the intellectually perceived stress from the cortex.

The connections to different parts and processes of the body only begins here. We have seen how the hypothalamus is affected by stress. We also know that the hypothalamus governs the endocrine system which regulates hormone secretion through the pituitary gland. Hormones, as we discussed, control enzymes, the biological catalysts of the body, as well as mitochondria, the energy transistors of the cells. A constant production of hormones should cause an eventual overstimulation of enzymes, leading to chemical failure in the cells. The enzymes control the nervous system which in turn governs behavior, so an enzyme failure will affect our behavior as well. But enzymes also direct ATP which carries life energy to all parts of every cell. Therefore, an enzyme failure also affects the quality of energy that gets transported within the cells. Because energy meridians and the nuclei of cells are connected, the entire acupuncture system of meridians will also be affected.[71]

Body fluids are the chief agents for homeostasis, and blood regulation has its own consciousness of wholeness, so any disturbance in the quality of blood will seriously affect the individual's health. The bloodstream, which carries the energy to all parts of the body, transports the quality of this life energy in health or illness. Muscles are the main agents for the circulation of bodily fluids, including blood. Body fluids are so sensitive to energy vibrations, they may even transmit the effects of muscle contraction of any one muscle to the rest of the musculature.

Therefore, in a series of intermingled connections, emotions affect the entire body down to the tiniest cell and even its internal components. There can be no doubt that a disturbance in our emotional expression leads to total disharmony in the body. Any held emotion, either in the muscles or tissues, sends waves of energy down to the most intricate part of our energy system. If we take the power of emotional response to the social and environmental levels, we find that emotions are also affected by external factors such as cultural milieu and, as we shall see later, noise pollution, lighting, and environmental radiations. Again, the hypothalamus appears to be the neuro-physiological mechanism which mediates the psychosocial influences on immunological reaction.

Taken as a whole, the above information indicates that by expanding or contracting energy fields in either direction, the most complete fields have an interlocking effect on the most micro-field and vice versa. From this perspective, all fields are united, with the emotional field functioning between the spirit and the body and acting as an energy mediator.

A reaffirmation of the principles of wholeness underlies the energetics of the PES process. Beginning with homeostasis and hemostasis,* the flow of life energy is maintained in almost all types of environments— physical, psychological, and social. The sympathetic and parasympathetic systems of the autonomic nervous system work in harmony to activate and relax the body as needed. Antibodies for specific antigens are created which are all generally similar to each other except at the "combining site" surface, where each antibody differs according to the corresponding antigens. For every antigen there is a corresponding antibody, similar to the matter and anti-matter match-up in subatomic physics. When defending the body, our energy system employs syntoxic and catatoxic stimuli as complementary methods of dealing with toxic stressors. Most of our physical symptoms are even attempts to complete a wholeness when direct expression of energy (mostly via emotions) has been blocked. The purpose of inflammation, for example, is to isolate an antigen so as to prevent its spreading. If our immune system is weak, however, we cannot effectively neutralize the antigen, so the symptom remains a struggle where a clear fight would have finished the battle.

In the brain, the reticular activating system (RAS), a mesh of nerve cells, is organized into a holistic network between the brain's cortex, the muscles, and the autonomic nervous system. In the words of Pelletier, "...the reticular system is one of the best pieces of neurophysiological evidence for a profound interconnection between mind and body."[72] Even though they are part of no specific body area, they form a whole through their PES functionalism. In fact, the entire mechanism of the PES process may be understood as a feedback-loop system** whereby one energy event triggers another. The cause-and-effect relationship of what came first is considered meaningless, because all phenomena are ultimately related in the long chain of energy interactions.*** In this regard, Pelletier is advocating a holistic diagnosis and treatment of (PES)

*Hemostasis is the stoppage of bleeding.
**A feedback-loop system is a process developed in cybernetics, the science of controls and communication in organisms and machines.
***This endless circle is used for automatic telephone recorders, so that a message is heard endlessly for every party that calls.

processes, as many of these are multi-determined and affect the entire system. He says of the isolation process of science:

> This is a productive but highly limited approach which neglects the multiplicity of factors outside the immune system which have a clear impact upon its functions.[73]

And of the PES process:

> ...it is assumed that a subtle mental or physical factor may have been the precipitating event, but after that event has occurred the entire system is affected and must be treated as a whole to restore equilibrium and health.[74]

And later:

> Only a holistic approach can help us predict and prevent psychosomatic disorders.[75]

Wholeness is not only an approach to PES; it is the basic underlying principle as to how it functions. Even doing isolated work when necessary, if seen from a holistic perspective, is in service of the larger whole. Nothing is outside the whole—only our illusions that this whole doesn't exist.

Health

Wholeness is a living process which manifests itself on all levels of energy. It is the integration and resulting harmony of existentially different but essentially similar energy manifestations. Each level, according to its own field properties and governed by its own laws of reality, vibrates within an energy frequency band which resonates with all other realms according to the laws of harmonics. Within each of these realms all subfields are brought together into a single, more complete field which expresses the gestalt of the whole. In this way, the wholeness of each subfield, gathered into the harmony of a larger field, and these fields, gathered into the life energy spectrum, combine to produce greater and greater wholeness.

One way of looking at this wholeness is to see it in terms of health. Both health and wholeness are derived from the same Indo-European root word "kailo," meaning whole or uninjured. We could therefore just as easily speak about the degree of health of each energy level as its degree of wholeness. We already speak of physical or emotional health and could just as readily refer to homeostasis as biochemical health or spiritual integrity as spiritual health as well. Health, like wholeness, is a state of being which demands an active consciousness in its functioning. When the physical body, emotional expression, and mental attitude are in harmony, the PES process manifests this health as synchronized thoughts, feelings, and actions—each being but a form of the others. Because there is no separation here, there is also no distress. Therefore, harmony in our everyday activities reflects our state of health.

Even our way of greeting each other has its roots in health and wholeness. From ancient times, to "hail" someone meant to greet them with health, as both are related. In Germany, to "greet God" (gruss Gott) when meeting someone really meant to greet the God or absolute wholeness in each other. The word "salutation," also used for greeting, still reflects its Latin root (salus) for health. The armies even ritualized this wish for health in their "salute" to the chief, as in the famous "hail Caesar." In German the infamous "Heil Hitler" expressed this wish for health and healing, as the German verb "heilen" means to heal. Politically speaking, we know one factor in Hitler's rise to power was his promise of bringing Germany together again; in other words, to heal the separation that existed.* Wholeness is therefore healing as well as health-inducing.

We also speak of wishing someone well or well-being, both of which are related to wholeness. A German drinking custom in Bavaria includes the saying "zum Wohl" (to your wholeness) when clanking glasses together. Other European countries also express this wish for health when washing away the day's dust. The French "sante," the Spanish "salud," and the Italian "salute" all connote the wish for well-being. Even sneezing in Germany will often produce a "Gesundheit!" (health) from your friends, derived from an expression for health used in the Middle Ages plague era.

Health takes on a spiritual dimension when we consider that wholeness and health are also related to the word "holy." In Latin "salvo" for health is related to salvare (L. to save), which is the basis for the word salvation. In a sense you were saved if you were whole. Holy people lived in this perpetual wholeness and were able to heal because of their spiritual health. On the physical level, ointments called *salves* were applied to heal wounds or other bodily injuries. Isn't wholeness really a "salve" to the injury we sustain by separating ourselves from the unity of life?

Another interesting connection with health is that of sound. In English, to be "sound" means to be healthy. This is where the medical practice of percussing the body or tapping for sound probably began.

*Interestingly, the Nazi swastika, an ancient symbol, meant unity, well-being, and luck.

In seventeenth century England, Dr. Robert Hooke found that healthy organs have a sound distinctly different from diseased ones. The modern rediscoverer of this technique, Dr. Abrams, founded Radionics. A similar principle is used by bats and, in a more technical way, with sonar underwater detection for ships or ultra-sonic waves for embryonic surveillance. By recording the sonic beams which bounce back from the intended object, a radiational feedback is produced.

Health, therefore, can be seen as an at-tune-ment of energy vibrations among the various energy fields. The old practice of atoning for one's sins was actually another aspect of wholeness in which sinners sought to produce an a-tone-ment or harmony with the divine whole, often called the ONE.* The word for sin in German (Sünde) is spiritually related to the word "sondern" (to be special); to sin, from its roots, meant to separate ourselves (G. absondern) from wholeness because of our wish to be special—this was, in fact, the original sin. Therefore, health of the spiritual field is really a oneness with the higher, more complete forces of energy, just as physical health is an attunement with the lower or less complete energies.** According to authors Allen et al., health is ultimately related to the functions such as cellular organic processes or our self-image—all being in tune with each other.[76] We might say that health on any level is the degree of attunement within its prescribed energy field and its degree of resonation among all the energy frequencies (or waves) within that field of operation. In the words of Henry Lindlahr, one of America's pioneers of natural medicine:

> Health is normal and harmonious vibration of the elements and forces composing the human entity on the physical, mental, and moral planes of being, in conformity with the constructive principle in Nature applied to individual life.[77]

The key to health on all levels is the harmony of its energy vibrations. Health is a state of harmony in which all energy vibrations are in dynamic sympathy (balance). It is maintained by standing waves which reinforce themselves continuously after being emitted from their core vibrations. These core vibrations produce waves which feedback to their energy field; all processes of this energy system work in unison to maintain our health.

*Muscle tonus, discussed earlier, is really a vibrational aliveness whose tension or stress creates a "music" of harmony, much like a well-tuned instrument.
**Pythagorus believed health to be the attunement of body and soul—hence his use of music and color to heal.

As everything in life vibrates, health is the rhythmical movement of these vibrations. Rhythms of pulsation are found in the heart and its circulatory system, and in the inhalation and exhalation of breath. Rhythms affect sleeping, working, eating, and fasting. Energy rhythms can be seen in acupuncture meridians as they move from organ to organ in a systematic process,* in the division of the body cells, and in the buildup and discharge of the menses. Health depends on the rhythmical movement of these and many other energy processes in the body. All must work in coordination for health to be maintained; none of the parts or systems can overshadow the others. In this harmony of health, a natural grace of movement develops which can be readily seen by the perceptive observer.

Looking at a dancer, for example, it is possible to tell whether he or she is in harmony from the inside-out or has been trained to move in mechanical synchronization. An inner harmony always shows itself as a dynamic balance which is not limited to any single movement. Rather, it is an organic movement of life energy flowing from one process to another. It is a harmony of equilibrium, a polarized homeostasis as energy moves through its maintenance and developmental cycles. In its movement, a wholeness is created which gathers at all times the various individual movements into a unity of grace and ease. In this regard, a subtle micro-movement called microment has been developed in Life Energy Therapy both as a diagnostic tool and as a healing process to recognize where our energetic balance is disturbed and thereby simultaneously show us the way to further wholeness.

Since health is the degree of wholeness of each energy level, we need to speak about relative degrees of health as well as an absolute health or ultimate wholeness. Relative health refers to a wholeness which is complete only on its own level of functioning but may not be on another level. For example, in clinical practice, it is quite common to see someone who is apparently physically healthy—lacking bodily symptoms of illness—who has great difficulty expressing emotions. Are such people healthy? Well, on a lower level the body appears healthy, but there is little emotional health. Therefore, we would have to say that physical health is a relative degree of wholeness, limited as it is to the lower energy levels. Such a bound state of controlled health often indicates a tremendous disturbance in the PES process between the body and emotions. In fact, because all the levels of energy are interconnected in high-level wholeness, the ability to maintain one realm of energy at an acceptable level of health without

*The word meridian is more precisely translated as "to guide the rhythmic manifestations of energy along definite paths." (Manfred Porkert, p. 161)

treatment, ritual, and belief.[79] Thus, early healers were both physi-cian and priest; these roles were not separate. This spiritual/physical unity persisted through the Egyptian era to the Greek period when the spiritual was philosophically divorced from the physical.

Some religions such as ancient Hebrew believed disease to be the wrath of God as a punishment for sin. Among the early medical sys-tems, the Chinese, for example, believed that disease was the result of an imbalance of two energy polarities, yin and yang, as well as the five passages, or elements as they are known in the West (wood, fire, earth, metal, and water). Health reflected the harmonious flow of life energy (chi) as it moved through complementary aspects such as the left/right, upper/lower, or internal/external sides of the body. Within this general bipolar movement, energy was thought to undergo a series of transformations depending on the five qualities described above. The Chinese elements are to be understood as five phases of evolu-tion which occur in the natural flow of life energy and which can be applied to all phenomena, regardless of variation in nature, such as the seasons, food, emotions, or parts of the body.

The Tibetans, whose physical medicine is derived in large part from the Chinese, also viewed disease from a spiritual perspective. Accord-ing to Buddhist thought, the roots of disease lie in three forms of igno-rance: ignorance of the essential structure of the human personality, ignorance of the true nature of the universe, and ignorance of our true self. As one anonymous lama (monk) put it:

Disease...has its roots in the good, the beautiful and the true. It is but a distorted reflection of divine possibilities.

It is in fact our distortion of wholeness which causes disease. Not wanting to see the light of truth, we ignore its laws and remain ignorant of our divine possibilities for more complete wholeness (holi-ness). Ultimately, disease is our lack of awareness of the whole, the ONE, and harmony of life. Sri Aurobindo called this nonawareness *subconscience.* Consciousness is the sharing of knowledge, the true science of life;* being subconscientious is a vague decision to avoid the whole or its potential for a fulfilling life.

Several Western doctors, like the Chinese, perceived disease as an imbalance of polarities. Hoffman (1664-1742) saw disease as a deficiency or excess of tonus, predating the later work of Wilhelm Reich with his "armor" concept of hypertonus muscles and Lillemor Johnsen's work

---

*Both science and con-sciousness are derived from the same Latin verb scire—to know.

with hypotonus muscles. (The Japanese massage art, *shiatsu*, also reflects this polarity of hypertonus (*jitsu*) and hypotonus (*kyo*).) Brown (1735-1788) later described disease as a result of deficiency or excess of stimulation, much in keeping with the Chinese view that diseases can be classified according to yang (excessive) or yin (deficient) conditions.

The Ayurvedic doctors of India and neighboring countries believed disease was the result of faulty proportions of energy qualities called *tridosha* (*vata*, *pitta*, and *kaph*), which as in the Chinese tradition referred to elements of transformation.

Similarly, Hippocrates believed that an irregular proportion of elements, known today as humours (blood, phlegm, yellow bile, and black bile), caused disease. Aristotle added to this by saying that four temperaments (biliary, sanguinary, phlegmatic, and melancholic) also played a large part in disease.* The Greek pneumatists blamed the airy spirit or pneuma. Hahnemann claimed disease was due to a weakness of the vital force, an aberration of health but not an entity unto itself.

In the 1500s, Fracastoro stated that disease was caused by contagion from infection, a view still held by most people today. However, it wasn't until the nineteenth century that the cell was discovered (Schwann), and it was shown by Virchow (1841-1908) that alterations of it were an essential factor in disease. During this period of great discovery, the almost ageless debate arose again about whether disease developed from within the organism or from outside factors. Pasteur, Lister, and Koch were in the forefront of those believing in exogenous (from the outside) disease. Their view has come to be known as the germ theory of disease. According to this belief, microbes which are air transported enter the body and cause disease.

Those who opposed the germ theory postulated that disease arises from within through a process of spontaneous generation. Adherents of this ancient belief argued that disease could arise in the body *de nova* (without cell parents). As opposed to the analytical, mechanistic approach of the germ theorists, the vitalists of the spontaneous generation thesis saw disease as an attempt by the body to restore wholeness. Therefore disease was an aspect of health. Experimentation done by F.A. Ponchet, who had traveled extensively to gather air from many parts of the world, showed that no germs as he defined them existed in the air. Pierre J. Béchamp demonstrated that microbes do exist in the air but are not morbid; otherwise, every wound or breath of air would pass disease on to us. On the contrary, his research

---

*For Avicenna, "temperament" referred to the pattern of energy qualities as a whole. (Shah, *The Sufis*, p. 129)

(such as asbestos) as important variables in understanding the nature of disease.

The more biological research is directed at discovering the nature of disease, the more we are led to the conclusion that a single-cause formulation for disease, as is currently defined, will be inadequate for a comprehensive theory. After a thorough review of the medical literature independently by Cassell and Engel on the cause of disease, Pelletier reports on

...the inadequacy of single-cause formulations or even multicausal considerations when these are limited to physical factors with other factors within the host often ignored or minimized.[81]

A new and promising approach to disease issues has been opened up by a new area of energy research called radiational physics. Western science has been increasingly interested in the relationship of radiations and disease. Thermography, for example, is a technique by which relative degrees of body heat are measured and displayed pictorially. These pictures reveal that cancer areas appear more red than other parts, indicating increased heat radiation. In a nonconventional approach to disease, Kirlian or electrophotography has revealed that disease processes can be recorded as a disturbed or diminished energy field. Dr. Burr in America, Dr. Inyushin in Russia, and Dr. Dimitrescu in Rumania all found that the biofield around each of us shows our degree of health or disease. When that field is disturbed it is possible to determine the exact location of the problem, before it manifests as disease in the physical body. Thus, the state of our fields dictates the present and future condition of the physical body. This supports my contention that we are fields first and bodies second; therefore, we become what our fields direct.

More recent work by researcher Harry Olfield in England with his "audio camera," a further development of Kirlian photography, has demonstrated that it is possible to both photograph and listen to disease based on a subtle field of energy that records such disturbances. Olfield found that cancer cells have a much higher level of energetic activity (15 times as much) than healthy tissue. But what about the role of energy fields in healing disease?

We know that certain animals, such as starfish and many amphibians, can regenerate limbs from this energy field. Dr. Robert Becker, curious about the regeneration possibility of such animals, found that they produce an energetic flow (which he calls "injury current") to that part of the body that has been lost or injured. Applying electrical stimulation, he has enabled so-called nonregenerating amphibians to grow new limbs. Dr. Wilson and his colleagues in London have used pulsed electromagnetic fields[82] to quicken the healing of nerves in mice. Acupuncture has been used for years to stimulate bone growth by increasing the flow of energy to the healing site. More recently in Germany, Dr. Werner Kraus has developed an apparatus called a magnetodyne, which has been used quite successfully in mending hard-to-heal bones.[83] Like Wilson, he uses pulsed electromagnetic fields. Dr. Studitsky in Moscow has even shown that when minced-up skeletal tissue is placed in the wound of a rat, the rat, without outside influence, can generate new muscle.[84] Like other types of living tissue, rat muscle may be responding to an energy field that governs its powers to regenerate.

Electrophotography shows that humans, unlike inorganic objects whose energy field is constant, have a well-organized but lively field that changes considerably according to mood, state of consciousness, intake of intoxicants (alcohol, drugs, tobacco), and atmospheric conditions. Research suggests that we can increase the healing effects of this field.

Dr. Popp, a German biophysicist, has presented a theory mentioned earlier that cells regulate themselves based on biosignals among each other. He proposed that disease results when these communication signals (infrared and sound) become disrupted. When this occurs, the cells attempt to normalize signal sending and encoding by a process of what could be called *repair resonance*. In this process the cells "sense" false signals by means of energy resonation and quickly attempt to destroy them. Disease may be seen as incompatible energy vibrations that produce faulty waves and incorrect information to the nucleus. According to this theory, cancer is a chronic disturbance of these information signals that ultimately creates an energy field other than the one created by healthy cells. Like others before them, Popp and his colleagues have found that cancer is a form of hyperenergy swinging oppositely from hypoenergy diseases (e.g., rheumatism), though both depart from the standing waves of "wellness" emitted by normal energetic activity. Dr. Tiller has even suggested that disease is an imbalance of conductivity between the positive and negative space/time frames. Where does all this lead us?

It leads us potentially to a very complex picture of disease, except for one thing. Like health, disease is a function of wholeness and can be described in terms of energy. Disease provides us with a multifaceted chance to learn about energy and eventually transform this knowledge into greater wholeness or health. Although we can view disease from various perspectives, we can integrate all of these with the use of energy concepts into a Life Energy Theory of disease.

If we review several of these perspectives, a fairly consistent picture of disease emerges. We can understand the native relationship to loss of soul in disease as a loss of harmony. Soul is the principle of universal wholeness; disease is an absence of soul, or wholeness whose harmony has been disturbed. When our personal harmony becomes disrupted, we have retreated from a wholeness that is regulated by the field of spirit. Spirit, I have contended, is an essential energy frequency (band) that identifies every object, person, or process. Therefore the belief that disease is caused when a spirit enters the body or is transferred is really an issue of personal identity. People possessed by a spirit are often young, naive, or religious and at some level either have insufficiently developed their identity or have denied it. When we lack the connection to our identity, we open the energy "door" for frequencies with which we do not resonate. This causes disease because health depends on the resonation of all energy frequencies according to the law of harmonics. That energy can be transmitted from one person to another has been well documented; more and more people are beginning to understand this truth. For both good and evil, the qualities of spirit may be exchanged—witness the numerous cults and religious systems throughout the world that practice such techniques. It is not, however, astounding that early peoples had a clear idea about the basics of disease and health, because they lived more in a state of wholeness than do civilized people today. Despite their superstitions, which tended to cloud the pure energy processes, native peoples knew wholeness.

The relationship between sin and disease is equally clear. If we remove the moralism behind the Christian idea of sin, disease can be seen as the consequence of our transgression against the laws of wholeness. No God need punish us—we do this ourselves. The idea of disease resulting from transgression is closer to the Indian notion of life consequences from the law of karma. All our actions are merely focal points along the circle of life energy movement. Therefore, the quality and consciousness of these deeds return to us to enrich or deplete our lives. There is no punishment, only the energy results of our actions.

Because health is balance, all our parts and functions must work in a complementary fashion. Whether this energy movement is polarized or cyclical, all phases of activity need to exhibit the rhythm of wholeness. Disease then can erupt when any energy polarity is disturbed, as in the yin/yang system, muscle tonus, stimulation, or breathing (air); biologically, this may focus on enzymes or other proteins and can be precipitated by extreme stress. In every case where life energy is disturbed, disease expresses itself. Poor nutrition creates poisons that must be discharged; lack of sunlight minimizes the ultraviolet rays necessary for health; and emotional stasis blocks the flow of energy, which in turn causes a disturbance of energy charge and discharge.

When the basic level of life energy is diminished, the body's ability to neutralize microbes arising from within or to defend against assaults arising from without is necessarily minimized. The normal communication signals thereafter become disturbed, and the standing waves of wholeness become totally disrupted.

Dis-ease cannot exist where there is harmony. Health is a coherence where all energy is brought together and focused. The result is a concentrated beam of light that has been known to the East for thousands of years on another energy level as the "one-pointedness" of meditation. Dis-ease may be understood as a function of light whereby our concentration, stillness, emotional clarity, and physical balance become diffused much the way a normal bulb scatters light. In this diffusion, the vibrational pattern of health or coherence becomes disturbed, and these energy patterns underlying all matter cause a breakdown. On the physical level, this would cause impairment of one or several organs; on the mental or psychological level it could cause neurosis or psychosis; and when aspects of both soma (body) and psyche (mind) are involved, a psychoemosomatic problem such as migraine headaches or some form of cancer could break out.

Often the symptoms of dis-ease are the latest manifestation of much deeper processes that have gone undetected. If you "break out" with breast cancer, it is not a part of you that has cancer; *the whole you* has fostered a cancerous process. Complete understanding of dis-ease necessitates what Pelletier describes as a multiversal approach, whereby not only physical influences such as germs are considered but also such factors as heredity, learning paradigms of illness (e.g., some sicknesses may be accepted while others are not), amounts and types of change,* patterns of emotional holding, social pressure, and a host of factors that affect how stress is interpreted. Much of our daily stress is unidentifiable due to noise pollution, atmospheric radiation, and unresolved emotional conflicts. Most patterns of holding are caused by unfinished energy processes (emotional and other) held in the body as vibrations. Outside stimulation and internal sensitivity simply trigger these held forces as they seek a release to complete their energy cycles. Unfortunately, few people have enough awareness of these factors or take the time for physical activity that would relieve

---

*Too much change in too short a period was found to be a good predictor of tendency to become ill (Pelletier, *Mind as Healer, Mind as Slayer*, p. 102).

a great deal of at least superficial stress; for both awareness and activity can lead to an understanding of deeper energy considerations. When we come to a greater stillness in our lives, we sense much more clearly the forces that affect us in daily life. In stillness we might feel a long held sadness or really hear the noise in our neighborhood. Busy, however, defending our held emotions, we keep ourselves away from a clear sense of simply what is. Stress virtually reflects this pent-up energy, leading to diseases of a physical/psychological nature.

I believe that dis-ease, regardless of form, must be understood in light of wholeness, which means that we must focus on the healthy aspects of dis-ease. We need to make diagnoses based on the whole person and his or her energy components, including sociopolitical and environmental milieus. We need to develop approaches to healing that involve mind, body, and spirit in ways that assumes everyone's responsibility for their present health status. To fully understand the energy components of health and dis-ease, we will need a closer, more integrated relationship among scientists of all disciplines. Until now, there has been almost no research on what keeps people healthy,* although there are volumes of data on illness. Is this only a coincidence or another statement about our fear of wholeness? We think that all forms of wholeness are dangerous because they lead us to changes that we may not accept; hence we resist the flow of energy, thereby slowing down (if not stopping) our evolution. Disease is a compromise in evolution. Simultaneously, energy is brought into movement and held back from complete expression; our disease is the compromise state—the combined product of an attempt at healing and our fear of evolving.

In closing Chapter Three we have added to our equation of energy:

Life Energy = intelligence
            = pattern
            = movement
            = rhythm
            = evolution
            = integration
            = emotion
            = degree of health
            = healing

*In Stockholm there is now planned such a pilot program under the leadership of physician Dr. Bjorn Lenke.

Chapter Four

Energy Radiations

You can go very far if you start very near. The nearest is you. We generally start with the farthest, the supreme principle, the greatest ideal, and get lost in some hazy dream of imaginative thought. But when you start very near, with the nearest, which is you, then the whole world is open, for you are the world. From the actual you must begin with what is happening now and the now is timeless.
—Krishnamurti*

If we take the next step from personal wholeness into our environment, we find that the same principles of life energy apply. The word *atmosphere*, for example, derived from atmo (Gk. breath or spirit) and sphere (Gk. ball or "as above"), reflects the concept that our environment is an extended realm of breath or spirit that is above us. But as the old Hermetic idiom suggests, "as above, so below"—our atmosphere is also us, and the nature of our breath (physical and metaphysical) becomes our environment. We often assume that what we define as "I" has little or no connection to what we call "other"— in this case, our milieu or environment. Gradually, however, we are realizing that our disregard for natural laws in the form of various pollutions has a definite effect upon us as individuals. When we are unaware of our surroundings and our impact on them, then our environment becomes us and our mistreatment. This is directly related to the law of wholes, which states that all isolated and unfinished processes, as well as pieces and parts, have a natural tendency to become whole. Because the law of wholes seeks completion through its resonance of like energy vibrations, the havoc we promote through our lack of awareness returns to us in like fashion.

*Reprinted by permission of the Krishnamurti Foundation. Copyright © by the Krishnamurti Foundation Trust Ltd.

an emotional barrier between the wearer and the outside world, they also block full-spectrum light (except artificial lenses) from being absorbed by the eyes.

Full-spectrum sunlight includes all the color frequencies and some ultraviolet and short-wave infrared radiations, with a strong emphasis in the blue-green range. In its descent to earth, sunlight becomes filtered through our atmosphere so that most short-wave ultraviolet rays do not penetrate. There has been much confusion about ultraviolet rays because of the lack of distinction between short- and long-wave ultraviolet. It is known that short-wave ultraviolet radiations are dangerous to health and life. In fact, hospitals use them to kill germs. But are they also killing us when they subject us to these rays indirectly?

Ott has shown that *long*-wave ultraviolet rays are not only not dangerous in small doses but are essential to health. When full-spectrum light was not available, or when special treatment was administered, long-wave ultraviolet radiation was given to people underexposed to sunlight; they benefited similarly to those who received more natural sunlight. This would indicate that long-wave ultraviolet is an essential part of full-spectrum light.

One danger, however, of exposure to ultraviolet rays is that we cannot always be sure that only long waves are radiating. Many sunlamps actually project short-wave ultraviolet, which can be lethal! With the increased popularity of solariums, we should know about control standards for sunlamps. Interestingly, although short-wave ultraviolet is generally dangerous to health, the trace amounts radiated through sunlight are actually necessary for health. We might compare this to chemical trace elements in the body, which are also important for well-being. In occult circles, ultraviolet light is believed to help people see the aura or etheric energy body.

When plants are grown with insufficient or incomplete light, they develop viruses. Although viruses may be injected into other victims, Ott contends that it is the poisons of faulty metabolism that are passed on and that these also afflict the new victim. Viruses may be the result of faulty processes of life energy, not the cause of disease itself. This would support the research done by Wilhelm Reich, Puharich, and Mischio Kushi (present leader of macrobiotics), all of whom contend that the virus is a self-developed process.

Research done by Ott with color filters to selectively screen out certain light frequencies has lent substantiation to this claim. Using blue filters on animal cells, he showed effects that closely resemble viruses, according to virologists observing his work. Ott also pointed out that the tomato virus usually breaks out after long periods of cloudy weather and low sunlight, even when the most sterile conditions exist. However, after a few days, tomato plants exposed to full-spectrum light and light foliar feeding came back to life and began producing normal tomatoes. This is quite unusual because afflicted plants are given almost no hope of recovery. If more research proves this to be true, then human virus might act in the same way. Because many physicians and scientists agree that cancers probably occur through virus, we can extrapolate that cancer might be shown to be a disease of metabolic disturbance caused by faulty nutrition and mal-illumination, as well as factors such as emotional blockage and environmental pollution. This brings us back to an important connection of the eyes as receptors of light, the pineal gland and its effect on the endocrine system and emotions.

Ott has also reported on several experiments with cancer patients who spent as much time as possible in the sun and tried to avoid all artificial sources of light. With one exception, all showed some improvement, most being completely cured. It appears that full-spectrum light has a positive, holistic effect on plants and animals, while incomplete light from artificial sources has a deleterious effect.

Artificial light, regardless of type, is always deficient in some important aspects of whole light that are essential to health. Ordinary incandescent light has virtually no ultraviolet light, lacks the blue end of the spectrum, and has a maximum of energy in the infrared range, which is why it becomes quite hot. Fluorescent lights operate on another principle by causing phosphor coating on the glass of the tube to fluoresce. The "warm white" version is strong in the orange-pink range.

Interestingly, a school in Niles, Illinois, reporting the highest rate of leukemia (a type of cancer) had two classrooms using such lighting. In addition, curtains were drawn so that no sunlight could enter because of a glare that penetrated the window glass. After administrators changed the lights to "cool white" type, opened the curtains more often, and used the lights less, no further cases were reported. Naturally, this raises many questions about lighting in schools, homes, and work environments.

Dr. Matthew Bradley and his assistant, Nancy Sharkey, at the National Cancer Institute Laboratory of Molecular Pharmacology in Bethesda, Maryland, have also found that fluorescent light can cause mutations of hamster chromosomes. These mutations may be partly responsible for the change of normal cells into carcinogenic ones.[5] A study by the German Green Cross Association states that fluorescent lights are a major source of headaches and eye pain in offices. According to their report, the more intense the light, the greater the danger.

They found that the combination of sunlight and artificial light is extremely dangerous to health.[6]

As if this isn't enough, fluorescent lights also flicker very quickly as the gas inside the bulbs is being charged. This is probably what causes a major part of office headaches, because these vibrations are unnatural and harmful to humans. Many reports indicate that such lights will also precipitate epileptic seizures. My experience has been that such seizures occur when there is a tremendous amount of emotional holding, the release of which is triggered in the brain via eye intake of this light. Because all emotions are also vibrations that should be released, holding on to these emotions builds up a sensitivity to stimulus activity like that produced by this fluorescent flickering.* According to computer research, it takes only one malfunctioning cell to set off a chain reaction of cells firing, which is what happens in a seizure.[7] It is quite possible that the disturbing vibration of fluorescent light may act as a trigger mechanism for held emotional energy.

Light is a field of influence whose degree of wholeness reflects how whole our environment is. Insufficient or isolated bands of light shift the balance of energy flow away from health toward disease. In such an atmosphere, it is more difficult for our spirit to express itself through the body or emotions. The result is a less lively way of being in the world. Ultimately, the light we use in everyday life should reflect as completely as possible on the physical level the wholeness of our spiritual potential.

Color

Another interesting aspect of light is what happens when only certain frequencies or colors of life energy are used. Research has shown that cells respond quite differently to a variety of colored filters. Most cells would respond in a natural pattern of energetic movements when exposed to sunlight. However, under filtered light, these same cells would move in more varied ways, breaking their usual patterns. Some would become inactive, while others would increase activity, and still others would be killed only by shifting the colored filters. With research in colors, we can be more precise as to how the use of different-frequencied light might affect our lives. We know from physics that color appears in objects because they reflect best those energy frequencies that correspond to a particular color or combin-

---

*This has also been observed in several cases where rock music from earphones has produced epileptic seizures in adolescents who never had seizures before.

ation of basic colors. In other words, a banana is green because of the chemical processes that reflect the wavelength of green. As it becomes more yellow and eventually brown, these processes shift frequencies and express this developmental movement. Research into the effects of red and blue have produced some interesting findings.

Red (pink)

Red is the densest of colors, representing a slow, long wave of energy. Research has shown that red light filters cause weakening and ultimately rupture of cell walls in both plants and animals. In addition, poor verbal response among humans and cancer, impotence, and aggressive behavior in male and female minks have been reported. Minks and pumpkins kept under red light produced all male offspring.

In hospital settings red is almost never used because it increases nervous tension and restlessness and has a strong afterimage. One exception is the use of pink in mental hospitals in California, based on the research of Dr. Schauss, former director of the Institute of Biosocial Research in Tacoma, Washington, who discovered that short exposures to pink light weakens muscle strength and creates docility.[8] Apparently only one percent of patients can resist its influence, even those who are color blind. Therefore, ward patients are put under the light if they become agitated; after 20 minutes of exposure, however, their behavior radically shifts and they become aggressive. No clear reason for the two contrary behaviors has been discovered.

It is interesting that people in many countries throughout the world typically dress female babies in pink. How this affects their docility and aggression has not been studied to my knowledge.

Psychologically, red produces claustrophobia in a closed room, although it is a compelling focal point if other colors are used to offset it. If toned down, red shades encourage a warm, reaching-out behavior. Red is a powerful, vitalizing color that is the most definitive color signal in nature. It appears to exacerbate disorders of posture and movement through pain thresholds. That red stimulates may seem to contradict its slow rhythm, but an ancient hermetic law of energy states that the form and function of an object are opposites. Likewise with colors, the frequency and function are opposites. So red vitalizes even though its rhythm is quite slow. Developmentally, red is useful and necessary in youth for activity, often giving way to blues for calm after the period of egocentricity is achieved.* In terms

*Period of egocentricity refers to a stage of development defined by Piaget.

of energy centers or chakras, red is connected with the sacrum, pelvis, and sexual desires.

Because both normal incandescent lights and fluorescent "warm" lights are high in this red range, more research is needed to see the direct effects of such frequencies on hyperactive children, injuries on the job, and heart disease. These types of artificial lights probably play a large part in our aggressive, competitive societies.

Blue

Toward the other end of the light spectrum is blue, which is energetically much quicker (higher frequency) than red because of its much smaller wavelength but produces calm. When blue filtered light was used during mating and/or early developmental periods for pumpkins and mink during research, only females of the species were produced. This was the opposite finding when red light was used, suggesting that each sex has a particular energy frequency that governs its evolution. Male mice under blue light became obese, but females did not. Mice of both sexes, however, showed higher cholesterol levels than those raised under red light. Vicious mink, when exposed to blue light, became quite tame and could be handled like house pets after 30 days of treatment.

In regard to human aggression, Gerrard and Hessey in 1932 apparently quieted down a violent crowd by using blue illumination.[9] Research done by Theo Gimbel in England has shown that blue reduces blood pressure, removes headaches, and regulates the harmonious development of tissue and body structure. Blue gives the feeling of space, which tends to minimize anxiety in hospital waiting rooms, though it can seem cold to the eye if used over large areas and may tend to cast a haze over details and objects in the environment.[10]

Psychologically, blue may cause withdrawal, especially in those who are shy, but it may help those who are active to achieve rest and calm. It may be particularly useful in places where massage or physical rehabilitation is done because it helps soften the body tissue, dissolving old physical structures — but only in those of a more rigid type. However, clients' oral tendencies would be reinforced because of blue's passive, flowing quality.

We could analyze each color according to its functional qualities if we had the space. But it should be clear that each frequency or mixture of color has an important effect in our everyday use of life energy. Conscious, harmonious selection of colors in our homes, work, schools, and clothes can greatly influence the deeper evolutionary processes of our lives.

Both light and color have been used successfully as treatment modalities in physical, psychological, and spiritual dis-ease. In the 1800s Niels Finsen of Denmark pioneered phototherapy by successfully treating tuberculosis of the skin with ultraviolet rays. Even earlier, Indian doctors treated jaundice in premature babies with direct exposure to sunlight; this is now being practiced by Western doctors. Dr. Cremer in England has shown that serum bilirubin, which causes jaundice, can be lowered by either direct sunlight or blue light treatment. This eliminates the need for blood transfusion in such cases.

Physicians have also effectively used light therapy in treating cold sores and fever blisters by dyeing the skin lesion and treating it with daylight fluorescent light. Through a process called photodynamic inactivation, the virus affecting these lesions becomes nonfunctional. Of special interest is *herpes simplex*, one type of this virus, because many scientists believe that it may be responsible for cervical cancer. In a study in Japan, a clear, positive association was found between carcinogenic hydrocarbons treated by ordinary tungsten light and the development of cancer.[11] This means that cancer-producing chemicals could become active with artificial light, and therefore light therapy could possibly be the treatment of future cancers.

In a study on alcoholism, it was found that rats kept in darkness on the weekends changed their preference from water to alcohol. When injections of the enzyme melatonin were given directly, the rats also became alcoholics. Melatonin is secreted from the pineal gland, a regulatory gland for light that is connected to the eyes' reception of light. Because more melatonin is secreted during dark periods, it seems likely that alcoholism might well respond to light therapy. If alcoholics are particularly deprived of healthy nutrition and sun light, light therapy and a balanced diet might prove to be a useful treatment. We know, for example, that in Scandinavia, where there are long periods of darkness, a considerable amount of alcohol is consumed. Combined with other factors such as history, religious taboos, emotional repression, and nutrition, darkness also contributes to alcoholism.

Psychiatrist Alfred I. Levy has shown that whole-light therapy, after only a few days of treatment, eases depression.[12] The late Colonel Dinshah Ghadiali developed a whole system of color therapy, called "spectrochrometry," used to treat various diseases, but he, like Wilhelm Reich and Ruth Drown, was forced to stop his practice because of infringement on accepted medical practice.

Future healers will probably be heavily involved with color and light, as were ancient peoples like the Egyptians, because of their direct, nondangerous effect when used correctly. This type of treatment is consistent with life energy principles of wholeness and minimal intervention.

Atmospheric Radiation

As we have discussed, light and color represent only a small part of the life energy spectrum of radiations. On the presently accepted electromagnetic spectrum, the smallest waves are considered to be cosmic rays. They consist of atomic nuclei, mostly protons and a sprinkling of heavier particles. These are known as primary radiations, and once they interact with the earth's atmosphere, they form other subatomic particles, including neutrons, which are called secondary radiation. The sources of these cosmic rays are the stars (major source), the Van Allen belts, and the sun.

We know that the sun has strong magnetic fields that are carried by solar winds. This wind is considered to be a breeze of electrified gas that transports the sun's magnetic influence to earth. Scientists have found an 11.1-year periodic cycle of solar activity that corresponds uncannily with volcanic eruptions, global flu epidemics, and wars. In addition, it has been found that the incidence of skin cancer rises dramatically three years after this 11.1-year periodic cycle. Some researchers believe that the bombardment of the earth's ozone layer by cosmic rays causes a depletion of this layer, which generally shields us from the dangerous short-wave ultraviolet rays. In fact, these solar influences are considered to be so serious that Russian patients (critical heart and mentally disturbed) are placed in shielded rooms at times of solar disruptions or solar-generated magnetic storms.

Energy researcher Georges Lakhovsky believed that cosmic rays in general also have healing properties. He found that cells are equivalent to oscillating circuits maintained by cosmic radiation. Disease, he said, is the disequilibrium of the cells caused by man-made radiation, among other things, which interfers with cosmic radiation. Lakhovsky's concept of cosmic radiation is similar to Reich's orgone, also a cosmic energy.

Like the sun, the planets and the moon have a direct impact on our lives. Studies have shown that cyclones, hurricanes, and earthquakes have a definite relationship to the position of the planets.[13] It is also known that more babies are born during a waxing than during a waning moon. Hemorrhaging is 82 percent more likely in hospital operations between the first and third quarters of the moon. Menstrual periods in healthy women also follow the monthly 28-day cycle. More recently, 23-day cycles (governing physical strength and energy), and

33-day cycles (controlling reasoning power and mental ability), have also been found.* When these cycles cross, there is a 7-8 percent greater accident proneness. The information on these cycles, called biorhythms, has been obtained in Switzerland and Germany, but it is currently being used in Japan and the United States as well to avoid unnecessary accidents by personnel in difficult cycle periods.

Much of the cosmic influence over our energy reflects the strength of magnetic force fields. We need to divide magnetic influences into two main categories, recognizing, however, that they are not separate from each other. The first are geomagnetic radiations that apparently affect us because of their magnitude, and the second affect us because of their subtlety. Large and intense magnetic forces work on a lower, more physical level of energy, while the subtler fields function on a higher-frequencied, more delicate energy level.

On the level of magnitude, Dr. Reiter, a German environmental physicist, has discovered what he called "spheric pulses," or electric discharges in the lowest level of the atmosphere (the troposphere) that emit electromagnetic pulses. These spherics easily penetrate buildings made of stone or concrete (metal less) and humans, and they apparently affect the birth rate, deaths, traffic and industrial accidents, and human reaction times.

Scientific speculation is that the magnetoreceptive apparatus is linked with the photoreceptive mechanism of light. It also appears that this receptivity to magnetic influence is not functionally separated from other parts of us. Here again we see apparent holism. In fact, research conducted independently by Dr. Kholodov and a researcher at the De La Warr Institute clearly indicates that isolated organs and tissues require a greater magnetic field than an entire organism. This would mean that the more integrated we are as people (emotionally, physically, and so on), the more sensitive we are to magnetic fields all around us. These fields in turn affect our behavior on a basic level, according to research physicist Victor Beasley:

> On the basis of current research it is now fairly certain that the intensity of magnetic energy required to evoke behavioral changes in most biological systems is relatively little.[14]

The weak or more subtle emanations may prove to have a greater impact on us than the stronger fields. This has been the opinion of scientists such as Madeline Barnothy and A. S. Presman. The

*Biological rhythms have been shown to be affected by light, gravity, barometric pressure, ion density, and the sun (Beasley, p. 98).

acknowledgment of slight field influences, like the ripening of fruit by the earth's magnetic field and the treatment by homeopathy, radionics, and color therapy, may prove to be a revolution in our way of living and our medical/psychotherapeutic treatments. On many levels the body blocks out huge doses as a defense mechanism but accepts smaller doses. Like homeopathic doses, chemical trace elements, and solar trace amounts of ultraviolet light, subtle magnetic fields may work on a nonphysical level of life energy that is much closer to our spirit. Therefore, if our consciousness is more present on this core level of energy, elemental doses of all radiations will affect us more strongly until we learn to transform these also. Wholeness provides us with a total closing that eventually leads us to let go all negative influences. According to Professor Frank Brown and Dr. Robert O. Becker, researchers in biomagnetic engineering, the bioelectrical field in the body provides the connection between the cosmic forces and human somatic/psychological functions.[15] How we respond to magnetic influences affects our entire physical and mental processes.

In addition to the magnetic influences from the sun, planets, and moon, other radiations affect life energy. Next to cosmic rays on the electromagnetic spectrum are gamma rays, which are produced from the spontaneous decay of radioactive substances. The greater the vibratory energy of these rays, the greater their penetration power into the body. Closely associated with gamma rays are alpha, beta, and neutron rays, with X-rays lower on the scale. With the exception of X-rays, these other rays are considered to be background radiation, which means that they are natural phenomena that are always present. We are being constantly bombarded with radiation from the cosmos, and all these radiations have their effects on us. Radiational physicist Dr. Hills believes that background radiation of wavelengths 13-80 cm. are absorbed by human beings via the chakras.[16] Aircrew members, for example, who fly closer and more often through these radiations, are technically considered to be radiation workers and as such are subject to strict controls about their allowed time in the sky.[17]

Of these cosmic radiations, beta rays penetrate the body the least. Alpha rays, on the other hand, can be swallowed with food that contains radioactive elements, as can neutron and gamma rays. This presents a tremendous problem because of our proliferation of nuclear fallout.* Unfortunately, nuclear blasts do not remain in the part of the world where they occur but are blown by the winds over

---

*Von Quintus remarks that atomic bombs, when exploded, cut a huge hole in the fine levels of energy that is not readily sealable and cause disease indirectly by negatively altering our energy environment.

the entire globe. This means that there is no such thing as *our* or *their* nuclear fallout but only ours together. What hurts them hurts all of us. We eat much of what falls to earth with our food. So even though we eat "health" foods grown on organic soil, we cannot stop radioactive fallout from ending up in our breakfast cereal. Clearly, more must be done on a political level. We know that strontium 90, one of the products of radioactive fallout, is attracted especially to milk and milk products because of its similarity to calcium. Once digested, this poison becomes stored in the bones. We also know that much of these nuclear wastes also become stored in human fat. Research has also shown that radiation of the nuclear type, in addition to X-rays, can cause mutations through chromosome breakage or direct ionization. The effects are cumulative, with gamma, neutron, and X-rays being the worst.

To get a clear picture of how we are being affected by these radiations, we have to speak a little about ions. Ions are electrical charges in the atmosphere that are produced when an electron has been lost ((+) positive ion) or gained ((-) negative ion) from an atom. There are technically two types of radiation connected with ions: ionizing and nonionizing. In nonionizing radiation the energy level of the orbital electrons is raised without the electrons actually being separated from the nucleus. These "excited" atoms are chemically reactive but have generally been thought to be less dangerous than ionizing radiation. However, as Dr. Zaret, an authority on radiant energy, points out, nonionizing radiation also affects DNA and may not be very different from ionizing radiation in its effects, though it differs in the way it causes radical atomic changes.[18]

Ionizing radiation is thought to be especially dangerous because, in this process, electrons are knocked out of their orbits away from the nucleus, thereby stimulating further ionizations, sometimes thousands more than the original radiation caused. The result is a high rate of chemical activity dangerous to living systems. Gamma, beta, alpha, neutron, and X-rays are all of this ionizing type. The ions associated with these radiations are classified as small ions, as opposed to large ions (dust) or medium ions (tiny particles). Normally, the destructive ionizing radiations of these small ions are kept in the Van Allen belts of geomagnetic fields that surround the earth. However, the gradual destruction of the ozone layer in the atmosphere through pollution, both nuclear and nonnuclear, has allowed more of these ions into our atmosphere.

As these ions enter our bodies, they displace electrons from the outer shells of the molecules they strike. This changes the chemical nature of who we are. On a biological level this means that our tissues become damaged to the degree of the intensity and type of radiation. This is why X-rays kill not only cancer cells but also living cells needed for defense. The most severely affected tissues are those that rapidly multiply, for example, lymph nodes, bone marrow, gonads, mucous of the alimentary tract, and epithelial layers of skin.

Apparently, the ionization by these radiations causes the nucleus in the cell to change. If the affected cell is a DNA molecule (the blueprint for life), all future biological offspring will be affected. This is why there is a high incidence of genetic mutations and uncontrolled cancer growths seen in tissue exposed to strong ionization. It may also be true that some chemical products of ionization create new toxins in the body, as occurs when water becomes hydrogen peroxide, a killer of microorganisms. Because a high percentage of the body is water, this presents a major threat to life.

High doses of ionizing radiation cause stoppage of mitotic dividing of cells necessary for life and may eventually lead to death. Lower doses may produce radiation sickness, nervous system irregularities, and a fall in white blood cells, which are essential for biological defense. Some interesting research has shown that oxygenated cells are three times more likely to be endangered by radiation than cells with lowered oxygen levels.[19] Breathing, which oxygenates the cells, actually makes us more vulnerable to injury. This might account for the fact that emotionally vulnerable people also breathe less as a built-in defense mechanism. When people are in the city, they breathe more shallowly than when they go to the country. It's possible that because of the level of poor air and fast lifestyle, city dwellers are breathing less fully and therefore feeling less emotionally as a built-in protection against toxins and emotional hurt.

Research performed in Russia and currently being duplicated in the United States by Leo Birenbaum, professor of electrical engineering at New York Polytechnic Institute, suggests that in addition to the quantitative effects of ionizing and nonionizing radiation, the frequency of such rays also plays an important role.[20] Studies have shown that biological processes may be differentially sensitive, both beneficially and adversely, to certain energy frequencies and not to others. This would support my contention that health and disease are functions of energy vibrations.

Ions play another important role in our health and well-being as part of a general atmospheric climate where we live and work. Generally, small ions effect atmospheric influences on us more than large or medium ions because of their mobility. Normally, the ratio of positive to negative ions in the atmosphere is 5 to 4, and their numbers may range from quite low in the cities (10 ions per cm³ air) to quite high at the mountaintops (1000 ions per cm³ air). At the shoreline the ratio changes so that 2 negative ions are present for every 1 positive ion. Research begun in the 1950s and continuing to the present has discovered that inhalation of positive ions produces swelling of nose mucous, irritation of the upper respiratory tract, feelings of uncomfortableness, slowing of mental processes, excess migraine, sick headache, swelling of the extremities, reduction of breathing by 30 percent, and depression, to name a few. Positive ions can be produced from several sources. In the cities they are created as air brushes against metal or as metal surfaces become heated. Naturally, in the cities where cars, equipment, and pipes are everywhere, we would expect a high ratio of positive ions. This is combined with the fact that pollutants (e.g., cigarette smoke and industrial waste) create large ions to which the small ions attach themselves. Consequently, the concentration of small ions falls and with it the rate of negative ions that are so important for health.

Another major source of positive ions is certain types of hot dry winds that are characteristic of many countries. In Germany they are known as Föhn, in California as Santa Ana, and in Italy as Sirocco. In all, about 15 countries experience negative effects from these winds. The Chinook winds in Canada sometimes measure a positive ion ratio of 35 to every negative ion. This tremendously imbalanced ratio causes a variety of health problems. Dr. Krueger, of the University of California at Berkeley, has discovered what might be the clue to these negative effects. Positive ions appear to release a neurohormone, serotonin, which if injected separately into the body also produces the same symptoms.

Negative ions act quite differently on the body. They improve the capacity to absorb and utilize oxygen, reduce anxiety, increase alpha brain wave output (also found during meditation), and increase the appetite and sexual desire. They also help precipitate dust, pollen, smoke, and germs out of the air. Because of the desirability of negative ions and their effect in treating respiratory infections and burn victims, negative ion therapy has become a new treatment modality. Dr. Sulman, a medical doctor in Jerusalem, has used this treatment for five years and reports a 75 percent success rate with patients exhibiting serotonin (positive ion neurohormone) symptoms. In addition, ion therapy has been proven to reduce germ counts by as much as 70 percent in 24 hours.

A major detriment to the natural ion therapy of fresh air is pollutants from nuclear wastes, chemical sewage, and industrial/transportational wastes. In a true holistic picture of ecology, all systems of air, water, and land must work harmoniously, for they return to us as supporters or deniers of life energy processes. Our atmosphere provides either what Reich called a life-positive (enhancing) or life-negative (destructive) milieu. Negative ions are life enhancing, while positive ions foster dis-ease. For the moment, we must say that our atmosphere is life negative, though new awareness is helping to change this condition.

One source of pollution is the fuel wastes of jet planes, which are causing thermopollution (heat) in the atmosphere. Over Chicago, for example, there has been a rise in temperature so that more ice is melting from the mountains, which could cause massive increases in water to overflow their present boundaries. At the same time, the weather has become more cloudy by 15-20 days a year. The Smithsonian Institute in Washington, D.C., looking into the reduction of sunlight, reported a loss of 14 percent during the past 60 years. This loss seems to be a combination of more cloud formation and lower sun intensity, despite the fact that the protective ozone layer is allowing more destructive short-wave ultraviolet rays through. A major factor in the destruction of the ozone layer is the use of aerosol containers for hair sprays and chemical cleaners, indirectly disturbing all the weather around the world.

This will have significant consequences for our lives according to recent findings on the effect of weather upon us. The science of biometeorology, which studies the interactions between humans and the weather, has only recently developed the tools to show the links between health and weather, although primitive man has always seen this connection. The Chinese speak about wind chi in their medicine as an explanation for a type of cold. Hippocrates, in 400 B.C., recorded more scientifically the psychological and physical reactions to hot and cold winds. Today new technology has broadened the picture immensely. Arthritis has been found to be aggravated by falling barometric pressure, as well as by an increase in humidity, supporting an old folk belief. Colds, however, are not caused directly by weather but probably result from stale air where viruses are contained. An interesting finding is that births are also directly affected by weather.

According to the American National Oceanic and Atmospheric Administration, the precise date and hour of our births are determined by weather! Their studies show that labor most often starts on days when "the temperature rises, barometric pressure stabilizes and high cloud cover appears." Births occur when "moist air gets into lower layers, pressure falls, clouds thicken, precipitation [may begin] and winds pick up." In fact, so clear were the relationships between behavior and weather that they divided weather conditions into six phases. Heart attacks ebb in phase 1 weather, which is cool, with high pressure and few clouds. Phase 2, characterized by beautiful skies, high pressure, and little wind, stimulates the body very little. In phase 3, women go into labor, learning problems and suicides peak. Between phases 3 and 4, most deaths occur, and in phase 4 birth occurs. In phase 5, where precipitation is accompanied by cold, gusty winds, rapidly rising pressure, and falling humidity, we become irritable and our resistance to disease is weakened. Phase 6, in which temperatures and humidity fall, pressure rises, and cloud cover is diminished, aggravates spasmodic diseases of the muscle.[21] Therefore, as we adversely affect our weather through pollution, we also affect a whole range of human behaviors. For, as we are seeing, weather and behavior are another whole that cannot be violated if we are to live in health.

A more recently identified pollution problem is that of a phenomenon called acid rain. Acid rain is a form of acid precipitation caused mainly by sulphur dioxide and nitrogen oxide emissions from the burning of fossil fuels such as coal, oil, and natural gas, as well as from motor exhausts (nitrogen oxide). When these flying pollutants mix with sunlight, oxygen, and water vapor, they develop into a "soup" of sulfuric and nitric acids in the atmosphere. When this acid falls back to earth in rainfall, its effects are devastating. In Norway 80 percent of the lakes in the southern part of the country have no fish. In Sweden some 4000 lakes have developed the same problems. In Bavaria, Germany, 3600 acres of evergreen forests have died because of acid rain. Even ground water is becoming polluted. In Sweden, where the buffeting capacity against acid rain is minimal, the damage seems the greatest. Drinking water becomes foul tasting and leads to diarrhea and corrosion of cooking appliances. One of the main problems in controlling acid rain is that many countries that suffer from its effects are the lowest producers. Sweden and Norway, for example, import 80-90 percent of their acid rain from the winds blowing from the Soviet Union, Germany, Belgium, France, and the United Kingdom. A good example of this was the recent nuclear disaster in Chernobyl, Russia, near Kiev, which exposed the entire world to radiational hazards.

In the sea pollutants of another kind disturb the flow of life energy. As atomic reactors continue to produce atomic energy from nuclear fission (the splitting of atomic nuclei), they need places to dump their atomic waste. In recent years it has become convenient to dump this waste into the sea. Almost all industrial countries are doing it, with the result that many of the coastlines of the United States, Britain, South Africa, the Far East, and Australia are strongly polluted with wastes. On the eastern shores of the United States, more than 260,000 times as much pollution was dumped in the ocean as was produced

Energy Radiations

Other earth and earth-related radiations have been known by early civilizations, but they are only now being more technically studied by conventional scientists. As early as 1930, von Pohl began some research into terrestrial radiation and disease using a divining rod.[28] Rambeau, in 1934, did similar work with a geophysical instrument that measured field strengths and came to similar conclusions. Both men found that the sick people they studied always lived in areas where the radiation from the earth was disturbed in some fundamental way. These areas of energetic disturbance have since come to be known as geopathogenic zones. Since then, more details about what constitutes these energy radiations have been accumulated.

A network of underground energy lines has recently been (re?)discovered by German researchers. Unlike waterways, this network is fairly regular across the entire globe, though differences in space between lines fluctuate with the distance from the equator. Dr. Manfred Curry, researcher and physician, found that this network of energy lines runs from northeast to southwest and from southeast to northwest, with an average distance between lines of about three and a half to four meters in Europe, although further north and south of the equator the lines are narrower. The lines themselves are about 75 centimeters wide, though they expand and contract a bit depending on the weather.[29]

Curry found that at places where two energy lines cross, there is an alternating positive and negative charge effect. Positively charged points of crossing cause normal cells as well as tumor cells (cancer producing) to grow, while negative crossing tend to lead to inflammation. Interestingly, these crossings, he found, regularly change their charge as though part of a huge magnetic balancing process.

Hartmann and his colleagues have come across another network, called the global network (Global-Gitternetz) or simply Hartmann network. This network runs north-south and east-west, independent of the Curry network. Like Curry lines, the Hartmann paths are orthagonal but measure about two and a half meters from east to west and two meters from north to south, with a breadth of about 21 centimeters. They are also weather related.

These network energies appear to be in the radio frequency band and function according to standing wave properties.[30] The most important effect of these energy networks on human health problems occurs when these lines also cross water pathways, although according to some practitioners of radiathesia (e.g., Kreitz), the entire energy line can have negative effects on health. The research gathered to date has been impressive in its documentation of clear biological effects on animals and humans on sites of the pathogenic disturbance zones.

Among the effects noted by physicist Herbert König in his comprehensive *Unsichtbare Umwelt*, translated roughly, *The Invisible World Around Us*, are change in infrared emission of humans, reduction in blood cells, development of blood abnormalities such as threads, granules, pustules, and small balls to the point of cancer, slowing down of reaction time,* nervousness, drop in blood pressure, and decrease in the immune system's response. In plants, the cores have been shown to fall out, and deficiencies and irregularities in growth and change of color were observed. Animals were observed to lose weight, flee from their nests (birds), and develop cancer on pathogenic points.

In humans the greatest effects seem to be on people whose vegetative system is extremely sensitive, who are emotionally disturbed, or who are affected by other environmental influences such as smoking, drinking, and city living, or who live in steel buildings. A principal effect is the weakening of the immune system. Thus, in addition to other harmful radiations from the atmosphere, including noise pollution, nuclear pollution, frequency pollution (various man)made frequencies), and emotional disharmony, the radiations from the earth also play an important part in our health.

From the other side of things, energy lines have been found that work positively toward greater wholeness. As is so often true, the negative aspects (in this case the harmful energy crossings) have been more researched than the positive or health-maintaining ones. We do know, however, that many ancient cultures knew about such energy lines and their radiations. Technically known as geodetic force lines, these energy pathways were known as ley lines to the Celts and Druids in England, as dragon lines in the Chinese Feng Shui or geomancy system, and as serpent trails to the medieval gnostics.[31] According to these traditions, the earth is webbed with invisible energy streams like a living body. In fact the Chinese saw in these lines a parallel to the acupuncture meridians of the body. Along these streams were positive and negative nodes that were differentiable by their effects. It was known, for example, that animals would often bear their offspring on these positive nodes, which were sometimes offshoots of the main line (called whorls). Other nodes were negative and worked like pathogenic zones, although some trees, like the weeping willow, preferred these sites.**

---

*This has been researched as well in relation to traffic accidents where these pathogenic points often exist.

**Blair has pointed out that the weeping willow is still used for magical ceremony, especially at full moon, when the power of the negative forces is greatest.

Where several of these positive energy lines come together, churches, temples, and ritual centers were established. In England, Stonehenge and Cumberland, and in Greece, the Delphi represent such hubs of energy focus. Jakob Lorber, a nineteenth-century German medium and proclaimed mystic had the insight that the earth is blanketed by fine lines of copper crystal in the form of triangular segments that hold the cosmic charge.[32] Perhaps future research will be able to discern more about the holistic aspects of these energy lines and their life-enhancing radiations in addition to their pathogenic aspects.

Household Radiation

Radiations in the home also affect us. Because the body is a semiconductor, it can be set into motion (physically, emotional, and so on) by any vibration that is strong enough or correctly tuned (more subtle energy). Among the sources of radiation that affect us the most are the appliances on which we have come to depend. High on the list is the television set. There are two main dangers to be aware of— positive ions and X-rays. Television sets charge the air near them with unhealthy positive ions, though its X-rays are even worse. A television set operates by emitting a stream of electrons onto a picture tube that translates these radiations into a picture. As these electrons are fired from a cathode gun (much like an X-ray machine), X-rays are given off. Unlike an X-ray machine, which is more focused, a television set spews radiation out in all directions, directly affecting those watching and indirectly affecting anyone else in the room or possibly even in the same building! The U.S. Department of Health, Education and Welfare (HEW) declared that although a safety limit of 0.5)milliroentgen of radiation per hour had been established, it was found that below this level down to zero, X-rays could still penetrate the body's tissues with a "subtle but harmful effect." It has further been shown that even trace amounts of X-rays are dangerous because they are cumulative.[33] According to Dr. Zaret, cathode ray tubes also emit ultraviolet radiation, which he says is the most mutagenic radiation known.[34]

Studies by John Ott have shown that TV radiations cause excessive growth and upturned roots in plants, as well as hyperactivity, agression, brain tissue damage, lethargy (after long exposures), and eventual death in small animals. People are, of course, not small animals, but Ott's studies have shown that human epithelial cells of the eye, which are connected to the pineal and pituitary glands as well as indirectly to the endocrine system, may be seriously endangered, even though no visible injury to the cells may appear. An example of the connection of the endocrine system to emotional and physical responses is watching television which may produce serious dangers not only to the eyes but through the eyes to our entire physical/emotional functioning. In a New York study of children who watch TV, television radiations have been cited in cases of general disease with symptoms of nervousness, fatigue, headache, loss of sleep, and vomiting. Two to three weeks later, without television watching, all symptoms disappeared. A study by the U.S. Federal Trade Commission stated that X-rays emitted from televisions have been shown to penetrate eyes, testes, and bone marrow. Television may even induce epileptic seizures, like fluorescent light, from the "flicker" effect of the picture tube. Color televisions have three cathode guns to one in a black-and-white set. This means that a much higher voltage is coming into color sets, and there is a greater danger of X-ray radiation on the output, especially if shielding is defective or missing.

With the interest in quick cooking, a new danger looms before us in the form of microwave ovens, which work by rapidly exciting food molecules from the inside in a push-and-pull effect of electromagnetic energy. Because of its efficiency, cooking takes only a fraction of the normal time. Previous health hazards in the form of leaking microwaves have been generally removed from newer microwave ovens, although older sets may still have some leaks. That microwaves are dangerous to health when directly absorbed is without question. Research has shown that microwave radiation can cause the following:

> Cataracts (clouding of the eye lenses), birth defects, sterility and possible death at high doses of exposure and at low levels of exposure such undesirable biological effects as irregular heart beat, blood flow and electricity in the brain, central nervous system disorders, changes to the blood's composition, headaches, stress, behavioral difficulties, and more.[35]

It is also known that cardiac pacemakers will be disrupted from their usual rhythm, nearly causing death to their wearers.[36] Therefore, all microwave appliances and hospital apparatus should be avoided by pacemaker wearers.

An additional danger is that such radiation is both additive (e.g., adds to a current inflammatory process) and cumulative (i.e., produces a buildup of exposure effects). The current U.S. safe exposure level for humans is 10 milliwatts per square centimeter of skin surface. However, since the setting of this standard, research animals have been killed with even less power. Although the thermal or "cooking" effects of microwave radiation are quickly observable, the "simmering" effects of longer-range molecular aberrations are less apparent though no less dangerous. So far we have no good, long-term studies of what happens when food is eaten from microwave processes or of the environmental effects of these radiations in our homes.

Air Conditioning

Another major danger to us is the generalized usage of air conditioning. Designed to keep us cool by taking the humidity (warm water) out of the air, air conditioning has caused other radiational and physiological hazards. Studies have shown that in the process of cooling the air, a condition of hypothermia (overcooling) is often produced. When this occurs the heart is slowed, edema (swelling) is encouraged, and acidosis (excess of acid) of the body results. Slowing the blood flow can lethally affect people with cardiac rhythm disturbances. Generally, with overcooling there is a depression of breathing, with a weak, prolonged expiratory phase. We know that even a small temperature loss can seriously affect the critical ability to judge and may even result in loss of consciousness in extreme cases.

Any drop in active breathing affects our mood as well as our emotional expression, because breathing charges the emotions, allowing us to more clearly perceive what we are feeling. Whereas television sets create positive ions, air conditioners remove all small ions from the air, thus destroying healthful negative ions. In addition, the use of air conditioners in hospitals spreads germs throughout the rooms, ironically in a setting that is supposed to be antiseptic. One way to improve this condition would be to use air conditioners sparingly when needed and install negative ionizers in the equipment, along with better filtration systems. If possible hospitals should be located in natural settings where fresh air would be a better substitute.

Electricity

Almost all of our household appliances are activated by electricity, which of course flows through wires. As a whole, these cables running throughout our residences create energy fields by their radiations. Despite the fact that all wire is somehow insulated, an electromagnetic network dependent on the intensity of the power and the geometric pattern of the laid cable is created. In the United States 110 volts with 60 Hertz is used, while in Europe generally 220 volts with 50 Hertz. Hertz is a measure of the frequency of electrical vibrations, while volts stand for the potential difference between two points on a conductor. Because of the nature of electricity, its poor isolation in wire, and the specific network of cable in each room, this electromagnetic field produces high-frequency signals, changing modulations (e.g., wind affects the cable), impulse-type radiations, and different field strengths in each room.[37]

The effects of these fields and field qualities on our life energy are numerous. The main disturbance to our system seems to be in processes that function by electromagnetic energy themselves. A principal target is nerve cells. We know that ion movement can be affected by electromagnetic fields and that ions in the body play a part in the stimulation of nerves.[38] Presman's research with electromagnetic fields and neurohormones indicates that the effect of these fields is often not specific, though principally affecting the nervous system. Dr. Zaret's research with different forms of radiation shows that these electric fields in our homes cause a negative effect on calcium metabolism in brain cells.[39] These effects probably result from the vibrational relationship between our personal vibratory pattern and the external field as it relates to water resonance, nerve receptors, and signal detection, all of which influence cell activity.

We could improve this state of affairs by insisting on better insulation (e.g., coaxial cable) that does not produce external fields, by unplugging electrical wires not in use, especially in the bedroom where rest is important, and by using small field neutralizers that have been tested for effectiveness. Unfortunately, many of these commercial apparatuses are simply nice ideas with little substantiation for their claims. Therefore, it is important to find ones that are truly effective.

Medical Radiation

In addition to household and office appliances, numerous radiation machines are used by the medical professions, all of which have an effect on our lives directly or indirectly. Because radiation waves don't just disappear after they are emitted, our technical use of various radiations means that these vibrations are constantly being added to background radiation.

All told, external and internal radiation from natural sources brings the average human dose to approximately 100 millirems per year or a lifetime dose of about 7,500 millirems. These doses alone would pose no problem. The potential for trouble develops only when we *add to* the natural radiation background. And this we do to an ever-increasing degree as scientific discoveries lead to technological advances...[and] increase our exposure to ionizing and non-ionizing radiation.[40]

The danger of this is that we also leave our awareness of radiation dangers in the background and find out too late what effects have been wrought on us. Our holism can be easily disturbed because we have not looked at the whole picture of radiation production, consumption, and waste.

One of the greatest exposure dangers to radiation comes directly from the diagnostic and treatment procedures of our medical and dental practitioners. Demographic information available for the United States in 1970 showed that about 65 percent of the total population is X-rayed every year, 80-90 percent of which comes from medical and dental X-rays. Theoretically, X-ray machines subject the patient to low doses of radiation, but as Dr. Mendelsohn has pointed out, thyroid cancer can develop after an amount of radiation equivalent to less than ten bitewing dental X-rays. If other parts of the body need examining, more radiation is needed, which means greater risk. The use of breast X-rays (called mammograms) is highly questionable because breast tissue is very sensitive to radiation and mammograms can cause more cancer than they will detect.[41] In addition to this is the unclear diagnostic reliability and validity of X-rays. According to Dr. Mendelsohn, a 1970 study has shown that radiologists themselves disagreed on the X-ray results about 20 percent of the time. Untrained physicians were found no less accurate than trained specialists in reading the results.

In cancer therapy high doses of X-rays may be administered (e.g., bone cancer), and some forms of cancer may even be treated with nuclear implants (e.g., cervical cancer). For many years even noncancerous diseases such as bursitis, arthritis, ulcer, warts, and acne were treated with X-ray, but this unwarranted treatment has declined in favor of other procedures.

We may also absorb radiation through radiopharmaceuticals, which are chemicals or drugs injected or taken orally to which a radioactive substance (radionuclide) has been added for diagnostic purposes. These drugs give off radiation from inside the body and theoretically enable doctors to diagnose a condition. Two recent developments of this type of diagnosis are the CAT (computer axial tomography) and PET (positron emission tomography). Both are nonsurgical scanning techniques that operate by taking pictures of the body through the radioactive residues left after injection or inhalation of radioactive elements. Although it is claimed that the radioactivity leaves the body within several minutes to several hours after entering it, the effect that such radioactive radiation has on the more subtle bodily processes or energy levels has not been determined.

Because X-rays have been implicated in the development of diabetes, cardiovascular disease, stroke, high blood pressure, and cataracts, in addition to childhood leukemia (due to prenatal radiation) and 4000 American deaths a year, we should be informed about the relation of benefits to hazards in X-ray usage.

Combined with other radiations from electron microscopes, ultraviolet lamps, infrared thermography (breast cancer detection), and, recently a beam of destructive radio signals being tested for cancer detection, hospitals are hotbeds of radiations, many of whose effects on the human body specifically and as background radiation generally have not been adequately assessed.

Sound

Of all the atmospheric influences on our energy, sound is perhaps the least considered, which is strange, because almost everyone is affected by it. Might we have become so used to hearing noise that we accept noise pollution as part of the background radiation? Sound is technically defined as a vibration of source transmission and effect perception that we know as hearing. The range of frequencies that we can hear ranges from 20-15,000 cycles per second, zero being the threshold for a young, healthy set of ears.

In addition to the ear, sound can enter the body through the skull, the torso, and the groin. Regardless of where sound enters, the signal is transmitted to every nerve center and organ of the body. This has the effect of maintaining an energy wholeness. After all, if each part of us is aware that sound stimuli are entering, we can respond in a complete manner, providing that there is already a measure of wholeness there. Noise is generally defined as sound that causes stress. But as Hans Selye pointed out, stress is necessary for life; only when stress becomes distress does a problem develop. For our purposes we can relate distress to disease and define noise as any frequency, or duration of frequencies, that leads us away from wholeness toward disease. Therefore, we will experience all sounds that resonate with our wholeness as pleasure, while we will experience dissonant sounds (noise) as unpleasant. Because each of us has a different basic energy frequency (spirit), what we experience as noise may differ considerably from person to person. Further, each of us functions on different levels of awareness. These too are energy frequencies and must be taken into consideration.

To measure noise acceptability limits, the U.S. Department of Labor has set standards for how loud sound stimuli might be without damage to hearing. The measurement for this sound is called decibels (db).

Table 4-1 gives you the limits.

Table 4-1

	Time		Intensity
for	8 hrs	not greater than	90 db
	4 hrs	''	95 db
	2 hrs	''	100 db
	1 hr	''	105 db
	30 min	''	110 db

We must consider noise from three aspects. The first is physical damage to hearing, the second is the emotional/psychological dis-ease, and the third is the effect on our wholeness. Physically speaking, any sound above 80 db can increase our hearing loss, and lower amplitudes over a longer period may do the same. Many household appliances approach this level and are increased by the vibratory transference to other household pieces such as the kitchen table (see Table 4-2). Farr, for example, says that a basic household sound of 58 db can be increased to more than 100 db in this way. Considering the number of appliances in the house and the level of noise produced by each, in addition to the noise next door or down the street, it isn't surprising how much damage is done to our hearing. Rock music, for example, often registers between 106 and 120 decibels, which presents a considerable danger to hearing, whereas the same intensity of a classical symphony (fortissimo) shows none. This is partly because higher frequencies are more piercing than low ones and are generally more annoying to our systems. In disease, high frequencies tend to produce headaches, while low frequencies tend to relax the large intestines, causing bowel movements.

We know that acoustic energy (noise) can damage cells by rupture in the tissues and by heating, strangely enough. Loud noise at a high enough frequency will produce heat that damages these delicate body tissues. On another level it has been found that noise raises blood pressure (you parents with children know what I mean), which severely affects heart diseases and creates a state of hypertension. The constant noise with which most people live in the cities leads to a vasoconstriction (tightening of the blood vessels) that remains even after the noise ceases. In fact noise that comes and goes like the trashmen at seven o'clock can be much worse than a steady background level because of its subtle shock effect. In addition, noise pollution may have the following effects on the body: blood pulse increases; the body temperature sinks; metabolism is increased; the adrenal glands secrete hormones; and electrical muscle activity is raised.[42] Constant noise prevents us from experiencing the deep levels of sleep that we need to stay healthy. People who cannot sleep deeply are chronically tired, have reduced energetic potential, and are more apt to become ill.

Table 4-2*

Intensity of Sounds Common in the Home**

Appliances Being Operated	Apartment A (db)	Apartment B (db)
Living Room†		
Quiet	50	50
Vacuum Cleaner (nozzle engaged on carpet)	72	72
Vacuum Cleaner (nozzle free)	81	73‡
Hi-Fi (loud but not vibrant)	80	75
Television (average volume)	—	68
Kitchen§		
Quiet	56	56
Stove Vent Fan	84‖	68‡
Stove Vent Fan and Dishwasher	88	71‡
Stove Vent Fan, Dishwasher, and Garbage Disposal	91	84‡
Garbage Disposal Empty	—	72
Garbage Disposal with Ice Cubes	—	78
Dishwasher Only	—	69
Bedroom		
Quiet	53	50
Air Conditioner (central system)	—	55
Air Conditioner and Air Filter Fan Unit	—	57
Bathroom		
Quiet	—	53
Ventilating Fan	—	63
Ventilating Fan and Toilet	—	72

*From "Medical Consequences of Environmental Home Noise" by Lee Farr in *People and Buildings* edited by Robert Gutman. Copyright © 1972 by Basic Books, Inc., Publishers. Reprinted by permission of the publisher.

**Measurements were made with a sound level meter (C scale). The apartments were in different buildings with different floor plans.

†Measurements were made 6 feet from the vacuum cleaner, 16 feet from the hi-fi, and 8 feet from the television.

‡Newer models.

§Measurements were made from the center of the kitchen.

‖Lower and steady sound productions. When hard materials such as bones were introduced into the disposal unit, the sound level rose to above 100 db.

Hearing loss from environmental noise pollution usually occurs in one of two ways: intense vibrations may blast the vital hair cells that transmit waves of sound information or cause a stress reaction in which the circulation of blood decreases, causing oxygen deprivation. Such deprivation, when it persists for more than a few minutes, leads to a greater susceptibility of mechanical damage to these hair cells. In each case dis-ease of energy vibrations results.

During the day, when you are relatively healthy, all this isn't even as bad psychologically as when you try to sleep at night or are physically ill. Emotional stress leads to the same oxygen deprivation as physical stress and thus can cause the same damage. It is interesting to note that native peoples retain their hearing almost intact into old age, thereby confirming that hearing loss is a phenomenon of civilization. Very few people today get the rest they need, especially in the hospital when they need it the most. Rest is often a matter of life and death. Very few hospitals have double doors or windows that would dampen the noise or allow carpets on the floors (for control of germs, they say). If we add to this the quality and types of materials used in building these edifices, plus the constant intrusion by the hospital staff, it is amazing that anyone gets any rest at all!

The implications of all this for our state of health or wholeness are quite far-reaching. Because wholeness is harmony, any disturbance of this peace naturally leads us away from wholeness. Once our wholeness is disrupted, we are open to all types of disease—physical, emotional, and so on. How can we talk about our "happy" homes or hospitals as places of health if they abound in disharmony through noise pollution? In fact today it might even be considered unnatural for anyone to want to stay in a hospital, or the home for that matter. Could this be why we are always on the move, buying one thing or another, traveling here and there only because we have become so frightened by the sound of silence?

Sound above 20,000 cycles per second is considered to be ultra(beyond)sound because we cannot generally hear it, though some animals do. Recent evidence, however, suggests that some people with high-frequency hearing can hear even radar sounds (which are microwaves) because of an uneven heating of the head by radiant energy.[43] These people hear clicks, buzzes, and hisses caused by thermoelastic pressure waves at ranges far above the accepted range of normal hearing (100 billion Hz). Ultrasound is used in prenatal diagnosis and a type of medical heat treatment called diathermy. Commenting on the dangers of ultrasound, Dr. Mendelsohn has said:

Ultrasound irradiation of red blood cells may change the ability of the cell membrane to pick up oxygen, thus impairing capacity of the cell to transfer oxygen to body tissues.[44]

And on ultrasound as used for prenatal examination through echo effects, he has said:

Animal studies have demonstrated circulatory problems, liver cell changes, alterations in brain enzymes and EEG patterns, delayed reflexes, emotional reactivity, reduction in immune antibodies and delayed neuromuscular development. There is a woeful dearth of careful long term studies in humans who were bombarded with ultrasound before birth.[45]

Ultrasonic waves, in conjunction with ultravisible light, have also been used to control crowds, with the result of illness, vomiting, and general disorientation of their willed behavior.[46]

In addition to the radiation sources mentioned above, here are a few in an endless list of other potential dangers: long-distance telephone microwave relay towers, police and weather stations, some computers, high-voltage electrostatic air filters, and FM radio and television broadcasting stations. We know that ultra-short-wave transmitters have been cited in behavioral disturbances in men working in front of them,[47] and that the ultrahigh frequencies from radio fields result in the accumulation of acetycholine along nerve fibers. Acetycholine is a chemical that produces hyperactivity in small quantities, while large doses lead to decreased activity. What else should we know? Dr. Adley, at the Brain Research Institute in Los Angeles, has demonstrated that even weak electrical fields affect the behavior of mice both positively and negatively.[48] Because many industrial machines and power lines also generate such fields, more research must be done to assess the effects.

Form

As we have discussed earlier, form is a vibratory pattern that gives the appearance of solidity because our senses are responding only to the physical effect of motion. As a wheel appears to be solid when spun quickly, so too our world of form is the illusion of existence for the deeper essence of life energy movement. In other words,

Stable forms are actually psychic representations within our consciousness arising from the interactions between our vibrating consciousness and other vibrating fields of energy.[49]

What we see and feel exists, but not the way we experience it. This
is the illusion upon which we also build our worlds. Forms are simply patterns of energy developed through us. Our collective state of
consciousness determines whether we develop forms that help or
work against our evolution. As French engineer Louis Turenne
pointed out, forms are different types of resonators for cosmic energy.
The shape of any object dictates the type of life energy that it distributes and attracts. This is also true of our bodies, organs, chakras, and
ideas. What are buildings, after all, but ideas that are expressed on
paper and later into material?

In addition, forms radiate and concentrate energy. It is well known
that pyramids, for example, gather energy and use this force to retard
disintegration. This is the secret behind mummification, a fact that
milk producers in France and Italy use in packaging their product.
The result is a longer product life without preservatives. Cameron has
shown that a cone, like a pyramid, will give off energy from its apex,
which can be extended by using wires.[50] Reichenbach had demonstrated earlier that crystals give off energy that can be seen and felt
by sensitives. Dr. Gerald Langham's work as a plant geneticist indicates that seeds, when placed in bottles similar in shape to themselves,
increase their germination strength years after storage, which leads
back to the old herbal concept of signatures. I have already mentioned
the treatment of cancer with thyme, which was thought by the Greeks
to resemble the thymus gland, one center of immunization. More
recently, Robert Pavlita in Czechoslovakia has developed a number
of psychotronic generators that function differently according to their
form and the mental programming of the operator but without any
electrical components.

In therapy the radiations from different forms have been used by
Buddhists in Colorado under the leadership of Trungpa Rinpoche to
treat various forms of neurosis. In a system called "space therapy,"
they put people into rooms especially designed to resonate with their
type of neurosis based on the Buddhist concept of "five families." In
principle this is quite similar to the theory of five elements in Chinese medicine, from which the Buddhist approach developed. Theo
Gimbel in England is doing similar work with form and color, also
using the five-elements theory in accordance with the five Platonic
solids: tetrahedron for choleric people, hexahedron for the phlegmatic,
octahedron for the sanguine person, icosahedron for the melancholic,

and the pentagondodecahedron for the centered individual. The collective experience of these people indicates that different forms of disease can be treated and healed with the appropriate energy radiation of form.

Architecture and Building Materials

In architecture form has been used to enhance qualities of life energy. Pyramidlike forms, for example, have been employed by the American Indians, the Chinese in their pagodas, the Aztecs, and of course the Egyptians. Many peoples who dwell in close proximity use the round form, such as the igloos of the Eskimos, the kraals of Africa, and the round houses of the Celtic tribes. More recently, architect Buckminster Fuller has created the geodesic dome, a circular structure made extensively of glass and wood. In the dome the inhabitants can see the sun during the entire day as it rises and sets on their habitat. Fuller developed this geodesic dome by taking a biological microstructure and reflecting this in the macrostructure of a building—a beautiful harmony of learning on one energy level and applying this knowledge on another. According to Fuller, only by experiencing the whole can we fully understand how any system really works. Analyzing the parts of a system, he said, can never give us an understanding of the whole. He used the term *synergy* for this holistic outlook.

Form reinforces our own life energies for better or for worse. Homes and office buildings that support wholeness provide an environment where it is easier for us to stay whole and stay within the cycles of life energy. Architect Gyorgy Doczi has proposed the term *dinergy* for the universal phenomenon of pattern creating based on the generative power of polarities in cooperation, for the words dia (meaning across) and energy. On the other hand, edifices that disturb our wholeness foster disease and disharmony. A huge apartment or office building, for example, made out of steel acts like a Faraday cage by energetically isolating the dwellers, thereby preventing them from exchanging energy with the outside environment. Thus energy charge is being pent up within the internal environment, which changes the energy balance.

An additional problem on the emotional level is that modern living has forced many people to lose contact with the ground. The ground provides both contact with an organic physical reality and an emotional rooting effect.* Lacking contact with the earth, we lose our

*This is despite the fact that steel buildings generally provide a good grounding from lightning, for example.

Energy Radiations

connectedness to our own biological roots and emotional grounding. The result is an emotional flightiness and irritability, great fluctuation in mood, nervousness, and general sense of existential loss, a kind of "not knowing where one is."

Despite the bleak picture in modern architecture, certain trends look promising. A few architects in England are applying the angles and forms of the Pythagorean theorem to enhance living, hospital, and schoolroom space by using/ \ angles to "ground" and practicalize occupants, while using\ /angles to predispose them to creativity, openness, and mood lightening.[51] In the United States hospital wards are being built with colors that have been shown to be effective for certain diseases, thus resonating a healing vibration in the entire atmosphere. John Ott has reported on office buildings that are using full-spectrum light and ultraviolet transmitting plastic windows. Their results show a decrease in worker illness, a 25 percent increase in production, and a better staff rapport. During a flu epidemic, for example, not a single worker had taken ill. More research must be done in this direction because the Hawthorne effect, for example, showed that any change in lighting may lead to a positive psychological effect. However, the increase of resistance to flu is certainly a significant finding, which Ott also found in a restaurant using ultraviolet lighting* for its effect on the white emblems of the waiters' coats.[52]

One major breakthrough in holistic architecture has been the work of Dr. Gerhard Moog and associates in Canada. Because of their total concept in building, they have been able to develop innovations that reduce building time, save money, save energy, increase safety, and reduce noise levels. All their buildings have an energy system that uses the recovered, stored, and recycled wastes given off by the buildings' lights, occupants, and office equipment. They don't even have furnaces! The temperature for the entire system and all security and safety mechanisms are controlled by a computer to minimize energy consumption.

The special glass used provides almost complete insulation from heat and cold and eliminates all drafts. This is accomplished by counteracting the heat or cold from the outside directly on the point of contact at the windows. Most systems "fight" the elements quite a distance from the exterior walls with heaters and air conditioners. Their usage of integrated ceiling design provides better lighting at one third the normal energy cost through the use of reflecting material to better distribute light. Special ceilings minimize the noise to a .92

*Ultraviolet light, known as black light, causes white objects to "glow" (fluoresce).

coefficient (1.0 is perfect), and the windows stop sound from bouncing off them.

Dr. Moog's work shows that holistic thinking is ecologically and personally sound as well as being practical. Wholeness is not an ideal but simply a comprehensive understanding of whatever endeavor we undertake. Moog has shown that these holistic systems save between a third and a half in energy costs, increase floor space from 4 to 10 percent, and provide a more humane environment with reduced noise levels.

Although such a system is a huge step in holism, there is more work to be done. More research, for example, must be done on the effects of building materials on us. We already know some things. Aluminum reflects visible and ultraviolet light very well, which means that it helps in growing plants. As a material often used for cooking, however, aluminum emits disharmonious vibrations to the food as measured radiathesically. Homeopaths know that aluminum can act as a slow, progressive poison after affecting the intestines. Symptoms are frequent passage of flatulence or obstinate constipation. Continued ingestion may lead to heart disease, clotting in blood vessels, ulceration, anemia, and debility.[53] Not every person is aluminum sensitive. One cause of the problem is that aluminum does not occur naturally as a metal in the soil but only in aluminum compounds. It is an extracted and refined metal, which may be a case of an element being isolated from its whole, causing dis-ease in those who are particularly sensitive to its vibration.

Corrugated iron reflects light poorly but, like tin, has a positive effect on plants when placed underground. As a building material, iron reflects noise, making it a noise pollution distributor. Copper is effective in inducing sleep and is a good conductor of electricity as well as life energy.[54] Lead has a devitalizing effect on life energy, though it is useful as a shield against cosmic radiations and medical X-ray equipment.

Concrete in homes and office buildings provides no warmth insulation, which gives it its "cold" feeling. It also allows no humidity to be processed (as does wood, for example), so it doesn't "breathe" with us. It also transmits almost every sound because of its poor absorption, making it also a noise pollution transmitter. Brick, though warmer than concrete, gives off radiations from the earth that may be harmful to health, depending on the type of earth that is used to make it.[55]

To date, the main energy problem with buildings is the lack of awareness and research on the effects of building and household interiors on our lives. Little concern has been paid to the myriad vibrations that we must neutralize every day if we are to remain healthy.

It is not a question of building edifices that are efficient but of creating structures that also support and extend our growth as spiritual beings. One large step would be a greater awareness of the problem and processes of energy radiation; the next step would be a revision of our building codes to include consideration for full-spectrum lighting, radiation-shielded walls, and air systems that support negative ions in the atmosphere. In addition, workplaces should offer the alternative of whole foods and vegetables to the usual processed food fare.

Material is also an energy form, and each one reflects specific energy qualities that we wear in our clothes and surround ourselves with in our homes, offices, and recreation areas. It is known, for example, that organic materials such as wool, cotton, silk, linen, and wood are good conductors of life energy, though wood and silk are not good electrical conductors.[56]

Cork and coconut fibers are better insulators for buildings than fiberglass, which is dangerous to health because of its harmful effects on the lungs. It has been thought that wool carpets could not be used in hospitals because they would increase the level of bacteria there. But research actually shows that no higher bacteria levels were found when wool was used as compared to synthetic fibers. Wool may even hold bacteria until it is cleaned. In addition, wool saves 12-13 percent in heating costs over synthetic fibers.[57]

Synthetic materials, on the other hand, are energetically dangerous because of the buildup of electrical charge that occurs. Dr. Reiter has shown that such materials may generate as much as 10,000 volts per centimeter. Carpets made of synthetics have measured as high as 15,000 volts per centimeter and can cause pain in some individuals, which is not surprising when you touch a metal doorknob after walking across such a carpet. The charge of highly isolated material such as synthetics from carpets, drapes, and other objects can lead to a damaging effect for air ions in living quarters.[58] Recently, one medical researcher showed that synthetic material worn in direct contact with the skin can lead to skin allergies.[59]

A wholeness perspective would advocate using natural fibers and materials wherever possible and emphasize the need for new uses of nature's resources, such as those from the sea, so as not to overtax our present supplies of land resources. In addition to those factors, holistic building must address such important areas of concern as how large our cities are,* how much fresh air and water is available, how

*Studies have shown that the fewer the people there are in a city, the lower the rate of disease (Dr. von Halle-Tischendorf).

quiet the living atmosphere is, how much space for parks and other green areas is provided, how much security from robbery and violence is provided, and how much isolation from unwanted radiant energies and environmental stress factors is provided.

Chapter Five

Medicine and Psychotherapy

Medicine

We have seen that forms give structure to energy processes that have come together in a whole. As such, they are the physical manifestations of an underlying gestalt that seeks greater concretization. This is true of hospitals and all other medical facilities. Hospitals were actually begun by the early Christians as part of the salvation for body and soul. They were so successful with their therapy of prayer and laying on of hands that a fourth-century emperor tried to restore pagan worship by setting up his own hospitals—without success. Later, hospitals became dormitories for the poor, derelicts, and travelers who had no other place to stay. From the Middle Ages to the eighteenth century, hospitals became refuges for the incurables, epileptics, the mad, and all those who basically awaited death. "Nobody," says Illich, "went to a hospital to restore his health." Doctors began to go to hospitals because it became easier to treat patients in one place. Today things seem to have greatly improved; however, a deeper look into the functioning of hospitals casts great doubt on their status as centers for health, for it is here that Western medicine really comes to light. Hospitals provide us with the form to observe the medical process as practiced by our twentieth-century health care practitioners.

Philosophically, Western medicine is still suffering from an anachronistic material form that is dead but lives on through the life-extending machines it has produced. The medical base of this materialism is the germ theory, which began in the era of Newton's classical physics and Descartes's rationalism. Both contributed to a mechanistic, dualistic Weltanschauung (world view), in which matter was considered indestructible, being made of atoms, the basic building blocks of the universe. In bacteriology Pasteur demonstrated that isolated microorganisms can be transposed to other animals, which will also be afflicted with the disease. This was proof enough to start Western medicine down the road to its present development. Because the germs were found prior to the development of disease, causal thinkers of the nineteenth century assumed that these micro-organisms must have caused the disease. This notion still prevails today, though the germ is becoming more and more difficult to defend as the sole agent of disease.

The result of this mechanistic thinking has spread to all parts of medicine. The body is generally seen as a great machine, with its numerous parts all performing their functions until one of them breaks down. Disease is said to occur when germs invade this machine, causing some of the parts to function improperly. When this happens, symptoms of the dysfunction appear as signs of what is going wrong. Different diseases are then classified by their characteristic symptoms. Because the types of symptoms are infinite, only the major ones are used to diagnose a particular disease. This leads to great difficulty when the symptoms are similar for different illnesses. Often a more complete diagnosis is called for, and it is usually done in a hospital or clinic.

Unfortunately, most diagnostic procedures used are still based on this mechanistic model. First, the people who examine us have been taught by working on sick or dead people. They have had little or no experience about what health is or with people who might be considered clinically healthy. This means that their emphasis in training has been on what has gone wrong or terminated in death. Second, the diagnostic procedures may not be accurate. Studies have shown that the electrocardiogram (EKG), a machine used for detecting heart problems, may be interpreted with variations up to 20 percent. Another study showed that the EKG indicated healthy readings in 25 percent of patients with proven cases of heart problems. All this inaccuracy may result from leakage of electricity from one machine to another, clinical incompetence, patient activity, and time of day, among other factors. The EEG (electroencephalogram), which measures brain waves and is used to indicate certain convulsive disorders, may show no abnormal graph for 20 percent of those with clinically established disorders. X-rays, as discussed in Chapter Four, are extremely dangerous to health, even at low levels of operation. And according to Dr. Mendelsohn, medical testing laboratories in the United States are "scandalously inaccurate." In some studies as much as 25 percent of the results were false, 5-12 percent of the labs found something wrong in healthy cases, and only 20 percent of the labs in a nationwide survey produced "acceptable" results 95 percent of the time. All this clearly indicates that there is a large margin for error in several important phases of the medical diagnosis. With the increase in medical technology and automation, this becomes a potentially greater threat to our health.

Another problem is that diagnoses are based on major symptoms that fit a statistical norm. That is, if two people have similar symptoms, there is no guarantee that they will be treated in the same way, and if they are treated equally, how do we know if the treatment fits for each? Statistically, the diagnosis may be accurate but totally miss the person with a treatment that deals only with major symptoms. On other less obvious (but often more important) levels, these treatments may do more harm than good because they don't fit. Because of this mechanistic model, many doctors assume that the problem must be on the physical level, though surveys of doctors have reported that 50-90 percent of the patients' problems are probably due to psychological factors. Many of these may actually be due to other causes affected by environmental pollution, spiritual healing crises, movement of higher energies (e.g., kundalini), nutritional deficiencies, and sociocultural norms. Because Western health care practitioners usually receive little, if any, psychological, nutritional, and cultural training (not to mention personal development work or spiritual training), it would be difficult for them to differentially diagnose anything other than physical diseases. Because they have usually seen and worked with only physical disease, they naturally tend to put every symptom into one of these norm categories. Even the idea of a norm is questionable. Norm comes from the Latin "norma," meaning square, which through the years has developed into a standard of usual states or conditions. Western medicine in large measure is treatment for the usual with mass statistics, generalized symptoms, and classified diseases. What if we don't fit the norm? What if there is no square in which to put us?

Next are the treatments. Because germs are thought to cause disease, they are the major points of intervention in Western medicine. Three major lines of *attack* are used: drug therapy, surgery, and radiation. Drug therapy is beset with problems and complications that are antithetical to health. Drugs used by Western medicine fall under the category of allopathy, which produces a cure by creating a condition opposite to the disease it is treating. As a principle, allopathy supports fighting between the germs and the drugs. This violent approach to therapy leads to more fighting, which, as in politics, is basically no solution. The effect of fighting germs with germicides (germ killers) is the development of stronger strains of germs that become resistant to germicides, which means that we must create new, more powerful

zations in letting out evil spirits (trephining). Though we might shudder at the thought of how these early operations were done, significant meaning was apparently attached to them, physically or psychologically. In modern medicine, amidst the many necessary and life-saving operations, a multitude of unnecessary and dangerous surgeries are performed. Estimates made by a U.S. congressional subcommittee suggest that 2.4 million unnecessary operations are performed each year. In addition to the staggering cost of $4 billion, twelve thousand lives were lost. Children and women account for an important percentage of the unnecessary surgery. Tonsillectomies (removal of the tonsils) account for about 30 percent of all surgery on children, 90 percent of which is considered unnecessary. In England, where tonsillectomies provide little financial incentive for physicians, the surgery rate is one half that of North America.[5]

Worse yet is the plight of women. Estimates suggest that one third to one half of all hysterectomies for removal of the uterus are unnecessary.[6] If current rates continue, half of all American women aged 65 and over could be without their uteruses. Episiotomy—the cutting of the perineum to widen the birth canal during birth—is another questionable surgical intervention. According to Dr. Mendelsohn, there is no evidence that this surgical procedure is necessary when the mother is consciously aiding delivery. Caesarean sections are also increasing, in part because of fetal monitoring by electronic equipment. Studies show that Caesareans are performed 3 to 4 times as often when this equipment rather than a simple stethoscope is used. Mendelsohn has pointed out that induced labor before an organic point of delivery can cause a natural distress for the baby, often resulting in a Caesarean. Are women becoming so much less flexible that an essentially natural process is becoming more difficult, or are doctors too ready to induce labor and cut when difficulties arise? Postoperative complications occur in half the women after such surgery and have a mortality rate of 26 times that for normal delivery. We really must question how important such operations are.

As for radiation treatment, much evidence has been uncovered concerning the dangers of such procedures and the questionableness of the need for such treatment. How can we justify the use of such radiation when there has been almost no research on the healthy radiations that come from a human being? By creating the external radiations of machines and then testing them on humans, we put the emphasis on the machines, not on us. Modern Western medicine has not yet accepted that humans also radiate energy, despite the work of researchers such as Burr and Tiller, as well as countless naturopaths and dousers using pendulums and dousing rods. Interestingly, in Germany, where healing practitioners (Heilpraktiker) work with such radiation, many medical doctors, after giving up on Western medicine to help themselves, go to the "competition." There must be something in these radiations, though very few of these doctors would admit to this fact. In the United States such information is denied because such radiational healing practices are illegal; nevertheless, there is a large underground movement that will eventually surface to become a recognized scientific pursuit.

One major criticism of orthodox medicine to these ancient but newly revived radiational techniques concerns research. Indeed, more standardized work must be done. One limitation on such research is that we really have only a few pieces of technical equipment that can measure some of these levels of energy or their emanations. By the same token, orthodox medicine, when seen from a real scientific point of view, lacks this precision in another way. According to Dr. Roberts, director of the U.S. National Bureau of Standards, one half or more of the data used in scientific research is unusable because it could not be proven that what was thought to be measured was in fact measured, nor was there evidence that potential error sources had been eliminated. These facts, combined with frauds in drug research, for example, do not justify considering such medical documentation as scientific. In addition, the closed-mindedness of many scientists and researchers to such themes as cancer and energy radiation does not befit the term scientific research. Researchers who are really looking for cancer cures should be open to all avenues, not only those presently accepted. Despite the fact that accepted avenues have shown little result, money continues to pour into such projects, while new areas of research such as nutrition and energetic radiation go unregarded. Such narrowness shows a basic fear of new ideas.

There is, however, a clear trend in medicine today to return to natural treatment. More and more doctors are becoming aware of the limits of their medicines and technological procedures. Patients too are becoming more aware of the dangers of modern medicine and are looking to alternative approaches. There is a boom in natural treatment of all types, ranging from chiropractic and osteopathic alignments* to preventive care, nutritional and vitamin therapies, fasting cures, massage (East and West), homeopathic and radionics treatments, color therapy, acupuncture, and so on. Many medical doctors are training with their former competitors, chiropractors (in the

---

*The art of adjusting bones for the benefit of energy flow has been known for at least 32 centuries by the Greeks, Chinese, and Hindus. It was formerly known as rachiotherapy (Ligeros, p. 53).

United States) and Heilpraktikers (in Germany), because of their success and knowledge of natural remedies. Clearly we need to return to the basis from which medicine began. We would be foolish to blame and criticize what has gone on in the past, and yet we should refuse to accept the abuses and unhealthy practices of modern medicine. Instead we must look clearly at the benefits and advances in modern medicine, especially those in emergency procedures and technical operations, while clearly disregarding what is unnecessary and not holistic. We could learn to look at diagnostic classifications of disease as a solid background in description, and at advances and further clarifications in anatomy and physiology as a solid base of body dynamics, without accepting this as the complete picture of human functioning/dysfunctioning. We could use all this to accept what fits in a new holistic model of health and discard what has proven to be unwarranted in theory, diagnosis and treatment.

All early medicine was based on wholeness. From the early associations of nature's movements—the blowing of the wind, the movement of the water, storms, earthquakes, eclipses of the sun and moon—with demons and gods, primitive man began to make connections between health/disease states and processes outside and inside himself. Among most primitive cultures the healer was both priest and physician because the cause of disease was considered supernatural. Therefore the medicine man or shaman served both roles because there was no distinction between physical disease and spiritual cause. This sense of wholeness reflects the early basis of unity between the spiritual and physical worlds. Modern medicine, unfortunately, has all but completely lost this connection to the spirit.

The roots of holistic medicine are located in the words themselves. A physician (L. physica: natural science) is basically a student of nature, while a doctor (L. docere: to teach) is a teacher. The practice of medicine (L. medicina: medi, healing, balance and cina, ingested substance) might be seen as the art of students and teachers of nature who facilitate the art of balance, one factor being ingested substances. If we go even further, we find that the Sanskrit root of medicine is medha, meaning wisdom. We are talking then about a practice in wisdom, whereby the balance or wholeness of life energy can be taught and learned by the study and practice of nature's processes. In the study of healing two symbols have been carried into the present. The first is R_x, which comes from an Egyptian word for the Eye of Horus and symbolizes healing. The other symbol is the insignia used for medicine in pharmacies and hospitals, called the caduceus. Though its roots have all but been forgotten, the caduceus was an Egyptian symbol for life and health, representing the two dynamic aspects of life energy: the left represents the feminine principle (lunar, contractive, yin, and Shakti), while the right stands for the masculine principle (solar, expansive, yang, and Shiva). Together the dynamic balance of both forms creates a wholeness in our expression and impression of life energy. A version of this symbol called the Staff of Aesculapius, with only one snake and energy movement, is also widely used.

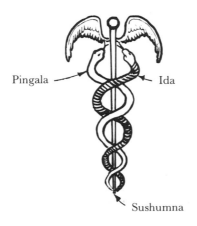

Figure 18. The Caduceus, the "winged snake staff," the sign or staff of Hermes. The Caduceus is the western counterpart to the energy canals and chakras in the human body according to the Indian system of Kundalini. The staff symbolizes the Sushumna-Nadi, the snakes of Ida- and Pingala-Nadis. Where the snakes cross there lie the six body chakras (the seventh chakra above the head is represented by the ball on top of the staff).

If we are to return to a wholeness of health and life, we must see the harmony and balance in all we do. This was essentially the basis for the healing practiced by Hippocrates, the father of modern medicine, who based his system on the concept of the organism as a unity (physis), unlike some of his predecessors, whose theories fostered separation. Among his theories, Hippocrates believed that a sick body will stimulate its own natural forces to reestablish good health and that the good physician will only intervene in the most natural way. In addition, he placed much emphasis on good diet, stress-free lifestyle, baths, and laying on of hands. He also believed in a healing energy that could pass from person to person and the science of chiropraxy. Though Hippocrates left no codified science of medicine that we know about, he developed the Hippocratic oath, which is still used by doctors today. Among the features of this oath are his promise to teach others at no cost, give prescriptions that do not cause injury, and give money to his teachers, should they need it. He also believed that drugs that produce similar symptoms in the healthy could cure the diseased. This idea of "similar curing similars" has been the major tenet of homeopathy, a system that was seen as a rival to the allopathic approach of orthodox medicine.

Like Hippocrates and Homer before him, Samuel Hahnemann believed that germs appear only after the person's system has been disturbed in some fundamental way. Unlike the mechanistic approach of the allopaths, homeopaths believe in a vitalist explanation of disease, saying that it is the body's attempt at healing. Physical symptoms are simply manifestations of this healing crisis, not the cause of the disease itself. In terms of energy, the vitalist approach is much closer to the current research in subatomic physics. Because matter has been shown to be a manifestation of energy, germs, like all living things, are extensions of an energy process. Therefore they cannot be the beginning of disease because energy is always in movement. So germs at most are a physical manifestation of an energy process that preceded their appearance and continues beyond it. Only in classical physics does a beginning and end even distinctly exist. This idea has not been supported by research. Indeed, quantum physicists find that nothing can be isolated but must instead be seen as a whole. Subatomic particles are constantly in motion, combining with one another, dividing through collisions, only to recombine again.

Hahnemann believed what the modern physicists find in their research, namely, that any research must consider the whole of the situation. Hahnemann, in his *Homeopathy*, considered all the symptoms of the patients, unlike his allopathic colleagues. He tested his drugs on healthy humans, whereas allopaths usually test on animals or sick humans. In addition, he considered several levels of energy in his diagnosis and treatment, finding that his drugs, often containing minuscule amounts of physical, chemical substances, worked simultaneously on a number of these levels. Orthodox medicine recognizes only the physical level and assumes that all disease begins on this level. But Dubrov's research has shown, for example, that cells communicate disease in nonphysical ways, proving that this single-level approach cannot be the whole truth. Hahnemann believed that this subtle level of energy is used in the self-healing process, which he supported through his physically weak but subtly potent medications. In Germany, Professor Hildebert Wagner has recently shown that the higher, more subtle dosages also have a biological effect on the immunology of organisms. In a practical comparison of allopathy and homeopathy during a severe cholera epidemic in the United States and Europe in 1832, homeopathy was found to be superior to allopathy.[7]

Ironically, several homeopathic principles and remedies are currently in use in orthodox medicine. Among these are the use of quinine in malaria treatment, mercury compounds for syphilis, X-rays for cancer (X-rays both cause and treat cancer), and iodine for thyroid conditions. Perhaps the most important use of homeopathic principles is that of vaccines in immunization. By administering a small dosage of a disease, it is possible to set up in the body a defense reaction to the disease later. This is a form of treatment by similars, which Edward Jenner independently substantiated at around the same time that Hahnemann formulated homeopathy. Even Emil A. Von Behring, discoverer of the tetanus antitoxin, spoke of this immunological finding:

And by what technical term could we more appropriately speak of this influence exerted by a SIMILAR virus, than by Hahnemann's word "Homeopathy"?[8]

If we turn briefly to Eastern medicine, we see the same holistic approach exemplified by homeopathy. The use of acupuncture, moxibustion, Shiatsu, and diet in the treatment of disease all reflect principles of balance, energy flow, interrelationship of organs with emotions, and self-help, as well as treatment by specialists. Eastern physicians' use of diagnosis, including a very intricate and accurate use of pulse diagnosis and the ingenious use of physical exercise to strengthen and treat the body, is truly a marvel to study and experience. In China it was customary to receive preventive medicine and change the diet with the coming of the different seasons, as well as to *not* pay the doctor if one got sick. If you got sick it meant that the doctor hadn't done his job!

Though many orthodox physicians have forgotten their roots in the holy (shamans), in the whole (Hippocrates), in the teaching (doctor), in the balance (medicine), in the unity of polarities (yin/yang), in the principles of nature (physician), and in the law of similars (homeopathy), the movement of harmony continues throughout orthodox medicine, even though many of those who practice holistic medicine are not accepted by the established powers. Homeopathic medicine is alive and well in Germany, and its costs are only a fraction of those of allopathic medicine. Both physicians and Heilpraktikers practice this art and science. Germany is one of the few places in the world where orthodox and nonorthodox treatment share a common healing heritage.

A number of other holistic influences on orthodox medicine are in use today. I have already mentioned the use of light and color therapy with neonatal jaundice, skin tuberculosis, cold sores, and blisters. Laying on of hands, called "therapeutic touch," has been demonstrated to positively affect both hemoglobin levels (Doris Krieger) and anxiety levels (Patricia Heidt) in patients. Both of these women are nurses using therapeutic touch in their practice, and Krieger has taught hundreds of other nurses and doctors to use this technique in their everyday duties. Megavitamin therapy has been used quite effectively with certain cases of schizophrenia, alcoholism, and hyperactivity.[9] Biofeedback, often called Western meditation, has been used quite extensively for pain reduction, hypertension, and cardiovascular dysfunctioning (e.g., blood circulation difficulties and arhythmic heart disorders). Biofeedback works on vitalist principles of feeding back technical data to the person about his body, which he can learn to alter or redirect. Thus both the disease and healing process are governed by alive communication between body and mind—a truly psychoemosomatic approach. Today, many medical clinics throughout the world are using biofeedback techniques to treat disease.

Western use of classical acupuncture has greatly increased since its inception in France, Germany, and later in the United States. Western researchers have also augmented their treatments with electrical stimulation of the needles, in addition to sonar and laser applications. Some Western doctors have also used hand manipulation of certain acupuncture points called "trigger points."

In Germany surgeons are using magnetic fields to increase the rapidity for healing of broken bones. Although these treatments are healing bones that have failed to respond to normal treatment and the rate of success is about 92 percent, this technique is still not accepted by the doctors' board as a proven method despite abundant physical proof that it works (e.g., X-rays before and after) and that it is currently being practiced in 21 clinics. Even though magnetic treatments have been practiced for ten years by several practitioners, all respected surgeons, the insurance companies refuse to pay for these treatments in Germany, where almost every bona fide medical treatment is covered.

When we look at the history of Western medicine, with its tremendous potential for integrative health practice, and then look at what has been done in the name of health, with unnecessary surgery, overuse and irresponsible use of drugs and radiation, we might become angry or give up. But it is easy to criticize the doctors (lumping them all together), the drug companies, or society for the present situation. Instead, we must clearly look at what we have allowed to happen to us, often as willing victims, and decide if we are now ready to do something about this set of events. We must look deeply into the true nature of medicine and health and decide which way our paths run—toward increased dependency or greater personal responsibility. One way we can move toward a more conscious and healthy lifestyle is to accept and support the positive and holistic procedures and people in medicine that foster a life-positive approach toward personal care while rejecting those that endanger our health and even our lives. Many of our health practitioners (doctors, nurses, chiropractors, Heilpraktikers, and so on) are truly interested in health in the purest sense of the word. We must support them with our knowledge and awareness while not blindly relying on them. Healing is something that only we can do, partly alone, and partly with the help of specialists.

Psychotherapy

As with medical therapy, we must reexamine the nature and practice of psychotherapy. There are so many misconceptions among professionals and laypeople alike. It is indeed surprising, for example, how many people still consider psychotherapy a treatment exclusively for the crazy or weak-willed. Part of the problem is tied to the history of psychotherapy, while another part is bound to what Thomas Szasz has called the myth of psychotherapy.

Western psychotherapy began as an offshoot of nineteenth-century medical practice and has still not managed to break itself completely free. Neurosis was generally seen as a medical problem caused by some malfunction of the nervous system. Hence the early treatment was based on the concepts that nerves exhibit electrical activity and therefore electrotherapy might prove useful. Even Sigmund Freud began his work as a neurologist and electrotherapist. The later development of shock therapy applied to the brain only served to reinforce this basically medical and physical view of neurosis. Then came psychosurgery, the most common of which is a lobotomy, in which the nerves between the thalamus and the cortex are cut. The result is usually a permanent passivity. One study in the United States showed that as of 1964, 50,000 lobotomies had already been performed, two thirds of them on women. Since then, new techniques for rendering parts of the brain inactive include ultrasonic waves, electrical coagulation, and implantation of radium seeds.[10] None of this, however, can be called psychotherapy. Modern psychosurgery is clearly separatist and serves only the purpose of societal control. Psychoactive drugs to enhance mood or depress excitation have also been added to the medical arsenal in the "fight" against "mental illness." At best psychoactive drugs control behavior while providing a measure of inorganic balance. At worst they may destroy energetic vitality (much of which is expressed in anger) and leave patients as "vegetables" in the back of some forgotten hospital ward. Under certain specific circumstances, these drugs may be warranted and useful for short periods to help stabilize a dangerous condition. However, the present medical distribution of drugs for all types of neurotic disturbances has proven unnecessary, dependency provoking, dangerous, and devitalizing to the real healing process.

In general, psychiatry is convinced that mental problems are a type of illness like other more organic diseases and should be so treated. Like their medical colleagues, psychiatrists are trained by working with dysfunctional people termed patients (L.: sick, suffering). This holds true for most other helping professions as well, despite the fact that numerous authors (Szasz, Laing, Goffman) have pointed out the "myth of mental illness."

Mental disturbance is not illness in the medical model, although some genetic and chemical qualities may coexist. As Freud pointed out, many states are multidetermined, the precise, singular cause of which may never be found. In fact, this incessant looking for *the* cause to everything, be it the origin of cancer or an emotional problem, keeps us in a mechanical model of cause and effect, thesis and antithesis, which results in linearity, rigidity, and ultimately splitting the nature of dis-ease. How can we expect to heal mental dis-ease (not illness), let alone acquire a clear picture about these states, if our processes of diagnosis and intervention are equally, if not more, disturbed than the problems themselves?

The unending looking for the "what" of dis-ease is ultimately an attempt to grasp an enemy that we then can do battle with—and of course defeat. This is where the roles of patient as possessed victim and psychotherapist as conqueror over evil arises. Of course the therapist, disguised as helper, is often looking for the mental "germ" that has caused the illness. Insistence on the medical/mechanical approach to problems, however, is not the only difficulty in psychotherapy today. Many of our professionals are poorly trained.

Good training will help teach an aspiring psychotherapist about his/her limitations as well as potentials. Holistic psychotherapy demands this balance. Many training programs throughout the world lack personal therapy. This essential part of the classical analytic schools has sometimes been lost in the proliferation of new psychotherapists. In India even the medical doctors were required to work with themselves—in ashrams (centers for spiritual study)—before completing their studies. Such inquiry is essential for clarity and purpose in therapeutic work.

Another feature of this self-inquiry is that we learn again to place the power of the healing in people, not in theories and techniques. Many therapies emphasize how their theories and techniques succeed but almost never how they fail. However, research consistently points out that the personal relationship between the therapist and therapee by far outweighs any theoretical orientation of the therapist.[11] Research with computers and laypeople as therapists also points to the same conclusion.[12] The *process* between both parties is the essential factor in therapeutic change, not the seeking of "germs." These germs may prove interesting but not essential. The learning process in therapeutic training, however, is not an intellectual one. According to Carl Rogers,

> Intellectual training [for psychotherapists] and the acquiring of information has I believe many valuable results—but becoming a therapist is not one of those results.[13]

Another problem besetting psychotherapy is the question of its usefulness. Some people see no use in therapy, either from their own negative experience or from misunderstanding what they have read in popular articles. On the other hand, therapy "addicts" almost live on therapy and cannot make any major life decision without first consulting their therapist. What these people learn in therapy has little to do with external reality and consequently generalizes very poorly.

Therapy has little place as a luxury, though it may become so even when therapist and client don't intend it. It is costly, time-consuming, and often disruptive (at least of old patterns).

Some clients feel that they are doing all they can by being in therapy—any kind of therapy—but this is often not the case. A therapy that helps us continue to fool ourselves with false supportive statements when confrontation is appropriate—or constant confrontation with what is not working in our lives instead of support for what is—is a luxury. The former is a luxury of self-indulgence, the latter a luxury of self-negation. Neither style will produce very effective results, though both may feed deeper needs on our part and that of the therapist.

Psychotherapy is also burdened by what I call a disease of process. It is customary in almost all hospitals and clinics, and in most private practices, to establish a clinical diagnosis for anyone seeking help. Diagnosing the problem usually means labeling the client in terms of disease,

believe that feeling pain or being aggressive is more important than other emotions.

Social psychologist Berkowitz has shown that angry retaliation against an aggressor may actually raise instead of lower the level of hostility. This suggests that how catharsis is carried out is as important, if not more so, than actually expressing an emotion. My clinical experience is that sadness, for example, can lead to other sadnesses ad infinitum if crying is not properly handled. Any emotional release can be used against wholeness, just as a healthy emotional expression can relieve many problems. It is not a question of catharting or not, but how one releases emotions, that shows its worth as a useful therapeutic process.

The therapy of behavior-oriented change is uninterested in insight because it is an intrapsychic factor that cannot be adequately measured by behavioral criteria. Like insight, behavioral change alone is limited as a criterion for developmental change. Therapies of behavioral change may deal only with external processes without touching the reason for these behaviors. In many cases the deeper problem simply shifts to other behaviors. Behavioral therapy seems most effective when a directed, focused treatment is needed, as in cases of phobia, socially inappropriate behavior, and short-term therapy. Over the past 20 years, behavioral therapy has become more holistic because of the need to extend and improve clinical results. Feelings and ideas are now often considered as internal behavior,[17] though many early behavioral theories did not consider them so because they are not external phenomena. A very effective type of behavioral therapy, called implosive therapy, even helps clients to confront their fears by experiencing them with full emotionality.[18] This is a type of catharsis. Because behavior modification has elements of correcting irrational ideas and direct expression of emotions, both insight and catharsis are also part of their behavior change.

From the insight side, even psychoanalysts modify behavior by establishing the rules of what is acceptable in terms of important material and by responding in supportive ways to acceptable content. In addition, says Strupp:

> The psychoanalytic psychotherapist's detachment and inscrutability as advocated by Freud permits him to exert a much more powerful influence as a change agent than a 'sharing' or self-disclosing attitude recommended by other therapists.[19]

Despite this, however,

As a model for producing changes in behavior the psychoanalytic model...has been fairly unimpressive.[20]

The lines that once divided insight, feeling, and behavioral therapy from each other are clearly eroding, because only in the whole does each manifestation of energy have meaning. Personal change and spiritual evolution cannot be isolated to any one part of us, because each energy process is related. Holistic psychotherapy demands a much broader perspective than any single package of theoretical constructs or techniques can supply.

The problem in psychotherapy today is not in the process but in the misunderstanding of its true nature. The word *therapy* comes from the Greek *therapeia*, meaning healing. The prefix *psycho* refers to the psyche, which means soul, spirit, and breath, as we have seen. So psychotherapy, is the art of healing the spirit through the wholeness of the soul using the medium of the breath. In principle and practice this is a far cry from anything we know as psychotherapy today. The concepts of soul and spirit have been reduced to psychological terms of the mind; and the breath, except for breath therapists and body psychotherapists, has been almost forgotten in the West. In the East, of course, the breath in yoga and exercises of Ki (for the martial arts) is very much alive.

Even the issues and themes of psychotherapy are confused by its own theoretical constructs. We often hear about a new "self-image," "bringing out one's personality," the importance of "strengthening weak ego functions," and "analyzing the character problems" in clinical settings. Though some of this work may be helpful, most of it actually supports the problems of separation from the whole by focusing on what I call trace problems and psychological limits (see Chapter 6).

The concept of self-image is tied ultimately to what an image is. The word *image* is derived from the Greek *mayos*, which is related to the Sanskrit word *maya*, for illusion. What sense is there in developing a better self-image or illusion of ourselves? We would only hold onto that like everything else. Holding on is a basic energy problem, which leads to both neurosis and physical disease. Therefore, work on our image has little to do with essence. We don't need an image of ourselves if we arc alive; we sense that living reality by just being. The same is true of personality. Personality is derived from the Latin *persona*, meaning mask. It too is an image that we show the world in some type of consistent way; it may be partly related to biophysical, organization, or unique qualities of a person, though it rarely concerns itself with the essence,* according to modern psychology.[21] A personality,

*Allport is an exception.

if it has any validity as a psychological concept, must be related to essence. It must represent a particular process of wholeness connected with our spirit; otherwise it is simply a description of internal/external behaviors. In any case personality work is still working with the extensions of wholeness but not the deeper energy problems or solutions, so deeper change and growth are minimized. Why should we work on having a better mask or performing certain roles? The true issues are in the basic expressions of absolute reality, which is spiritual by nature. Therefore a psychotherapy of the personality can bring little meaningful evolution.

What about character? Like personality, character only has validity because of its relationship to wholeness. It is generally defined as the aggregate of features, traits, and attitudes that form the individual. Originally in psychoanalysis, character traits were believed to develop from socially conditioned primitive impulses. Wilhelm Reich showed that character has more than traits to it by representing it as a typical mode of reaction. Character formation occurs, he believed, as a result of the threatening outer world and repression of instinctual urges. Psychotherapy of the character came to be known as character analysis after Reich.

The word *character* is derived from the Greek word for engraving instrument (charakter). Character is something etched into us. But *what* is etched into *what?* Subsequent therapeutic research has found that in addition to a major mode of dealing with life situations, there are other "character" behaviors that are related though distinct. If we examine the nature of character, we find first that we cannot work with only one set of character traits because other ways of dealing with the world are related. This means that a comprehensive therapy must deal with other sets of behaviors (minicharacters?) as well. Second, in therapy we are working with people in evolution, not characters alone. It is quite possible to work on the character(s) and never humanly touch the person behind that character, not to mention his/her spirit. Third, the energy involved in the character behaviors and attitudes is the least alive because it is the most fixed. Therefore, therapy on this level encounters resistance from the beginning. Fourth, character therapy work essentially deals with the most negative and least open part of the person, so little emphasis is paid to the dynamic, exciting, and healthy parts of the person. Finally, character behaviors are best understood as energy processes. This allows us to talk about an oral, hysterical process without labeling anyone as an oral character, for example. Thus we can use all the movements of energy within a person as a dynamic network of interrelations without getting stuck in analyzing single sets of behaviors. Every person is a mixture of character processes anyway.

The ego is another main aspect of Western therapy. Most theorists describe it as the executive of the personality, which realistically selects and responds to environmental stimuli for the purpose of integration. Its main task is to mediate between the instinctual demands of the id and the conditions of the surrounding environment. Other theorists describe the ego as the conscious mind (Jung), the determiner of the individual's adjustment (Murray), the developer of congruent behavior (Allport), and the director of conscious behavior (ego analysts). Unfortunately, even though the ego plays an important role in human development, it has never been seen for what it is— simply a manifestation of wholeness on the psychological level of energy. As such, it is only one of many processes in which wholeness is active. However, it has been separated out of a larger wholeness and given too important a place in psychological theory. It is often referred to as a small computer in the brain.

Let us not forget that these concepts are simply constructs to describe processes that have many parallels on other energy levels. However, because the psychological dimension in man has been emphasized instead of, say, the spirit, the ego has undeservedly stood apart from other holistic processes.

This isolation of certain parts of wholeness has been the main problem of psychological theory and psychotherapy. Basically, any aspect of image, personality, character, or ego that has worth in a psychotherapeutic context is related to some aspect of wholeness. Each is only a particular perspective related to a larger order.* As a whole they are best described as organized patterns of energy that are extended in action. They are no more important than other processes of wholeness.

Psychotherapy is itself in a process of evolution. Throughout the years we have learned a considerable amount about this special interaction. Despite the limited potential of insight, Freud opened up many therapeutic roads for the rest of us to pursue. His study on transference from patient to therapist and the therapist's own counterproductive attitudes (countertransferences) is still a useful perspective on therapeutic energy exchange. His work with defenses and resistances revealed much about energy blockages and how they might be alleviated in continued therapy. Freud's interest in the systematization of technique, notably interpretation, provided a basis for timing

*The philosophy of scholasticism, for example, also believed that the ego was comprised of the whole man, body and soul.

and focus that is essential for therapeutic work in general and energy work in particular if translated into process and movement concepts. As has been shown elsewhere,[22] the psychoanalytic model, when revised, can be used quite well to describe how energy becomes perceptually focused or withdrawn with attention to stimuli.

Alfred Adler introduced the concepts of a lifestyle and the creative self by which we supposedly make our own personality, two concepts that were the antithesis of the Freudian doctrines of man as victim. Adler's interest in the birth order of the child and social position revealed two other aspects of therapeutic importance. Jung's emphasis on the aims and aspirations of the client (teleology) led us to consider the future in therapy. His interest in the racial and universal aspects (collective unconsciousness) of life, as well as his study of Eastern life principles, considerably broadened the scope of therapeutic work. From this research he developed the concept of the "self,"—the part in us that seeks wholeness.

Wilhelm Reich demonstrated the importance of working with the body and mind as a functional unity. In addition to his brilliant clinical work with individuals, Reich made the connection from the individual through the social to the cosmic levels in his study of weather, atmospheric orgone, and nuclear radiation. He clearly showed that life energy is a physical phenomenon that can be measured and used in therapy.

Carl Rogers, founder of client-centered therapy, has shown us the need for a *human* therapist (warm, empathic, trustworthy, responding) in the therapeutic relationship. Under client-centered therapy, the medicalized and passive "patient" became the client, an active partner in the dyadic relationship. From behavioral modification therapy we learned about the quality of reinforcer and a greater precision in researching and describing what actually happens in therapy. Suddenly the *results* of therapy became important—this was the beginning of the end for luxury therapy that produced little change.

In the 1920s Psychodrama introduced the possibilities of group work, role reversals, the existence of our own internal roles, and later sociodrama, where a real-life social situation is expressed in drama. The group phenomenon has been extended in studies of group process and later in encounter therapy, which emphasizes confrontation, both positive and negative. This has opened up the use of group energy as a place for feedback, sharing, and emotional release.

Founded on the teachings of Gestalt psychology, Zen Buddhism, and Wilhelm Reich among others, Gestalt therapy has brought us the continuum of awareness and the concept of the "here and now." It emphasizes an existential experience of time and space as it applies to a totality of identification and responsibility for life. Besides bringing to therapy a practical, spontaneous, moment-to-moment awareness, Fritz Perls, one of the founders of Gestalt therapy, brought humor and vivacity to therapy, both of which were generally lacking.

Although they are almost unknown in the West, we have much to learn from Eastern methods of psychotherapy, developed from the Oriental traditions of religion, philosophy, and lifestyle. Norita therapy, for example, emphasizes living productively despite symptoms of disease by becoming less attached to the symptoms and becoming more involved in meaningful activity. Naikan therapy has shown how introspection can lead to an awareness of how unappreciative we have been in life; it reinterprets the past by providing a fresh meaning of gratefulness to it. It is not based on the insight of "why" things are, as in causality, but on a new perspective about the meaning of people in one's life.

A host of other therapies and therapeutic influences could be mentioned, but for our purposes, suffice it to say that psychotherapeutic methods and processes are not isolated events but have developed and grown from one another and have been part of a continuing flow of life energy themselves. Each has contributed to a more complete understanding of the therapeutic process. Each has been a specific form of energy manifestation that was important in its time, a vital part of the *form-geist*.

Today we need forms and processes that more appropriately resonate with current advances in understanding. This need is particularly apparent in the field of psychotherapy. Two foci of this necessity have emerged. First we need a more comprehensive perspective about the nature of psychotherapy and the levels of dis-ease that it purports to treat. Our present approaches are in general extremely limited in their scope as to the origin of dis-ease. Most problems are seen as being based exclusively in psychological dynamics. But let us not forget, that psych-ology has its roots in the logos of the psyche or the wholeness (order) of the soul, spirit, mind, and breath. The dynamics of so-called psychological processes represent only one level of energy. Other considerations include disturbances of the spirit, body, society, and environment. A comprehensive psychothcrapy demands an extremely broad overview of what the wholeness of the psyche really means, and present forms rarely include such a far-reaching perspective. Because of their limited vision, they deal with a very narrow range of problems. Even Western systems with theoretical roots in cosmic phenomena or Eastern philosophies have had difficulty integrating this background into the practical foreground of therapeutic technique and lifestyle.

In addition, many types of therapy compete with others for the position as *the* therapy for the cure of neurosis or anything else. Unfortunately, there is no ideal therapy, just as there is no singular path to evolution. Most forms of therapy work best with certain kinds of problems and people. Psychotherapy should let go of this competitive stance and clearly look at which therapeutic processes work best for which people and why. Implied here is a common basis of operation from which to compare different methods and processes.

Another major deterrent to greater wholeness in psychotherapy has been its disconnection with the natural sciences. Professionals on both sides have often assumed that the methods and knowledge of the "other" have little to do with one's own area of interest. Nothing could be further from the truth.

Psychotherapists and scientists could learn from Eastern and Western mysticism, which provide a way (Tao), philosophy, and experience of wholeness invaluable for a complete concept of healing. As Capra so aptly commented in *The Tao of Physics* through a paraphrase of an old Chinese saying:

Mystics understand the roots of the Tao but not its branches; scientists understand its branches but not its roots. Science does not need mysticism and mysticism does not need science, but man needs both.[23]

If wholeness exists, the laws (logos) of this harmony should be applicable in every area because they are all related. One reason for the separation among the sciences and their disconnection to mystical thought has been the lack of a common language, which is mandatory if greater integration is to take place. This work suggests that the concept of life energy would provide such a basis. Thus, whether we talk about chemical or physical reactions, emotions, behavior, or consciousness, we could describe all of these in energy terms. An important factor in this ancient/new vernacular would be the inclusion of qualitative aspects of energy as described in this text, as well as the usual quantitative factors. The main focus of this language would be process, not content, befitting both the nature of life energy and the direct relationship of process to wholeness.

Once an interdisciplinary language based on energy has been established and the perspective of psychotherapy has been broadened, the second principal need of psychotherapy must be fulfilled. This is the necessity for developing a specific form of psychotherapy that could take this new, widened overview and the integrated language of process and involve them in a practical system of therapy and lifestyle.

In order to have a wide range of application and benefit from the evolution of psychotherapeutic knowledge, this new form should be rooted in both the ancient wisdom of the past and the scientific research of the present. The ancient knowledge has proven to be meaningful throughout the years in various cultures concerning the energy relationship of man, his environment, and his therapeutic interaction. This new form of psychotherapy should also be based on both the natural and metaphysical sciences (e.g., radiational physics), because together they provide a comprehensive understanding of the physical and nonphysical world.

In addition, this new form should make some radical and some transformational changes in the current practice of psychotherapy. It must return to its roots as a healing art because its functional parameters would be expanded to all areas of personal wholeness. Psychology, as the term is currently used, would be insufficient by itself as the new therapy's focus of activity. Instead therapy would be based on the dynamic processes of the spirit and the evolution of the soul. In *The Myth of Psychotherapy* Thomas Szasz has made the same point:

Psychotherapy is a modern, scientific sounding name for what used to be called the 'cure of souls.'[24]

And later:

The essence of all therapy...[is] spiritual healing.[25]

The concepts of soul and spirit bring a wholeness to psychotherapy that is missing in its current practice. Ironically, the word *psychiatrist* comes from a reshuffling of "the healer of the soul" (iatros tes psyches).

From this broadened perspective, psychotherapy cannot be limited to insight, behavior, emotions, mind, ego, personality, character, and image. It is more than the "healing words" (iatrologic) of Szasz, who sees psychotherapy best described as a combination of rhetoric and logic. After all, therapy (healing) is more than a logical sales "pitch." Though words can be healing when connected to a larger whole, present therapeutic use often supports dis-ease by talking about issues instead of wholeness and the blocks that we put in the way.

A new therapy must both broaden current theories and practices and be open to radically new concepts. As a beginning, psychotherapy in the service of evolution must look beyond the ego to other, more complete levels of wholeness. In these realms the concentration on the "I" aspects of who we are must give way to simply *the whole*, in which no individual interests or needs exist. In Sanskrit ego means

"I, the doer." Higher evolution insists on reaching a stillness in which the doing quality of life is quieted. This doesn't mean that nothing is done; it does mean that no-thing is done. In effect, while there is no doing from a personal point of view, everything is done as an energy flow. So the ego is best understood as an organizational process of wholeness that yields in higher states of evolution to more complete processes.

On the physical level, we should emphasize the importance of the body in any process of healing. Although this seems rather obvious, most therapies still deny its importance. What is being "healed" in the mind if the body isn't there? Can we really believe that the head is not part of the body? But we must see the body in its true nature. Nonpsychotherapeutic body work often separates the body from the mind and emotions, as though a restructuring of the body form were enough. This realignment can certainly be helpful, but is has little to do with spiritual evolution when done separately from the whole. The body as form is only one manifestation of life energy; it has no essence outside the spirit.

Body approaches that do include emotions and insight in their work often fail to understand that it is not the body that must be stressed or "released," for "we are our bodies" only on the physical level. Stressing certain parts of the body to bring out specific emotions is based on the erroneous assumption that particular emotions as content are held in the body. The truth is that if you work in a distinct way with muscles, different emotions emerge. A good example of this is the masseter muscle of the jaw. In muscular-oriented stress therapy, pushing on this muscle usually brings out anger. However, if you massage this muscle gently or start minute vibrations there, sadness, sexual feelings, or fear will emerge. So which emotion is being held there? Clearly, no particular emotion, only energy, because emotions are processes, not content.

All emotions are related and quickly move from one expression to another depending on how we work with them. From our point of view, holding energy in the musculature is a function of energy patterns, not bound content. After all, the only reason that a muscle holds anything is because the energy of awareness is there. Repression of emotions in the muscles only works at all because of a continuous supply of energy invested in that boundness. When we are sick or under hypnosis, the musculature of the armoring lessens or disappears completely. Are we to believe that the character structure that supposedly corresponds to muscular armoring and helps defend us suddenly vanishes? And what about neurosis? Are we any less neurotic because our armoring isn't palpable? In some ways yes, because in sickness we don't have the physical energy to be as psychologically disturbed. In other ways no, because the neurosis is a pattern of disease that remains within. But in both cases neurosis is an energy pattern manifest only because of an energy investment and maintained internally because of the interwoven quality of energy activity. So it is not the muscular holding that is the neurosis but the energy pattern that is disturbed and manifests itself on the exterior as muscular armor.

But even the concept of armoring isn't completely true because, for example, oral character processes show hypotonic muscles, while hysterical dynamics often show a separation between binding tissue and the muscle itself. These manifestations could hardly be called hypertonic muscular armoring, and yet people exhibiting these characteristics are also evidently neurotic. Armoring cannot be either the cause or the main expression of neurosis if not all neurotics display it. The use of stress exercises to break through such muscular rigidity is a mechanistic treatment of an extension of a dysfunctional energy pattern, not a direct treatment of the problem itself. Emotional holding is a continual process that results from a diseased energy pattern. It is only diseased because insufficient awareness is brought to the pattern. Therefore, the more awareness that is awakened, the greater is the likelihood of changing the pattern. Once the pattern is changed, there is nothing for the muscles to hold—they move toward wholeness, not away from emotional expression. If we go into the matter more deeply, even muscles are not strictly content; they are not matter, as the classical Newtonian physicists believed, but energy processes.

If we magnify a muscle cell, at a certain point it disappears as substance and all that is seen is movement. On only one level of reality does a muscle appear to be matter. Fundamentally, like all matter, a muscle is an interconnecting net of energy fields in movement.

Chladni and later Jenny have shown through their form resonations that the most active aspects of life energy have no structure at all, while the least active are what we call form. This means that the body's form (i.e., its muscular structure) is less "alive" than the energy fields that form it. The body is really a composite field that exists only through a specific manifestation of consciousness that is reinforced over time; it is an energy cassette in biological form. Change therefore is quickest and most direct when therapy confronts the state of consciousness that comes through this form. In a transpersonal sense the body is a transformer of energy and functions as a medium for concretization for both higher and lower frequencies.

Despite the usefulness of emotional expression as a process in therapy, we must revise our concepts of emotions. Almost all emotional/

body psychotherapies see emotions as held content that must be discharged in some type of cathartic process. My work with acupuncture and other subtle energy systems has shown that we can rebalance energy—even dysfunctional emotional processes—by nonemotionally treating the energy flow instead of the emotions themselves. This demonstrated that emotions are one expression of energy but certainly not the most basic. Later I will show that emotions are often released in Life Energy Therapy as part of a "letting through" process of the *healing channel*. I never look for emotions in therapy, nor do I believe that their expression is the best or only road to wholeness. However, when they are part of a natural process of healing, emotions are important to express in a focused way.

There is another important consideration here. Because emotions are energy processes, it is sometimes more important to recycle their energy than to blow it off or away in catharsis. In addition, many of our emotions are derived from situational reactions to things that we cannot accept. If we learn to see the *real*, to accept life just as it is, we will have fewer emotional reactions and therefore fewer emotions to hold back (or express for that matter). Holistic therapy should be interested first in becoming aware of held emotions, then understanding the message behind that holding, and, when appropriate, letting go of the held energy there. Each emotion has a bodily and evolutionary purpose and is therefore important to express when appropriate. This appropriateness has nothing to do with social norms but with wholeness. Someone who holds back anger may need to learn to express it in direct, nondestructive ways. However, if someone is still angry after his/her fury is expressed, the problem is probably not in the anger but in the frustration caused by nonacceptance. Effective therapy consists of correctly assessing the problem and dealing with held emotions in the most appropriate way for each person.

From a spiritual point of view, we must accept our emotions just as they are while learning to distinguish resonant emotions from noise or noninformational ones. We must also be able to transform emotions, because remaining stuck in emotional consciousness alone will prevent us from further evolving. In fact many of our emotions are expressions of energy that come from a cultural inheritance or from another lifetime, neither of which has to do with our spiritual essence. By learning to let these through, we free energy for the purpose of evolution.

Further, the new therapeutic form must extend itself in several new modes. Diagnosis must be developed in a direct relationship to the therapeutic work. Unlike the present systems where the diagnosis is a strait jacket of clinical categories, an energy diagnosis would focus on patterns of movement that are directly amenable to change. The therapist thus becomes a change agent whose focus is energy and evolves into an *energist* whose training is multifaceted. First and foremost, an energist bases his learning on his own personal experience of energy within himself and with others. He has learned to be spontaneous and clear and has shown himself able to transform many forms of energy. His knowledge includes information (based on personal experience) on the nature and movement of life energy and its relation to the spirit, the body, nutrition, politics, and culture, as well as the usual psychological dynamics, but understood from an energy and evolution perspective. Because no two people can do energy work alike, an energist has learned to trust his spontaneous contact with the energy that moves in him and his clients instead of relying on techniques. The basis of this learning is spiritual development and the observed laws of nature. Advanced energists become consultants to many types of organizations, not only because of their content knowledge but because of their process understanding and its connection to wholeness.

One system that meets both the general and specific requirements of an energy-based psychotherapy already exists. In addition to psychotherapy, it is currently being used in such areas as pedagogy, economics, organizational consultation, theater, dance, and art. This system is called the Life Energy Process.

Chapter Six

Life Energy Process®

Introduction to Life Energy Therapy (L.E.T.)

Despite the recognition that the art and science of therapy were in need of greater wholeness if they were to truly evolve, my research into the nature of psychotherapy revealed that some measure of integration was already present. Western forms of therapy were more similar than dissimilar, both in theory and practice, if one went deeper into their processes. Further, it became evident that Eastern forms of therapy such as acupuncture, Aikido, Tai Chi, and Yoga, also work with similar processes, though on a different level. What was needed was a common denominator for Eastern and Western systems. I discovered that I could achieve such a synthesis of therapy modalities by using the concept of "energy," because each method can be related directly or indirectly to energy processes. It was simply a question of translating described theory and practical techniques into energy terminology.

As is often the case in movements of awareness, the determined need for greater wholeness in psychotherapy was quickly followed by a discovery that made the next step possible. I found a new therapeutic process that had its roots in the ancient wisdom of energy but could also be used in a practical way in modern therapy.

"Energy" the research concept became "life energy" the dynamic principle and later evolved into the Life Energy Process. One aspect of this process became Life Energy Therapy (L.E.T.), the system of therapy that I would like to describe in the next few pages.

As L.E.T. was evolving, several important conclusions became apparent. First, to be practical as a psychotherapy, L.E.T. had to return to the concept of healing that was implicit in the origins of therapy but that had been lost over the years through degeneration of wholeness. Little by little, an erosion of unity has taken place, resulting in the present specialization of mind, body, emotion, and spirit therapies. Second, because the essence of therapy is spiritual, L.E.T. had to be based in this realm while also working on other levels of energy as extensions of the spirit. The Western emphasis on ego functioning, for example, would have to be expanded to realms where being and egolessness were also important. In short, I saw in L.E.T. a form of healing that transcended the accepted limits of psychotherapy by being based on the processes of the spirit; a system as steeped in the philosophical/religious traditions of the past as it was connected with the latest research in physics; a method as practical as it was theoretical; and an approach to life that balanced the unity of life's functions with the potential for individual focus—all of which would return to the original concept of therapy as wholeness.

The basic idea of Life Energy Therapy can be found in the name itself. If we see life as a state of animation characterized by processes of movement, then everything in the universe has a certain life, although this may not be biological.* Even inanimate objects vibrate and express themselves in movement, according to the new physics. Therefore we can see everything as a process of life whose existence fosters movements of wholeness. Energy is the medium for this activity, as we have seen, and therapy is one process that makes whole or heals. If we extend these healing movements over time and simultaneously consider them in a spiritual framework, they automatically lead to evolution. Life Energy Therapy, then, is the study of energy as a vital medium of life and the practice of its movement as it leads to greater wholeness in spiritual evolution.

In L.E.T. we are interested in the origins, the roots of all phenomena that express their essence. This therapy is therefore a radical (L. *radix*, root) approach that goes beneath the forms of disease to the real energy problem, which is always related to a separation from wholeness. The therapy or healing of such disease must therefore go beyond the individual goals of psychotherapy to achieve its results. True healing goes beyond psychological freedom, emotional expression, behavioral change, body work, assertiveness, and pleasure, and yet it works with all of these when appropriate. Its foremost orientation is wholeness, and all aspects of therapy are directed to increasing that wholeness as it moves in its evolutionary phases. Evolution resembles a standing wave that rises in energy levels as each degree of wholeness is experienced. Our focus in L.E.T. is to be involved with evolution, just as the universal whole has become involved in matter so that its ascent

---

*Reich has shown in his biomedical research that the division between organic and inorganic matter may be developmental, not essential.

in evolution may be more complete. Therapy is essentially a process that brings us back to a wholeness that we already know; everything that we need to learn in order to heal ourselves is already there. We have only to rediscover it. Both the nature of our problems and the means to solve them are built into the process of wholeness. Using energy principles in therapy helps us acquire a comprehensive overview of how our lives function and how they are related to the universal order. Because space is limited, I will describe only some of the main characteristics and processes that constitute L.E.T.

Awareness

The basic process in L.E.T. is awareness because only change with awareness leads to evolution. If we return to its roots, we find that awareness is related to the observation of truth. It is a kind of watchfulness based on a spontaneity in the moment. Because of the flow of life energy, whatever we become aware of increases the energy flow in the direction of the object of focus. Therefore everything in our awareness is charged with a degree of energy. Because life energy is unlimited, our ability to be aware has no bounds, and because the tendency of all processes is towards wholeness, we are automatically led to greater awareness. Therefore being aware and becoming more aware are natural processes that evolve by themselves. So why aren't we more aware of ourselves and the world around us?

The answer lies in our fear of wholeness. Because we know some place within us about this wholeness, we also know that if we became more aware, we would eventually perceive those parts of us that we don't want to see. So we keep ourselves unaware of these parts by developing a perceptual neurosis; in other words, we learn to be unaware.

The nature of wholeness is such that we are organically led to be aware of all things that are true or real. Our lives, then, are really processes of becoming aware of the permanent truths or absolute reality. However, because we fear the simplicity and power of absolute reality, we train our attention to become aware of only those phenomena that resonate with our level of consciousness. Needless to say, our awareness usually stays on a low level of relative reality in which we concern ourselves with daily chores and pleasures but avoid the messages of essence or absoluteness.

By becoming more aware, we open the doors of perception to the possibility of seeing more in us and the world in which we live. So awareness is really the first step in the process of change and evolution. Change without awareness is simply idle motion looking for meaning; it is change for change's sake, but we do not evolve. Greater awareness brings more aliveness to the healthy and unhealthy parts of ourselves by creating true excitement. This happens when we see more clearly where and who we are, where our difficulties lie, and eventually our possibilities for change. All this of course takes time. It is not a question of seeing what is difficult for us only once; this is only the opening. True awareness is seeing and staying with this perception until we are led to movement. Sometimes this may mean sitting with a painful feeling until we cry. Or this focus in awareness may help us see how a difficult marriage has really helped us grow as a person. Maybe we become aware that we need to change jobs because our present one is no longer fulfilling. In all cases awareness charges and therefore makes more alive the nature of our difficulties so that their solutions become possible.

In L.E.T. we help facilitate the experience of awareness through physical movements especially designed to bring us more in touch with the universally whole part of ourselves. We use physical contact, verbal feedback, and meditation to support this process. The focus of the awareness work is centered on the degree of wholeness that is already present and only secondarily on the blockage of wholeness. This is important because the emphasis on wholeness first energizes and therefore supports the integration that already exists. We should only focus on energy blockages to help eliminate their disturbance, and only in relation to wholeness; otherwise disease, not wholeness, becomes reinforced.

Awareness work brings to full clarity how we avoid ourselves and the greater wholeness by sometimes emphasizing the most simple truth of how a flower looks or how water runs in a stream. Gradually we can accept all reality just as it is, without avoiding parts of it, even those aspects of us that are hard to accept. Perhaps for the first time we become aware of how we run away from the simplicity or beauty of wholeness, fearful that its completeness will overwhelm or blind us. Ironically, because we fear the light of truth, we keep ourselves blind by our own ignorance that this wholeness exists. We have usually learned to turn away from wholeness because for our parents, and our society, wholeness also appears dangerous. After all, there can be no control of wholeness. Control exists only in separation. Socially our attempts to control cultural mores or human behaviors are really expressions of fear of an organic order. Because we don't feel this order in our bodies or see it in nature with our eyes, we try to enforce it with our will. Law and order advocates, for example, are frightened by their own inner urges; they need everything to be in order because they fear that any living process will shake their fragile reality to pieces. Their order is an "as if" wholeness whose natural rhythms have been disturbed. On a larger scale, many of us have managed to survive physically by separating ourselves from wholeness, only to be haunted later by the disease of separation. In this splitting from absolute reality, we have denied ourselves an essential aspect of existence. The field of wholeness constantly sends us messages to come back to its completeness in the stubbed toe, the destroyed relationship, and the cancer we develop. Some of us hear these messages; others do not. In any case it is not by chance but by personal choice. Those of us who hear do so because the desire for wholeness overrides the difficulties in coming home. We know that we will face unpleasant things along the path, but the completion of the circle seems worth the effort. Interestingly, it is not the "hard times" that nearly prevent us from further wholeness but the joy of being complete!

In the process of becoming aware, our avoidance lessens; we begin to confront and accept who we are. Difficulties and possibilities, pains and pleasures, all become open to experience. Gradually we find new focus in life. What was once scattered in the running away now creates new wholeness in the stillness. Perhaps a tedious relationship takes on new meaning, or perhaps we learn that it is time to say goodbye to this contact, knowing that we no longer fit together in a new emerging whole. In our pain and excitement we keep going deeper into ourselves; this is the movement of awareness.

In therapy we gradually bring life energy into areas of body, emotions, and spirit that were previously undercharged. A psychoemosomatic unity begins to develop as consciousness is raised.

For us to experience a particular state of consciousness or shared knowledge, awareness, or the perception of truth, must take place first. Naturally we cannot begin by perceiving ultimate truth, but every process of awareness intensifies the movement toward it. Though awareness is a continuous process, experience of different levels of consciousness is a discontinuous process that develops as the energy of awareness is maintained in focal perception. By keeping ourselves centered in awareness, we increase the intensity of energy gathered at points of attention until a quantitative increment produces a qualitative change and our consciousness becomes altered. This is an essential aspect of healing:

> For a lasting, permanent and complete cure it is essential to raise the permanent level of consciousness.[1]

Because awareness and consciousness are experiences of wholeness, along the way of healing we are automatically led to further evolution as the flow of life energy seeks greater and greater completeness. Many people intuitively feel this inner movement, but because it is unknown to them, they tend to block its flow. They mistakenly assume that awareness of an unidentified process in themselves will necessarily lead to an unwanted change. Naturally they feel pushed to action, so they resist awareness of this process as a way of blocking the need to act. By its nature, awareness fosters action of wholeness as an extension of its perception of truth. However, this manifestation of truth is always related to appropriate movement. It is never forced or hurried because it operates according to our natural rhythms. Likewise we can be aware of everything and take no action whatsoever. Once this "must" to act has been dissolved, we are free to act or not. The result is an excitement of awareness. Open to observe everything and yet to not act on it, we experience the freedom of true potentiality. This is the kind of quiet potency that leads to an energy presence in someone. Observers sense the honesty, clarity, and power of such an aware person. He/she need not do anything, because everything is done through its own organization. Awareness leads to this absolute order where no control is necessary. The restraint of control (F. *contre*, against, and roller, roll) is superfluous when we stay in the natural flow of awareness. Life simply "rolls" by itself when it is undisturbed by our distractions of unawareness. I speak about an internal roll of order or introl in which we flow with the natural movement of energy. This flow of awareness is usually broken when we are led to experiences that are too pleasurable or painful for our level of consciousness. At these points we deny the truth of our experience and learn to be unaware.

A good example of this occurs in therapy when verbal feedback is given. Many people have learned that an observation of their actions by someone else, usually a parent, led to criticism, and now they expect that all observation and comment must be critical. But even criticism (Gk. *kritikos*) from its energy movement is simply a skill in judging and need not be the insult that it is usually perceived to be.

Awareness is by nature a nonjudgmental process that leads only to truth. Criticism can exist only when we are living in polarity. Truth, however, knows no such dichotomy. But it does know difference, as relative aspects of our lives tell us. Whereas criticism focuses on difference, good or bad, truth sees all superficial difference as relative aspects of the same wholeness. In therapy we must sense with our whole self this distinction between awareness and criticism. Awareness leads to more complete consciousness and evolution; criticism leads only to an energy "ping-pong" of attack and defense.

Staying with awareness as it moves in the healing process necessitates a focusing of life energy, which often leads to a focal point called a "burning-point" in German (Brennpunkt). Awareness brings the fire to attention that both excites our perception and sterilizes the pain in our visions like fire sterilizes a wound. Being aware is a fascinating experience, and it requires the courage of a true pioneer to stay focused at difficult times. The true seeker does not concern him/herself with the polarities of life; he/she is interested and imbued with the intent and power of being aware.

Trace Problems

The process of awareness shows exactly how we keep ourselves away from wholeness. Particularly in the initial phases of discovery, we tend to focus on our difficulties, whether this is the problematic relationship with our spouse or partner, our job situation, or some physical ailment. Sometimes this leads to a criticism of ourselves and our world until we learn to accept reality as it is. In psychotherapy this awareness is heightened because the therapist helps us look at ourselves in a new way. Unfortunately, most therapies direct their treatment efforts toward these life difficulties, which are considered to be behavioral dysfunctions (by the behavioristic schools) or overt manifestations of deeper, repressed impulses (by the psychoanalytic schools). Some therapies see problems as manifestations of unfinished gestalts (Gestalt therapy) or the result of unexpressed emotions (e.g., bioenergetic and primal therapies). To a limited degree, there is truth in all these approaches, but we need a more complete understanding of human problems.

Almost all the problems that we are aware of are not the real difficulties at all. They are only extensions of the real problems. I call what we see "trace problems" because of their minimal connection hints at the deeper source (see Figure 19). They are ripples of dysfunctional energy that arise from a deeper source like bubbles in water rising to the surface. They are the existential effects of a disturbance in our connection to essence, nothing more. The more we pay attention to these apparent difficulties, the more energy we actually invest in their existence. That is, the more important we make these problems, the longer we support their existence.

From an L.E.T. perspective, problems are expressions of energy imbalances that result from a basic disharmony on their level of functioning. This means that there are different degrees of problems. Not all difficulties are on the same level of consciousness, so working with

ENERGY PROBLEM CONE

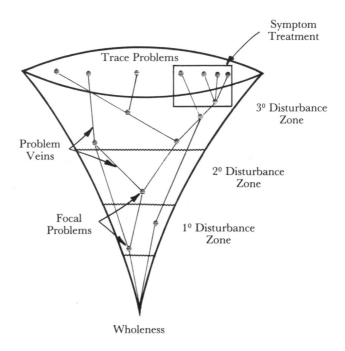

Figure 19.

them requires different sensitivities of diagnosis and treatment. For example, say you fell down yesterday and hurt your left knee. Normally you might go to a doctor or another healing practitioner. You get bandaged up and the problem is solved. Not necessarily. Often such accidents have a deeper significance. In conventional psychotherapy you might be asked to look at the motivation for hurting yourself or the need for attention. In L.E.T. we look more closely at the energetic importance. On the physical level the knee is a shock absorber. Emotionally it is connected to fear because of the tendency to stiffen the knee when we want to appear strong. When we are afraid to fall physically or emotionally, we lock the knee as a defense. Defensive people always have stiff legs because the mobility in the knee joint has been hampered. In terms of character processes, such people tend to be rigid. Now let's go further. The knee is also connected to the kidneys in Eastern medicine; the emotion represented by the kidneys is also fear. Therefore we see the emotional and physical connection of the knee to the kidneys and fear.

In L.E.T. we go even further. The left knee is also connected to the receptive (not passive) side of the body. This means that one energy movement flows from left to right up the left leg, through the pelvis, and then down the right leg. We would check this flow. The knee is also the yang side of a minor energy chakra on the other side. An energy diagnosis would determine if this is working properly. Then we would explore the problem further on the spiritual level. Kidneys are related to forgiveness, and problems with them often result from an energetic holding. Not wanting to forgive someone, we hold a grudge against them; this holding hurts us, not the other person. An energy diagnosis would then determine with the client the "life message" of falling down on the left knee. What was important for you to learn? How can you go further on your path? A small incident like falling down clearly has connections to many energy levels, all of which we must explore to get a comprehensive picture. We need to go much further than even the most advanced psychology can take us. Energy principles allow us to understand the problem and the solution on different energy levels.

The ultimate cause of these problems is a splitting from wholeness, which may have been necessary at an earlier time in our lives to survive. Children, for example, who do not make this split often die because of the tremendous pain they experience when they feel unwanted, unloved, or unable to grow freely. To physically survive, most of us have split from our own wholeness. In so doing, however, we opened up a pathway to dis-ease that we have totally "forgotten" about on a conscious level. We act as though life still has its original wholeness—until we begin to receive other signals, like falling down. We are sent life messages that express themselves as trace problems. These messages tell us that our wholeness is disturbed. They are often necessary to show us where we have left the path of wholeness so that we might return to completeness by becoming aware. Naturally, staying unaware prevents us from truly seeing these messages and therefore from really healing ourselves.

Trace problems are developed over time as the basic split from wholeness deepens and becomes more elaborated into "problem veins." In other words, trace problems are only the latest manifestations of a basic energy dysfunction that began long ago. Its roots are not psychological but spiritual. The psychological aspects of a problem are second- or third-degree energy causes but never the primary cause. This is why a psychotherapy that works on the psychological level can never get to the real problem. Of course the trace problem may seem to disappear, but the energetic disturbance remains on a deeper level. A strictly medical approach to all forms of disease is usually a "band-aid therapy" that covers over or removes the symptom but doesn't touch the roots of the problem. After all, how can a person's inability to forgive be cured with a fresh bandage on the knee? Now, medically treating the wound combined with psychologically treating the third-degree energy cause, plus addressing the spiritual split, creates a total approach to the problem.

Trace problems seem very real on the surface. They exist in our physical lives as concrete problems, but below the surface we find a different story. At their roots all problems have the same energy disturbance—separation from wholeness. In fact their physical existence depends on an energy source that they themselves cannot provide. Trace problems exist because of an energy flow that is continually sent in these directions. Without this flow there would be no problem. Have you ever tried to force yourself to be neurotic? Neurosis and its disturbed processes can only exist if energy supports them. If we didn't have a natural tension (stress) in our muscles, we would collapse because the bones could not support themselves; the same is true of trace problems. They need our support to exist. In the Buddhist tradition, suffering arises when we stop the flow of life by clinging to the illusions (traces) of form. The dis-ease of life's difficulties is the result of blocking the flow of life energy; it is not the natural state. The energy supporting all disease is the life force of wholeness that has been diverted from its course.

Because energy is constantly in motion, a departure from wholeness leads energy into the path of disease. By a process of expansion and elaboration, our problems move from first- to third-degree disturbances in a type of *disease harmonics*, manifesting themselves as trace problems that we become aware of as bubbles on the surface of our lives. All first-degree disturbances are principal splits from wholeness. These may develop even as a young baby or a fetus in this lifetime, though we bring many of these splits into this life from previous incarnations. Such splits in their second-degree manifestations are represented by the schizophrenic separation from physical reality. Because of their heightened sensitivity to wholeness and the subsequent pain at the separation from it, people often develop schizophrenic splits as an attempt to protect themselves. Throughout the process of elaboration, energy gathers itself into nodules (called *focal problems*) along the problem veins, much like acupuncture points along energy meridians. Focal problems are units of disharmony that are attempts to encapsulate the disease. Just as an infection in the body will often develop a boil with pus in an attempt to control the sphere of damage.

Let's say that you were born with an inflamed kidney. This would be a focal problem. For whatever reason, this life message told you that kidneys and all things connected with them would be an area of focus for you in this lifetime. Often these messages come from a previous life. Going back in a past-life therapy deals at most with the particulars of the situation that may have led to the kidney focus. The still deeper problem, namely, the need to learn forgiveness, still wouldn't be touched. In fact focusing too much on a particular physical problem may even prevent us from dealing with the spiritual message because the symptom as signal is alleviated.

Perhaps the early inflammation is treated medically, and the problem seems to disappear. But because the energy disturbance has not been resolved, you later have knee problems. You fall down several times in your life, always on the left side. Only the left knee has arthritis. In a car accident the left knee is cut, and so forth. Until we learn to understand these messages, the problem remains, even though the trace aspect of it may change.

In L.E.T. we see each symptom or problem as a manifestation of a disharmony between awareness and expression. When deeper energy processes become blocked in awareness, their expression in the physical world must take on the character of some type of indirect expression. Because we are not in full awareness, we develop symptoms and/or problems that show us more completely what those deeper dysfunctions are. Because symptoms are still expressions, albeit indirect ones, physical problems are really compromises between expression and repression. Not fully expressed but not fully repressed, the symptom manifests itself as an unaware middle way.

Many therapies base their theories of neurosis on the mechanism of repression. They contend that we repress what we don't want to confront as instincts, impulses, or emotions. In L.E.T. we see this idea as being only half the story. If we look at the energetics of repression, we find that in this process life energy, which otherwise would express itself, is being bound inside. We believe that repression and all that is held bound by it is really being used by us to avoid greater wholeness. Repression doesn't make us neurotic; the fear of wholeness does. Repression is an intermediary stage in the process.

Fear of wholeness shifts the entire idea of problems into a spiritual realm. Letting go of our problems is tantamount to letting go of our attachment to disease. Disease complicates life because it disturbs clarity and confuses our basic rhythms. We have come to believe that complexity equals sophistication. We even say that someone is "simple," meaning that he/she is not very bright. Therefore simplicity is equivalent to dumbness and lack of sophistication. Wholeness is by nature simple, though very intelligent, and therein lies our problem. We don't know how to be simple in an intelligent way; hence we prefer the complexity of disease and confusion. Add to this another difficulty: because we know somewhere about the state of wholeness and the fact that we have lost it, we are not eager to have it again. It's a bit like knowing that you can only fall to the ground if you fly with joy. Staying on the ground prevents the fall. Most of us are afraid to fall, which means that we are afraid to fly. Unlike hysteria or superficial "kicks," wholeness is connected to both the earth and sky. We cannot fall from wholeness; we can only go away from it as Adam and Eve symbolically did in Paradise.

Like neurosis, many psychotherapies support the idea of an unconscious as it relate to our daily problems. They insist that repressed elements of the mind not conscious to us, like phantoms in a cave, motivate our problematic behavior, feelings, and ideas. Jung even posited a collective unconscious by which the total experience of man as a race is inherited as a potentiality by each member of that race. From a wholeness point of view, this concept is incomplete. Though many features, including racial memories, are passed on from one species member to another, the division between conscious and unconscious is arbitrary and separative. If we were not aware enough to avoid all these elements at some level, we would surely "bump" into them in one of our wanderings through the mind. For the mind is both a product of consciousness and a function of wholeness. Isolating one or a hundred elements of consciousness can only be done with another process of awareness. Otherwise, the natural state of mental harmony would reform itself again. Therefore, if we didn't know what actually bothered us, we couldn't block its exit. If we weren't aware of our racial memories, how could we actualize their potentiality? These acts take a certain degree of consciousness. Our research has shown that if we could dismiss our repressive mechanisms, we could automatically become whole. During the healing process, a period of unsettlement generally occurs as the newly released energy seeks a balance in itself. Many people know this, which is why they are afraid of being overwhelmed or overcharged.

Therefore, we must be aware of what we block or what we have done racially. This means that our awareness, though perhaps minimal, is still connected to the energy of the "known," and therefore no separation exists. Repression is only a tool of our fear, but even repression is a process of awareness. Not everything is repressed, so how do we know what to repress? Repression, therefore, cannot be the problem; nor can the content of "unconsciousness," because we know what the content is anyway. The deeper and therefore essential problem that gives power to repression mechanisms is the split from wholeness. The unconscious, repression, and neurosis are all terms that we use to explain our unwillingness to confront wholeness. By themselves they have no power but operate only in the range of third-degree causality. Our insistent focusing on life's problems is a way of staying diseased. The basic fear of wholeness ties this investment of energy to disturbance. In wholeness and health there are no problems; so if we were whole, we would have no complaints about life. What would we do if we couldn't complain? Our problems keep us busy. But can wholeness be so frightening that we would do almost anything in our power to avoid it?

In L.E.T. we focus on the fear of wholeness instead of the repression, because once we allow more wholeness, we have no need to repress anything. It is amazing how quickly neurosis is "healed" when we accept wholeness. From a neurotic point of view, repression actually does us a service by binding the life energy that we are afraid to experience. In L.E.T. we go beyond this neurotic theater by delving directly into the separation from wholeness. Therefore, whether our problems manifest themselves as physical complaints, psychological confusion, social unrest, existential anxiety, or spiritual trepidation, the energy process remains the same.

From a spiritual perspective, trace problems are chances to become aware—learning situations in which we are provided with concrete foci for our deeper energy disturbances. Life's difficulties become evolution's possibilities. In essence there are no problems as we define them. Trace problems, for example, are only structures of situations that we can make into problems or not. A problem (Gr. proballein: to lay or throw before) is simply an energy pattern that lies before us. Trace problems are only forms of life energy that meet us in awareness on our path toward wholeness. Once we increase awareness and initiate an understanding of trace problems, therapy moves into a third phase, called energy patterning.

Energy Patterns

In uncovering the energy dynamics of trace problems, I found that all our difficulties are related not only in essence by their separation from wholeness but also to each other by a similar disease vibration. Though we seem to have many problems in life with our work, social relationships, and personal health, they stem from the same disturbed energy processes, known as *energy patterns*. For each person, disease is a unique process that can be described as a type of vibration,* movement, and rhythm that does not resonate with their spirit. Every problem that we experience is a manifestation of these energy patterns, whereby each pattern develops into several trace problems (see Figure 20), all with the same energy disturbance. Thus, by a process of extension, the original problem of separation from wholeness becomes projected into our contact with the world and creates a problem form that looks like it comes from outside us. It looks like the problems find *us*, although the opposite is really true. We radiate the disturbance that eventuates in a form in our everyday lives, which we then call a problem. In addition, each culture has a prominence of certain energy patterns; therefore our disturbances are apt to be stronger when we live in a culture whose problems resonate with ours. The opposite situation might occur when we live in a culture whose patterns are quite contrary to ours; this often produces a disease between the culture and us. We either have to leave the culture or learn to adjust to it. A healthy adjustment is not to vibrate the same cultural dis-ease but to return to our own vibration (spirit) and let go of the cultural disturbance.

Because life energy is always in motion, our original split from wholeness becomes elaborated through other energy patterns, all related to the original cause. These patterns function as disease harmonics in which each unique pattern remains in a proportional frequency relationship to the original disease. By a still further elaboration, each energy pattern creates several trace problems, which are different forms of the same energy disturbance in a particular frequency range. These findings suggested to me that it was possible to organize trace problems into larger groupings based on the similarity of these patterns. Let's say, for example, that you came to therapy with contact difficulties at social functions. In the course of therapy through energy patterning, you learn that all activities that require you to go over an energy boundary are likewise difficult. You realize that your lack of assertiveness at work and your inability to experience full sexual pleasure are related. Even your diet and lifestyle support the problem. Now you begin to get a larger picture of the deeper energy disturbance that creates the individual trace problems. Therapy has helped you rediscover the pattern: after you allow a certain amount of energy to charge an activity, instead of doing it completely

*This has also been suggested by nonpsychotherapeutic approaches such as radionics.

(like being assertive or having an orgasm), you shift the focus and no resolution occurs. You are always frustrated and don't know why.

ENERGY PATTERNS

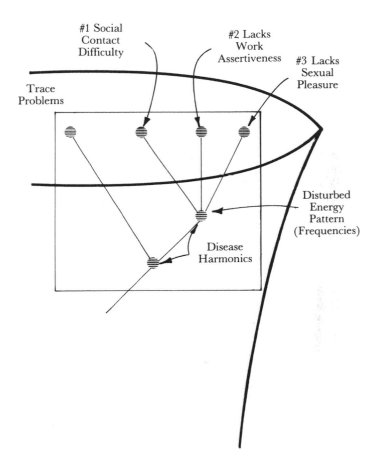

Figure 20.

Once the energy pattern emerges, the therapy proceeds to help you experience the feeling of going over the energy barrier. Slowly you begin to trust your ability to go further into an activity, which gradually translates into a healthy assertiveness, greater confidence, and more sexual pleasure. The advantage of uncovering these patterns is that instead of dealing with a number of problems one by one, you can concentrate on changing the energy pattern from which all the problems result. This shortens therapy considerably.

Part of our work is to help uncover the nature of these patterns. Practically speaking, we do this by reversing the process shown in the energy problem cone (Figure 19). Unlike homeopathy, where the diseases often manifest themselves in reverse order of occurrence, disturbances of wholeness are multileveled. In the healing process patterns of disease can emerge from many of these levels and from any time period simultaneously. Therefore, in contrast to the problem veins, healing veins develop anew in a nonsequential order. Our experience has shown that processes of healing and patterns of disease emerge as we are able to deal with them. We cannot force or direct them in a linear way; that would disturb the healing organic process. Life energy knows its way back to wholeness; it is a universal path well worn by many before us. We must begin by using the presenting problems as background information for the development of a problem understanding. In the course of therapy a pattern of these difficulties begins to emerge without our explicitly looking for it. We allow the pattern to emerge as needed. To do this, we translate the symptoms/problems into energy processes and then gradually begin to collate these processes. The development of an energy pattern is facilitated by an understanding of the laws of energy as they apply to everyday situations, our philosophies of living, functions of the body, nutritional requirements, and so on. Again, we rediscover these patterns only in relation to wholeness. We are interested, for example, in seeing how energy patterns were "as if" attempts to develop wholeness. Perhaps a series of problems was important to increase our awareness of the energy pattern that we would not have noticed had only one trace problem broken out. The greater number of trace problems might have led us to therapy, which eventually led us to greater wholeness.

Even individual problems are based on wholeness. Perhaps the difficulty with sexual pleasure forced us to consider our relationship to our body or to patterns we learned from our parents. This understanding led us to be more concerned about our pleasure and about letting go of our parents. Therapy can be quite helpful in this direction, not by simply understanding but by going through the direct experience with the help of an energist. In L.E.T. we go beyond the symptoms to the energy processes from which they arise, knowing that a trace problem can exist only if there is an energy network to support it.

Once this network has been uncovered and rechanneled, the disease disappears.

The existence of energy patterns makes it clear that disease, like health, is interwoven into the fabric of our lives. I call this connectedness the *life energy weave*. Like a piece of material with both vertical and horizontal strands, a network of energy processes is formed from their criss-cross interaction.* However, instead of linear strands, the radiations of energy fields and various energy centers, including the microcenters of acupuncture points, interface with each other just as raindrops create minute waves in a lake. In health these radiations interfere positively in harmony, whereas in disease they interfere negatively against each other. In the interaction of this energy, network forms are created like higher-level nodal points that both maintain the quality of interference and stabilize its radiations. One form that is most interesting for us here is the body. In health the energy network produces a body that vibrates this same positive interference within. Naturally, in disease the body reflects its negative interference. We create our bodies based on the quality of energy interference within us. Over time, health or disease becomes "woven" into our bodies and lifestyles based on the relationship of energy vibrations. This is also why a supportive environment with minimal harmful radiations is important, because these radiations too become part of us.

Earlier we discussed that disease is not a one-time process but a consistent radiation of disharmony. Most medical experts agree, for example, that cancer may be present in the body for up to eight years before a physical sign appears. However, once this pattern of cancer is dissolved, cancer as the physical disease cannot exist, to which many cases of spontaneous recovery attest. We cannot have an isolated cancer of the breast, lungs, stomach, and so on. These localizations are only the sites of emergence. Cancer is a disturbance of the whole. All our bodily, emotional, social, and spiritual functions are united by the life energy weave, so any aspect of disease will affect all other parts of us. If this disharmony becomes chronic, disease is woven into our everyday activities as an extension of the internal disease. After a while we cannot even differentiate between health and disease because we have no clear perception of what health is. Socially, we have so woven disease into our societies that it is accepted as normal to be sick and/or neurotic and/or drug abusive (e.g., alcohol, pills, and so on). Thus, despite the fact that information about psychology,

*The Egyptians believed that knowledge is formed by the same criss-cross qualities of information.

psychotherapy, and substance abuse is more available now than ever before, the rate of emotional disturbance and drug dependency is ever increasing.

Patterns of disease are replicated over and over because they have become so ingrained in our lives that we rarely experience this disease directly. They have become energy cassettes, playing backward and forward over and over until we are lulled into a false sense of security.* Even though these cassettes are not songs of harmony, they provide many of us with a busy-ness (business); after all, if we can spend most of our time attending to problems, we have little left for dealing with our fear of wholeness. Despite this, these cassettes bind energy and therefore are also holistic unto themselves, even though they cause disturbance in the larger whole because of their isolation. In fact all disease is "as if" wholeness. So therapy should be oriented not toward removing disease but toward transforming a negatively interfering and therefore destructive network of "ersatz" (substitute) wholeness into a positive expression of health. By looking at all disease as an attempt at wholeness, we minimize resistance to change because we have not attacked disease as an enemy but have accompanied it into true wholeness like an Aikido movement. In actual therapy trace problems are gradually drained of energy and disappear like healed wounds.

Essential Perception

Another reason why trace problems are so aggravating is that we have little connection to their meaning. We often hear, "Why did that have to happen to me?" Very few people understand that problems are chances for growth. Our problems often seem insurmountable because we do not have a clear overview of their place in our evolution. Further, we are led to believe that problems are to be avoided; mistakes shouldn't happen. The media tell us to keep cool, dismiss pain with two aspirin, and develop self-confidence by denying our deepest fears. But why? Life's difficulties, even minor pains, can be significant messages to us of deeper energy processes that are often necessary for our further development. Nature has no accidents, only rhythms of change that function according to energy laws. Can we really believe that our problems are outside these laws?

*In Transactional Analysis an equivalent of emotional cassettes are called "racket feelings." In L.E.T., however, cassettes are repeated energy patterns that are not only emotional but physical, spiritual, social, and so on.

By becoming increasingly aware, by seeing life's symptoms for what they are, as well as being open to the cause and pattern of our disharmony, we make several important steps in melting our dis-ease. In L.E.T. we speak about the gradual rediscovery of this basic knowledge as "re-search," because at a particular level, we already know the wisdom of energy in its function and dysfunction. It is only a question of making aware processes with which we have little contact at the present time. In therapy complement to the research of energy patterns is the development of a new perspective about what these processes mean in our lives. Because this new perspective allows us to see more clearly the real meaning of our difficulties, we call this process *essential perception.*

Though a few enlightened people develop this clarity, for most of us the path toward such direct experience of the real is a long and involved process. As Bhagavan* Ramana Maharshi pointed out, what is real is that which doesn't change. The absolute real in this sense is the ageless wisdom of simply what is. Naturally, our ability to see such absolute truth depends on our level of consciousness. However, as a complementary aspect of pattern researching, we can develop greater and greater clarity as a result of continual focus. Meditation is the most direct approach to essential perception, but meditation is a state of awareness, only one aspect of which is receptively sitting to meditate. Essential perception is a state of mental stillness as well as a state of bodily aliveness. In effect it is a total involvement in becoming conscious of simply and precisely how things are. This truth of reality is probably best expressed by Zen Buddhism:

> Rain on bamboo
> Wind in the firs
> They speak
> The truth of Zen.

Though essential perception cannot be trained per se, it can be learned. In that sense it is a holistic art that we develop with experience by directly applying it in living life more completely. As we usually perceive it, physical reality is simply the latest form of deeper energy processes that are ageless. Essential perception allows us to cut through the form of physical reality to discover the spiritual or essential meaning underlying its existence. The original meaning

*The title Bhagavan is roughly equivalent to "God" and is a name given by the people to revered saints; it is never taken on by the person himself, as one popular teacher has recently done.

of Aristotelian form, as you might recall, was the design of essence. From this perspective the physical world is the design of essence or soul as it manifests itself on the physical plane of matter. The ability to use essential perception has direct application in psychotherapy as well as in everyday situations. Consider the following example.

I once led an international, professional workshop on an island off the coast of Spain in which one member was receiving personal feedback about her irresponsible behavior. On the one hand, she wanted the feedback, but on the other hand, she was frightened that the negative feedback might overwhelm her. Being "sensitive" professionals, many people in the group were trying to help her sort out her personal issues, being sympathetic to her feelings and generally trying to facilitate a good but productive experience. It was getting to be late at night and all the professional "help" had led to a lot of conversation but very little therapeutic movement. After I made a few process comments, it became clear that almost everyone was caught in a web of helping, rendered impotent by their very efforts to solve the dilemma of the one professional's ambivalence. Given the lateness of the hour, I asked them to sit and meditate for a few minutes together. When I called them back to a group discussion, they discovered that there was now total agreement about the situation, whereas just minutes before the opposite had been the case. They all agreed that trying to be helpful was feeding the helplessness of this woman and that it would be best to let her fully experience the situation without further interference.

In effect they had let go of the trying, the analysis, and the helping and had come to the essence of the matter without needing words. Essential perception is the observation and experience of this wholeness as reality in a direct and unobstructed way. It is going beyond what lies before our eyes to the energy process within. Practically speaking, essential perception evolves by initially bringing awareness to all parts of us that had been denied. This raises the energy level at these focal points of awareness. Increasingly, we open to greater subtlety in life. Like its complement (energy disturbances), we can experience essential perception in degrees arising from the level of trace problems to ultimate oneness called by Sri Aurobindo, an Indian sage, cosmic oneness (see Figure 21).

An increase in awareness that is held in focus leads to a rise in consciousness. The higher and more complete the consciousness, the higher the degree of essential perception. As we become more able to use essential perception, the meaning of our difficulties in life becomes clearer. Our understanding of each problem, once we have come through it, helps us further along the path of evolution. If we stay aware of this process, we experience more complete degrees of perception. Trivial, less important issues cease to waste our time; we can see our needs more clearly and eventually even let go of these at higher, more complete levels. Even biological needs such as eating and sleeping cease to have the same importance because these are desires connected with physical reality. As we move away from depending on this physical realm, physical needs diminish.

ESSENTIAL PERCEPTION CONE

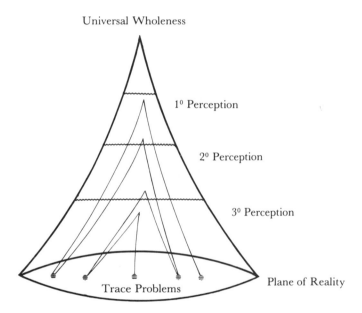

Figure 21.

On a communication level essential perception lets us go beyond the words of a conversation to see the real process of emotion or motivation beneath. Without analyzing, the "real" dialogue emerges as we see the verbal games drop away and we come to an honest contact.

On the spiritual level our attention is drawn ever higher as we see the reason for our existence from a larger perspective. We become so interested in wholeness that anything not whole becomes less relevant. We may find ourselves needing different kinds of friends whose way is also wholeness. Gradually we become more aware that our problems, which is why we should have a correct perspective on them. From a spiritual viewpoint, this separation from objects and processes in our world is usually called detachment. This should not be confused with a schizoid detachment, which is a severe energy disturbance manifest as a lack of emotional connectedness.

One difficulty here is that detachment refers to a disconnection from wholeness. Though detachment is an appropriate term for the schizoid separation from unity, it is not appropriate for a process of spiritual development. Any separation from wholeness causes disease because an energy field is disturbed. We might more properly refer to this disidentification with our problems and other worldly dependencies as a *transtachment* that goes beyond these physical fixations but does not separate from them. In spiritual transtachment we still see the connection to our difficulties in life, though we do not depend on them to identify ourselves. Therefore we are free of their binding power. Separation from the physical world only creates a polarity, even if the intention is to make us free. We cannot experience freedom by denying a connection of any type. Spiritual transtachment is therefore a more complete form of wholeness because it accepts our trace problems but sees them through the lens of essential perception.

Denying or disconnecting ourselves from these problems only invests more energy in their existence. Only by accepting and then going beyond manifest forms to the essence of their spiritual message can we truly evolve beyond them. As an energy process, transtachment gathers the forces of trace problems and goes beyond their level to our spirit core, where life energy is channeled and amplified for the purpose of evolution. Detachment is a going away from attachment, which is in itself another attachment; but transtachment is going toward wholeness by accepting and then going beyond our relative reality to the absolute truth of oneness.

By combining the process of energy patterning with the perspective of a developing essential perception, we experience a more complete whole in the dimensions of healing and evolution (see Figure 22). Our research indicates that the more deeply we inquire into the nature of our diseased patterns, the clearer we become about how we have led ourselves away from wholeness. Ironically, as we more fully experience the nature of our separation, we become more whole, because separation can exist only in unawareness. Just as the night helps us appreciate the day, each awareness of our split from wholeness brings us back to the light of oneness.

Similarly, as we perceive more and more clearly the meaning of these difficulties, our courage to uncover more of these patterns is greater until we realize a complete understanding of energy move-

PERCEPTION DISTURBANCE DIAMOND

Wholeness

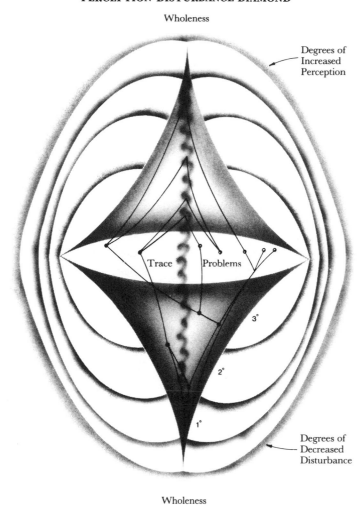

Degrees of
Increased
Perception

Trace Problems

3°

2°

1°

Degrees of
Decreased
Disturbance

Wholeness

Figure 22.

ment. By experiencing a new perspective on our problems, we become free from them on their level of existence. Now we can see them as part of an energy film that runs through us if we let it, or parallel to us if we become aware. In each case there is a connection but in the

288	*Life Energy Process*

"living film" we *are* the difficulties we experience, whereas in the "situation film" we experience the learning situation of life's difficulties as different but not separated from our spiritual essence. Essential perception allows us to see that we are not the problems that we experience because we are by nature without problems; at the same time it shows us that this situation film is necessary for our evolution. Without it we couldn't confront the discrepancy between our essence and our existence.

Thus energy patterning and essential perception are two aspects of the same totality that we can apprehend from both lower and higher research experiences, because "lower" and "higher" don't exist in the nonpolarized harmony of wholeness. Even the sphere of self-inquiry that Sri Aurobindo spoke about in his *Integral Yoga*, is described as descending into the lower energy realm from the awareness of the higher, unlike most types of Indian approaches to level opening, which recommend the opposite direction. In wholeness lower is higher, and vice versa, just as the patterning of disease complements essential perception.

We must allow these two energy processes to come together if we are to have complete health. Those who get stuck in one direction fail to realize the wholeness that is possible when we experience both. Many people in psychotherapy look endlessly for the causes of their dissatisfactions without seeing the meaning of these messages. In fact this infinite search for causes becomes *the* problem, which is supported by too many therapists. This leads to a life negativity where the only important things are problems and their analysis. Others go in a pseudospiritual direction by avoiding all the negativity of life as though life had no rubbish. They would like to lead the "holy" life. But holiness has its roots in wholeness and can never be experienced when we deny part of that whole. True spirituality involves going to the essence of all things, even the negative, perhaps even especially the negative, because here we hide from ourselves and ultimately our own evolution.

Healing Channel

On the path of evolution, becoming whole and maintaining our health requires an intensive effort of awareness, not because the change and evolution processes are so difficult but because we have lost contact with the naturalness of their harmony. When we fall outside wholeness, our powers of restoration and repair are minimized because not all of our energy is available in a focused way. Fortunately, however, except in extreme cases of degeneration, healing is a natural process that will constantly lead us in the direction of wholeness, if we let it. When animals are ill, for example, they seek rest and avoid eating. Some even apply dressings of down or feathers, secure broken bones by ligament splints, or cut veins to bleed themselves (e.g., the hippopotamus) when needed.[2] Likewise, when we are ill, our body knows how to heal itself. Naturally we can help alleviate the symptoms, but the healing process is automatic. Even in many cases of cancer, the fact that recovery is possible without drugs or surgery suggests that our ability to heal ourselves is quite powerful.*

In studying the process of how this natural healing takes place, I discovered a pathway of life energy that I call the *healing channel*. It is not a physical canal like the nerves or blood vessels, nor is it as directed as an acupuncture meridian. Rather it is an energy passage that operates through vibratory resonance between our individual wholeness (Atman) and the universal soul (Brahman). It acts as a channel for the specific frequency band of our spirit, much like a radio receives transmission from its station source. In our case the station is the universal field and the receiver is the body. This channel is unique for each person and we can learn how to reconnect ourselves to it, even after many years of separation. It is a vibratory state of consciousness in which all parts of us resonate together as they personally express the harmony of the whole. The healing channel serves as a medium for energy alignment, whereby all energy processes operating within us experience a complete unison despite their specific frequencies. This is made possible by the harmonics of energy vibrations as all waves, regardless of their size and speed, come together at the end of their cycles. You might picture these waves as two men who are going to Paris. One drives his car directly from Munich to Paris, while the other flies the same route but stops along the way. Both men take the same route and reach Paris at the same time, despite taking different ways to get there.

Though the healing channel is not physical in nature, it is related to our physical body as the chakras are connected to nerve plexi. One of its important relationships to the body is through the spine. As we have discussed, the spine protects the cerebrospinal fluid, which transmits subtle waves of energy throughout the torso and the brain, connecting all our organs. Spinal alignment helps the healing channel function on the physical plane, although the channel is not dependent on the spine. Likewise, when the body is structurally aligned through the musculature, we can move more effectively and in better harmony

*Dr. A. Sattilaro, for example, cured himself of terminal cancer with a macrobiotic diet.

network of processes that we can tap into at all times by tuning to the correct vibrational band. Mediums of all types, including radiathesists, can tune into aspects of this field and receive clear, coherent beams of information.

The more we can tune into this universal field, the more complete is the information we receive. Enlightenment might be seen as a state of contact with this universal field in which all the information from past, present, and future bound in its energy processes is available. This is why all highly evolved people, despite personal and cultural differences, always relate the same basic truths. Each has opened this healing channel to the absolute reality of wholeness. This universal field itself serves as an endless feedback system for the maintenance of order in the universe as we know it, while simultaneously preserving an ageless wisdom of energy processes and the principles that govern their functioning. This source provides a constant supply of data to those of us who are open to such knowledge.

I believe that this phenomenon of energy channels is not restricted to biologically living things. Radio, television, and other communication devices all operate with similar channeling media. Subatomic physicists have also discovered what they call reaction channels, which are in principle very similar to healing channels. According to theoretical physics, the reactions of "strongly interacting" nuclear particles called hadrons are best described as a flow of energy through certain channels.[3] In the collision of these hadrons, extremely short-lived phenomena called *resonances* are formed, although they soon disintegrate. According to Capra:

> A resonance is a particle but not an object. It is much better described as an event, an occurrence or a happening.[4]

The likelihood that a hadron collision will produce such a resonance depends on the frequency of probability waves.

> When this energy or frequency reaches a certain value, the channel begins to resonate; the vibrations of the probability wave suddenly become very strong and thus cause a sharp increase in the reaction probability. Most reaction channels have several resonance energies, each of them corresponding to the mass of an ephemeral intermediate hadron state which is formed when the energy of the colliding particles reaches the resonance value.[5]

The healing channel acts as a reaction channel for energy processes on all levels. As our spirit interacts with other fields, it creates focal points of awareness like the nodal points of electromagnetic fields, the acupoints of energy meridians, and perhaps like the hadrons of subatomic physics. Spiritual resonances may be ultrashort-lived events that communicate messages of consciousness to us if we are open to them. These may be subtle contacts with absolute wholeness that appear and disappear in our lives and eventually lead us further in our evolution. As in the world of subatomic particles, we have several resonance energies in the healing channel that directly relate to specific energy levels. Depending on our level of consciousness, there is a greater or lesser probability that we will contact certain of these levels. The more evolved we are, the greater the probability of resonating with the higher energies of the more complete realms. Spiritual resonances may give us a continual chance to follow the path of wholeness or remain in our lower-level reactions. The existence of subatomic reaction channels and technological electromagnetic channels are certainly not proof of a healing channel, but they do suggest that such a mechanism of transmission is not an isolated phenomenon.

As I see it, the healing channel is really a gift that unites us with the universal intelligence. All the actions that take place in this energy cavity are messages to us that this connection exists. We must be able to see this fact, however; otherwise we cannot take advantage of its help in everyday life, nor in our further evolution.

Most of us have to learn how to reconnect ourselves to this channel. Though some of us may have opened one resonance avenue, we fail to see that this is only a fraction of what is possible. There is even a tremendous danger that in experiencing one aspect of the healing channel, we assume that we are in contact with the whole. Many people on the spiritual path lose their way because of what they think are "their" powers or because they are misled by teachers who pretend to experience the whole. Though it is almost impossible not to lose our way sometimes without the help of an enlightened teacher, closer contact with our healing channel will help us stay on our path.

We must first bring our awareness to an experience of the healing channel. When we become truly aware of the experience and results of being in this channel, we can more easily return to it even when we have gone away. Like a path that we've traveled before, wholeness is a known that we need only rediscover. The next step is learning how we slip out of this channel. Because wholeness is our true nature and the healing channel is an important connection to absolute wholeness, it is natural for us to remain in this channel. We don't really have to "do" anything to get back into it; we must become aware of how we become unnatural, that is, how we remove ourselves from this wholeness. We need only become aware of how we block an essentially natural process and learn to stop preventing ourselves from enjoying its benefits. All of our complaints about our parents, cultures, unpleasant experiences, need for repression, and so on are excuses for not being in our channel.

Technically, when we attune ourselves to this healing energy, we feel a resonation with something that is more whole than we as personalities could ever be. We begin to sense the difference between external and internal vibrations that resonate with our spirit and those that simply resonate with our held energy. The latter lead to a *resonance of re-action*, while the former direct us to a *resonance of harmony*. Vibrations that have little or no meaning for us will have nothing to resonate with and thus will have little or no effect on us. Because everything in life vibrates, however, our spirit field must constantly process all these different oscillations and determine which ones are important. Each influential set of vibrations transmits information, so what we become attuned to gives us information about what is important for us. Becoming aware of the types and content of the communication we act on or re-act to is a major process in our development. What we are attuned to and are touched by shows us where we are in our evolution. If we are always bothered by particular noises or persons, our disturbance often indicates some unaccepted part of us that resonates on a level of little awareness. We are what disturbs us!

When we are out of attunement, almost all energy frequencies will resonate with our own dis-ease because we lack a clear sending and receiving signal of the spirit as it comes through the healing channel. In information theory stimuli that are unimportant to us are known as noise. Being attuned creates a high information-to-noise ratio, while being out of attunement creates a low information-to-noise ratio. With a low ratio, we cannot see clearly what is important for us in life. So many stimuli impinge on us, but we don't know to what if anything to respond. Therefore we become despondent or hysterical and respond to very little or everything. Under stress, the ratio of information is low because the pressure to act minimizes the organic receiving and sending functions. In some cases we fail to respond to important information, while in others we respond excessively to the unimportant. Mostly we do both, which creates a back-and-forth oscillation of dis-ease at both poles. It is no wonder that the psychoemosomatic process degenerates into physical and psychological disturbances, because the body, as a vibrational amplifier, becomes the product of a disrupted energy pattern in the life energy weave.

If our evolution is on the less complete levels of consciousness, we will tune ourselves automatically to lower, slower energy vibrations. For example, we might be caught in sadness and anger on the emotional level or in physical activity to the exclusion of spiritual interests. Perhaps this low level resonates with all that is diseased—we seek the sordid, the perverse, and the destructive in life for our amusement, instead of uplifting activity. Disease is the attunement to vibrations that are not synergetic with our spirit frequency.

John Ott has suggested that in the plant world, chloroplasts and pigment granules are used to natural light and that they are adversely affected by any other light. So it is for us too. Because we are naturally attuned to wholeness on all levels, any vibration that is not holistic will affect us adversely, unless our consciousness is so complete that we can transform potentially deleterious radiations into healthful ones.

Interpersonally our attunement to others constitutes rapport or sympathy with another. You may have experienced a first meeting with someone in which this attunement occurred. Immediately, you felt a oneness: conversation was easy, your interests were similar, and you could wholly communicate how you felt. Perhaps you easily shared your intimate experiences, as though there were no barriers between the two of you. This is a good example of how one person's channel can attune itself to another's; a flow of life energy was allowed that created instant wholeness and rapport. As the holistic resonance of such a contact continues, both people tend to become more alike. We can readily see this in loving couples who have been together for a long time. Little by little, they take on habits and patterns of the other as the energy seeks a unity from the polarity of two.

In L.E.T. the processes of awareness, energy patterns, and essential perception are directly related to the healing channel (see Figure 23). When we experience what being in this channel feels like, we become aware of life situations that show us we were there in the past. You may recall moments when everything you did seemed to correspond perfectly. Perhaps you found your job or your partner by simply being in the right place at the right time. We often attribute such events to chance or accident. This is easy to accept when it happens infrequently, but when we begin to experience it more and more of the time, we sense that there is another order operating. In an energy sense every accident is due to happen.

In the healing channel there are no decisions to make, no will to exercise, and no seeking. There is only what is. The longer we stay in this channel, the simpler life becomes because our increased awareness sensitizes us to the experience of being in harmony with ourselves and everything around us. Everything not in harmony with us is more clearly experienced as not-us and becomes increasingly unacceptable.

THE HEALING CHANNEL

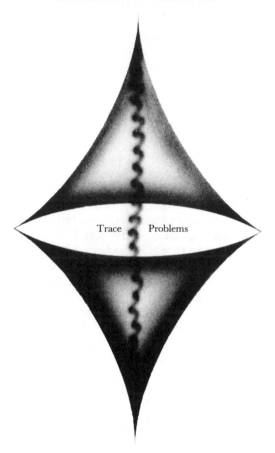

Figure 23.

If you are a smoker, smoking automatically becomes unpleasant because it is based on disease. Likewise, we change our food and drinking habits as we adjust to what feels appropriate for us. Unwhole behaviors are less tolerated; whole experiences feel more correct. Behaviors that do not fit into this new developing order are simply left behind as anachronistic when we direct the energy that animates them into behaviors of wholeness. Naturally we begin to see the patterns of disease and health much more quickly; at the same time, the healing channel lifts us upward as we make contact with the higher energies. Our perception becomes more essential as we contact only those situations that help us to grow. All other situations become less interesting. The extremes of our wandering behavior fall away as we come to see exactly what is important for us.

In therapy learning about the healing channel involves increasing awareness, attuning to the frequency of wholeness, staying focused in this resonation, and, finally, "letting through" of life energy. As a process, letting through consists of learning not to polarize energy into categories of prejudice but simply to stay in wholeness.* It is letting the energy show us what it needs to do for our evolution. This of course means letting go of our will, which wants to direct life. In the healing channel we do not need will because we do not have to direct life (even if we could); life is full of unfolding situations and chances to evolve that are provided for us according to our level of consciousness. By letting through, we allow the flow of energy to show us what we need to live and grow. Life energy always goes to places that are most open at any given time in the evolution process. This is quite in contrast to the process of "working through" developed by Freud and used today by many psychotherapies. As Freud described it:

> One must allow the patient time to get to know this resistance [the need to repeat a neurotic process in the transference] of which he is ignorant, to work through it, to overcome it, by continuing the work according to the analytic rule in defiance of it. Only when it has come to its height can one, with the patient's cooperation, discover the repressed instinctual trends which are feeding the resistance; and only by living them through in this way will the patient be convinced of their existence and their power.[6]

In letting through we don't need to overcome any resistance because the resistance is a formation of an energy blockage. We need only become aware of it until we can accept it, and life energy flows again. In letting through, energy flows into focal points of energy interaction that create an intensity of feeling, ideas, behaviors, and so on, all of which exist to teach us. Healing is automatic; it is built into energy fields on all levels of existence. We need only contact the healing channel and allow it to show us our life by staying aware and focused in its experience.

*This letting through process for the energist is simply called "channeling."

If we could simply accept life energy as it comes through us, we would not need therapy. But because we have difficulties with this process (which could be the most simple), we often need a focused process like therapy to help us return to wholeness. Because we have held back our energy for so long, it is difficult now to simply let go of it. This blocked energy has become woven into our bodies, personalities, roles, attitudes, feelings, and behaviors. To let go of these is really to learn how to die. Form develops because energy is crystallized, and most of what we call "us" has been crystallized to the point of petrification. Letting go of that very stable form is extremely difficult. Our total life is actually a form of energy processes that eventually fades away into death. Like physical life, the form of our being (not the being or self) must die so that new energy can be liberated. Matter is always developing and dissolving, from the smallest subatomic particle to the largest cosmic star. In between these extremes, the body, personality, and other units of personal wholeness constantly undergo death and rebirth. The creation and destruction of cells and the change in our personalities are witness to this fact on different levels of energy.

True evolution in our lifetime is the progressive letting go of form— all form—until physical death separates us from the body. So we must learn how to die by letting go of our held (dead) processes. These may come out as bodily fluids and wastes, colors, dreams, physical symptoms, emotions, or simply as energy vibrations that shake and clean the body. We have held energy for so long that we have become virtual energy reservoirs, where our muscles and connecting tissue form the dam. Physically this muscular holding is an energy cassette, just as are reactionary emotions or fixed ideas. By letting go of this held energy, we dissolve the cassette and free energy for new spontaneous movement. This energy movement will often express itself as an emotional explosion as we contact our death and expand into life. Death is both the extension of disease (i.e., the separation from wholeness) and the liberation from form in its return back to the spirit. Ironically, death is the key to life. For in our ability to die, to let go of form, we are truly alive. Many people confuse this death of form with a physical death. In therapy form-death feels like death of the body, but it is not. It feels that way because we have identified with all our forms, including the body, as us. Letting through and allowing one form after another to die is a liberation of the spirit, body, and emotions as we come to the true self beneath all its illusions.

Integrative Movement

As a result of living more and more in the healing channel, a new way of expressing ourselves begins to emerge. It might be described as a total involvement in what we do, whether we are eating, working, meditating, or loving. I have called this total involvement *integrative movement*. From the Eastern perspective, this movement is related to the right action of the Buddhists in general or the total awareness of the Zen Buddhists in particular. Right action should be understood not in terms of "right and wrong" but in terms of appropriate action. Integrative movement is a quality of wholeness in our activity (stillness is also activity) characterized by a strong personal center usually called hara, or specifically, tan den in the East. The hara is both a main source of energy focusing in the body and the visceral seat of emotions and personal identity. A strong hara expresses itself in knowing who we are and what we need at all times; all problems in therapy related to identity and life decisions show up clinically as a weak hara.

Integrative movement always begins in the hara. It connects all our activity with meaningfulness; that is when we act from the hara in the process of integrative movement, we sense the connection to what we do as the whole of us responds. This is especially apparent in the martial arts, where life energy is stimulated and exercised as a power to be used in total sensing and movement. No move is wasted because we sense at every moment what is appropriate without analyzing. In fact analysis is too slow to be integrative. Analysis breaks down and separates, so it is not holistic and can never be the source of integrative movement. Rather, integrative movement is knowing at the right time and place exactly which type of activity we need. It is a sensing of wholeness and the extension of this unity into movement. So integrative movement is organically connected to the healing channel and its information about wholeness and well-being. Most important, integrative movement fosters further evolution by supporting us in focusing this wholeness in a practical, directed way, situation after situation, in a continuum of connected activity. No step is wasted because all movement is focused on the whole.

In L.E.T. we use many types of physical movement to stimulate the opening up of blocked life energy, including stretching, reflex quickening, strengthening, energizing, flexibility, and specially designed movements for particular energy chakras, meridians, and other energy pathways/centers. Once the energy has been awakened and brought into movement, it seeks its own flow based on the emerging energy focus of the moment. Sometimes the energy moves into the undercharged hands/feet or expresses itself as a whole body warmth. At other times an emotion suddenly emerges from an old memory. There may simply be a light trembling that brings physical or emotional coldness to the surface. One person may become aware that he has cut off his aggressive feelings and therefore has undercharged hands; another may learn about the coldness she took in from her mother and still retains deep inside. In all cases a new understanding takes place between physical manifestations and their personal meaning to our lives. The form of each manifestation is unique to the individual because each of us has a specific path, although our collective path is the same—wholeness.

Therapy is a personal road even if it occurs in group work. In groups the initial movements that stimulate the energy for all participants focus themselves in a particular way for each individual. The movements themselves are secondary to the flow of the energy, which means that we have no set movements that group members perform. They arise spontaneously from the combined experience of the group and group energist. This emphasis on movement instead of exercise and the importance of spontaneous movements distinguishes our work from group exercise programs or set therapeutic exercises.* Movement for us is awareness in activity. The importance of movement is its fostering of awareness, not its goal orientation; that is, we don't perform a movement to achieve any particular goal. Movement is only another aspect of awareness that brings our personal processes into focus. Even the masters of Tai Chi and Aikido, who practice the same movements over and over, do not seek perfection in the movement but total involvement in the process until there is no separation between the art of movement and the practitioner. One becomes the chi or ki—the flow of life energy. This gives the true martial artist tremendous strength and courage, and a tremendous sense of wholeness. Integrative movement has just such a quality. It takes the process of wholeness from its connection to the healing channel and distributes this awareness to all parts of us, making us whole.

In movement a participant may begin to feel the separation of breathing and movement, the split of the right and left sides of the body, the lack of focus in the movement, the pattern of holding back emotion, the fear of wholeness, the dependency on doing what others do, or the tendency to go away instead of into emotions.

Integrative movement is activity with a high level of awareness;

*The Felderkrais method of neuromuscular training also emphasizes movement instead of exercise, though it is not based on a spiritual, emotional, or psychotherapeutic orientation, as is L.E.T.

in fact this heightened awareness in all that we do is the actual healing agent. The movement brings the quality of awareness to light, but the awareness is the healing process. The intention of integrative movement is simply to do everything as completely as possible with no concern for how long, how often, or how perfect the movement is done. This approach is distinct from, say, stress exercises in some body-oriented psychotherapies in which the intent is to stress the muscles until the emotions break through the muscular armoring. But stress only works at all because the pain of an exercise focuses awareness. If we don't allow ourselves to feel any pain, nothing will happen to us. But because the physical pain becomes so great, most people are drawn to heightened awareness. Working, however, with schizoid or rigid processes (rigidity is also based on a deeper schizoid process), stress exercises require a tremendous amount of time to have any effect because of the separation of the body and emotions. In stress exercises one is designed to elicit anger, the next sadness, and still another fear. In L.E.T. we use movements that work with deprogrammation and process orientation instead of goals and programmed exercise-emotion relationships. We encourage the excitement of awareness, aliveness, and growth instead of pain or stress. Life has enough distress without our adding to it. Knowledge of energy dysfunction does not require stress; the knowledge of energy dynamics, patterns of health and disease, and the healing process are enough. By forcing the body in stress, we mistrust our ability to come out of our energy shells. It shows a basic lack of respect for the child in us who developed his/her armor for protection.

Microments

In L.E.T. we therefore prefer to work directly on the energy field level. Even when we touch the body, it is understood that this contact is only the interface of energy fields on a physical level. We have developed a special type of micromovement, called *microments*, that work directly with energy processes and their patterns and, minimally, with the external musculature. We have found that the subtle body movements, not the heavy muscular ones, have the most direct relationship with patterns of disease and health.* Additionally, we have discovered that the internal orientation of energy patterns and

---

*This is especially important because much of our disease is pre- and subverbal, being derived from prenatal experiences, subtle interactions with our parents and energy influences of our environments (e.g., lights, noise, and so on).

dynamics, when extended, causes the muscular holding on the outside and that both the external and internal processes maintain a reciprocal feedback system. So in L.E.T. we work to open up the external energy level through dynamic movements and the internal level through subtle movements. By working on both internal and external energy processes, we can proceed with therapy much more quickly.

Because the concept of microments is a new one, I'd like to describe it in a little more detail. Microments are simply patterns of movements that are done very slowly and in an established rhythm of some polarity such as left and right or up and down. In shifting from one polarity to another, awareness is brought to every minute activity. In this process subtle vibrations that form the pattern of internal activity are brought to the surface. As they emerge, these minute vibrations function as tiny waves that develop into larger waves and consequently larger vibrations as they expand into the space of the external body structure. This naturally also brings the tissues and muscles into vibration, all without stress. Technically microments tap into the energy pattern that makes up the body and they directly contact the healing channel. All vibrations that are not holistic are driven to the exterior for discharge or expulsion. In this way disease is forced out of the wholeness, much like darkness is "driven out" by light.

There is scientific support for the idea that small phenomena can effect larger ones. In biochemistry trace elements of such minerals as fluorine, iodine, and zinc are found only in small amounts in the body, though they play a very important role in health. This is also true of the trace radiation of ultraviolet rays from the sun. We have discussed how subtle magnetic field influences may eventually prove to have a greater effect on us than medium-range influences, precisely because of their triggering mechanisms. This has been demonstrated in homeopathy with minute doses and has been supported by research in physics as well. We know, for example, that when particles from space (gamma ray photons) decay, they cause a radiation that produces still more photons in an effect called a "cascade shower." Closer to earth, this concept has been used in engineering as "cascade amplification," in which a small initial energy will lead to macrosized energy. A common use is the opening of a two-ton bank vault door through the interruption of a light beam.

Quantum physicist Evan Harris Walker has mathematically demonstrated that events in the brain are governed by a higher order (synonymous for him with consciousness) and that brain neurotransmitters, key elements in how the brain functions, can be affected by the "tunneling through" of a single electron. According to Walker, once an electron has come through the barrier, such as found in the brain's presynaptic membrane, a delicate electrical potential is charged and a large flow of electrons is possible. This large flow has been called the cascade amplification of the brain. This is quite significant because graded, slow-potential charges wax and wane at the synaptic junctions between neurons. If this delicate balance can be affected, then neurons would begin firing and behavior could be affected. It is also significant that the most recent brain research has concluded that all brain synapses are essentially alike and seem to function differently only in regard to a subtle as yet physically undefined influence. All indications are that consciousness (though not accepted by physical science) is the best candidate for this subtle process. If this proves to be true, then our state of awareness could influence the delicate electrical potential of the brain's presynaptic membrane, thereby affecting neurotransmitters and eventually behavior. How might this be possible?

Einstein formulated a theory of light energy in which the higher the frequency of the photon, the higher will be its state of energy ($Et = \hbar$ where energy (E) times time (t) is equal to Planch's constant ($\hbar$), which represents the fixed interaction between energy and time). This means that a high frequency or rate of vibration will generate a high amount of energy. In the concept of angular momentum, (A = mvL, where angular momentum (A) is equal to mass (m) times velocity (v) times the radius of a turning object (L)) physicists have shown that a small radius can store an infinite amount of energy.[7] One example of this is the ice skater who spins faster and faster as she draws her arms into the body, creating a smaller radius.

If we look at the research and theory from physics as a whole, it seems possible that microments function by both raising the vibrations of energy through awareness and reducing the radius of physical movement, each of which produces high amounts of energy. In terms of healing, the intensity of this energy could affect delicate presynaptic potentials, and we would begin to change our behavior. In addition, the patterns of disease woven into the fabric of the body cannot exist in a field of wholeness. Microments, by connecting with the subtle but powerful healing channel, allow us to contact the universal consciousness of the Absolute Reality or Soul. The key element here is our state of consciousness acting through the integrative movement of the microprocesses that unite our spirit in the medium of the healing channel to the universal energy field of the cosmos.

As Chladni has demonstrated, form (in this case the body) is the least vibratory aspect of energy. By working with the external form (body) and the internal vibrations (healing channel), we interconnect the physical body with the internal healing energies in the spiritual experience of wholeness. In this harmony our body and mental attitudes change, as well as our relationship to our feelings and behavior, because all these are manifestations of energy patterns. When these patterns become more whole in their synchronization with the order of our energy fields at all levels of relative reality, all disease patterns break down and gradually die out. Microments allow us to become aware of finer and finer adjustments to the healing channel until we feel an attunement. When this happens, all the information needed to live and evolve is provided to us in a similar process of information theory as a triggering mechanism. In its application to microments, our fine attunement to the appropriate frequency band (the spirit) yields universal information from even the slightest initial energy.

A main point about L.E.T. is that change is basically an automatic process that requires a certain relearning for most people. The principal obstacles to this natural process are our fear of change, our illusions, our belief in the existence of one reality, and our stubbornness to let go of old habits and ideas. Most of all, we must understand that our fear of wholeness keeps us investing energy in destructive patterns, some of which may even be the therapies that are supposed to help us. Our need to suffer is falsely based on the illusion that enduring life's difficulties is necessary for growth. In L.E.T. we see another alternative, and that is to turn to the universal source from which all change emanates. Its wholeness is everywhere to be seen for those with eyes for such harmony; we need only discover how to reconnect with its simplicity and wisdom. This requires a tremendous perseverance of awareness that involves neither suffering nor frustration. It does require clarity, focus, and a fervent desire to evolve, as well as an openness to a radical departure from preconceived ideas.

Chapter Seven

Conclusion

Throughout this book, I have suggested that Life Energy is a powerful explanatory concept for understanding the religious and healing practices of many civilizations throughout history, as well as the natural relationship of the spirit, body, and emotions to the conscious experience of wholeness. Such comprehensiveness is possible because this force is present in all phenomena as both the essence and medium for their expression in our existential world of physical form. In addition, I believe that Life Energy is an extremely important concept in examining and ultimately comprehending the physis or true nature of science, particularly physics as it might be applied to the study of health and wholeness. The new physics, for example, is confirming many ancient beliefs in the nature of the universe that we can reapply in our time if we see them from the perspective of Life Energy. Automatically, the physical and metaphysical worlds are brought together in a new synthesis. The coming together of these aspects of Life Energy is no coincidence, although we have lacked a common language with which to describe the functioning of this whole. By describing all processes as unique manifestations of energy on different levels of reality we can specifically relate all of these to one another. The result is a newly rediscovered wholeness that is both precise and complete, unlike most explanatory models, which provide either great detail or an overview but not both. This is certainly true of therapy and science. To date very few models of health have combined the balance of both polarities in a clear and concise manner. Technique or theory has usually prevailed in a lopsided emphasis, to the detriment of a complete approach.

The time has come for a new integration between specification and comprehensiveness. This new completeness is consistent with ancient wisdom—experienced in almost all civilizations through religious and healing procedures—and with modern research in subatomic physics and psychotronics. In this new wholeness a philosophy of energism emerges in which we can describe all aspects of the whole in energy terms. This has far-reaching consequences for both the therapies and the sciences. Modern medicine, for example, would have to reexamine its treatment procedures of symptom alleviation in favor of true curing by going to the roots of disease. The emphasis would be on preventive care, minimizing side effects in any medicinal preparation, and more research into holistic remedies that support the body's own processes of defense and regeneration.

In a new holism of therapeutics, psychotherapy must extend its theoretical and practical boundaries to include transpersonal dimensions of evolution and a greater acceptance of body-oriented approaches to complement the overemphasized mind (insight) processes. By using the language and concepts of Life Energy we can simplify the often confusing and misunderstood connections between physical and metaphysical realms.

A new holism would force us to reevaluate our ideas about science and mysticism, which are generally seen as separate fields of experience. Although there are differences in the two perspectives, such distinctions imply neither a lack of connectedness nor an inability to learn from one another. In fact, if the laws of wholeness are consistent, there *must* be a relatedness between science and mysticism that we have been until recently unwilling to rediscover.

Superficially, science appears more structured, linear, and rational than the more holistic, abstract, and intuitive path of mysticism. Scientists have usually been more interested in gathering "objective" content data to develop a whole, while mystics begin with the whole and observe its details. We should not, however, become attached to these generalizations. Every research project, for example, is predominantly based on subjective and intuitive processes of design, conclusions, and extrapolations. Even the machines used to objectify results are the products of subjectivity, while their data are measured in subjectively chosen units. To standardize that subjectivity so that everyone agrees that a meter is so long and no longer or shorter lends itself to greater but certainly not absolute objectivity.

Theoretical physics has necessarily stepped outside the realms of the linear and natural world to speculate about such unknowns as white holes and points of singularity, while modern physics has shifted its emphasis away from content-oriented science to a more useful process-oriented approach. Quantum physics stresses the need to look at the whole instead of the particular pieces of the universe, which again shows that the integral perspective of the mystical world is also present in the scientific sphere.

Likewise, the metaphysics of mysticism has always used "scientific" elements in its theory and practice through its insistence on the observation of reality, its research into the nature of knowledge, and its verification of cosmic "laws" through an elevation of consciousness—all processes related to scientific method.

In fact the "spirit" of science and the "science" of mysticism form the basis of how the physical and metaphysical worlds function with each other. A body without the animation of a spirit or a process of the soul without physical concretization would be incomplete as part of the evolution/involution cycle of Life Energy.

If we take science to its extreme, we are automatically led into the spiritual world because it is the absolute basis of the phenomena that science studies. However, most scientists never go this far. Even our machines, which we develop out of a particular need in the physical world, are end products of a certain consciousness. With a more complete consciousness, we could build machines that are more holistic and ecologically sound. Let us not forget that the limitations lie not in the machines per se but in our level of consciousness. For this reason, the mystical experience can help provide our world with more appropriate extensions of wholeness instead of the polluting devices we now build.

Of course the mystical experience is not necessary to produce a less polluting world, but a new sense of wholeness is necessary and we can effectively experience this through spiritual practice. There is no inherent separation between the inner world of spiritual growth and the outer world of everyday life. The spiritual perspective gives meaning to our daily situations, while physical reality ensures the consistency of our spiritual focus through our trials and errors.

This physical world of illusions forces us to confront ourselves through our creation and destruction of forms and the difficulties that arise from these processes. Our so-called problems are really messages of awareness that we receive as we pass from one stage of consciousness to another. They are both signs of where we interfere with the flow of energy and tests of initiation to show us if we are ready for the next steps of development. In order to grow, we need these continual shocks to awaken us from our lethargy and conceit.

Ironically, we seek the security of world peace, emotional harmony, and financial stability while denying the wholeness that makes these possible. In our schizophrenia we create conflicts in all sectors of life, which we then must resolve. By busying ourselves with problem solving and new understanding, we effectively prevent ourselves from experiencing the wholeness that already exists. Because we have so little consciousness of this universal whole, we are frightened to live in its completeness. We are scared to let go of our "theater" with each other, our chit-chat about the weather and the neighbors, and our obsession with ideals. Letting go of our business would force us to be *real.*

Our present age is a perfect one for coming to terms with our paradoxical behavior. We are continually confronted with our need to stay in conflict—between our bodies and emotions, in our social relationships, and in our political strife—all of which are splits from wholeness. Our land, seas, and air, are becoming increasingly polluted because we will not be holistic in our production/consumption of energy resources and goals. Our environment has spoken to us in messages of disruption and catastrophe. Are we ready to listen?

We say that we want peace. So why do we consistently create problems for ourselves and others? And why do we think that peace is only a political issue, outside our own personal wars?

We could spend our research funds on holistic medicine that would benefit both the receivers *and* the producers of people-compatible drugs and treatments—but we usually don't. We could build machines that are quieter, less intrusive, and more ecologically holistic—but we usually don't. Such holism is possible—if we really want it.

We must decide to remain part of the problem of dis-ease or become part of the solution in wholeness. We cannot do both. Wholeness is a clear path of spirit that seeks a reunion with an eternal completeness. It cannot accept anything less. Our consciousness of wholeness as the universal field of Life Energy is the beginning of a transformation from difficulties to possibilities. Only in its completeness are we connected with our true spiritual self and the peace that it radiates.

Especially now, in these times of division and isolation, we need pioneers willing to see the wholeness in life and live according to its precepts, despite the fact that others may not fully understand this path. Lack of acceptance should not matter. If we are living wholly instead of playing with the fantasy and ideas *about* wholeness, our path will be clearly marked. Wholeness is the message of our ancient journey that we must bring to light again and again. It demands our attention NOW.

Notes

Chapter One. History of Energy

Part One. The East

1. Patton, "Aircraft of the Pharaohs," *Omni*, 4:12 (1982).
2. Lamy, *Egyptian Mysteries*.
3. Flannagan, *Pyramid Power*.
4. Allen et al., *Energy, Matter and Form*, p. 195.
5. Ibid.
6. Hackmann, *Chinesische Philosophie*, p. 26.
7. Berk, *Chinese Healing Arts*, p. 2.
8. Motoyama, "Electrophysiological and Preliminary Biochemical Studies of Skin Properties in Relation to Acupuncture Meridians," *Research for Religion and Parapsychology* 6 (1980).
9. Allen et al., *Energy, Matter and Form*, p. 16.
10. Ibid, p. 25.
11. Love, *The Quantum Gods*.
12. von Quintus, *Durchbruch zum Ursprung*.
13. Portnoy, "Spinoza, the Outcast Philosopher," *Holland Herald* (17:10 1982).
14. Shah. *The Sufis*.

Part Two. The West

1. Pierrakos, *Human Energy Systems Theory*.
2. Lucoff (Airola, ed.), *Health Secrets from Europe*.
3. Kent (Vithoulkas), *Homeopathy*.
4. Reich, *The Cancer Biopathy*, p. 15.
5. Krippner and Rubin, *The Kirlian Aura*, p. 165.

Chapter Two. Toward a Physics of Life Energy

1. Zukav, *The Dancing Wu Li Masters*, p. 212.
2. Capra, *Tao of Physics*, p. 6.
3. Ibid, p. 57.
4. Año, "Mind and the Quantum," *Bulletin Today* (December 1981).
5. Capra, *Tao of Physics*, p. 60.
6. Freedman and van Nieuwenhuizen, "Supergravity and the Unification of the Laws of Physics," *Particles and Fields*.
7. Hills, *Nuclear Evolution: Discovery of the Rainbow Body*, p. 787.
8. Motoyama, "The Mechanics by Which Psi-Ability Manifests Itself," *Impact of Science on Society* 24 (1974), p. 321.
9. Tiller, "Toward a Future Medicine," *Proceedings of the Association for Research and Enlightenment Medical Symposium* (January 1976).
10. Allen et al., *Energy, Matter and Form*, p. 105.
11. Tiller, "Creating a New Functional Model," unpublished.
12. Justa-Smith, "The Influence of Enzyme Growth by the 'Laying-on-of-Hands,'" *Dimensions of Healing Symposium Proceedings* (1972).
13. Ostrander and Schroeder, *Psychic Discoveries Behind the Iron Curtain*.
14. Dudley, "The Rediscovery of Ether," *Future Science*, p. 189.
15. Gallimore, *The Handbook of Unusual Energies*.
16. Zukav, *The Dancing Wu Li Masters*, p. 278.
17. Pelletier, *Towards a Science of Consciousness*, p. 47.
18. Ibid.
19. As quoted in Allen et al., *Energy, Matter and Form*, p. 86.
20. Talbot, *Mysticism and the New Physics*, p. 7.

21. Toben, Sarfatti and Wolf, *Space-Time and Beyond.*
22. Zukav, *The Dancing Wu Li Masters.*
23. Globus, "Consciousness and Brain," *Archives of General Psychiatry* 29 (1973).
24. Quoted in Zukav, *The Dancing Wu Li Masters,* p. 88.
25. Quoted in Capra, *Tao of Physics,* p. 280.
26. Tiller, "Consciousness, Radiation," *Proceedings of A.M.P. Symposium* (September 1972).
27. Bohm, *Wholeness and the Implicate Order,* pp. xi-xii.
28. Quoted in Zukav, *The Dancing Wu Li Masters,* p. 323.
29. Ibid, p. 315.
30. Ibid, p. 118.
31. Einstein, *The Evolution of Physics,* p. 243.
32. Dubrov, "Biogravitation and Psychotronics," *Future Science,* p. 231.
33. Capra, *Tao of Physics,* p. 200.
34. Kunz, "On the Symmetry Principle," *Main Currents in Modern Thought* 22:4 (1966), p. 200.
35. Pelletier, *Toward a Science of Consciousness.*
36. Allen et al., *Energy, Matter and Form.*
37. Ibid, p. 122.
38. Sarfatti, unpublished manuscript quoted in Zukav, *The Dancing Wu Li Masters,* p. 213.
39. Daniels, "The Possibility of a New Force in Nature," *I.E.E.E. Regional Electromagnetic Compatability Symposium Record,* p. 37.
40. Bentov, *Stalking the Wild Pendulum,* p. 59.
41. Capra, *Tao of Physics,* p. 67.

Chapter Three. Wholeness and Energy

1. Three Initiates, *The Kybalion,* p. 220.
2. Beasley, *Your Electro-Vibratory Body,* p. 11.
3. Tiller, "Consciousness, Radiation and the Developing Sensory System," *Proceedings from A.P.M. Symposium* (September 1972).
4. Bradley, *Endings.*
5. Krippner and Rubin, *The Kirlian Aura.*
6. De La Warr, "Power of Thought," p. 22.
7. Ibid. from original work by Albert Abrams.
8. Allen et al., *Energy, Matter and Form,* p. 209.
9. Blair, *Rhythms of Vision.*
10. Tiller, Conference on the Physics of Consciousness, Newton, Mass., 1975.
11. Tiller, "Toward a Future Medicine," *Phoenix* 1:1 (Summer, 1977).
12. Forbes, "Changes in Body Water and Electrolyte During Growth and Development," *Body Composition in Animals and Man.*
13. Snively, *The Sea of Life.*
14. Beasley, *Your Electro-Vibratory Body,* p. 14.
15. Pykett, "NMR Imaging in Medicine," *Scientific American* 246:5 (1982).
16. Blair, *Rhythms of Vision,* p. 50.
17. Zackrisson, "3000 Åriga Frön Fran Mosse Började Gro," *Dagens Nyheter* (November 11, 1982).
18. Beasley, *Your Electro-Vibratory Body,* p. 17.
19. Barnothy, *Biological Effects of Magnetic Fields,* p. 15.

20. Dixon, "The Master Code," *Omni* 4:12 (1982), p. 18.
21. Davies, "Clones vs. Cancer," *Omni* 4:12 (1982).
22. Beasley, *Your Electro-Vibratory Body*, p. 20.
23. Allen et al., *Energy, Matter and Form*, p. 59.
24. Koestler, *Janus*, p. 199.
25. Nossal, *Antigens, Lymphoid Cells, and the Immune Response*, pp. 264-5.
26. Waddington, *Structure of the Genes*.
27. Lee, *The Herb Renaissance*.
28. Allen et al., *Energy, Matter and Form*, p. 119.
29. Quoted in Allen et al., *Energy, Matter and Form*, p. 118.
30. Allen et al., *Energy, Matter and Form*, p. 8.
31. Lakhovsky, *The Secret of Life-Cosmic Rays and Radiations of Living Beings*.
32. Beasley, *Your Electro-Vibratory Body*, p. 22.
33. Allen et al., *Energy, Matter and Form*, p. 115.
34. Becker, "Relationship of Geo-Magnetic Environment to Biology," *New York State Journal of Medicine* (August 1, 1963).
35. Goddavage, "Man, the Biomagnetic Animal," *Fate* (July 1964).
36. Ponte, "Biomagnetism: The Force that Shapes Our Lives," *Reader's Digest* (November, 1982).
37. Baker in Panatti, *Breakthroughs*, p. 133.
38. Beasley, *Your Electro-Vibratory Body*, p. 104.
39. Ibid.
40. Ibid.
41. Goddavage, "Man, the Biomagnetic Animal."
42. Bhattacharya in Davis and Bhattacharya, "Magnet and Magnetic Fields or Healing by Magnets."
43. Ibid.
44. McLean in Goddavage, "Man, the Biomagnetic Animal."
45. Davis in Davis and Bhattacharya, "Magnet and Magnetic Fields."
46. Beasley, *Your Electro-Vibratory Body*, p. 105.
47. Pierrakos, *Human Energy Systems Theory*.
48. Beasley, *Your Electro-Vibratory Body*, p. 106.
49. Allen et al., *Energy, Matter and Form*, p. 112.
50. Ibid, pp. 216-217.
51. Barnothy, *Biological Effects of Magnetic Fields*, p. 196.
52. McFarland, *Physiological Psychology*, p. 291.
53. Cited in Beasley, *Your Electro-Vibratory Body*, p. 115.
54. Rubin and Katz, "Auroratone Films for the Treatment of Psychotic Depressions," *Journal of Clinical Psychology* 2:4 (1946).
55. Chapman, *The Body Fluids and Their Functions*.
56. Bridges, "Emotional Development in Early Infancy," *Child Development* 3 (1932).
57. Selye, *Stress Without Distress*, p. 135.
58. Schneider, *Revolution in the Body-Mind*, p. 28.
59. Osborne, *The Teachings of Bhagavan Sri Ramana Maharshi*.
60. Spees, "A Thymos Primer," *Journal of American Medical Association* 207 (1969), p. 1436.
61. Ricciutti, *Emotional Development in the First Two Years*.
62. Bohm, *Wholeness and the Implicate Order*, p. 197.

63. Guyton, *Basic Human Physiology.*
64. Cited in Cannon, *Wisdom of the Body,* p. 21.
65. Pelletier, *Mind as Healer, Mind as Slayer.*
66. Anakraut and Solomon, "From the Symbolic Stimulus to the Pathophysiological Response," *International Journal of Psychiatry in Medicine* 5 (1975).
67. Pelletier, *Mind as Healer, Mind as Slayer.*
68. Baltimore quoted in "Psychology Tomorrow: The Nobel View," *Psychology Today* 16:12 (1982), p. 31.
69. Pelletier, *Mind as Healer, Mind as Slayer,* p. 45.
70. Gray, *Gray's Anatomy.*
71. Allen et al., *Energy, Matter and Form,* p. 17
72. Pelletier, *Mind as Healer, Mind as Slayer.*
73. Ibid, p. 67.
74. Ibid, p. 42.
75. Ibid, p. 77.
76. Allen et al., *Energy, Matter and Form,* p. 182.
77. Lindlahr, *Philosophy of Natural Therapeutics,* p. 23.
78. Zinlardo, "Cognitive Control," quoted in Pelletier, *Mind as Healer, Mind as Slayer.*
79. Kingston, *Healing Without Medicine.*
80. Pelletier, *Holistic Medicine,* p. 98.
81. Ibid.
82. Mishlove, *Roots of Consciousness.*
83. Kötke, "Heil aus dem Tunnel," *Stern* (No. 3, 1981), p. 127.
84. Mishlove, *Roots of Consciousness.*

Chapter Four. Energy Radiations

1. Benoit et al. in Ott, *Health and Light,* p. 150.
2. Ott, *Health and Light,* p. 103.
3. Ibid, p. 150.
4. Ibid, p. 80.
5. N.Y. Times quoted in Allen et al., *Energy, Matter and Form,* p. 28.
6. "Kopfschmerzen durch falsches Licht," *Vital Magazine,* (Oktober, 1981), S. 46.
7. Maurer, "Computer Epilepsy," *Omni* 4:12 (1982) p.49.
8. Elias, "Using Colors to Alter Behavior," *Los Angeles Times* (August 3, 1980), part v3.
9. Gimbel, *Healing Through Color,* p. 78.
10. Mahnke, "Color in Medical Facilities," *Interior Design* 52 (1981), pp. 256-64.
11. Takayama and Ojima, "Photosensitizing Activity of Carcinogenic and Non-carcinogenic Polycyclic Hydrocarbons on Cultured Cells," *Japanese Journal of Genetics,* 44 (1969), pp.231-40.
12. Hellman, "Kann Licht Depressionen heilen?" *Psychologie Heute* (November 1982).
13. Blair, *Rhythms of Vision,* p. 56.
14. Beasley, *Your Electro-Vibratory Body,* p. 82.
15. Goddavage, "Man, the Biomagnetic Animal."
16. Beasley, *Your Electro-Vibratory Body,* p. 163.
17. Ecker and Branesco, *Radiation.*
18. Marsh, *The Way Technology Works.*
19. Hall, *Radiobiology for the Radiobiolgist.*
20. Marsh, *The Way Technology Works.*
21. Panatti, *Breakthroughs.*
22. Eckardt, "Strahlend geht das Meer zugrunde," *Stern* (Juli 8, 1982).
23. König, *Unsichtbare Umwelt.*
24. von Quintus, *Durchbruch zum Ursprung.*

25. Bachler, *Erfahrungen einer Rutengängerin.*
26. Böhm, *Wholeness and the Implicate Order.*
27. Ibid.
28. Hartmann, *Krankheit als Standortproblem.*
29. Bachler, *Erfahrungen einer Rutengängerin.*
30. Kreitz, *Die Krankheitsursache.*
31. Blair, *Rhythms of Vision.*
32. von Quintus, *Durchbruch zum Ursprung.*
33. Ott, *Health and Light.*
34. Marsh, *The Way Technology Works.*
35. Ibid., p. 90.
36. Ecker and Branesco, *Radiation.*
37. König, *Unsichtbare Umwelt.*
38. Ibid.
39. Marsh, *The Way Technology Works.*
40. Ecker and Branesco, *Radiation,* p. 48.
41. Mendelsohn, *Confessions of a Medical Heretic.*
42. König, *Unsichtbare Umwelt.*
43. Kending, "Listening to Radar," *Psychology Today* 16:12 (1982), p. 80.
44. Mendelsohn, *Confessions of a Medical Heretic.*
45. Ibid.
46. Beasley, *Your Electro-Vibratory Body,* p. 110.
47. Tromp, *Psychical Physics.*
48. Beasley, *Your Electro-Vibratory Body.*
49. Allen et al., *Energy, Matter and Form,* p. 170.
50. King, Serge, "Neoenergy and Geometric Forms" in *Future Science,* pp. 184-90.
51. Blair, *Rhythms of Vision.*
52. Ott, *Health and Light,* p. 10.
53. Tomlinson, *Medical Divination.*
54. Eeman, *Cooperative Healing.*
55. Ecker and Branesco, *Radiation.*
56. Mann, *Orgone, Reich and Eros.*
57. Weeks, "Hospitals," *Architectural Review* 168 (1980) p.55.
58. König, *Unsichtbare Umwelt.*
59. "Kopfschmerzen durch falsches Licht," S. 46.

Chapter Five. Medicine and Psychotherapy

1. Mendelsohn, *Confessions of a Medical Heretic,* pp. 52-53.
2. Wade, "Drug Rehabilitation," *Science* 179 (1973), pp. 775-77.
3. *Physicians' Desk Reference.*
4. Illich, *Medical Nemesis, the Expropriation of Health,* p. 44.
5. Vayda, "A Comparison of Surgical Rates in Canada and in England and Wales," *New England Journal of Medicine,* 289 (1973), pp. 1224-29.
6. Doyle, "Unnecessary Hysterectomies," *Journal of the American Medical Association,* (151) 1953, pp. 360-65.
7. Coulter, *Divided Legacy.*
8. Behring, "Modern Pthisiogenic and Ptisiotherapeutic Problems in Historical Illumination," Section V.
9. Adams and Murray, *Megavitamin Therapy.*
10. Illich, *Medical Nemesis, the Expropriation of Health,* p. 32.
11. Strupp; Bergin and Garfield, *Handbook of Psychotherapy and Behavior Change.*
12. Lang, "A Psychophysiological Analysis of Fear Reduction using an Automated Desensitizing Procedure," *Journal of Abnormal Psychology* 76 (1970), pp. 220-34.
13. Rogers quoted in Orstein, *The Psychology of Consciousness,* p. 67.

14. Bergin and Garfield, *Handbook of Psychotherapy and Behavior Change.*

15. Strupp, Fox and Lessler, *Patients View Their Psychotherapy.*

16. Strupp, "Towards a Reformulation of the Psychotherapeutic Influence," *International Journal of Pschiatry* 3 (1973), p. 292.

17. Ford and Urban, *Systems of Psychotherapy*; Lazarus, *Behavior Therapy and Beyond*; Agras, *Behavior Modification.*

18. Stampfl, "Implosive Therapy; Part I: The Theory" in *Behavior Modification Techniques in the Treatment of Emotional Disorders.*

19. Ibid, p. 301.

20. Ibid, p. 293.

21. Hall and Lindzey, *Theories of Personality.*

22. Sabetti, *Psychoanalysis as an Energy Process: Theory.*

23. Capra, *Tao of Physics*, p. 297.

24. Szasz, *The Myth of Psychotherapy*, p. 25.

25. Ibid.

Chapter Six. Life Energy Process

1. Westlake, *Pattern of Health*, p. 145.

2. Edgar, *The Origins of the Healing Art.*

3. Capra, *Tao of Physics.*

4. Ibid, p. 259.

5. Ibid.

6. Pelletier, *Toward a Science of Consciousness*, pp. 58-60.

7. Freud, "Analysis Terminable and Interminable," in *Therapy and Technique*, p. 165.

References

Ackerman, Eugene. *Biophysical Science.* Englewood Cliffs; N.J.: Prentice-Hall, 1962.

Adams, Ruth and Murray, Frank. *Megavitamin Therapy.* New York: Larchmont Books, 1973.

Agras, W. Stewart, ed. *Behavior Modification: Principles and Cinical Applications.* 2nd ed. Boston: Little, Brown, 1978.

Aichelburg, Peter C. and Sexl, Roman U., eds. *Albert Einstein.* Braunschweig: Viehweg, 1979.

Airola, Paavo. *Health Secrets from Europe.* New York: Arco Publishing, 1975.

Allen, Phil; Bearne, Alastair; and Smith, Roger. *Energy, Matter and Form.* Boulder Creek, Calif.: University of the Trees Press, 1977.

Allport, G.W. *Personality: A Psychological Interpretation.* New York: Hall, 1937.

Anakraut, A. and Solomon, G.F. "From the Symbolic Stimulus to the Pathophysiological Response: Immune Mechanisms." *International Journal of Psychiatry in Medicine* 5 (1975): 541-63.

Año Ed. T. "Mind and the Quantum: Two Universes or One?" *Bulletin Today* (December 28, 1981).

Averill, J.R. "Autonomic Response Patterns During Sadness and Mirth." *Psychophysiology* 5 (1969): 399-414.

Babbitt, Edwin D. *The Principles of Light and Color; the Classical Study of the Healing Power of Color.* New Hyde Park, N.Y.: University Books, 1967.

Bach, Edward, *Blumen, die unsere Seele heilen.* München: Hugendubel, 1979.

Bach, Edward. *The Twelve Healers.* London: C.W. Danill, 1977.

Bachler, Käthe. *Erfahrungen einer Rutengängerin.* Wien: Veritas Verlag, 1980.

Backster, Cleve. "Evidence of Primary Perception in Plant Life." *International Journal of Parapsychology* 10:4 (1968): 329-48.

Bailey, Alice. *The Soul and its Mechanism.* New York: Lewis Publishing, 1965.

Bailey, M., and Zabrisky, L. "Changes in Proteins During Growth and Development in Animals." In *Body Composition in Animals and Man,* edited by Gilbert Forbes. Washington, D.C.: National Academy of Sciences, 1968.

Baltimore, David. Quoted in "Psychology Tomorrow: The Nobel View." *Psychology Today* 16:12 (1982): 21-31.

Baranski, J.L. "The Frequency Spectrum and the Principle of Resonance Absorption." *North American Aviation* (1963).

Barnothy, Madeline, ed. *Biological Effects of Magnetic Fields.* New York: Plenum Press, 1964.

Baron, Robert Alex. *The Tyranny of Noise.* New York: St. Martin's Press, 1970.

Basbam, A.L. "The Practice of Medicine in Ancient and Medieval India." *In Asian Medical Systems: A Comparative Study,* edited by Leslie Charles. Berkeley: University of California Press, 1976.

Bayes, K. *The Therapeutic Effect of Environment on Emotionally Disturbed and Mentally Subnormal Children.* London: Unwin, 1967.

Beasley, Victor. *Your Electro-Vibratory Body.* Boulder Creek, Calif.: University of the Trees Press, 1978.

Becker, F. "Focus on the News: Empowering Body to Regenerate." *Medical World News* (September 1, 1972).

Becker, R.D. and Murray, D.G. "The Electrical Control System Regulating Fracture Healing in Amphibians." *Clinical Orthopaedics and Related Research* 75 (1970):169.

Becker, Robert O. "Relationship of Geo-Magnetic Environment to Biology." *New York State Journal of Medicine.* August 1, 1963.

Behring, von, Emil Adolph. "Modern Pthisiogenic and Pthisiotherapeutic Problems in Historical Illumination." *Section V:* New York, 1906.

Benoit, Jacques and Assenmacher, Ivan. "The Control by Visible Radiations of the Gonadotropic Activity of the Duck Hypophysis." *Recent Progress in Hormone Research,* 15 (1955): 143-64.

Bentov, Itzhak. *Stalking the Wild Pendulum.* New York: Dutton, 1977.

Bergin, A.E. and Garfield, S.L., eds. *Handbook of Psychotherapy and Behavior Change.* New York: Wiley, 1971.

Berk, William, ed. *Chinese Healing Arts, Internal Kung Fu.* Culver City, Calif.: Peace Press, 1979.

Berkowitz, Leonard. *Aggression: A Social Psychological Analysis.* New York: McGraw-Hill, 1962.

Bessenich, Frieda. *Zur Methode der empfindlichen Kristallisation.* Dornach: Philosophisch-Anthroposophischer Verlag, 1960.

Beynam, Laurence. "Quantum Physics and the Paranormal." *Astrologia,* 1 (1975).

Blair, Lawrence. *Rhythms of Vision.* New York: Schocken Books, 1976.

Böhm, Helmut. "Die Infrarotphotographie im Dienste der Radiästhesie." Radiästhesie-Kongress in Puchberg, Austria, 1973.

Bohm, David. *Wholeness and the Implicate Order.* London: Routledge & Kegan Paul, 1980.

Bohm, David. Lecture at the University of California, Berkeley, April 6, 1977, quoted in Gary Zukav, *The Dancing Wu Li Masters.* New York: Morrow, 1979.

Bohm, David and Riley, B. "On the Intuitive Understanding of Nonlocality as Implied by Quantum Theory." Preprint. London: University of London (1974).

Bolen, Jean Shinoda. *The Tao of Psychology.* San Francisco: Harper & Row, 1979.

Boling, Nick. "Tree ESP." *Omni* 5:3 (1982) 42.

Bourne, L., and Ekstrand, B. *Psychology.* New York: Holt, Rinehart & Winston, 1979.

Bradley, Buff. *Endings.* Reading, Mass.: Addison Wesley, 1979.

Breggin, Peter. "The Return of Lobotomy and Psychosurgery." *U.S. Congressional Record* 118 (February 24, 1972) 5567-77.

Bridges, K.M.B. "Emotional Development in Early Infancy." *Child Development* 3 (1932):324-41.

Brodsky, G. *From Eden to Aquarius.* New York: Bantam Books, 1974.

Bulger, R., ed. *Hippocrates Revisited.* New York: Medion Press, 1973.

Burns, William. *Noise and Man.* Philadelphia: Lippencott, 1969.

Burrows, Graham D. and Pennerstein, L. *Handbook of Hypnosis and Psychosomatic Medicine.* New York: Elsevier/North Holland Biomedical Press, 1980.

Butler, W.E. *The Magician: His Training and Work.* New York, Weiser, 1971.

Camp, John. *The Healer's Art.* New York: Taplinger, 1977.

Cannon, Walter B. *The Wisdom of the Body.* New York: Norton, 1932.

Capek, Milic. *The Philosophical Impact of Contemporary Physics.* Princeton, N.J.: Van Nostrand, 1961.

Capra, Fritjof. *The Tao of Physics.* New York: Bantam Books, 1977.

Capra, Fritjof. *The Turning Point: Science, Society and the Rising Culture.* New York: Simon & Schuster, 1982.

Chapman, Garth. *The Body Fluids and Their Functions.* Southampton, England: Camelot Press, 1980.

Cirlot, Juan E. *Dictionary of Symbols.* New York: Philosophical Library, 1962.

Condrau, Gion. *Einführung in die Psychotherapie.* München: Kindler Taschenbücher, 1974.

Coulter, Harris L. *The Divided Legacy.* 2d ed. Richmond, Calif.: North Atlantic Books, 1982.

Cousins, Norman. *Anatomy of an Illness as Perceived by the Patient.* New York: Norton, 1979.

Daniels, Rexford. "The Possibility of a New Force in Nature." In *I.E.E.E. Regional Electromagnetic Compatibility Symposium Record,* October 6-8, 1970, Texas (70 c 28 EMC).

Dantsig, N.M.; Lazarer, D.N.; and Sokolov, M.V. "Ultraviolet Installations of Beneficial Action." Washington, D.C.: International Committee on Illumination, 1967.

Davies, Owen. "Clones vs. Cancer." *Omni* 4:12 (1982):89-92.

Davis, A.R. and Battacharya, A.K. "Magnet and Magnetic Fields or Healing by Magnets." Calcutta: KLM Private, 1976.

Davis, George. *Radiation and Life.* Ames, Iowa: Iowa State University Press, 1967.

Dean, D. "Pletismograph Recording of ESP Responses." *International Journal of Neuropsychology* 2:5 (1966).

De Chardin, Pierre Teilhard. *The Phenomenon of Man.* New York: Harper & Brothers, 1959.

De La Warr, George. "Power of Thought." Reprint of paper read to Oxford University Scientific Society, May 5, 1961.

Dhawan, P.D. "The Tribasic Concept of Ayurveda—Explained in Terms of Allopathy." In *Theories and Philosophies of Medicine.* New Delhi: Institute of History and Medical Research, 1973.

Dhyanyogi Shri Madhusudandasji. *Shakti.* Pasadena, Calif.: Dhyanyoga Center, 1979.

Dixon, Bernard. "The Master Code." *Omni* 4:12 (1982):18.

Doczi, György. *The Power of Limits.* Boulder, Colo.: Shambhala, 1981.

Dollard, J., et al. *Frustration and Aggression.* New Haven, Conn.: Yale University Press, 1939.

Dorland, W.A. Newman. *Illustrated Medical Dictionary.* 24th ed. Philadelphia: W.B. Saunders, 1965.

Doyle, James. "Unnecessary Hysterectomies." *Journal of the American Medical Association.* 151(1953):360-65.

Dreyfuss, Henry. *Symbol Sourcebook.* New York: McGraw-Hill, 1972.

Dubrov, Alexander. "Biogravitation and Psychotronics." In *Future Science,* edited by John White and Stanley Krippner, 229-44. New York: Anchor Books, 1977.

Dudley, H.C. "The Rediscovery of Ether." In *Future Science,* edited by John White and Stanley Krippner, 184-90. New York: Anchor Books, 1977.

Dunbar, F. *Mind and Body: Psychosomatic Medicine.* New York: Random House, 1947.

Eccles, John C. *Facing Reality.* New York: Springer Verlag, 1970.

Eckardt, Nikolaus. "Strahlend geht das Meer zugrunde." *Stern* 28 (Juli 8, 1982).

Ecker, Martin and Branesco, Martin. *Radiation.* New York: Random House, 1981.

Edgar, Irving. *The Origins of the Healing Art.* New York: Philosophical Library, 1978.

Eeman, L.E. *Cooperative Healing.* London: Frederick Muller, 1947.

Einstein, Albert and Infeld, Leopold. *The Evolution of Physics.* New York: Simon & Schuster, 1938.

Elias, M. "Using Colors to Alter Behavior." *Los Angeles Times* (August 3, 1980), part V3.

Enge, L. *Introduction to Atomic Physics.* Reading, Mass.: Addison Wesley, 1972.

Engel, G. "Unified Concept of Health and Disease." *Perspectives in Biology and Medicine* 3 (1960), 459-85.

Evans-Wentz, W.Y. *Tibetan Yoga and Secret Doctrines.* London: Oxford University Press, 1958.

Farr, Lee. "Medical Consequences of Environmental Home Noise." In *People and Buildings,* edited by Robert Gutman, 202-11. New York: Basic Books, 1972.

Feller, R.P.; Burney, S.W.; and Sharon, I.M. "Some Effects of Light on the Golden Hamster." *IADR Abstracts.* New York: International Association of Dental Research, 1970.

Flanagan, G. Pat. *Pyramid Power.* Glendale, Calif.: Pyramid Publishers, 1974.

Flannagan, J.L. *Speech Analysis, Synthesis and Perception.* Berlin: Springer Verlag, 1965.

Forbes, Gilbert. "Changes in Body Water and Electrolyte During Growth and Development." In *Body Composition in Animals and Man,* edited by Gilbert Forbes. Washington, D.C.: National Academy of Sciences, 1968.

Ford, Donald. and Urban, Hugh B. *Systems of Psychotherapy: A Comparative Study.* New York: Wiley, 1963.

Forwald, H. *Mind, Matter and Gravitation.* New York: Parapsychology Foundation, 1969.

Freedman, D. and van Nieuwenhuizen, P. "Supergravity and the Unification of the Laws of Physics." In *Particles and Fields,* 121-33. San Francisco: Freeman, 1980.

French, A. *Vibrations and Waves.* New York: Norton, 1971.

Freud, Sigmund. "Analysis Terminable and Interminable." In *Therapy and Technique, The Collected Papers of Sigmund Freud.* New York: Collier Books, 1963.

Fuller, Buckminster. *Synergetics.* New York: MacMillan, 1975.

Gallert, Mark. *New Light on Therapeutic Energies.* London: James Clark, 1966.

Gallimore, J.G. *The Handbook of Unusual Energies.* Mokelumne Hill, Calif.: Health Research, 1976.

Gimbel, Theo. *Healing Through Color.* Essex, England: C.W. Danill, 1980.

Glazewski, A. "The Music of Crystals, Plants and Human Beings." Reprint from *Radio Perception* (September 1951).

Globus, Gordon G. "Consciousness and Brain." *Archives of General Psychiatry* 29 (1973):153-57.

Goddavage, Joseph. "Man, the Biomagnetic Animal." 17:7 *Fate* (1964:29-36).

Goethe, von, J.W. *Theory of Color.* Cambridge, Mass.: M.I.T. Press, 1970 (first published 1840).

Goffman, Erving. *The Presentation of Self in Everyday Life.* London: Penguin, 1971.

Goldwag, E., ed. *Inner Balance, Power of Holistic Healing.* Englewood Cliffs, N.J.: Prentice-Hall, 1979.

Gordon, William. *Synectics.* New York: MacMillan, 1961.

Grad, Bernard. "The Influence of an Unorthodox Method of Wound Healing in Mice." *International Journal of Parapsychology* (Spring 1961):5-24.

Grad, Bernard. "A Telekinetic Effect on Plant Growth." *International Journal of Parapsychology* 5 (1964):117-133.

Grad, Bernard. "The Laying on of Hands: Implications for Psychotherapy." *Journal of the American Society for Psychical Research* 61 (1967):286-305.

Gray, Henry. *Gray's Anatomy.* 35th ed. London: Longman, 1973.

Grollman, Sigmund. *The Human Body.* New York: MacMillan, 1978.

Guirdbam, A. *The Nature of Healing.* London: George Allen & Unwin Ltd., 1964.

Gurvich, Alexander G. *Die Mitogenetische Strahlung.* Jena: Fischer Verlag, 1959.

Gutslein, B. "Neural Factors Contributing to Atherogenesis." *Science* 199 (1978):449-51.

Guyton, A. *Basic Human Physiology.* Philadelphia: Saunders, 1977.

Hackmann, Heinrich. *Chinesische Philosophie.* München: E. Reinhardt, 1927.

Hahnemann, Samuel. *Organon der rationellen Heilkunst.* Dresden: Arnoldische Buchhandlung, 1810.

Hahnemann, Samuel. "Versuch über ein neues Prinzip zur Auffindung der Heilkräfte der Arzneisubstanzen, nebst einigen Blicken auf die bisherigen." *Journal der practischen Arzneykunde und Wundarzneykunst,* Berlin 2, (1796):391-439; 465-651.

Hall, Calvin and Lindzey, Gardner. *Theories of Personality.* New York: Wiley, 1970.

Hall, Eric. *Radiobiology for the Radiobiologist.* Hagerstown, Md.: Harper & Row Medical Dept., 1978.

Halle-Tischendorf, L. von. "Städtebau und Medizin." *Forum, Städte, Hygiene* 6 (November/Dezember 1981).

Hameroff, Stuart Roy. "Chi: A Neural Hologram? Microtubules, Bio-holography and Acupunture." *American Journal of Chinese Medicine,* 2 (1974):163-70.

Harrison, Jane E. *Prolegomena to the Study of Greek Religion.* New York: Noonday, 1955.

Hartmann, E. *Krankheit als Standortproblem.* Heidelberg: Haug, 1967.

Harvalik, Z.V. "Sensitivity Tests on a Dowser Exposed to Artifical D.C. Magnetic Fields." *American Dowser* 14:1, 4 (1974).

Heidt, Patricia. "Effect of Therapeutic Touch on Anxicty Level of Hospitalized Patients." *Nursing Research,* 30:1 (1981): 32-37.

Hellman, Hal. "Kann Licht Depressionen heilen?" *Psychologie Heute* (November 1982):44-47.

Hill, Ann, ed. *A Visual Encyclopedia of Unconventional Medicine.* New York: Crown, 1979.

Hills, Christopher. *Nuclear Evolution: Discovery of the Rainbow Body.* Boulder Creek, Calif.: University of the Trees Press, 1977.

Holroyd, Stuart and Powell, Neil. *Geheimnisvolle Wissenschaften.* London: Aldus Books, 1978.

Holzer, Hans. *Beyond Medicine.* Chicago: Henry Regnery, 1973.

Illich, Ivan. *Medical Nemesis, the Expropriation of Health.* London: Calder & Boyars, 1975.

Inglis, Brian. *Fringe Medicine.* London: Faber & Faber, 1964.

Jaynes, Julian. *The Origins of Consciousness in the Breakdown of the Bicameral Mind.* Boston: Houghton Mifflin, 1976.

Jenkins, David. "Psychological and Social Precursors of Coronary Disease." *New England Journal of Medicine* 284 (1971):307.

Jenner, Edward. *An Inquiry into the Causes and Effects of the Variolae Vaccine, a Disease Known by the Name of Cow-Pox.* London: Sampson Low, 1798.

Jenny, Hans. *Cymatics.* New York: Schocken Books, 1975.

Johnsen, Lillemor. *Psychic Aspects of Muscular Testing and Therapy.* Oslo: Sem & Stenersen, 1969.

Justa-Smith, Sister. "The Influence of Enzyme Growth by the 'Laying-on-of-Hands.'" *Dimensions of Healing Symposium Proceedings.* Los Altos, Calif.: Academy of Parapsychology, 1972.

Karagulla, S. *Breakthrough to Creativity.* Los Angeles: De Vorss, 1967.

Kending, Frank. "Listening to Radar." 16:12 *Psychology Today* (1982):80.

Kervan, C. *Transmutations a Faible Energie (Naturelles et Biologiques).* Paris: Librarie Maloine, 1972.

Khanna, Madhu. *Das Grosse Yantra-Buch.* Freiburg im Breisgau: Aurum Verlag, 1980.

Kiev, Ari. "The Psychotherapeutic Aspects of Primitive Medicine." *Human Organization* 21:1 (1962):25-29.

King, Francis and Kingston, Jeremy. *Östliche Lebensart und medizinische Rätsel*. London: Aldus Books, 1978.

King, Serge. "Neoenergy and Geometric Forms." In *Future Science*, edited by John White and Stanley Krippner, 184-90. New York: Anchor Books, 1977.

Kingston, Jeremy. *Healing Without Medicine*. London: Aldus Books, 1976.

König, Herbert. *Unsichtbare Umwelt*. München: Herbert L. König (Eigenverlag), Arcisstrasse 21, 8000 München 2, 1980.

Koestler, Arthur. *Janus: A Summing Up*. New York: Random House, 1978.

Kötke, Rainer. "Heil aus dem Tunnel." *Stern* 3 (1981):127.

"Kopfschmerzen durch flasches Licht." *Vital Magazine* (Oktober, 1981):46.

Kreitz, Hanjo. *Die Krankheitsursache*. München: Herold Verlag, 1982.

Krieger, Dolores. "Therapeutic Touch: An Imprimatur of Nursing." 75:5 *American Journal of Nursing* (1975):784-87.

Krieger, Dolores. "Healing by Laying on of Hands as a Facilitator of Bioenergetic Change: The Response of In-Vivo Human Hemoglobin." *International Journal of Psychoenergetic Systems* 1 (1976):121-29.

Krippner, Stanley and Rubin, Daniel. *The Kirlian Aura*. New York: Anchor Books, 1974.

Krishnamurti, Jiddu. *The Awakening of Intelligence*. New York: Aron Books, 1973.

Kryter, Karl. *The Effects of Noise on Man*. New York: Academic Press, 1970.

Kunz, F.L. "On the Symmetry Principle." 22:4 *Main Currents in Modern Thought* (1966):92-96.

Kurtsin, I.T. *Theoretical Principles of Psychosomatic Medicine*. New York: Wiley, 1976.

Kushi, Mischio. *Acupuncture, Ancient and Future Worlds*. Boston: Tao Publications, 1973.

Kybalion. *Eine Studie über die hermetische Philosophic des alten Ägyptens und Griechenlands*. Haar: Akasha, 1981.

Laing, Ronald D. *The Politics of Experience*. London: Penguin, 1970.

Lakhovsky, Georges. *L'Oscillation Cellulaire*. Paris: G. Doin, 1931.

Lakhovsky, Georges. *The Secret of Life-Cosmic Rays and Radiations of Living Beings*. London: Heinemann Medical Books, 1939.

Lamy, Lucy. *Egyptian Mysteries*. New York: Crossroad Publishing, 1981.

Lane, Earle, ed. *Electrophotography*. San Francisco: And/Or Press, 1975.

Lang, P. "A Psychophysiological Analysis of Fear Reduction Using an Automated Desensitizing Procedure." *Journal of Abnormal Psychology* 76 (1970):220-34.

La Patra, Jack. *Healing, the Coming Revolution in Holistic Medicine*. New York: McGraw-Hill, 1978.

Lazarus, Arnold A. *Behavior Therapy and Beyond*. New York: McGraw-Hill, 1971.

Lazarus, Richard. "Little Hassles Can Be Hazardous to Health." *Psychology Today* 15:7 (1981):58-62.

Lee, Paul. *The Herb Renaissance: A National Correspondence Course* (unpublished).

Levi, Eliphas. *Transzendentale Magie*. Basel: Sphinx Verlag, 1977.

Lewis, Howard R. and Lewis, Martha E. *Psychosomatics*. New York: Viking Press, 1972.

Ligeros, K. *How Ancient Healing Governs Modern Therapeutics*. New York: Putnam, 1937.

Lindlahr, Henry. *Philosophy of Natural Therapeutics*. Chicago: Lindlahr, 1922.

Long, Max F. *The Secret Science at Work*. Los Angeles: De Vorss, 1953.

Love, Jeff. *The Quantum Gods*. New York: Samuel Weiser, 1979.

Mahnke, Frank. "Color in Medical Facilities." *Interior Design* 52:4 (1981):256-64.

Main, Iain. *Vibrations and Waves in Physics*. Cambridge, England: Cambridge University Press, 1978.

Malan, D.J. *Physics of Lightning*. London: English Universities Press, 1963.

Mann, W. Eduard. *Orgone, Reich and Eros*. New York: Simon & Schuster, 1973.

Marsh, Ken. *The Way Technology Works*. New York: Simon & Schuster, 1982.

Maurer, Allan. "Computer Epilepsy." *Omni* 4:12 (1982):49.

McFarland, Richard. *Physiological Psychology*. Palo Alto, Calif.: Mayfield, 1981.

Mendelsohn, Robert. *Confessions of a Medical Heretic*. New York: Warner Books, 1979.

Mendelsohn, Robert. "Ultrasound." *Let's Live* 49:4 (1981):133.

Middleton, J., ed. *Magic, Witchcraft and Curing*. Austin, Texas: University of Texas Press, 1976.

Mishlove, Jeffry. *Roots of Consciousness*. New York: Random House, 1975.

Moses, Paul. *The Voice of Neurosis*. New York: Green & Stratton, 1954.

Moss, Ralph. *The Cancer Syndrome*. New York: Grove Press, 1982.

Moss, Thelma. *The Probability of the Impossible.* Los Angeles: J.P. Tarcher, 1974.

Motoyama, Hiroshi. "Electrophysiological and Preliminary Biochemical Studies of Skin Properties in Relation to Acupuncture Meridians." *Research for Religion and Parapsychology* 6 (1980).

Motoyama, Hiroshi. "The Mechanism by Which Psi-Ability Manifests Itself." *Impact of Science on Society* 24 (1974):321.

Musès, Charles. "Paraphysics: A New View of Ourselves and the Cosmos." In *Future Science,* edited by John White and Stanley Krippner, 280-88. New York: Anchor Books, 1977.

Neuburger, Max. "The Doctrine of the Healing Power of Nature Throughout the Course of Time." Translated by Dr. Linn J. Boyd. Unpublished Ph.D. thesis, University of Kansas (Lawrence), 1933.

New York Times. "Fluorescent Light's Effect on Cells." Quoted in *San Francisco Chronicle,* April 28, 1977.

Nossal, Gustav J.V. and Ada, G.L. *Antigens, Lymphoid Cells, and the Immune Response.* New York: Academic Press, 1971.

Oesterreicher-Mollmo, Marianne. *Herder Lexikon—Symbole.* Freiburg im Breisgau: Verlag Herder, 1978.

Ornstein, Robert. *The Psychology of Consciousness.* San Francisco: W.H. Freeman, 1972.

Osborne, Arthur. *The Teachings of Bhagavan Sri Ramana Maharshi in His Own Words.* Tiruvanvamalai: Sri Ramanasramam, 1977.

Ostrander, S. and Schroeder, L. *Psychic Discoveries Behind the Iron Curtain.* Englewood Cliffs, N.J.: Prentice-Hall, 1970.

Ott, John. *Health and Light.* New York: Pocket Books, 1977.

Otto, H. and Knight, J. *Dimensions in Wholistic Healing.* Chicago: Nelson-Hall, 1979.

Pàlos, Stephan. *The Chinese Art of Healing.* New York: Bantam Books, 1971.

Panatti, Charles. *Breakthroughs.* New York: Berkley Books, 1980.

Patton, Robert. "Aircraft of the Pharaohs." *Omni* 4:12 (1982):52-60.

Pawlicki, J.B. *How to Build a Flying Saucer.* Englewood Cliffs, N.J.: Prentice-Hall, 1981.

Pelletier, Kenneth. *Holistic Medicine.* New York: Merloyd Lawrence, 1979.

Pelletier, Kenneth. *Mind as Healer, Mind as Slayer.* New York: Delacorte, 1977.

Pelletier, Kenneth. *Toward a Science of Consciousness.* New York: Dell Publishing, 1978.

Penrose, Roger. "Black Holes." In *Albert Einstein,* edited by Peter C. Aichelburg and Roman U. Sexl, 33-50. Braunschweig/Wiesbaden: Friedrich Vieweg & Sohn, 1979.

Pfeiffer, E. *Sensitive Crystallization Processes.* Philadelphia: Graphic Crafts, 1968.

Physicians' Desk Reference. 28th ed. Oradell, N.J.: Medical Economics Co., 1974.

Picardi, G. *The Chemical Basis of Medical Climatology.* London: G.T. Thomas, 1962.

Pierce, J.R. *Almost All About Waves.* Cambridge, Mass.: M.I.T. Press, 1974.

Pierrakos, John. *Human Energy Systems Theory.* New York: Institute for the New Age of Man, 1976.

Pitt, Valerie, ed. *The Penguin Dictionary of Physics.* New York: Penguin, 1977.

Ponte, Lowell. "Biomagnetism: The Force that Shapes Our Lives." *Reader's Digest.* November, 1982.

Popp, F.A. "So könte Krebs entstehen." *Bild der Wissenschaft* 1 (1976).

Porkert, Manfred. "Chinese Medicine: A Traditional Healing Science." In *Ways of Health,* edited by David S. Sobel. New York: Harcourt Brace Jovanovich, 1979.

Porter, T. and Mikellides, B. *Color for Architecture.* New York: Van Nostrand Rheinhold, 1976.

Portnoy, Ethel. "Spinoza, the Outcast Philosopher." *Holland Herald* 17:10 (1982).

Presman, A.S. *Electromagnetic Fields and Life.* New York: Plenum Press, 1970.

Puharich, Andrija. *Beyond Telepathy.* New York: Anchor Books, 1973.

Puharich, Andrija. "The Search for a Common Denominator in Medicine and Healing." *Proceedings of the Dimensions of Healing Symposium.* Los Altos, Calif.: Academy of Parapsychology and Medicine, 1973.

Purce, Jill. *The Mystic Spiral Journey of the Soul.* London: Thames and Hudson, 1974.

Pykett, Ian. "NMR Imaging in Medicine." *Scientific American* 246:5 (1982):54-64.

Rabi, Isidor. Associated Press release, December 30, 1939.

Radionic Centre Organization. *Mind and Matter.* Oxford, 1965.

Rambeau, V. "Besteht ein Zusammenhang zwischen der Tektonik der Erde und dem Krankheitsproblem?" *Wetter, Boden, Mensche* 7 (1969):341-54.

Rattemeyer, M., and Popp, F.A. "Evidence of Photon Emmision from DNA in Living Systems." *Naturwissenschaften* 68 (1981):572.

Reich, Wilhelm. *Character Analysis.* New York: Farrar, Straus & Giroux, 1949.

Reich, Wilhelm. *The Cancer Biopathy*. New York: Farrar, Straus & Giroux, 1973.

Reichenbach, Baron Karl von. *The Mysterious Odic Force*. New York: Samuel Weiser, 1977.

Reiser, Oliver. *Cosmic Humanism*. Cambridge, Mass.: Schenkman, 1966.

Reynolds, David. *The Quiet Therapies*. Honolulu: University of Hawaii Press, 1980.

Ricciutti, Henry N. *Emotional Development in the First Two Years*. (ERIC ED 039936) Ithaca, N.Y.: Cornell University, Cornell Research Program in Early Childhood Education, 1969.

Rieff, Philip, ed. *Therapy and Technique*. New York: Collier, 1963.

Roddie, Jan C.; Wallace, M.; and William, F.M. *The Physiology of Disease*. London: Lloyd-Luke, 1975.

Rubin, Herbert E. and Katz, Elias. "Auroratone Films for the Treatment of Psychotic Depressions in an Army General Hospital." 2:4 *Journal of Clincial Psychology* (1946):333-40.

Runes, Dagobert. *Dictionary of Philosophy*. Paterson, N.J.: Littlefield, Adams & Co., 1962.

Russell, Edward. "The Fields of Life." In *Future Science*, edited by John White and Stanley Krippner, 59-72. New York: Anchor Books, 1977.

Russell, Edward. *Report of Radionics: Science of the Future*. London: Neville Spearman, 1973.

Sabbagha, Rudy E. *Ultrasound in High-Risk Obstetrics*. Philadelphia: Lea and Feliger, 1979.

Sabetti, Stephano. *Energy Concepts of Life Energy Therapy*. Munich: Trautenwolfstrasse 3, 8000 München 40, Life Energy Publications, 1978.

Sabetti, Stephano. *Life Energy: A Psychotherapeutic Evolution*. Munich: Life Energy Publications, 1978.

Sabetti, Stephano. *Life Energy Therapy: An Introduction*. Munich: Life Energy Publications, 1978.

Sabetti, Stephano. *Manifestations of Energy*. Munich: Life Energy Publications, 1979.

Sabetti, Stephano. *Transpersonal Dimensions*. Munich: Life Energy Publications, 1985.

Sattilaro, A. *Recalled by Life*. Boston: Houghton Mifflin, 1982.

Schackter, S. and Singer, J.E. "Cognitive, Social and Physiological Determinants of Emotional States." *Psychological Review* 69 (1962):379-99.

Schneider, A. and Tarskis, B. *Physiological Psychology*. New York: Random House, 1980.

Schneider, P. *Revolution in the Body-Mind*. New York: The Alexa Press, 1976.

Schnitzer, L.E. "Diagnostic Ultrasound: Basic Principles." In *Obstetric Ultrasound: Applications and Principles*, edited by W.S. van Bergen. Menlo Park, Calif.: Addison Wesley, 1980.

Schwenk, Theodore. *Sensitive Chaos*. New York: Schocken Books, 1976.

Scientific and Technical Congress of Radionics and Radiasthesia. *Proceedings*. London: Markham House, 1950.

Selye, Hans. *Stress Without Distress*. Philadelpha: Lippincott, 1974.

Shah, Idries. *The Sufis*. Garden City, N.Y.: Doubleday, 1964.

Shah, Lt. Col. "The Constitution of Medicine." In *Theories and Philosophies of Medicine*. New Delhi: Institute of History and Medical Research, 1973.

Shapiro, Marc. "Mesmer, Reich and the Living Process." *Creative Process Bulletin of the Interscience Institute*, 4:2 (June 1965).

Sheldrake, Rupert. "A New Science of Life." 90:1258 *New Scientist Magazine* (June 18, 1981):766-68.

Siegman, A.E. *An Introduction to Lasers and Masers*. New York: McGraw-Hill, 1971.

Sigerist, Henry E. *A History of Medicine. Vol. II: Early Greek, Hindu and Persian Medicine*. New York: Oxford University Press, 1961.

Simpson, D.P. *Cassell's Latin Dictionary*. New York: MacMillan, 1979.

Slager, U. *Space Medicine*. Englewood Cliffs, N.J.: Prentice-Hall, 1962.

Snively, W.D. *The Sea of Life*. New York: David McKay, 1969.

Solomon, R.L. and Corbit, J. "An Opponent-Process Theory of Motivation." *Journal of Abnormal Psychology*. 83 (1973): 158-71.

Soo, Chee. *Tao of Long Life: The Chinese Art of Chang Ming*. London: Gordon and Cremones, 1979.

Spees, Everett. "A Thymos Primer." *Journal of the American Medical Association (JAMA)* 207 (1969):1436-39.

Stampfl, T.G. "Implosive Therapy; Part I: The Theory." In *Behavior Modification Techniques in the Treatment of Emotional Disorders*, edited by Stewart G. Armitage. Battle Creek, Mich.: V.A. Publications, 1967.

Stone, R.B. and Stone, L. *Hawaiian and Polynesian Miracle Health Secrets*. New York: Parker, 1980.

Strauss, A., ed. *Where Medicine Fails*. New Brunswick, N.J.: Transaction Books, 1970.

Strong, Leonell. "The Possible Effect of the Oil of Thyme on the Incidence of Spontaneous Cancer in Mice." *American Journal of Cancer* 23 (1935):297-99.

Strupp, Hans. "Towards a Reformulation of the Psychotherapeutic Influence." *International Journal of Psychiatry*, 3 (1973): 263-354.

Strupp, Hans; Fox, Ronald; and Lessler, Ken. *Patients View Their Psychotherapy*. Baltimore: John Hopkins Press, 1969.

Sulman, F.G. "Health, Weather and Climate." *International Journal of Biometeorogy*. 18 (1974):313-18.

Swann, I. *To Kiss Earth Good-Bye*. New York: Hawthorne Books, 1975.

Symonds, Percival. "A Comprehensive Theory of Psychotherapy." *American Journal of Orthopsychiatry* 24 (1954):697-712.

Szasz, Thomas. *The Myth of Mental Illness*. New York: Harper & Row, 1974.

Szasz, Thomas. *The Myth of Psychotherapy*. Garden City, N. Y.: Anchor Press, 1979.

Szent-Györgi, A. *Introduction to a Sub-Molecular Biology*. New York: Academic Press, 1960.

Takayama, S. and Ojima, Y. "Photosensitizing Activity of Carcinogenic and Non-carcinogenic Polycyclic Hydrocarbons on Cultured Cells." *Japanese Journal of Genetics* 44 (1969): 231-40.

Talbot, Michael. *Mysticism and the New Physics*. New York: Bantam, 1981.

Tansley, David. *Subtle Body*. London: Thames and Hudson, 1977.

Targ, R. and Putoff, H. "Information Transmission Under Conditions of Sensory Shielding." *Nature* 252 (1974):602.

Taylor, J. *Superminds*. London: Macmillan, 1975.

Thomas, Lewis. *Lives of a Cell*. New York: Bantam Books, 1974.

Thomson, W. *Natural Medicine*. New York: McGraw-Hill, 1978.

Thorwald, Jürgen. *Science and Secrets of Early Medicine*. New York: Harcourt Brace Jovanovich, 1969.

Three Initiates. *The Kybalion*. (The Yogi Publication Society) Chicago: Masonic Temple, 1912.

Tiller, William. Conference on the Physics of Consciousness, Newton, Mass., 1975. Lecture.

Tiller, William. "Consciousness, Radiation and the Developing Sensory System." In *Proceedings of A.P.M. Symposium on Dimensions of Healing*, Stanford University, Palo Alto, Calif., September 1972a.

Tiller, William. "Creating a New Functional Model of Body Healing Energies." (Unpublished), Stanford University, Palo Alto, Calif., 1976b.

Tiller, William. "Radionics, Radiasthesia and Physics." In *Proceedings of the Varieties of Healing Experience Symposium*, Academy of Parapsychology and Medicine, Los Altos, Calif., 1972b.

Tiller, William. "Toward a Future Medicine Based Upon Controlled Energy Fields." In *Proceedings of the Association for Research and Enlightenment Medical Symposium*, Phoenix, Ariz., January 1976a.

Tiller, William. "Toward a Future Medicine Based On Controlled Energy Fields." *Phoenix*, 1:1 (Summer 1977).

Tillich, Paul. *The Courage to Be*. New Haven, Conn.: Yale University Press, 1952.

Toben, B.; Sarfatti, J.; and Wolf, F. *Space-Time and Beyond*. New York: Dutton, 1975.

Tomlinson, H. *Medical Divination*. Bradford, Holsworthy, England: Health Science Press, 1966.

Tromp, S.W. *Psychical Physics*. Amsterdam: Elsevier, 1949.

Tyberg, Judith. *Sanskrit Keys to the Wisdom Religion*. San Diego, Calif.: Point Loma, 1968.

Vayda, E. "A Comparison of Surgical Rates in Canada and in England and Wales." *New England Journal of Medicine* 289 (1973):1224-29.

Veith, Ilza. *Huang Ti Nei Ching Su Wên*. The Yellow Emperor's Classic of Internal Medicine. Berkeley, Calif.: University of California Press, 1949.

Verlag, H. *The Power of Breath*. Whittier, Calif.: Doty Trade Press, 1958.

Vishnudevananda, Suami. *The Complete Illustrated Book of Yoga*. New York: Bell Publishing Co., 1960.

Vithoulkas, George. *Homeopathy*. New York: Avon Books, 1971.

von Quintus, Icilius. *Durchbruch zum Ursprung* (Unpublished).

Waddington, Conrad Hal. *The Strategy of the Genes: A Discussion of Some Aspects of Theoretical Biology*. London: G. Allen & Unwin, 1957.

Wade, Nicolas. "Drug Regulation: Food and Drug Administration Replies to Charges by Economists and Industry." *Science* 179 (1973):775-77.

Wagner, Hildebert. Wissenschaftliches Institut für Pharmaceutische Biologie, Karlstrasse 29, 8000 München 2, personal communication.

Walker, Benjamin. *Encyclopedia of Metaphysical Medicine*. London: Routledge & Kegan Paul, 1978.

Walker, Evan Harris. "The Nature of Consciousness." *Mathematical Biosciences* 7 (1970):131-78.

Watkins, Alfred. *The Old Straight Track*. New York: Ballantine, 1973.

Watson, Lyall. *Supernature*. New York: Bantam Books, 1974.

Weeks, R. "Hospitals." *Architectural Review* 168 (1980):55.

Weizsacker, von, C.F. "Einstein's Importance to Physics, Philosophy and Politics." In *Albert Einstein*, edited by Peter C. Aichelburg and Roman U. Sexl, 159-68. Braunschweig/Wiesbaden: Friedrich Vieweg & Sohn, 1979.

Westbrook, A. and Ratli, O. *Aikido and the Dynamic Sphere*. Rutland, Vt.: Charles E. Tuttle, 1970.

Westlake, Aubrey. *The Pattern of Health*. London: Vincent Stuart, 1961.

White, John and Krippner, Stanley, eds. *Future Science*. New York: Anchor Books, 1977.

Wilson, O.E. *On Human Nature*. Cambridge, Mass.: Harvard University Press, 1978.

Wong, K. and Lien-Teh, W. *History of Chinese Medicine*. China: National Quarantine Service, 1936.

Woolridge, D.E. *The Machinery of the Brain*. New York: McGraw-Hill, 1963.

Young, Arthur. *The Reflexive Universe: Evolution of Consciousness*. New York: Delacorte Press, 1976.

Zackrisson, Olle. "3000 Åriga Frön Från Mosse Började Gro." *Dagens Nyheter* (November 11, 1982).

Zarel, Milton. "A Doctor's View of Electromagnetism." In *The Way Technology Works*, edited by Ken Marsh, 89-94. New York: Simon & Schuster, 1982.

Zukav, Gary. *The Dancing Wu Li Masters*. New York: Morrow, 1979.

Index

Publications by Dr. Stephano Sabetti

The Wholeness Principle: Exploring the Life Energy Process. This new book presents the historical background and scientific foundation of Dr. Sabetti's Life Energy Therapy. $12.95 paperback
345 pages, English $19.95 hardcover

Life Energy: A Psychotherapeutic Evolution / Psychotherapeutische Entwicklung
This article discusses the development of Life Energy in Reichian and Bioenergetic Therapies and shows its further evolution in Life Energy Therapy (L.E.T.) as created by Dr. Sabetti.
18 pages, English (E) or German (G) $3/DM 5,-

Life Energy Therapy: An Introduction / Einführung in die Life Energy Therapy
This basic introduction explains the philosophical and theoretical foundation of L.E.T. as a synthesis of Eastern and Western energy concepts in body psychotherapy.
13 pages, English or German $3/DM 5,-

Energy Concepts of Life Energy Therapy / Life Energy Therapy— Energie-Konzepte
In this article Dr. Sabetti explains several of the main energy concepts which are used in the theory and practice of L.E.T.
18 pages, English or German $3/DM 5,-

Manifestations of Energy / Energie-Manifestationen
One of the main tenets of L.E.T. is that there are many forms and levels of energy which affect us and that any attempt at healing must consider all of these. This article describes many of these levels.
28 pages, English or German $3/DM 5-

Transpersonal Dimensions / Transpersonale Dimensionen
Discusses the transpersonal aspects of Life Energy Therapy in relationship to physics, and the concepts of trace problems, energy patterns, the healing channel, and micro-movements.
9 pages, English or German $3/DM 5,-

Life Energy Live
An actual transcript of the film *Life Energy Therapy*, in which Dr. Sabetti alternately works therapeutically with Mary, his client, and explains what is happening energetically in the interaction. Mary, an artist, describes her own experience with the work at the end of the film.
20 pages English $3.00

Gestalt Therapy Energized: (I) Theory and (II) Therapy
In the first article the concepts of repression and neurosis are discussed in Life Energy terms, as well as the flux of perception in the Life Energy Cycle. In the article dealing with therapy the role of the patient and Gestalt Therapy techniques are discussed in the light of energy concepts.
25 pages each English $3.00 each

Psychoanalysis as an Energy Process: (I) Theory and (II) Therapy
Explores the theory of neurosis and repression in Freud's system as energy processes in (I), while in (II) Freudian therapy is examined in relation to energy concepts from the points of view of the analyst, the patient, and techniques.
I: 12 pages; II: 19 pages English $3.00 each

Perceptual Energy
Discusses Freud's Topographical System of Conscious, Preconscious and Unconscious in the light of perceptual psychology, using energy and attention as explanatory concepts.
19 pages English $3.00

Behavior Modification (Wolpe) as an Energy Process as Demonstrated with Reciprocal Inhibition
Describes the theory of neurosis, neurotic responses (e.g., displacement, avoidance, etc.) and their therapy in energy and attention terms.
23 pages English $3.00

Common Ground: Comparative Study of Psychoanalysis, Gestalt Therapy and Reciprocal Inhibition
Compares the techniques of Psychoanalysis, Gestalt Therapy and Behavior Modification (Wolpe) in energy and attention concepts.
28 pages English $3.00

Emotions on Trial
Mental "illness" and criminality are seen as two attempts to relieve personal helplessness in the face of societal controls which repress personal variance, especially emotional expression.
18 pages English $3.00

Organizational Energy / Energie der Organisation
Organizations can be seen as energy systems whose basic wholeness is disturbed by all blockages of energy flow. This article discusses the role of top management, the concept of wholearchy, organizational field, the process of change, and the path of transformation.
25 pages, English or German $3/DM 5,-

Shinkido Massage
Describes the background and practice of this special art of massage developed by Dr. Sabetti. Bringing energy waves in the body into movement, resonation through Shinkido massage promotes physical health, fosters emotional expression, enhances sensual pleasure and supports spiritual evolution.
20 pages English $3.00

Lebensenergie
Presents both theory and research which support the idea of a universal wholeness in religion, philosophy, physics, the body, emotions, the environment, medicine and psychology.
316 pages, German   DM 32,-

The price of the paperback edition of *The Wholeness Principle* is $12.95. Costs given below include the book, postage and handling (and sales tax for California residents).

Purchases from outside the U.S. must be in U.S. dollars. With regular handling allow six to eight weeks delivery.

Make checks payable to Life Energy Media, 14755 Ventura Blvd., Suite 1908, Sherman Oaks, CA 91403.

----

*Please send my copy (copies) of *The Wholeness Principle* by Dr. Stephano Sabetti to:

Name _____

Address _____

_____

Profession _____ Tel: _____

I have enclosed my check □ money order □ for:
Payment must be U.S. dollars.

	Cost per Copy	No. Copies	Cost
California residents (including sales tax)			
—Regular handling	$16.64	_____	_____
—First Class	$18.64	_____	_____
U.S.—Regular handling	$15.80	_____	_____
—First Class	$17.80	_____	_____
Europe—Regular handling	$16.40	_____	_____
—Air Mail	$27.40	_____	_____

Other Publications:

Title	Cost (including sales tax)	No. Copies	Cost
_____	CA $4.93	_____	_____
_____	CA $4.93	_____	_____
_____	CA $4.93	_____	_____
	(no tax)		
_____	U.S. $4.75	_____	_____
_____	U.S. $4.75	_____	_____
_____	U.S. $4.75	_____	_____

Total Enclosed _____

□ Please include me in mailings on future events sponsored by the Institute for Life Energy.